Grammar
of Freedom/
Five Lessons

Works from
the Arteast 2000+ Collection
Moderna galerija,
Ljubljana

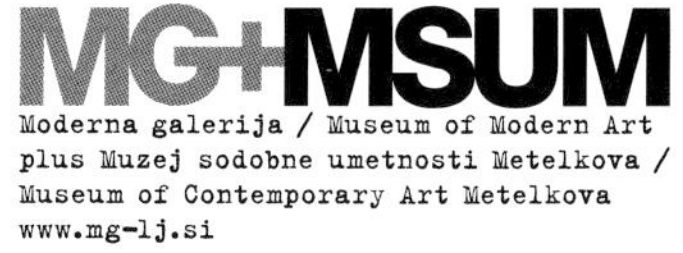

Moderna galerija / Museum of Modern Art
plus Muzej sodobne umetnosti Metelkova /
Museum of Contemporary Art Metelkova
www.mg-lj.si

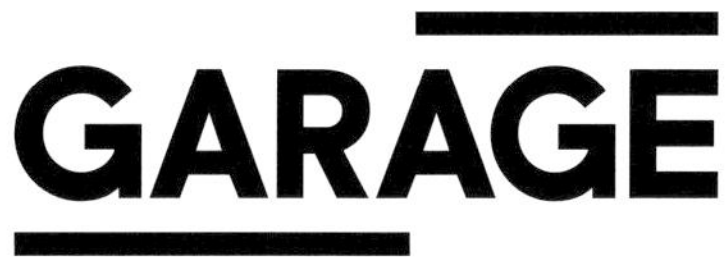

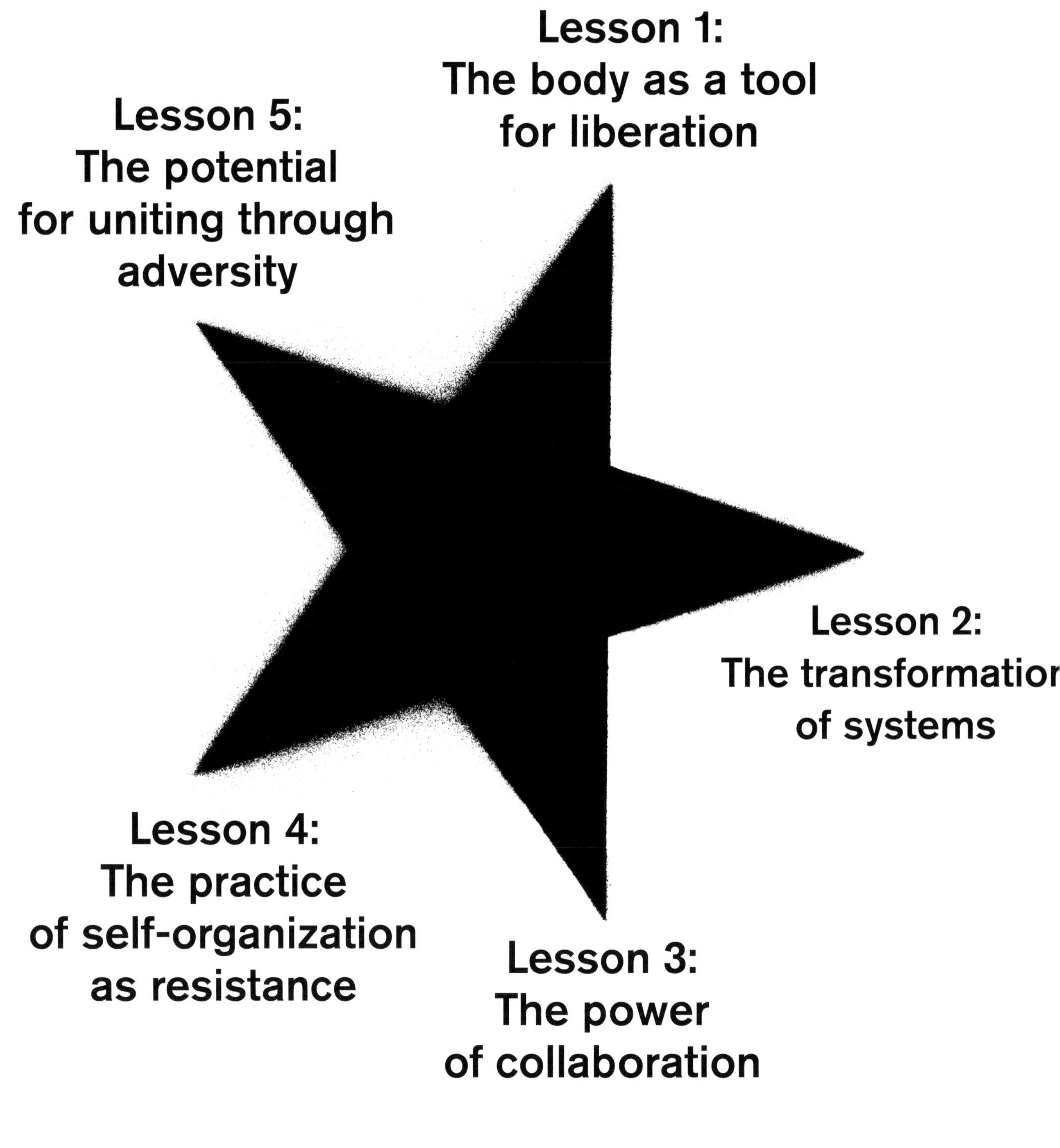

Lesson 1:
The body as a tool
for liberation
Lesson 2:
The transformation
of systems
Lesson 3:
The power
of collaboration
Lesson 4:
The practice
of self-organization
as resistance
Lesson 5:
The potential
for uniting through
adversity

Preface

It gives me great pride that Garage Museum of Contemporary Art is the first institution in Russia to develop a collaboration with Moderna galerija in Ljubljana. Such a partnership is long overdue, not only for what audiences in Moscow have to gain from the opportunity to see a compelling collection of art, but also because of the benefits that an exchange like the one we have undertaken can bring to the Museum.

When I founded Garage eight years ago, it was through a wish to provide an internationally oriented platform that could provide access to the people, art, and ideas that are making history. As the plans for the Museum have grown and evolved, it has become increasingly evident that this also means taking responsibility for leading the debate as to what "international" means in Russia today. While it is always important to showcase great art from Europe and the United States, it is perhaps even more relevant to expand our horizons and present work from places that are challenging and expanding what art can do and say. Ironically, for this exhibition it has meant looking closer to home and recognizing that there are worlds within worlds on our doorstep that are only just beginning to be explored.

My thanks go to Zdenka Badovinac, Director of Moderna galerija, and her team for this opportunity to create another landmark project in Garage's development.

Dasha Zhukova
Founder
Garage Museum of Contemporary Art

Introduction

In summer 2013, when Zdenka Badovinac and I first discussed the idea of producing a show for Garage selected from Moderna galerija's Arteast 2000+ Collection, the motivation was simple: never before in Russia had there been an exhibition dedicated to presenting art from Eastern Europe in a way that integrated Russian artists into the story. In fact, the suggestion that Russia had any connection to, or interest in Eastern Europe was conspicuously absent in art museums. Despite twenty-or-so years of a global "former East" debate, and even after the former USSR and former Yugoslavia collapsed almost simultaneously in the early 1990s, there was little institutional acknowledgement of Russia having an integral role in the artistic identity of the region.

It was time to rectify this situation. "Better late than never!" we said, as we raised a glass to our new shared mission.

At that time, little did either of us know that the show would actually be *ahead* of its time for Moscow, insofar as the current political situation had not yet transpired. Now the project is presented while the conversation about how art practices can respond to the present real world situations in Russia—in relation to Ukraine, to the new so-called Cold War, to the financial crisis, to sanctions, to boycotts—has barely begun. The exhibition *Grammar of Freedom/Five Lessons* offers at least the start of an enquiry, providing evidence that artists from across the region have been striving to address remarkably similar situations, albeit in widely different contexts, for decades.

As the first museum initiative anywhere in the world to focus on the work of Eastern European postwar avant-garde artists, the Arteast 2000+ Collection has gained a reputation for providing an extensive overview of art from the region but with an international perspective. More specifically, the collection reveals how artists have responded to their lived experiences, from the aftermath of World War II, through the post-socialist transition of the 1990s, to the current context of global neoliberal capitalism. As a result, it offers rare insight into shared sociopolitical concerns between intergenerational artists who could otherwise be seen to have little in common.

Grammar of Freedom/Five Lessons is a selection of more than 70 artists and art collectives from Eastern Europe and countries constituting the former USSR, with works ranging from the 1960s to the present. As the title suggests, the show is organized around five "lessons" that form a series of propositions to be questioned and explored through the juxtaposition of the selected works. Together, they propose a "grammar," or set of tools, that shed light on how artistic strategies have created resistance to—or provided alternative commentaries on—a range of social and political situations. In this way, the exhibition reveals how artists have historically sought liberty and considers how their approaches may resonate today.

This project is the second in a multi-year series of exhibitions and events at Garage that investigate the potential functions of a collection relative to the broader activities of a contemporary museum. Instigated in 2014, two years after Garage Archive Collection was established, the series is part of Garage's "live" research enterprise, wherein historical precedents and current cultural conditions are explored in-depth, with the public, to share the production of knowledge during the nascent development of the Museum. At the heart of the venture is a desire to think through the characteristics of Garage's own collection—which is the first public archive in the country related to the development of Russian contemporary art from the 1950s through to the present—and understand better its possibilities as a resource, not just in its material form but also as a repository of experience. The occasion to learn from the Arteast 2000+ Collection and develop an exhibition, education program, catalog, and international conference that focus on Russian art in the framework of its political and geographic location has been integral to better understanding the ways that Garage can uniquely contribute to the creative life of Moscow today.

Kate Fowle
Chief Curator
Garage Museum of Contemporary Art

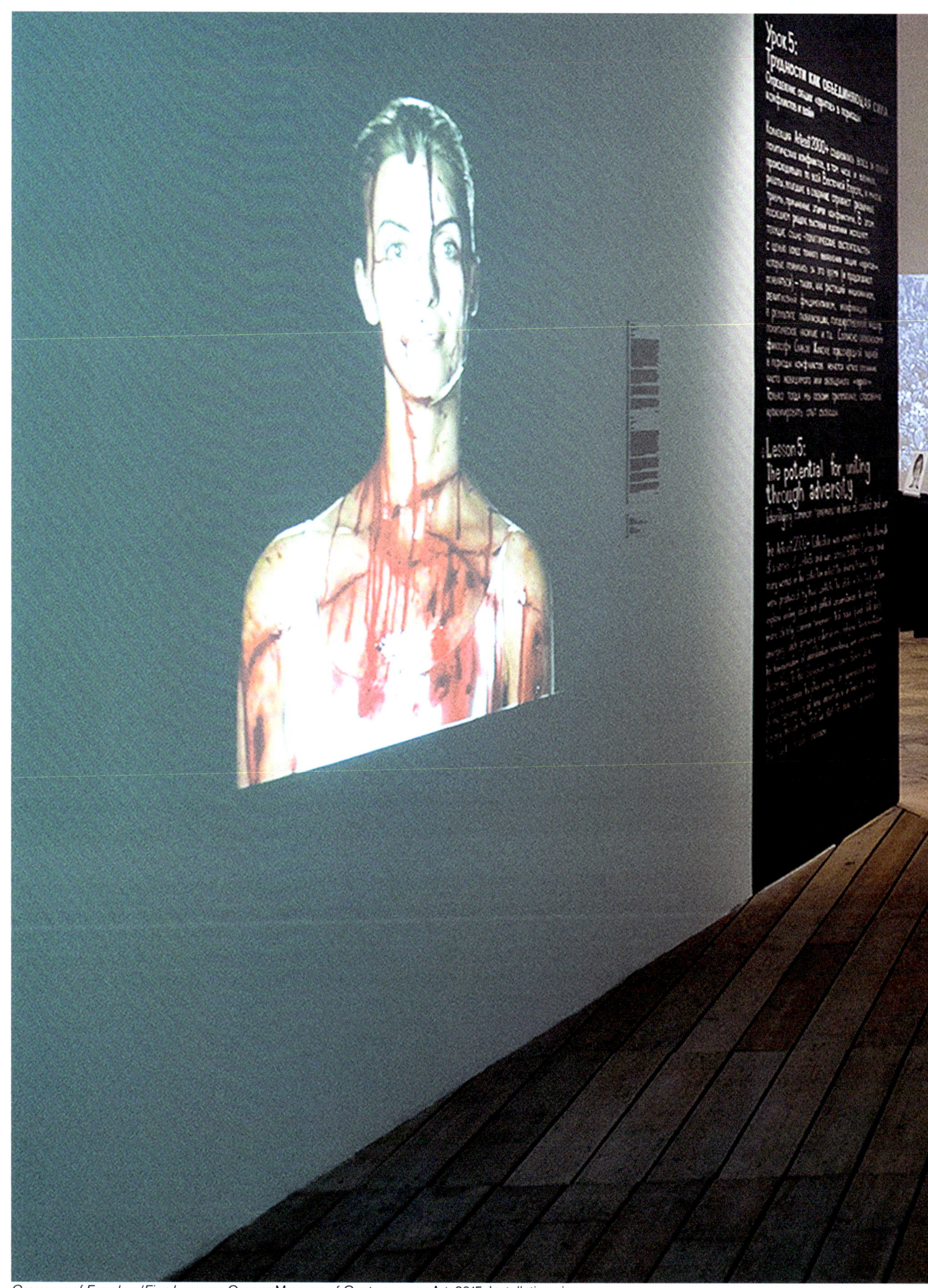

Grammar of Freedom/Five Lessons, Garage Museum of Contemporary Art, 2015. Installation view
© Garage Museum of Contemporary Art

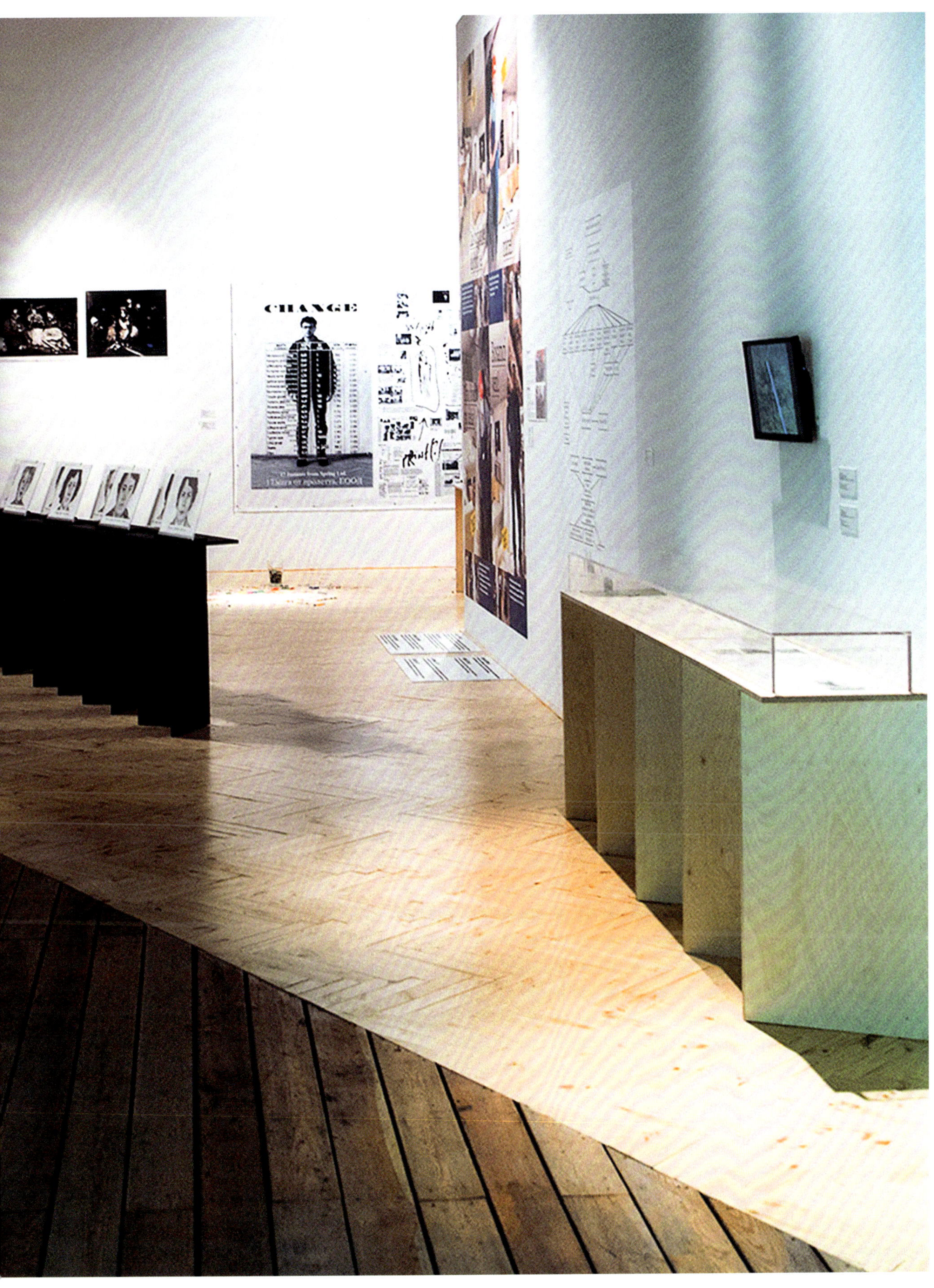

CHANGE

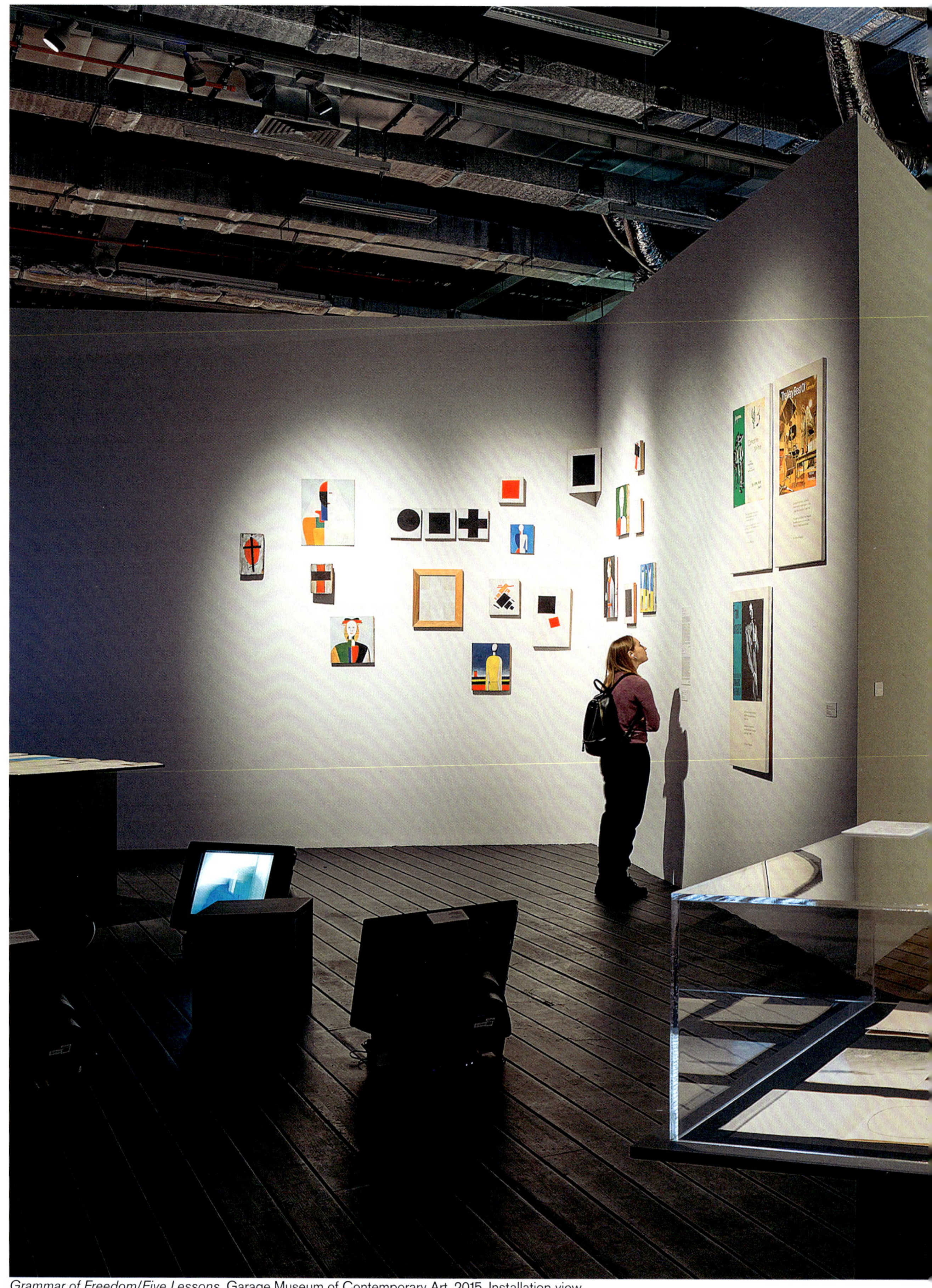

Grammar of Freedom/Five Lessons, Garage Museum of Contemporary Art, 2015. Installation view
© Garage Museum of Contemporary Art

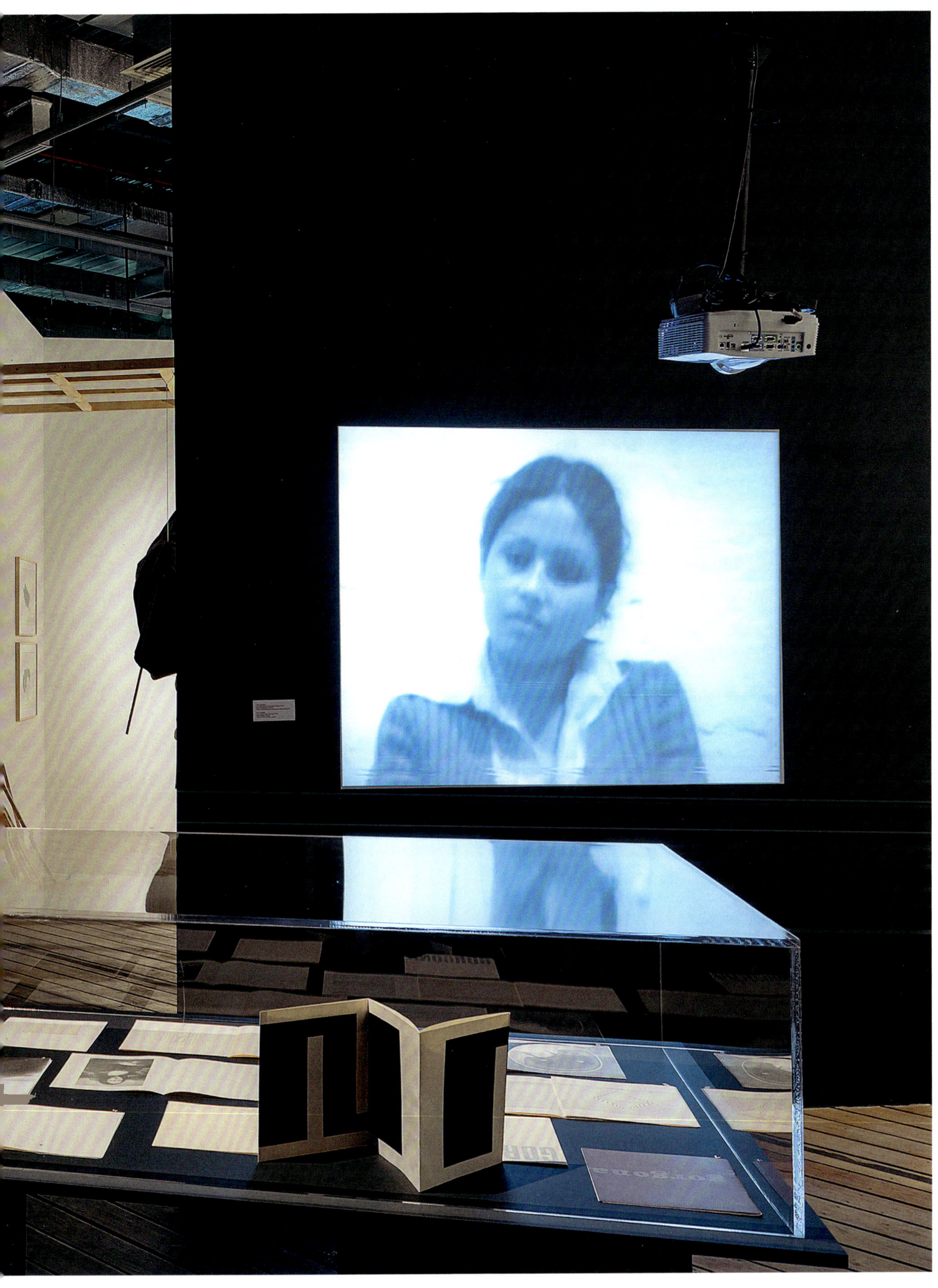

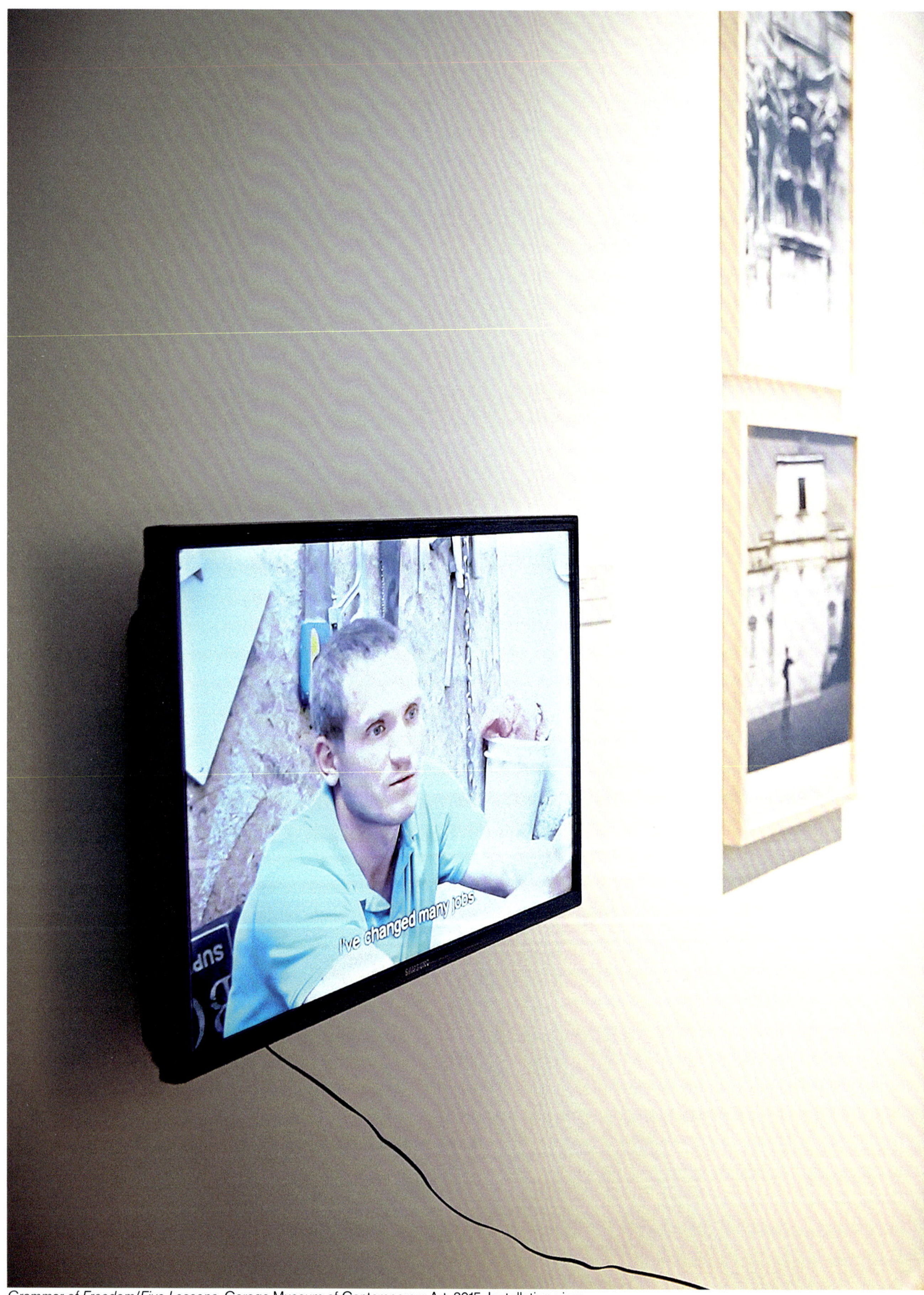

Grammar of Freedom/Five Lessons, Garage Museum of Contemporary Art, 2015. Installation view
© Garage Museum of Contemporary Art

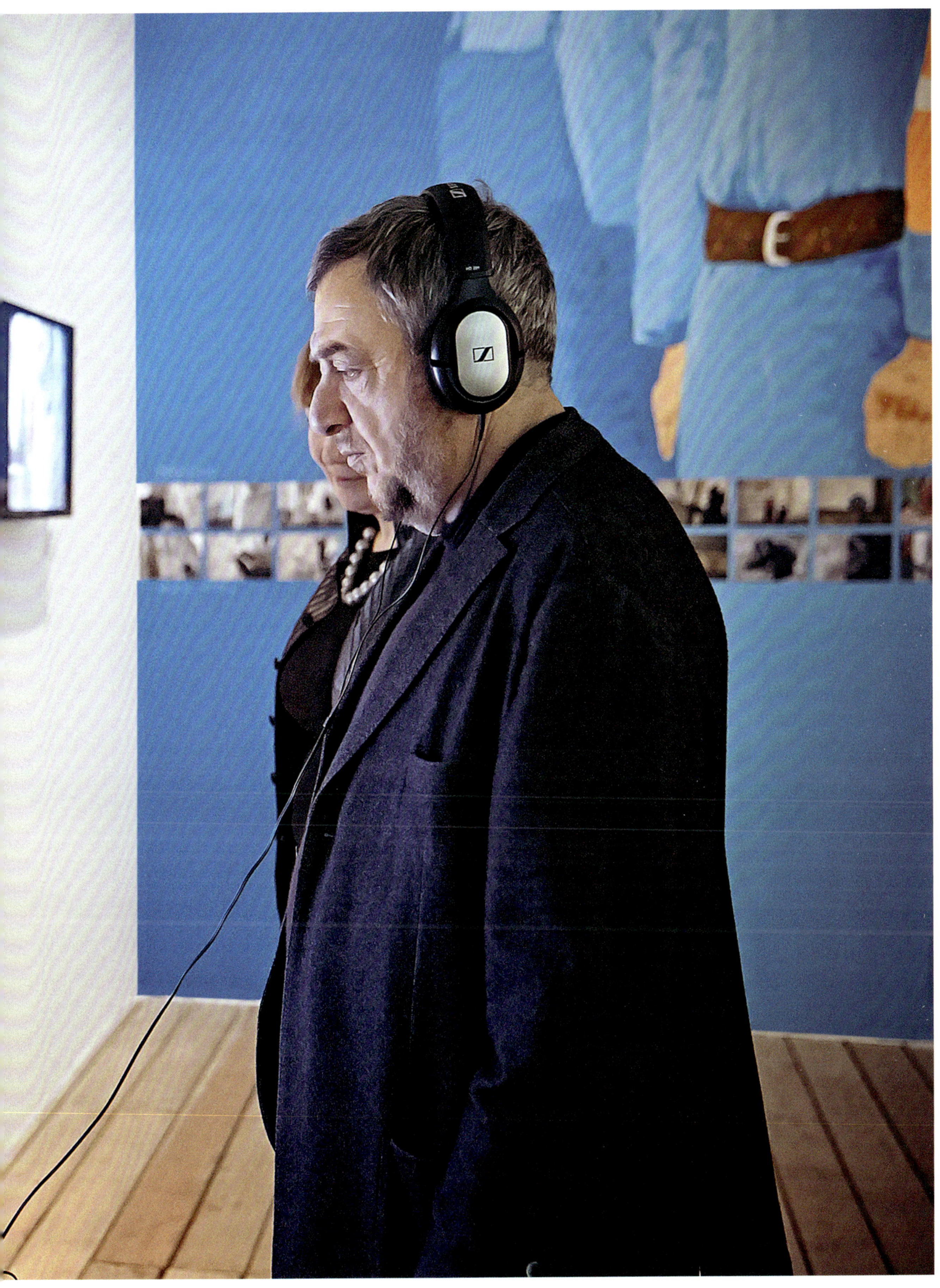

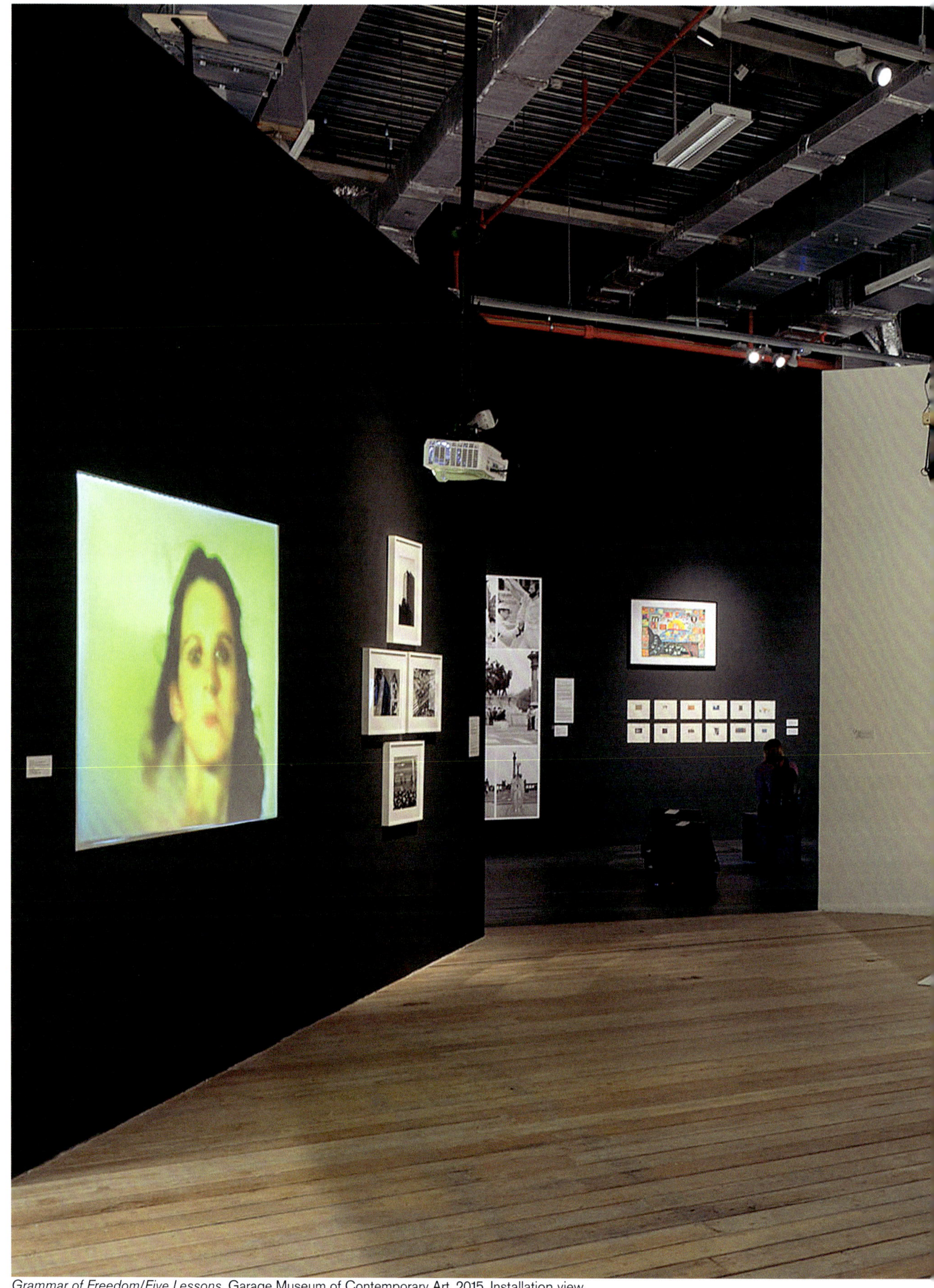

Grammar of Freedom/Five Lessons, Garage Museum of Contemporary Art, 2015. Installation view

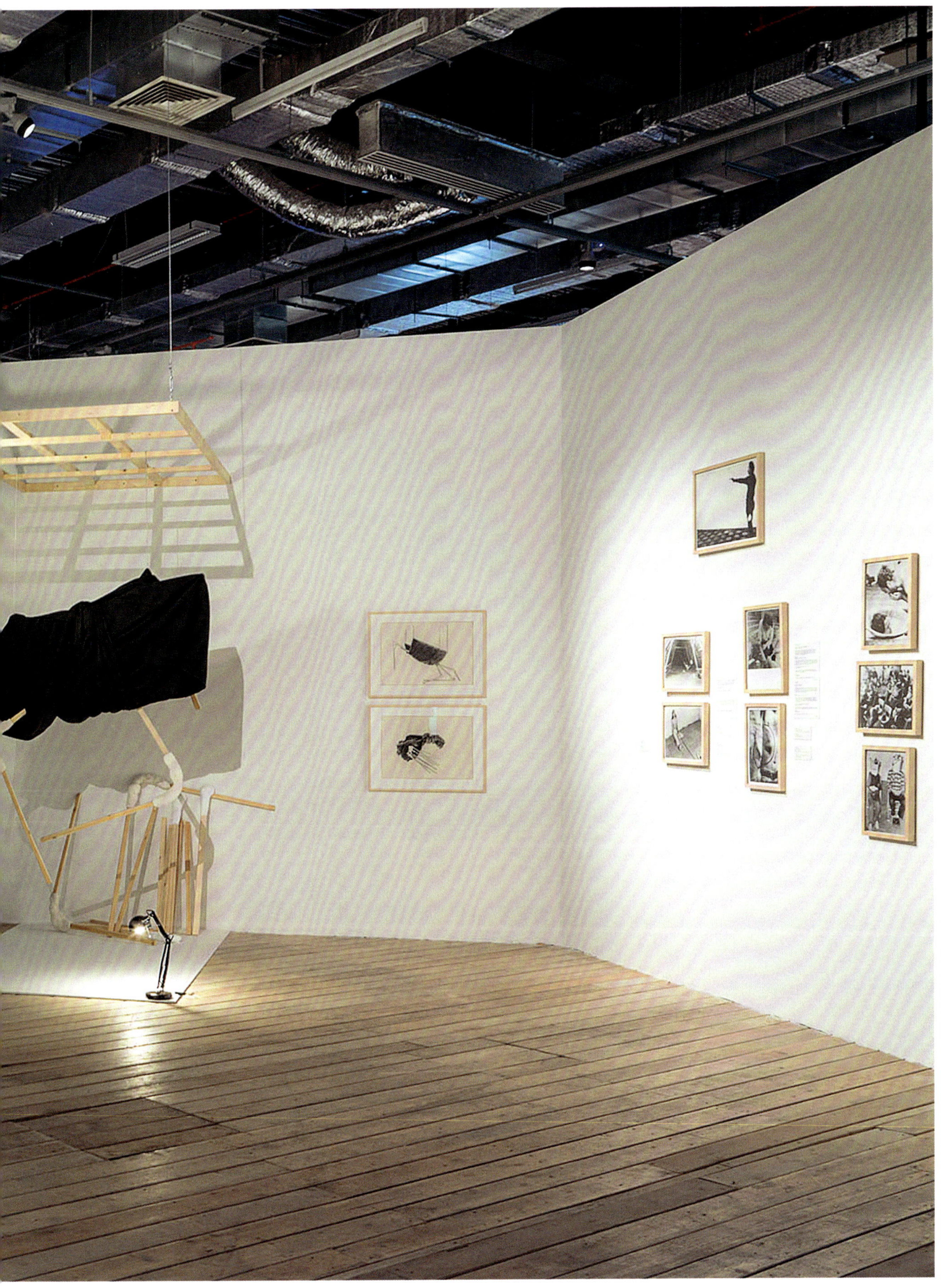

The Big and the Small /
The Arteast 2000+ Collection as
a tool for new cultural production

The Big and the Small / not a role but a tool

In 2000, Moderna galerija in Ljubljana founded
the first collection of Eastern European postwar avant-
garde art. The fact that this collection originated
in the East, as well as the redefinition of the historical
canon that started with its foundation, triggered
processes of redefining the existing model of cultural
production and creating a new one. The collection
became a permanent platform for two very important
and closely intertwined endeavors: on the one hand,
it has been working towards a greater visibility for
Eastern European art and analyzing its sociopolitical
and cultural contexts for fifteen years; on the other,
it has been consistently involved in the emergence
of new forms of cultural production.

For a long time, the collection did not have a proper space
for presentation, as the Moderna galerija building was too
small. This situation only changed in 2011, when Moderna
galerija acquired another building, part of the former
barracks of the Yugoslav army, and created a new unit,
the Museum of Contemporary Art Metelkova. This marked
the beginning of a new phase in the history of the main
Slovenian museum of modern art, founded in 1948 as
Moderna galerija. Its division into two units—the museum
of modern art and the museum of contemporary art—
necessitated defining the difference between modern
and contemporary as the difference between the historic
modernist style and something that is not only being
created today, but represents a style in itself. The
Arteast 2000+ Collection became the heart of the new
Museum of Contemporary Art Metelkova, thereby also
contributing to the definition of contemporaneity. Through
the activities of this collection and through the museum,
this contemporaneity is defined as something devoid of
a universal character. Contemporaneity is a condition that
is both a constituent part of a concrete locality and in
constant dialogue with other localities. We live in a global
world, but we communicate with it from a determined
point, establishing connections with other localities
through various resonances based on shared interests,
urgencies and similarities.

Arteast 2000+ is a collection bringing together art from
former socialist countries in a process of historicization,
not only to confer greater visibility on a previously
marginalized region, even less to declare some sort of
fixed common Eastern European identity, but primarily

in order to serve as a tool for research into the material
conditions of artistic production, of musealization, and
of distribution of art in the Eastern European region in
comparison with other contexts. With its critical perspective
on material conditions, both in the local space and in its
incorporation in wider geopolitical dynamics, the collection
has developed different approaches to musealization and
created various narratives.

Over the last fifteen years, the Arteast 2000+ Collection
has been presented as a tool for the analysis of various
instances of micro-politics and geo-politics, for exploring
new models of historicization and a more equitable
exchange of ideas in the international space, and for
inter-regional integration.

Before explaining the concept of collections as tools and
illustrating it with individual presentations of Arteast 2000+,
let me draw attention to the series of Arteast exhibitions,
which has represented a meaningful complement
to the collection, helped accelerate the processes
of historicization of the Eastern European region, and
indicated points of contact with other cultural spaces
in the world. In a sense, the series was anticipated
by the exhibition *The Body and the East: From the 1960s
to the Present*, staged at Moderna galerija in 1998, which
represented the first relatively complete overview of
performative practices in Eastern Europe. So far, there have
been four exhibitions staged as part of the series. The first
one was *Form-Specific* (2003), which deconstructed
the myth of the abstract form as universal, presenting
it rather as specific and committed to the sociopolitical
context and to various artistic traditions. The next one was
7 Sins: Ljubljana—Moscow (2004), in which curators from
Moscow and Ljubljana, Viktor Misiano, Igor Zabel, and
myself, played with stereotypes of the Eastern European
mentality, such as laziness, cynicism, collectivism,
utopianism, love of the West, lack of professionalism,
and masochism, pointing out how these vices could also be
virtues. The third was *Interrupted Histories* (2006), focusing
on the self-historicization of Eastern European artists and
partly, also, of Middle Eastern artists. The last was *Arteast
Collection 2000+23* (2006), also featured below among
the displays of the collection. While in *Interrupted Histories*
artists played the roles of archivists and curators, in *Arteast
Collection 2000+23* they took on the roles of selectors,
suggesting works for the Arteast 2000+ Collection. These
last two exhibitions foregrounded another function of art,
harmonized with the specific needs of its local space. Both
emphasized informal artistic methods of historicization,
which in Eastern Europe have often provided an alternative
for the lack of serious institutional efforts (and in places
still do). Such parallel histories have found their place
in the Arteast 2000+ Collection as well.

Below, I will clarify these different ways of understanding
the collection as a tool, illustrating them with its various
displays, from its founding in 2000 to the latest exhibition,
Grammar of Freedom/Five Lessons at Garage Museum

of Contemporary Art in Moscow (2015). Among other things, this exhibition foregrounds, in a particular way, the relation between the big and the small, which can be seen as the key metaphor of the Arteast 2000+ Collection.

In this context, the big and the small point to the diversity of relations, which are nevertheless interlinked through the constant struggle for independence and sovereignty on the part of the weaker party. However, the big and the small also frequently swap roles, since it is often the small that causes shifts and fractures the big.

This relation also characterizes the cooperation between small Ljubljana and big Moscow, a small nation and a big one. The alliance emphasizes that within unequal relations, there are always forces on both sides that oppose the dominant poles of antagonism and that, identifying the common enemy and each other's similar visions, attempt to imagine a better world. The collaboration between the art scenes of Ljubljana and Moscow has become a tradition, again and again seeking similar experiences based on which it attempts to find alternative solutions to various problems in the world of art as well as more generally. More recently, it again makes sense to revisit the shared experience of the disintegration of two former multinational states: the Soviet Union and Yugoslavia. Through the history of various conflicts, for instance the last Balkan war or the ones following the disintegration of the Soviet Union, including the last Russian-Ukrainian conflict, we learn the importance of cooperation among intellectuals and artists in identifying the common enemy among the warring parties, the enemy that, at least in the cases mentioned above, appears to lurk in imperialist tendencies, in nationalism and capitalism.

The relation between the big and the small describes relations of power, where the small is, among other things, associated with the private in relation to the official, with the relation between art and state, freedom and lack of freedom. The small seems to be absolutely powerless in the face of the big, yet this is not necessarily the case, as shown precisely by art. Art shows that before something changes in reality, it has to be imagined in a micro-situation. When the big becomes hegemonic and starts to stifle our freedom, one way to rebel against it is by using our own small grammars of freedom.

The Arteast 2000+ Collection as a tool for new cultural production

Arteast 2000+ is a pioneering collection of Eastern European art, informed from its inception by a prevalent interest in Eastern European avant-gardes. The emancipatory potential of this art has also become our principal frame of reference for developing the concept of the collection as a tool.

Let me illustrate this with a few examples of the policy of exhibiting Arteast 2000+:

The collection as a tool to enter into dialogue with the world: The collection was first exhibited in 2000 in an unrenovated former military barracks in Ljubljana. The aim was for Moderna galerija to introduce its new collection as symbolic capital with which it was entering into dialogue with the West. Subtitled *Eastern European Art in Dialogue with the West*, the exhibition included works by Western artists that were part of the museum collection, though not as numerous or as systematically collected as Eastern European art.[1]

The collection as a tool of self-definition: The second display of the Arteast 2000+ Collection was in Innsbruck, Austria in 2001. Since the venue had glass walls, which, naturally, precluded a standard installation, we displayed it in crates specially designed both for transport and display. There existed an explicit interest in presenting Eastern European art in the West, but not under the same conditions as Western art. Conceiving the display in shipping crates pointed to a tactic adopted by the East, of turning unfavorable conditions into an advantage.[2]

The collection as a tool for/of interactivity: Entitled *Arteast Collection 2000+23*, the third staging of the collection was at Moderna galerija in 2006. The exhibition was conceived together with *Maska*, a performing arts journal then celebrating its 100th issue. We invited 50 artists who had been presented in *Maska* to collaborate; they were asked to choose a work from the Arteast 2000+ Collection and then propose a work of their own to be included in the collection in 2023, when *Maska* will celebrate its 200th issue. The fact that 50 new works will be included in the collection in 2023 as a direct result of this project speaks of how the institution's role as the selector of works in the collection has, in this case, been delegated to associates. [3]

The collection as a tool for producing new knowledge about the region and its art system: The *Museum of Parallel Narratives* was staged in the frame of the museum confederation L'Internationale[(1)] at MACBA, Barcelona in 2011. The represented period matched L'Internationale's long-term research program on postwar avant-garde art between 1957 and 1986. This was a time when dictatorial regimes of various kinds ruled over a large part of the world, but it was also marked by the postwar belief in the new modern era, in which advanced technologies played an increasingly dominant role, the world was better connected by new transportation and communication systems, and the mass media were gaining power. Eastern European postwar avant-gardes were not explicitly or overtly political. Rather than expressing open criticism, they strove to create micro-political situations with art. Accordingly, the works in the exhibition were divided into a number of distinct groups.

— **Body art and other forms of performance art:** *Marina Abramović, Geta Brătescu, Ion Grigorescu, Tibor Hajas, Sanja Iveković, KwieKulik, Jan Mlčoch, Karel Miler, Petr Štembera, Ilja Šoškić,* and *Raša Todosijević.* These artists intensified the experience of social isolation, marginalization, and vulnerability.[4]

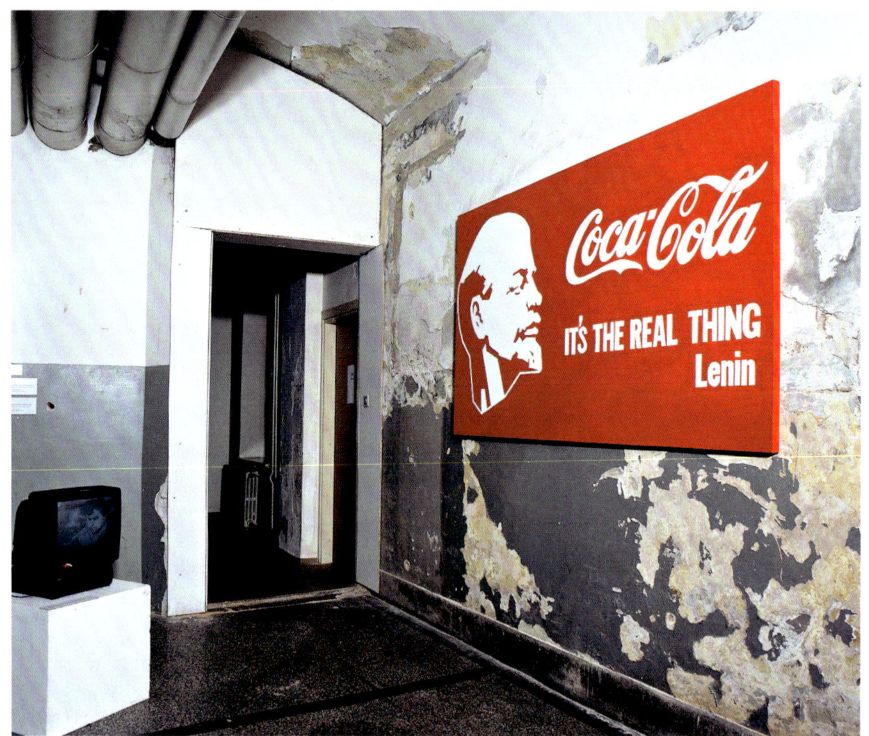

Coca-Cola
IT'S THE REAL THING
Lenin

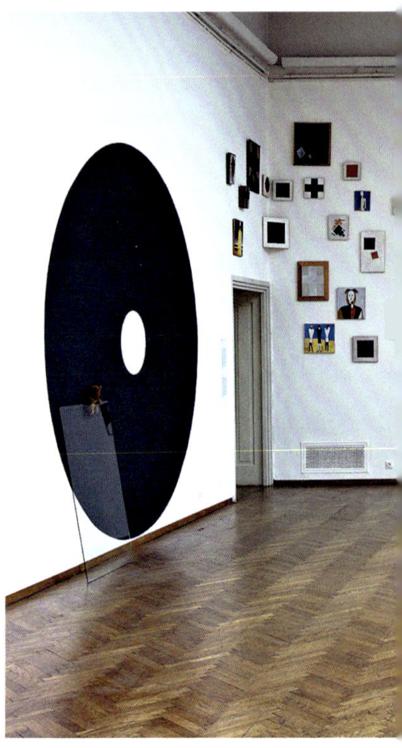

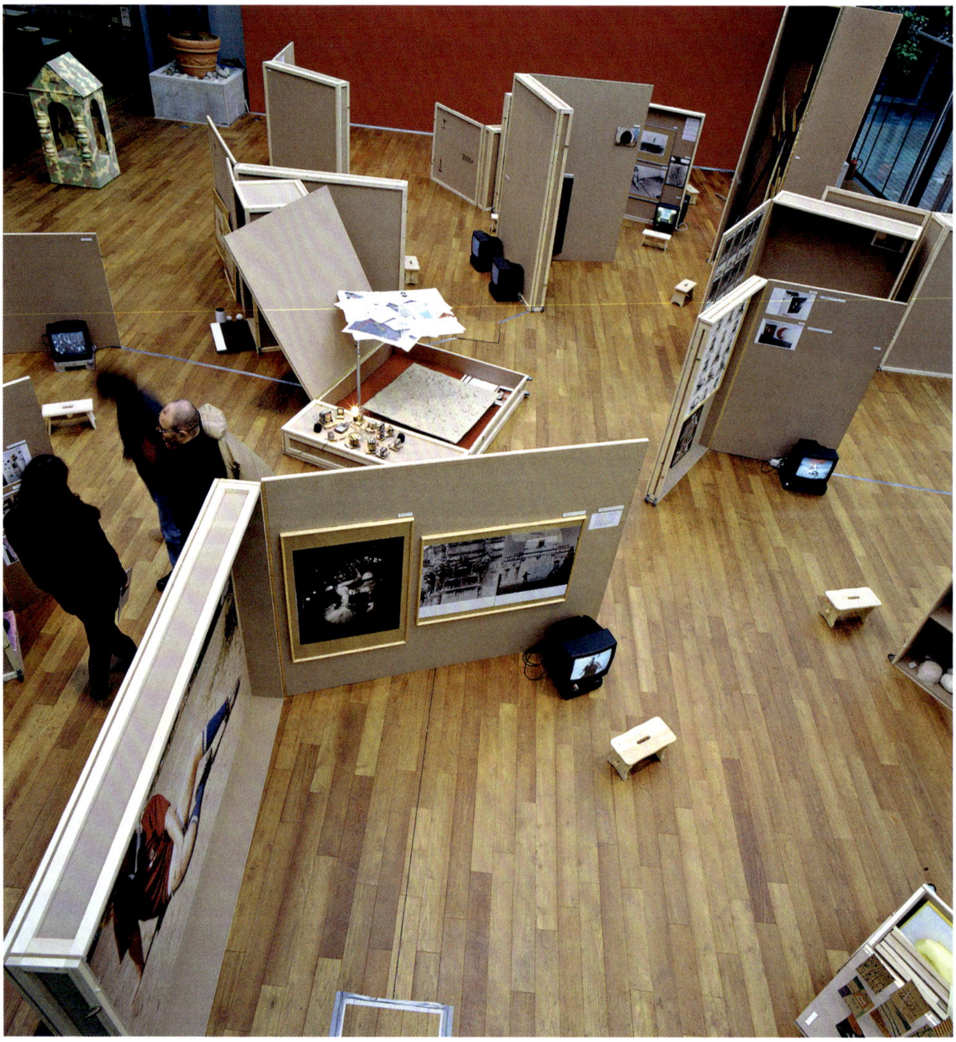

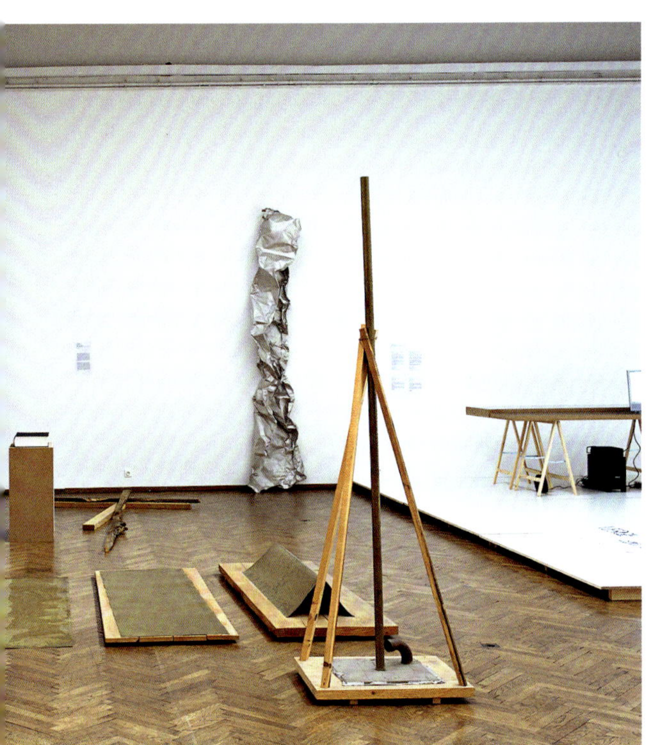

1. Alexandr Kosolapov, *Lenin Coca-Cola*, 1980
Exhibition: *Arteast 2000+: The Art of Eastern Europe in Dialogue with the West*, exhibition in the then still unrenovated museum premises on Metelkova Street (now the Museum of Contemporary Art Metelkova), Ljubljana, 2000
Photo: Lado Mlekuž, Matija Pavlovec
© Moderna galerija, Ljubljana

2. Exhibition: *Arteast 2000+: The Art of Eastern Europe*, Orangerie Congress, Innsbruck, 2001
Photo: Alex Nuding
© Moderna galerija, Ljubljana

3. Exhibition: *Arteast Collection 2000+23*, Moderna galerija, Ljubljana, 2006
From left:
Dmitri Prigov, *Pulsing Black*, 1998;
Kazimir Malevich, *The Last Futurist Exhibition*, Belgrade, 1985–1986;
Ivan Kožarić, *Installation*, 1996
Photo: Dejan Habicht, Matija Pavlovec
© Moderna galerija, Ljubljana

— **Specific forms of happenings and rituals:** *Stano Filko, Alex Mlynarčik*, and *Vlasta Delimar and Željko Jerman*. Real-time excerpts from "found" society, in which the artists observed various relationships and themselves as well, trapped in different social contradictions. [5]

— **Collective methods of work as a central theme in art:** *Josip Vaništa [Gorgona], Neue Slowenische Kunst, OHO, Walter de Maria*, and *Andrei Monastyrsky*. Through these actions a method of group work was developed that offered an alternative to the dominant ideology of collectivism. [6]

— **Actions in public space:** *Braco Dimitrijević, Tomislav Gotovac, Jiři Kovanda, Milan Knižak, Paul Neagu, OHO [Naško Križnar, Milenko Matanović, David Nez*, and *Drago Dellabernardina]*, and *Goran Trbuljak*. Many street actions, sometimes just minimal departures from everyday routine, or provocations, helped to shift the boundaries of the permissible in the minds of passersby. [7]

— **The use of language as materiality:** *Stanislaw Droždž, Dimitrije Bašičević Mangelos, Josip Vaništa [Gorgona], Julije Knifer, Miklós Erdély, OHO [Marko Pogačnik, I. G. Plamen, Franci Zagorčnik], Ana Nuša and Srečo Dragan, Vlado Martek, Jiři Valoch*, and *Endre Tót*. Presenting an opposing position to established modernist forms of art, these works were generally directed against the art establishment and the non-ideological nature of things as things. [8]

— **The media image in the socialist socio-political context:** *OM Production, Natalia LL, Tomislav Gotovac, Sanja Iveković and Dalibor Martinis*, and *Josef Robakowski*. When mass media images appeared in artworks, they served as comments on the duality between the ideology of modesty in socialist society and the unrealized desire for glamour. [9]

— **Totalitarianism as a theme and over-identification:** *Borghesia, Ion Grigorescu, Marina Gržinić and Aina Šmid, Neue Slowenische Kunst [the groups IRWIN, Laibach, the Scipion Nasice Sisters Theater*, and *New Collectivism]; Komar and Melamid, Alexander Kosolapov, Mladen Stilinović, Kazimir Malevich of Belgrade, Ilya Kabakov*, and *Vladimir Kupriyanov*. The retro-avant-garde and Sots Art artists especially, but also certain representatives of the alternative culture of the 1980s, combined the imaginaries of different totalitarian societies in order to draw attention to the ever stronger and ever more obvious contradictions in socialist society. [10]

— **Diagrams relating to the musealization of Eastern European art:** These primarily contained information about the presence of works by individual artists in public and private collections over several decades (until the present). By answering questions about their works' presence in different collections the artists provided an important report on the workings of the art system in the region. Despite the fact that the disastrous results

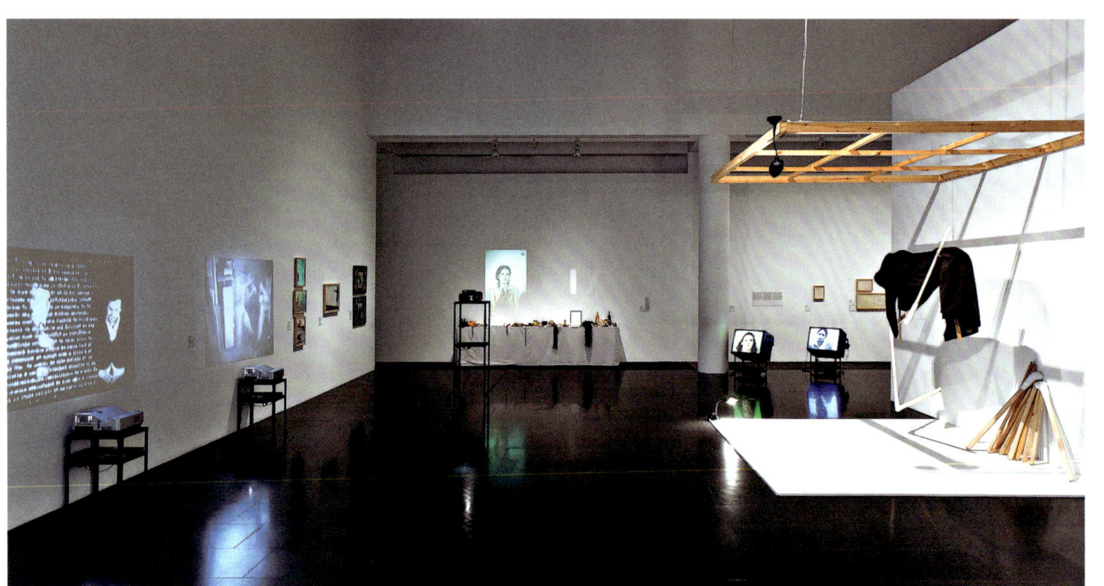

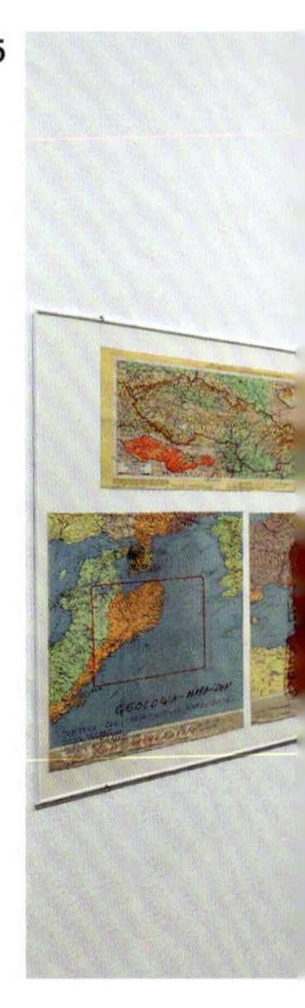

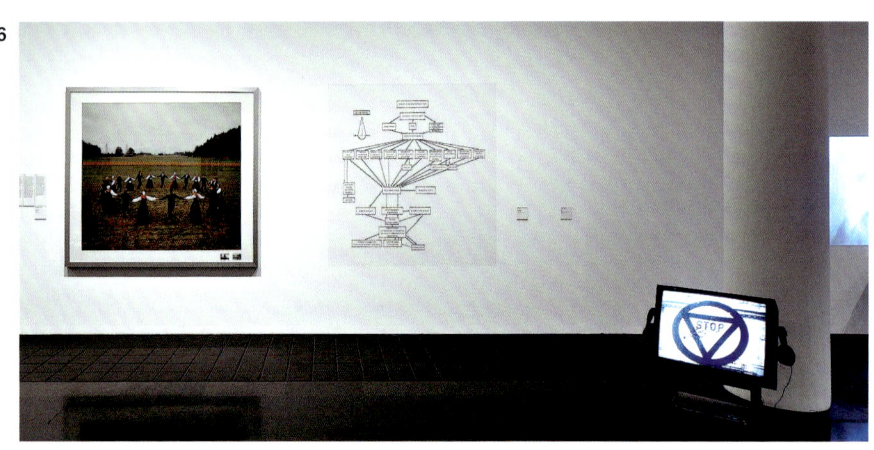

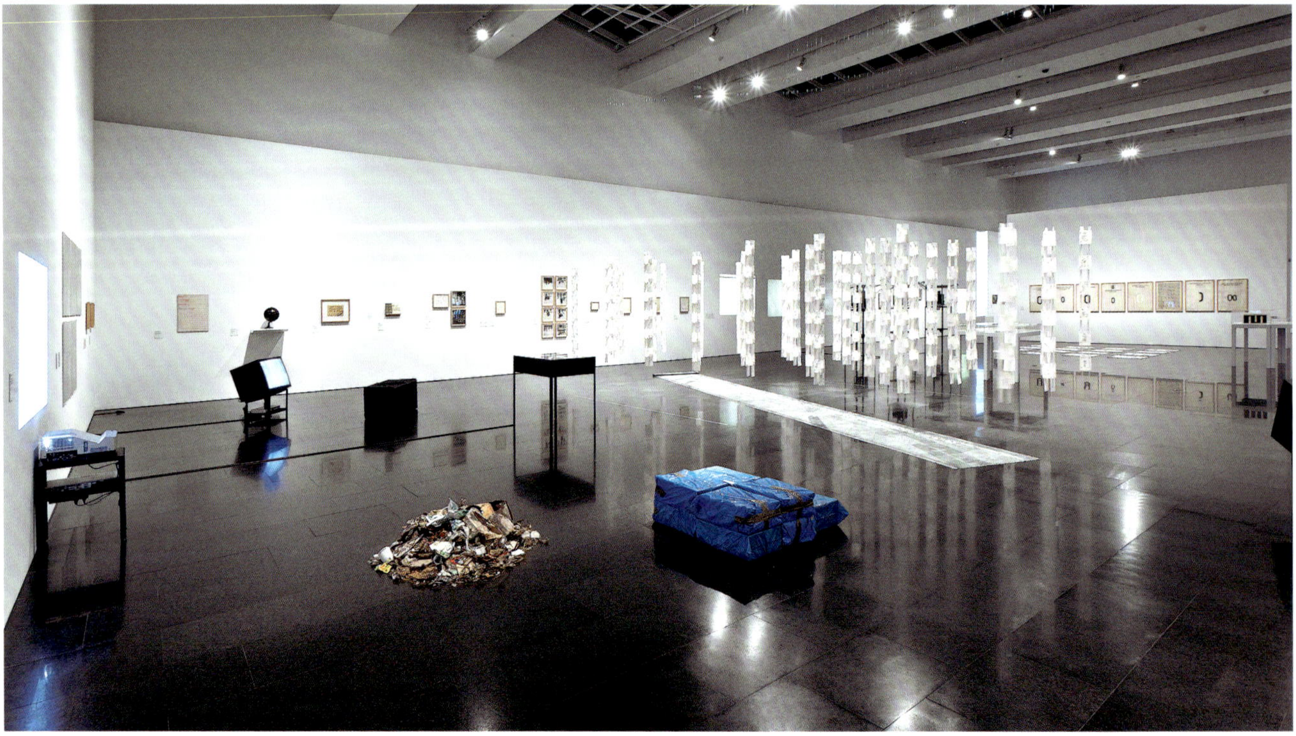

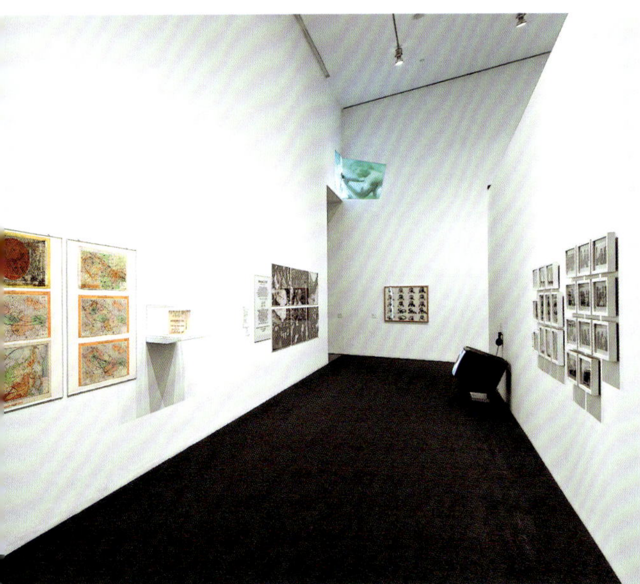

4. Body art and other forms of
performance art
Exhibition: *Museum
of Parallel Narratives*, MACBA,
Barcelona, 2011
From left:
Ion Grigorescu, videos;
Marina Abramović, *Rhythm 0*, 1974;
Geta Brătescu, *No to Violence*,
1974
Photo: Rafael Vargas
Courtesy of the MACBA Study
Center

5. Specific forms of happenings
and rituals
Exhibition: *Museum
of Parallel Narratives*, MACBA,
Barcelona, 2011
Stano Filko, *HAPPSOC III: Altar
of Contemporaneity*, 1966
Photo: Rafael Vargas
Courtesy of the MACBA Study
Center

6. Collective methods of working
became the central theme of art
Exhibition: *Museum
of Parallel Narratives*, MACBA,
Barcelona, 2011
From left:
IRWIN, *Panorama NSK*, 1997;
Neue Slowenische Kunst (NSK),
The NSK Organigram, 1984
Photo: Rafael Vargas
Courtesy of the MACBA Study
Center

7. Actions in public spaces
Exhibition: *Museum
of Parallel Narratives*, MACBA,
Barcelona, 2011
Tomislav Gotovac, *Cleaning Public
Spaces*, 1981–1989/*Homage to
Christo*, 1981–1989
Photo: Rafael Vargas
Courtesy of the MACBA Study
Center

for the 1960s, 1970s, and 1980s have improved slightly over the past twenty years, the arithmetic mean of the results gathered by the *Questionnaires* remains somewhere around zero. [11]

The collection as a tool to define the idea of a museum of contemporary art and of contemporaneity:
The exhibition *The Present and Presence* marked the opening of the new Museum of Contemporary Art Metelkova in 2011. It centered on various ideas of time (*Lived Time, Future Time, No Future, War Time, Ideological Time, Dominant Time, Quantitative Time, Creative Time, Time of the Absent Museum, Retro Time, Time of Passage*). It defined contemporaneity as presence and the present. "Presence" here means an active relationship with one's own time, and "the present," the period in which we live. Contemporary art must belong at one and the same time both to the present and to presence. We can say that our present started in the late 1980s with increased circulation of global capital and the ubiquity of digital technologies. For Eastern Europe, this period represents another turning point as well, marked by the fall of the communist regimes, the emergence of new sovereign states, and also war. While the present relates to chronological time, that is not necessarily true of presence, which means an individual's active position; it can also be interpreted as participation—for the artist, this is presence in real time; for the viewer, presence in the artwork; and for the historian, presence through participating in a multitude of histories. A contemporary art museum is no longer based on a universal concept of art and its autonomous logic, but instead follows the authentic interest of a given space. Authentic interest looks for local priorities and their consonance with similar examples in the world. [12]

The collection as a tool for a critique of the conditions of contemporary art: *The Present and Presence / Repetition* is a series of exhibitions that we have staged since 2012, based on the concept of repetition. Our new Museum of Contemporary Art Metelkova opened in late 2011. A month later we were informed that we would not be getting any additional funding for the program in the new building. With almost no money we thus decided to repeat the exhibition that was still on display, the one we had opened our new museum with. In our manifesto of repetition we described repeating as a form of "recycling" in a crisis—a critical reaction to existing local and global conditions. Our repetition aims to draw critical attention to the ever more quickly changing exhibitions and other art events that happen today, as well as to the too-fast and too-superficial consumption of intellectual content and to the importance of re-reading. Repetition is also one of the fundamental features of contemporary art (just think of the video loop, the use of documentation, popular art genres such as re-enactment, and such curatorial buzzwords as "redefine," "rethink," and "revisit"). For us especially, it was also important to emphasize the fact that repetition is a crucial principle in

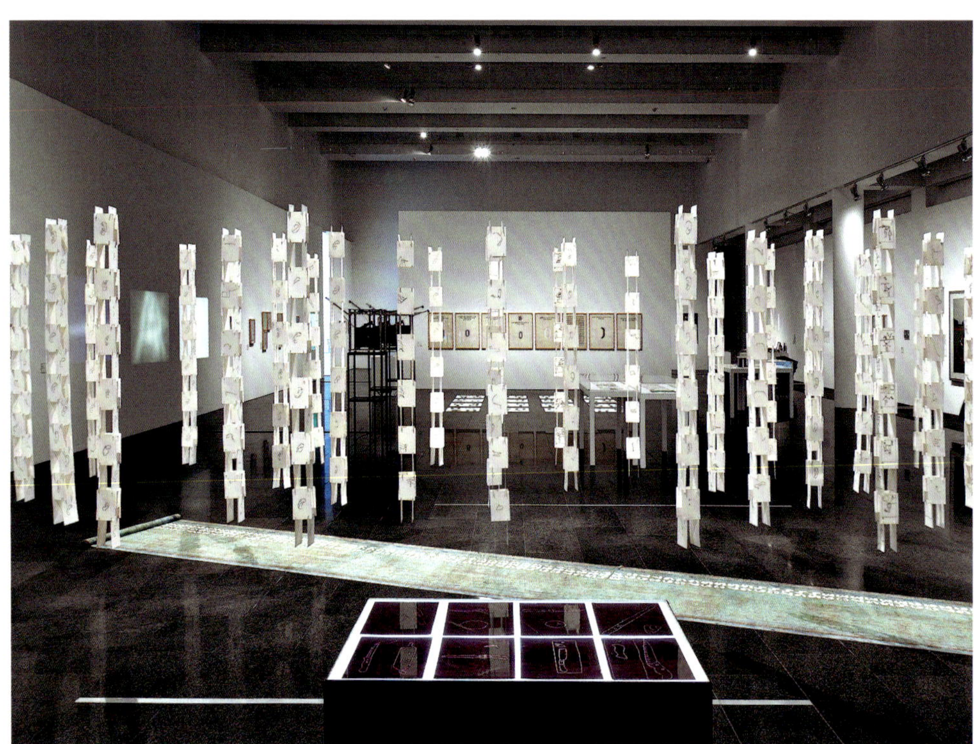

10

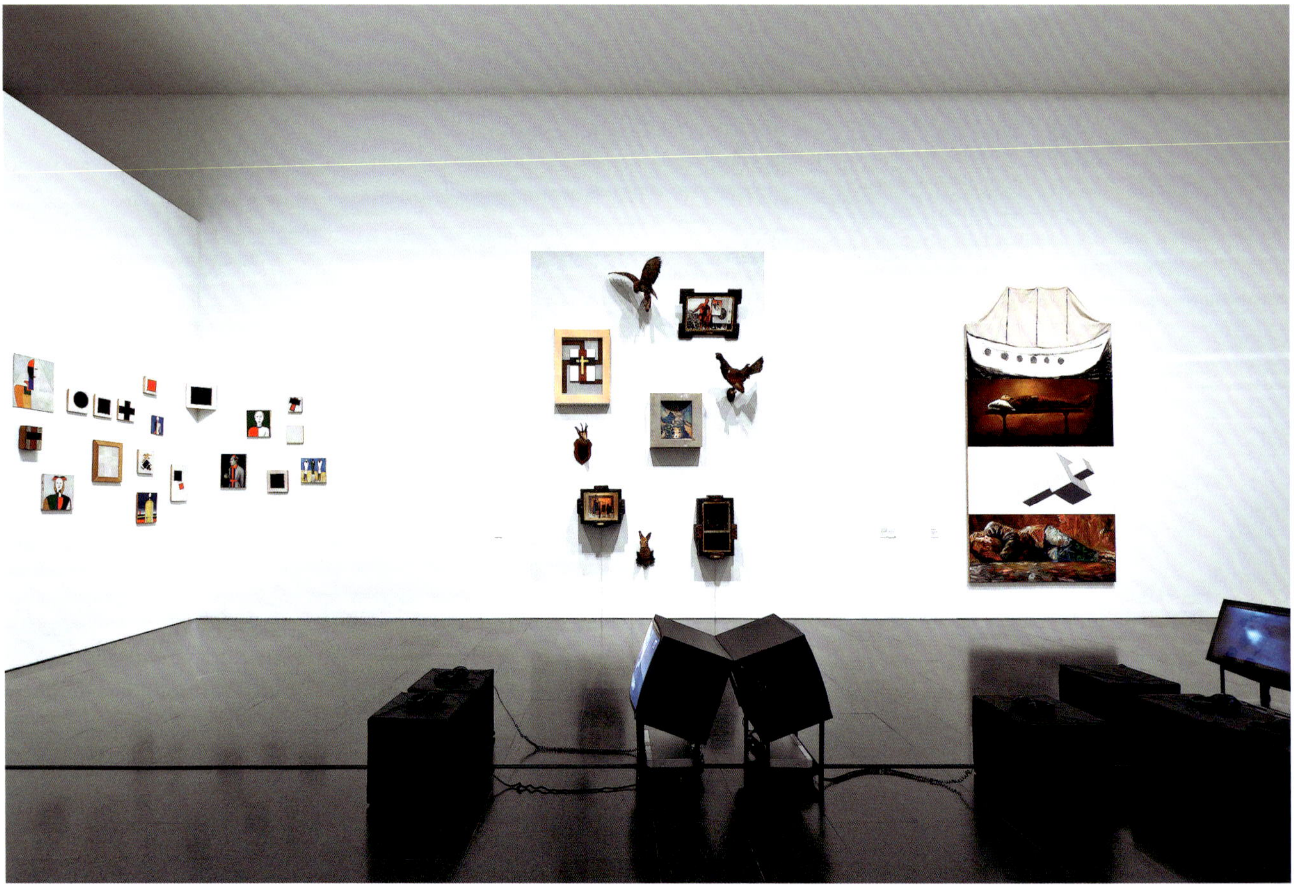

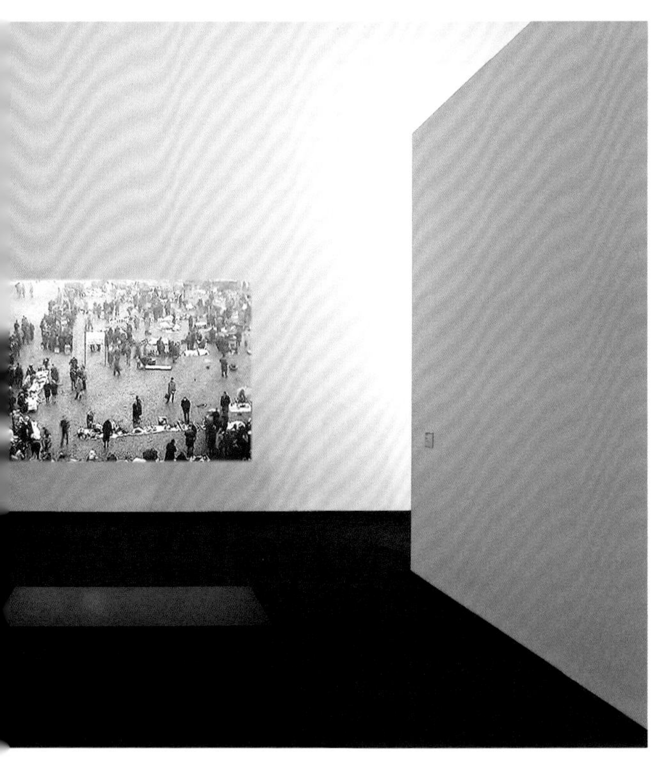

the creation of a history, for which a developed art system is needed. Repetition is driven by trauma, and here we are principally interested in two traumas associated with the territory of Eastern European art: the trauma of the absence of a developed art system and the trauma of the unrealized emancipatory ideals of communism.[13]

The collection as a tool for fighting the common enemy. The exhibition *Grammar of Freedom/Five Lessons* prepared for Garage Museum of Contemporary Art in Moscow (2015) continues in the vein of the collection policy, underlining two aspects:

— The dialogue between Eastern European artists, in this case particularly between Yugoslav and Russian artists, in the light of references to the Russian historical avant-garde and contemporary common projects by artists from different parts of the region;

— The search for artistic freedom in various periods, first in the context of the stifling conditions under the socialist regimes, then during the war in the 1990s (in the territory of the former Yugoslavia), and now in the time of global neoliberal capitalism and new conflicts (particularly between Russia and Ukraine).

The exhibition is organized as five lessons, enabling the viewer to navigate both the dialogue between Yugoslav and Russian artists and the timeline of the postwar Eastern European avant-gardes.

The first lesson is entitled *The body as a tool for liberation* and explores how artists have used the connection of the physical to the psychological "self" to draw attention to external situations. The second—*The transformation of systems*—focuses on the machinations of the art world with all its inherent inequities and paradoxes, to reveal how artists have found creative ways to make their voices heard locally, regionally, and internationally. The next section—*The power of collaboration*—accentuates the pivotal role that collaborative practice has played in amplifying artists' concepts and ideas. The fourth lesson, called *The practice of self-organization as resistance*, critiques the conditions of labor and champions various forms of self-organization. Finally, *The potential for uniting through adversity* highlights the need—particularly in times of conflict and war—to recognize common "enemies" such as nationalism, aspects of the global capitalist system, and religious fundamentalism.

Grammar not as a role but as a tool

Given that grammar sets rules for writing and speaking, the question is whether "a grammar of freedom" is not a contradiction in terms. We have already said in the introduction that the relation between the big and the small is not absolute but rather depends on the circumstances. By the same token, we can say that rules in general are similarly dependent on life.

8. The use of language as materiality
Exhibition: *Museum of Parallel Narratives*, MACBA, Barcelona, 2011
OHO, Marko Pogačnik, *Programmed Environment*, 1969
Photo: Rafael Vargas
Courtesy of the MACBA Study Center

9. The media image in the socialist socio-political context
Exhibition: *Museum of Parallel Narratives*, MACBA, Barcelona, 2011
Józef Robakowski, *The Market*, 1970
Photo: Rafael Vargas
Courtesy of the MACBA Study Center

10. Totalitarianism as a theme
Exhibition: *Museum of Parallel Narratives*, MACBA, Barcelona, 2011
From left:
Kazimir Malevich, *The Last Futurist Exhibition*, Belgrade, 1985–1986;
IRWIN, *Kapital*, 1984–2000;
Komar and Melamid, *Smooth Sailing with Lenin*, 1985
Photo: Rafael Vargas
Courtesy of the MACBA Study Center

1.) KOLIKO VAŠIH DEL JE BILO V VAŠI DRŽAVI VKLJUČENIH V / HOW MANY OF YOUR WORKS WERE INCLUDED IN YOUR LOCAL (NATIONAL)

A) zbirke javnih muzejev / public museums' collections

	umetniki, ki so začeli delati v 60. letih 20. stol. / artists who started working in the 1960s	umetniki, ki so začeli delati v 70. letih 20. stol. / artists who started working in the 1970s	umetniki, ki so začeli delati v 80. letih 20. stol. / artists who started working in the 1980s	umetniki, ki so začeli delati v 90. letih 20. stol. / artists who started working in the 1990s	umetniki, ki so začeli delati v 21. stol. / artists who started working in the 2000s	skupno število odgovorov vseh umetnikov / the sum total of answers by all of the artists	najpogostejši odgovor za posamezno desetletje / the majority answer for the individual decade
v 60. letih 20. stol. / in the 1960s	7A, 2B, 1C					7A, 2B, 1C	A
v 70. letih 20. stol. / in the 1970s	3A, 3B, 3C, 1E	10A, 3B, 1C, 1D, 2E				13A, 6B, 4C, 1D, 3E	A
v 80. letih 20. stol. / in the 1980s	2A, 3B, 2C, 2D, 1E	8A, 4B, 3C, 2D	7A, 3B, 3C, 3E			17A, 10B, 8C, 4D, 4E	A
v 90. letih 20. stol. / in the 1990s	2A, 1B, 2C, 3D, 2E	4A, 1B, 2C, 8D, 1E	5A, 5B, 3C, 1D, 2E	2A, 10B, 1C, 1D		13A, 17B, 8C, 13D, 5E	B
v 21. stoletju / in the 2000s	1A, 1B, 3C, 5E	4A, 3B, 3C, 3D, 5E	8B, 3C, 3D, 3E	4A, 6B, 2C, 1D, 1E	1A, 2B, 1C	10A, 20B, 12C, 7D, 14E	B

B) zasebne zbirke / private collections

	umetniki, ki so začeli delati v 60. letih 20. stol. / artists who started working in the 1960s	umetniki, ki so začeli delati v 70. letih 20. stol. / artists who started working in the 1970s	umetniki, ki so začeli delati v 80. letih 20. stol. / artists who started working in the 1980s	umetniki, ki so začeli delati v 90. letih 20. stol. / artists who started working in the 1990s	umetniki, ki so začeli delati v 21. stol. / artists who started working in the 2000s	skupno število odgovorov vseh umetnikov / the sum total of answers by all of the artists	najpogostejši odgovor za posamezno desetletje / the majority answer for the individual decade
v 60. letih 20. stol. / in the 1960s	5A, 5B					5A, 5B	A
v 70. letih 20. stol. / in the 1970s	3A, 1B, 1C, 3D, 2E	12A, 1B, 2C, 1D, 2D				15A, 2B, 3C, 5D, 2E	A
v 80. letih 20. stol. / in the 1980s	2A, 1B, 1C, 1D, 5E	8A, 2B, 2C, 4D, 1E	6A, 3B, 1C, 1D, 5E			16A, 6B, 4C, 6D, 11E	A
v 90. letih 20. stol. / in the 1990s	2A, 2C, 2D, 4E	9A, 2B, 2D, 3E	5A, 3B, 2C, 2D, 5E	5A, 3B, 2C, 2D, 2E		21A, 8B, 6C, 8D, 14E	A
v 21. stoletju / in the 2000s	1A, 1B, 2C, 1D, 4E	7A, 2B, 1C, 1D, 5E	3A, 5B, 2C, 1D, 6E	2A, 4B, 3C, 3D, 2E	2B, 1D, 1E	13A, 14B, 8C, 7D, 18E	E

C) zbirke drugih umetnikov / other artists' collections

	umetniki, ki so začeli delati v 60. letih 20. stol. / artists who started working in the 1960s	umetniki, ki so začeli delati v 70. letih 20. stol. / artists who started working in the 1970s	umetniki, ki so začeli delati v 80. letih 20. stol. / artists who started working in the 1980s	umetniki, ki so začeli delati v 90. letih 20. stol. / artists who started working in the 1990s	umetniki, ki so začeli delati v 21. stol. / artists who started working in the 2000s	skupno število odgovorov vseh umetnikov / the sum total of answers by all of the artists	najpogostejši odgovor za posamezno desetletje / the majority answer for the individual decade
v 60. letih 20. stol. / in the 1960s	6A, 2B, 2C					6A, 2B, 2C	A
v 70. letih 20. stol. / in the 1970s	5A, 2C, 1D, 2E	9A, 6B, 1C, 1E				14A, 6B, 3C, 1D, 3E	A
v 80. letih 20. stol. / in the 1980s	4A, 2B, 1D, 3E	9A, 2B, 2C, 2D, 1E	6A, 2B, 3C, 4D, 2E			19A, 6B, 5C, 7D, 6E	A
v 90. letih 20. stol. / in the 1990s	5A, 1C, 3E	8A, 5B, 1C, 2E	6A, 2B, 2C, 3D, 4E	7A, 2B, 1C, 4D		26A, 9B, 5C, 7D, 9E	A
v 21. stoletju / in the 2000s	5A, 1C, 3E	8A, 3B, 3C, 2E	8A, 2B, 1C, 2D, 4E	7A, 1B, 2C, 3D, 1E	2A, 1B, 1E	30A, 7B, 7C, 5D, 11E	A

<table>
<tr><td colspan="2" rowspan="2">1-3 dela / works
3-5 del / works
5-10 del / works
več kot 10 del / more than 10 works</td><td colspan="8" align="center">VADIM FIŠKIN</td></tr>
<tr><td colspan="3" align="center">v domovini / locally</td><td colspan="5" align="center">mednarodno / internationally</td></tr>
<tr><td rowspan="2">javni muzeji / public museums</td><td colspan="2">zasebne zbirke / private collections</td><td rowspan="2">javni muzeji / public museums</td><td colspan="4">zasebne zbirke / private collections</td></tr>
<tr><td rowspan="2">zbiralci / collectors</td><td rowspan="2">umetniki / other artists</td><td colspan="2">zbiratelji / collectors</td><td colspan="2">umetniki / other artists</td></tr>
<tr><td></td><td></td><td></td><td></td><td>Zahod / the West</td><td>drugod / the rest</td><td>Zahod / the West</td><td>drugod / the rest</td><td>Zahod / the West</td><td>drugod / the rest</td></tr>
<tr><td>v 60. letih 20. stol. / in the 1960s</td><td></td><td></td><td></td><td></td><td></td><td></td><td></td><td></td><td></td></tr>
<tr><td>v 70. letih 20. stol. / in the 1970s</td><td></td><td></td><td></td><td></td><td></td><td></td><td></td><td></td><td></td></tr>
<tr><td>v 80. letih 20. stol. / in the 1980s</td><td></td><td></td><td></td><td></td><td></td><td></td><td></td><td></td><td></td></tr>
<tr><td>v 90. letih 20. stol. / in the 1990s</td><td></td><td></td><td></td><td></td><td></td><td></td><td></td><td></td><td></td></tr>
<tr><td>v 21. stoletju / in the 21ʰ c.</td><td></td><td></td><td></td><td></td><td></td><td></td><td></td><td></td><td></td></tr>
</table>

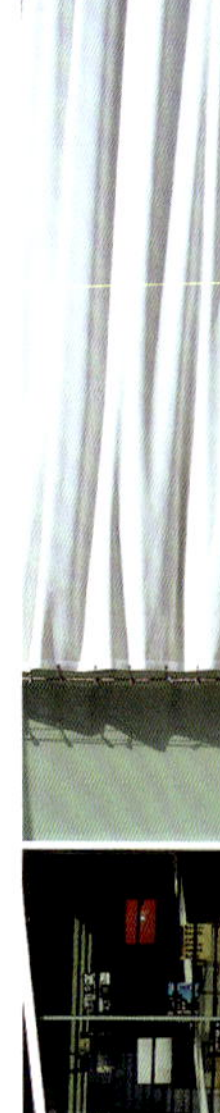

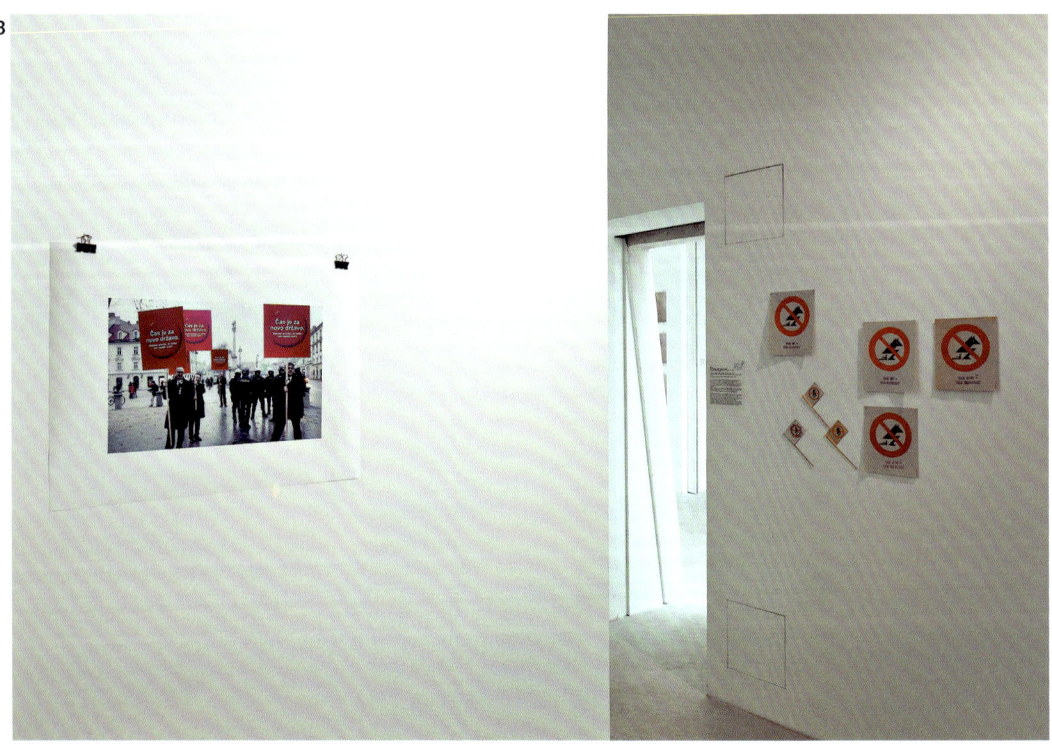

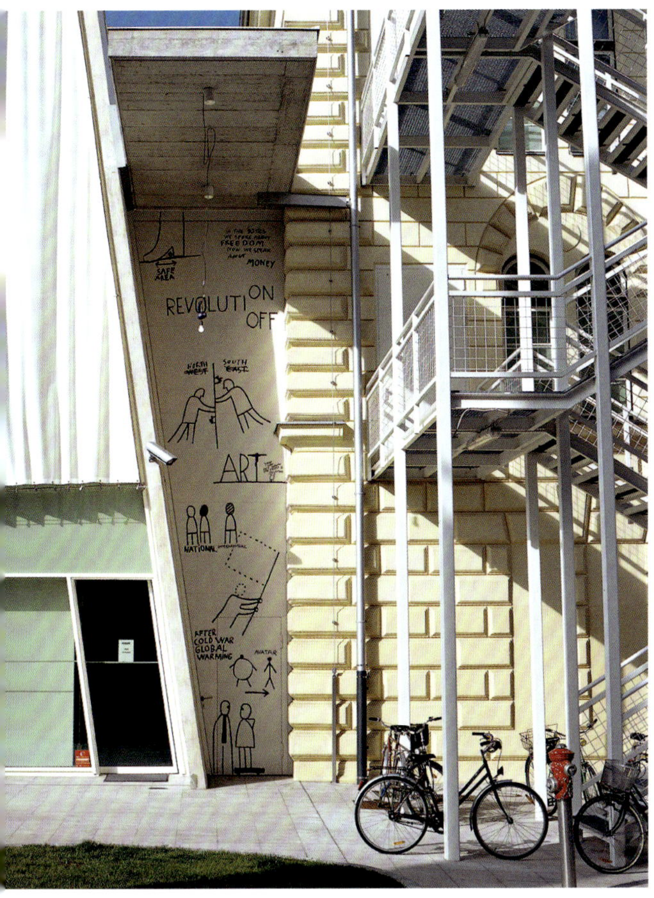

The Arteast 2000+ Collection presents art from a region not yet contained in the system of dominant history, that is, the system of established rules. We can safely say that the history of Eastern Europe has not yet been written, and hence is situated somewhere between rules and life. Giorgio Agamben describes the relationship between the rule and life: "Neither written word nor living voice, the rule constantly moves between these polarities, in search of an ideal of the perfect common life that [it] is precisely meant to define."[2]

On the one hand, the Moscow staging of the Arteast 2000+ Collection speaks about the lessons in the grammar of freedom that we receive from the art in the collection, and on the other hand, about the uses of the collection itself in similar emancipatory processes. Both the art and its collection foreground the use of the grammar, that is the use of the language of art and of the collection, which can keep changing and is therefore free.

Art collections are formed on the basis of certain classification systems with the purpose of representing art which fits the categories included in such systems. Any instrumentality of such a collection, whether ideological, political, or commercial, is usually hidden from view. We could say that the particularity of Arteast 2000+ is that it reveals itself as a tool for something beyond a seemingly neutral presentation of art. It is fairly rare for a collection to present itself as a tool, since it remains in the interest of ideology and of capital to show things in their function as spectacles, separate from their profanity. Agamben[3] speaks of how profanity restores to free usage that which, divorced from primary behaviors, has become either sacred or merchandise, or limited to its exhibition value. In a way, for Agamben, profanation means a demusealization of the world, or at least the demusealization of the world where the museum had become part of the general spectacle. The use of our collection could thus be understood as a deactivation of the apparent neutrality of the collection, that is, the deactivation of its own musealization. Arteast 2000+, then, can be thought of in terms of profane musealization and hence in terms of its liberating potential.

Zdenka Badovinac
Director Moderna galerija, Ljubljana

11. *Questionnaires*, 2011–2012
© Moderna galerija, Ljubljana

12. Museum of Contemporary Art Metelkova (MSUM), Ljubljana
Dan Perjovschi, *In 1990 We Spoke About Freedom, Now We Speak About Money*, 2011
Photo: Dejan Habicht
© Moderna galerija, Ljubljana

13. Exhibition: *Present and Presence / Repetition 3: The Street*, Museum of Contemporary Art Metelkova (MSUM), Ljubljana, 2013
From left:
IRWIN, *Time for a New State*, 2012;
Škart, *Your Shit–Your Responsibility*, 2000
Photo: Dejan Habicht
© Moderna galerija, Ljubljana

(1) L'Internationale is a confederation of six modern and contemporary art institutions. It proposes a space for art within a non-hierarchical and decentralized internationalism, based on the values of difference and horizontal exchange among a constellation of cultural agents, locally rooted and globally connected. It brings together six major European museums: Moderna galerija (MG+MSUM, Ljubljana, Slovenia); Museo Nacional Centro de Arte Reina Sofía (MNCARS, Madrid, Spain); Museu d'Art Contemporani de Barcelona (MACBA, Barcelona, Spain); Museum van Hedendaagse Kunst Antwerpen (M HKA, Antwerp, Belgium); SALT (Istanbul and Ankara, Turkey) and Van Abbemuseum (VAM, Eindhoven, The Netherlands).

(2) Giorgio Agamben, *The Highest Poverty: Monastic Rules and Form-of-Life* (Stanford, Stanford University Press, 2013), 75.
(3) Giorgio Agamben, *Profanations*, (New York: Zone Books, 2007).

I KNOW YOU
ARE HERE
READING
BUT YOU HAVE
NO IDEA
WHERE I AM. [1]

In his recollections describing the short but crucial three years before the Chapel Studio[2] was forcibly closed down in 1973, the influential Hungarian artist Gyorgy Galantai tells of his regular exchanges with the police, which led to the elaboration of a set of useful tactical considerations. In order to carry out his plan and transform the Studio into a "small Hungarian Documenta," he frequently came face-to-face with the "strange cultural creatures" who persistently searched for overtly political works. Stating that it was not an exhibition and placing "private property" signs did not stop them, so he started adopting various other strategies. One of the most important, according to Galantai, was never to confront the authorities head on. Aware that their ideology was based on Marxist dialectics he staged lectures on related subjects and learned the rhetoric so well that he could out speak them by virtue of his knowledge. When, in 1979, Galantai and Júlia Klaniczay went on to found the Artpool project,[3] its survival was based on these intuitively accumulated tactics. Their "uncensorable" apartment-institution worked "with an exact aim and direction, sensitively detecting changes and adjusting accordingly."[4] Today, the Artpool Art Research Center is still active and producing an archive of art from East-Central Europe, a testimony to the fact that a sense of vigilance, intuition, and adjustment is as important as the friendship and love that kept it running. What mattered was to retain a memory of the inconvenient histories which the state wanted simply erased. Instead Galantai and Klaniczay meticulously recorded and distributed them, while also generating new histories, giving the right to lesser-known narratives to be preserved and re-visited at a later date.

Contemporary art in Russia today also falls under the rubric of "inconvenient histories" and remains a marginal, unpopular field, exposed to continuous pressures, not only locally but also from the international art community. In Moscow, the few publicly-minded art institutions employ various tactics to deal with such pressures, and they are often spontaneously administrated in reaction to a new ruling, to circumvent state or religious censorship, budget cuts, or legal restrictions affecting culture such as the recent law concerning film and video screenings.[5] To this local control are added external constraints such as boycotts by international artists and institutions of events in Russia and a refusal to lend works of art on the part of international museums. All of these "withdrawals" seriously threaten the access to contemporary culture locally and the development of a dialogue beyond the immediate community. A generally pessimistic mood regarding the future in Moscow is vocalized by many local cultural practitioners, taking into account the escalating clashes in Ukraine, the menace of war between the two nations, the economic crisis, and, ultimately, the (self-inflicted?) isolation of Russia from the world. The risk of an exodus is very palpable, especially among the younger, post-Soviet generation. In this rather gloomy atmosphere, one of the most positive twists on the various dark perspectives was expressed recently by the Russian historian Alexander Shubin (not without irony and bitterness): "At the very least, we have Putin to thank for freeing history from point zero."[6]

At this time, when constructing history is tantamount to parsing mediatized quotation, staging an exhibition called *Grammar of Freedom* that revisits how artists have historically responded to real world situations and inequities seems a timely and relevant "tactical consideration." An even more important aspect is that the "grammar" of strategies proposed is based on a new model of historicization that is uniquely Eastern European; it has become increasingly evident to those of us working in Russian art institutions that we need to look at something other than the canonic American or European models of museum collections. In fact, we need to invent something of our own.

This process is already underway—particularly through the privately-funded but publicly-minded museums—but to turn to examples within the territory that share a socialist past with Russia; to explore scenarios that remain culturally overlooked and yet are still relevant now; to understand how exchanges happen on a sporadic, unregulated basis but endure, is to delve deeper into the legacies that we can learn through and from.

It is interesting to analyze the different types of contemporaneity in relation to the concept of timeliness. If on a basic level contemporaneity evokes the irrevocable time that is close to us, that is "with us," being timely becomes all the more an act of punctuation, of rupturing any comfortable perception of being "with time." In socially and politically charged environments such as Russia today, timeliness seems under constant threat. This process is governed not only by an inability to see clearly what the present is but, first and foremost, by an apparent breakdown when trying to catch up with the speed at which events develop. This could be the very definition of the term, and yet it is interesting

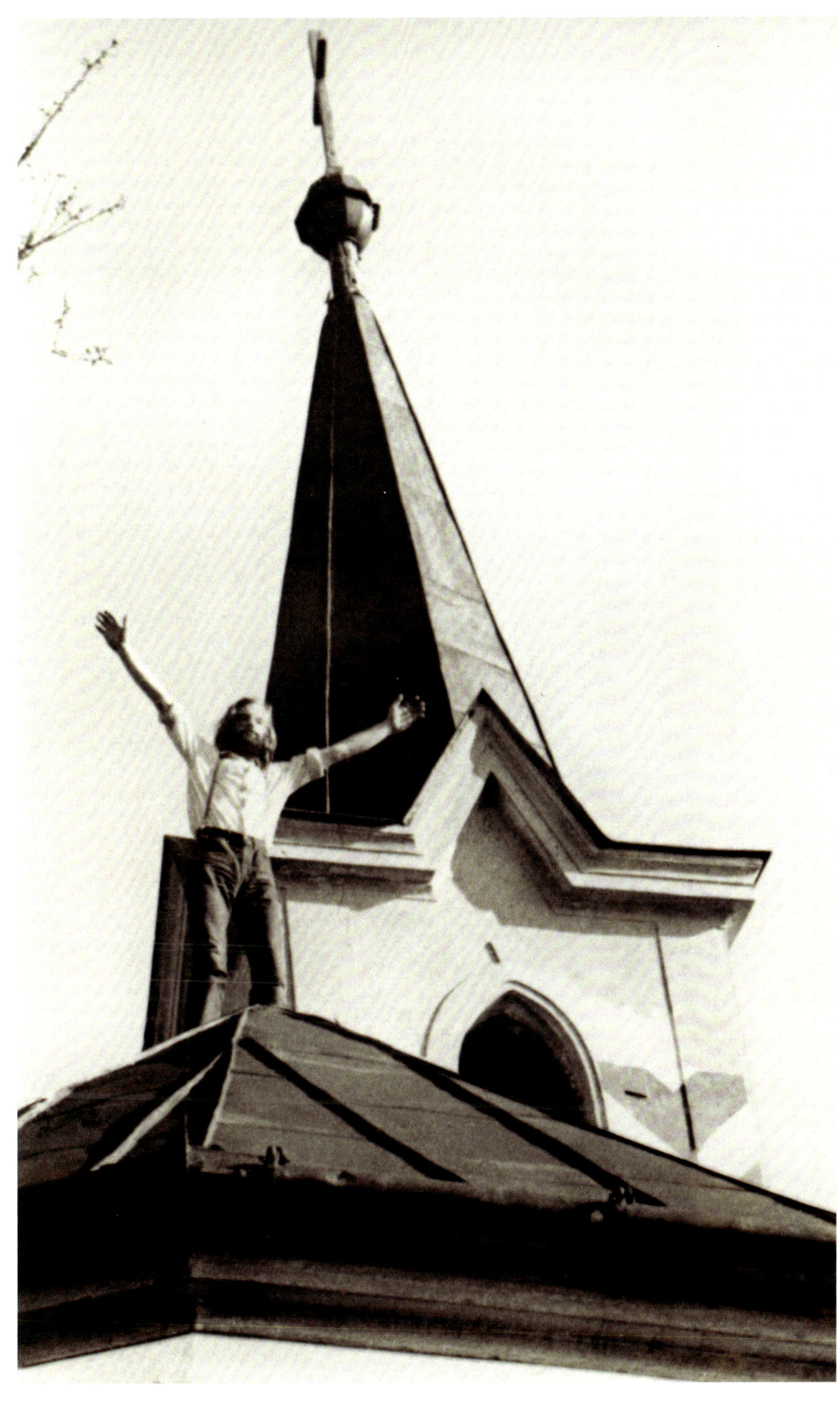

György Galántai on the roof of his Chapel Studio in 1973
© Artpool Art Research Center

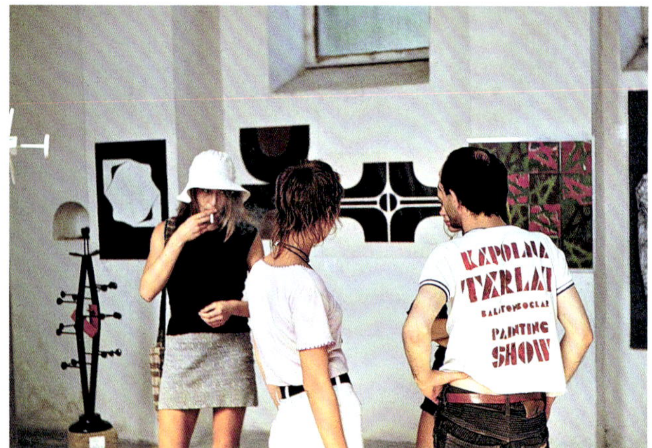

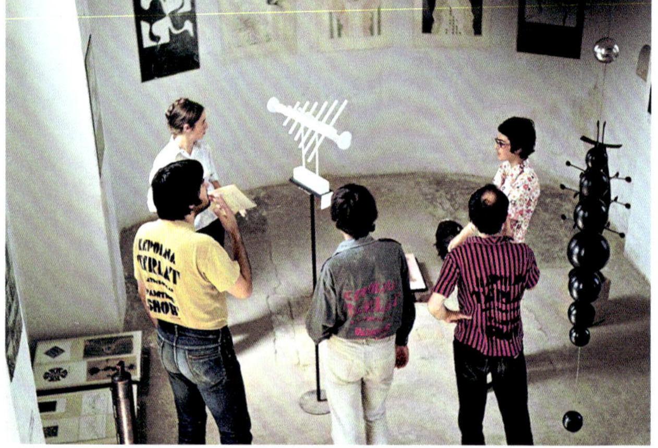

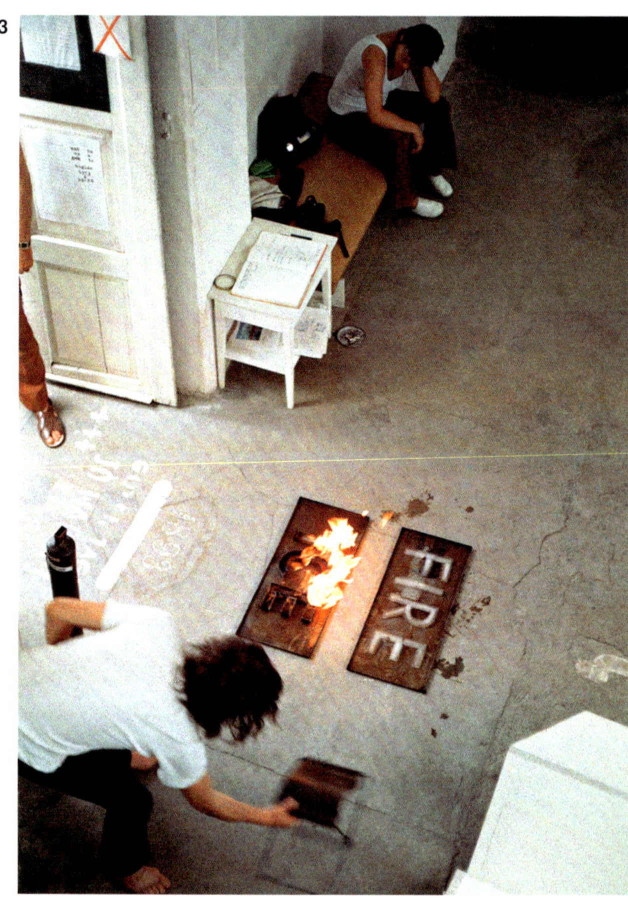

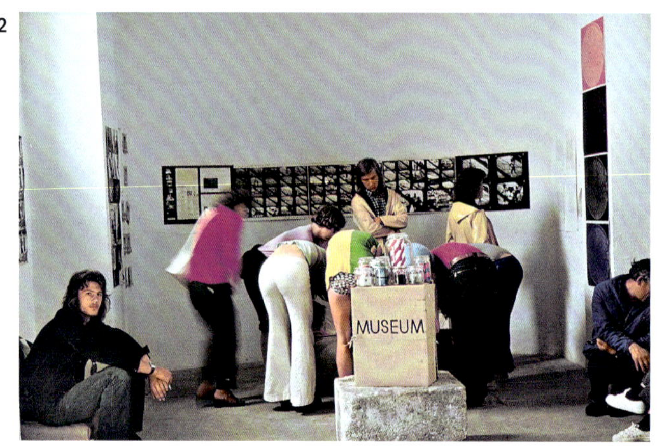

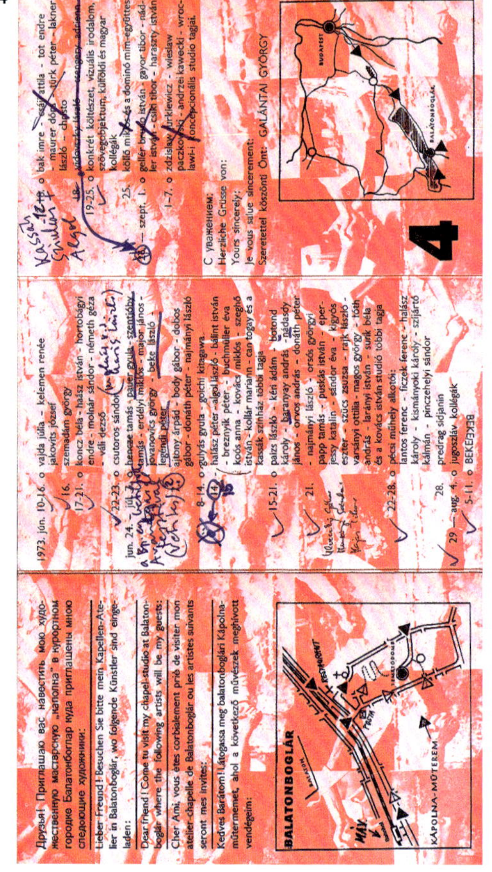

Друзья! Приглашаю вас навестить мою художественную мастерскую „капопна" в курортном городке Балатонбоглар куда приглашены мною следующие художники:

Lieber Freund! Besuchen Sie bitte mein Kapellen-Atelier in Balatonboglár, wo folgende Künstler sind eingeladen:

Dear friend! Come tu visit my chapel-studio at Balatonboglár where the following artists will be my guests:

Cher Ami, vous étes corbialement prié de visiter mon atelier-chapelle de Balatonboglár ou les artistes suivants seront mes invités:

Kedves Barátom! Látogassa meg balatonboglári Kápolna-műtermemet, ahol a következő művészek meghívott vendégeim:

1973. jún. 10-16. o vajda júlia – kelemen renée – jakovits józsef
16. szemadám györgy
17-21. o koncz béla – haász istván – hortobágyi endre – molnár sándor – németh géza – váli dezső
22-23. o csutoros sándor
jún. 24. o hencze tamás – pauer gyula – szentjóby tamás – erdélyi miklós – major jános – jovanovics györgy – beke lászló – legéndi péter
ajtony árpád – body gábor – dobos gábor – donáth péter – najmányi lászló
8-14. o gulyás gyula – goichi kitagawa – halász péter – algol lászló – bálint istván – breznyik péter – buchmüller éva – koós anna – kovács miklós – szeghő istván – kollár mariann – can togay és a kassák színház többi tagja
15-21. o palzs lászló – kéri ádám – botond károly – baranyay andrás – nádasdy jános – orvos andrás – donáth péter
21. – najmányi lászló – orsós györgyi – papp tamás – puskás istván – eper-jessy katalin – sándor éva – kigyós eszter – szücs zsuzsa – rajk lászló – varsányi ottilia – magos györgy – tóth andrás – larányi istván – surik béla – és a kovács istván studió többi tagja
22-28. o pécsi műhely alkotói: lantos ferenc – ficzek ferenc – halász károly – kismányoki károly – szijártó kálmán – pinczehelyi sándor
28. predrag sidjanin
aug. 4. o jugoszláv kollégák
5-11. o BEKÉRZSB

o bak imre – császár attila – tot endre – maurer dóra – türk péter – lakner lászló – christo
18. o vidovszky lászló – szengey adrienn
19-25. o konkrét költészet, vizuális irodalom, szövegobjektum, külföldi és magyar kollégák
25. o költő miklós és a dominó mim-együttes
szept. 1. o gellér b. istván – gayor tibor – nádler istván – csiki tibor – haraszty istván
1-7. o zdzislaw jurkiewicz – wieslaw paczkowski – andrzei kawecki – wroclawi-i koncepcionális studio tagjai.

С уважением:
Herzliche Grüsse von:
Yours sincerely:
Je vous salue sincerement:
Szeretettel köszönti Önt: GALÁNTAI GYÖRGY

to explore whether there are models or possibilities for contemporary institutions to accommodate the demands of the time for different types of speed of interaction with art, as well as presenting, articulating, and, in general, supporting artistic practices.

This issue was acutely felt when Garage organized an exhibition relating to the 2013–2014 Maidan demonstrations by three Ukrainian artists—Nikita Kadan, Lada Nakonechnaya, and Mykola Ridnyi—planned to run simultaneously with *Grammar of Freedom*. In fact, the project could be seen as a double failure, because at first the show was due to open in March 2014, coinciding with the deployment of the Russian army in Ukraine, to which the artists responded by withdrawing from the program. Then, after postponing the project to 2015, a second withdrawal followed, as the conflict between the two nations deepened. Refusing the exhibition format as an adequate form of communicating something at the forefront of "active history," the artists instead flew to Russia and held a discussion with the local public. In this arena they expressed a set of very relevant preoccupations, such as in the present time can an artist continue to do what they normally do under the conditions of war? What transpired were ruminations on how one can remain true to oneself and communicate or formulate anything in public, especially through an artwork, when by the time it is done, one's emotions, thoughts, and beliefs have

strayed in another direction, swamped by the merciless flow of events. For the participants, the distance in time needed to "produce" a meaningful response in the form of art has yet to materialize. Here we can see an interesting parallel with the Arteast 2000+ Collection and *Grammar of Freedom*, wherein with the benefit of a critical distance in time the display does not become less connected to the present, but instead leaves us feeling that the past has not only caught up with the present but that it has actually, uncannily surpassed it, even before it actually happened.

In the case of the Ukrainian artists, or the beginnings of the Artpool project mentioned earlier, where intuitive tactics are the bravest assets, a bare, raw contemporaneity transpires whose vector goes against the grain of its time; another contemporaneity, described through the collection, combines many different temporalities at once, clashing and confronting each other. *Grammar of Freedom* looks at a past that is filtered through the emotions, confusion, and inarticulateness of the present. In this palpable clash lies its timeliness. As Galantai once said, "ART ALWAYS WORKS COUNTER TO ITS MILIEU, OTHERWISE IT COULD NOT CHANGE IT." (1985)

Snejana Krasteva
Curator
Garage Museum of Contemporary Art

1. Chapel Studio interior 1971, with visitors wearing self printed T-shirts that advertise the exhibitions
Photos: György Galántai
© Artpool Art Research Center

2. Chapel Studio interior 1973
Photo: György Galántai
© Artpool Art Research Center

3. *FIRE/ICE* — a concrete poetry action by Tibor Gáyor at the Chapel Studio in 1973
Photo: Dora Maurer
© Artpool Art Research Center

4. György Galántai's invitation to his Chapel Studio in Balatonboglár for the 1973 summer events
© Artpool Art Research Center

(1) This text was written on a plinth next to two others, each with a different text. The work is by Hungarian artist Gyula Pauer and is entitled *Conception Works* (1973). Pauer was arrested and questioned about this work. For further information see http://mek.oszk.hu/13000/13024/13024.pdf, p. 32.

(2) The Chapel Studio was a space Galantai rented and transformed into an underground venue for showcasing Hungarian, and occasionally foreign, artists. It was located in a chapel in the small town of Balatonboglár, some 150 km south of Budapest. In the three years it existed, it was instrumental in the development of conceptual practices in Hungary.

(3) Artpool project was established in Galantai and Klaniczay's apartment in Budapest. It opened its doors publicly under its current name in 1992, after the change of regime. Until then, it operated as an underground initiative dedicated to collecting and disseminating materials and archives concerning Hungarian unofficial art life since the 1960s.

(4) For Galantai telling the story of Artpool, see http://mek.oszk.hu/13000/13024/13024.Pdf, p. 15.

(5) Since 2014, public institutions wishing to screen films or video works have to obtain "screening permissions" from a special state agency.

(6) Alexander Shubin in conversation during a closed-door discussion at Garage, held on January 26, 2015. Shubin is Head of the Institute of History of Russia, Ukraine and Belarus in the World History Institute of The Russian Academy of Sciences, Moscow.

The Moscow-Ljubljana Axis

What we might call the Moscow-Ljubljana Axis began to take shape at the very beginning of the post-communist era. I recall how, at the tail end of the 1980s, Boris Groys was on his first visit to Moscow after he had emigrated and enthusiastically told us about the artists of the IRWIN group, which was then unknown in the Russian capital. He described the collective rituals of these Ljubljana artists—their tendency to wear uniforms and march in formation, to raise and lower a flag every day, and so on. He depicted IRWIN as a kind of simulated totalitarian sect and gave a theoretical interpretation in his article "Irwin: More Totalitarian than Totalitarianism." Later on, when we became better acquainted with the work of these artists, several discrepancies between Groys description and the reality of the group became clear, but without a doubt his story sparked enormous curiosity in Moscow about the Ljubljana artists. In the 1990s, when I began to send invitations to international artists for the Apt-Art International project (international exhibitions in Moscow apartments), one of them winged its way to IRWIN in Ljubljana. Their response was the *NSK Embassy Moscow*, one of the most significant events in the city in the 1990s.[1] Establishing themselves in a rented apartment at 12 Leninsky Prospekt in June 1992, the artists worked tirelessly, holding numerous lectures, shows, performances, dialogs, and discussions. Key figures from the artistic and intellectual worlds of Slovenia and Moscow visited throughout the month.

This dialog between the Russian artistic and intellectual scenes and Ljubljana, which engaged a wide array of artists, continued and became a mature network of contacts and joint initiatives. In 1996, IRWIN took part in my Stockholm exhibition *Interpol*, which caused a huge international scandal. Materials from the project and a number of analytical responses to it were then collected in a book, *Interpol: The Art Exhibition which Divided East and West*, published by IRWIN and *Moscow Art Magazine*. Also in 1996 IRWIN made the *Transnacionala* project in the United States, a coast to coast trip in two trailers with three Russian artists—Vadim Fishkin (who at that time lived in Ljubljana), Yuri Leiderman, and Alexander Brener. As part of this "road project," the Ljubljana and Russian artists met with American colleagues, had tense discussions with them, and endlessly argued among themselves. A year later,

Brener performed his extreme action in Amsterdam's Stedeljik Museum, spray painting a green dollar sign on Malevich's *White Square*, as a result of which he was arrested and taken to court. During the trial, IRWIN ran a support campaign for the Moscow artist (he was a Moscow artist back then), explaining his intellectual stance and the essence of his poetics. This experience of dialog with Russian art, which ran deep in Ljubljana, and the general sense of becoming adept on the international scene was summarized by the renowned Ljubljana curator and theorist Igor Zabel in his famous text "We and the Others." It was first read at a Moscow conference in 1997, and in 1998 it was published in a new form in issue 22 of *Moscow Art Magazine*.[2] Finally, also in 1998, I wrote a detailed piece for a catalog accompanying IRWIN's *Transnacionala* project in which I defined the relationship between art figures from Moscow and Ljubljana in terms of the concept of friendship.[3]

Ljubljana's Museum of Modern Art, or Moderna galerija, was at the wellspring of this chain of events and human connections (the list and descriptions of which could go on). In its dealings with the artistic process, this museum never kept a safe distance. From the beginning it saw its mission as creating situations rather than drawing lessons from what had happened, and initiating a process rather than pinning down facts. Even though there was no understanding then, in the early 1990s, of what exactly this "new institutionalism" was, Moderna galerija was already part of a small circle of innovative European museums that had created a new institutional model. Incidentally, the model was far from a set of abstract, normative principles that were to be universally applied. More accurately—and especially as was the case with Moderna galerija—it was a kind of spontaneously occurring methodology that arose from an analytical, but also sometimes intuitive, reaction to the dynamics of the artistic situation. This suggests the first characteristic of Ljubljana's "new internationalism"—Moderna galerija, unlike globalized contemporary art factories (like a kind of ill-starred Tate Modern), is rooted in the anthropological dimension. This is why my excursus into the history of personal connections between a group of people from Moscow and Ljubljana is so relevant in this context. In its strategic decisions, the Ljubljana museum relied quite heavily on what occurred in this circle (and others)—on the ideas discussed and created there. In some cases, it reacted to them sometimes before they became texts or artworks, capturing them while they were still living, oral pieces of knowledge. When I complimented his text "We and the Others," Zabel, who together with the museum's director Zdenka Badovinac played a key role in shaping Moderna galerija, replied, "What are you talking about? All I did was put on paper the things that Ljubljana artists have been discussing for ages."

With these words Zabel did not so much understate the importance of his own authorship as—and this is methodologically crucial—acknowledge that the character of contemporary knowledge is social and relational rather than elitist and abstract. Hence the Ljubljana museum's consistent strategy of hosting discussions. It was adopted very early, long before it became commonplace among modern institutions. At the same time, as I realized after participating in a number of these events, at Moderna galerija they were always lively and engaging, unlike the way discussions were and continue to be held in most contemporary institutions (formally and dogmatically). The public events—if they were planned as such, because often there was just an internal exchange of ideas—were informal insofar as they had an air of comfortable and informative conviviality. This interweaving of the public and the intimate, the professional and the personal, which characterized the Ljubljana meetings, was very similar to the way life unfolded at the NSK Embassy. It seems easy to explain this analogy by referring to the fact that, as experts maintain, the new institutionalism was based largely on the earlier relational practices of contemporary artists.[4]

However, based on my observations with regard to Ljubljana, we do not have before us a case of succession or borrowing, but a parallel and countervailing movement: at the same time that artists moved in the direction of artistic mastery of social practices, curators and institutions moved in the direction of face-to-face relations, employing in their work living, as well as academic, knowledge. In other words, in Ljubljana neither artists nor museums followed the logic of the conveyor belt. Rather they aimed to create communities—confidential communities soldered with friendship.

In this case, it would be wrong to equate the concept of friendship with something exclusively psychological and intimate. Friendship is an extremely efficient productive resource. Built into collaborative work, friendship allows one to see the other more fully and have a more intense relationship, rather than simply a professional one. In friendship the relationship remains even when the actual work on a joint project is finished, allowing one to make continued use of expertise and ideas. The fact that in Ljubljana the productive resource of friendly relations, or more precisely that which Aristotle would call political relations, is used so ably is very telling. Here the openness of institutions to the sphere of informal relations might be explained as a natural product of the weakness of the local art system, of its insufficient autonomy from the sphere of living communication. But Moderna galerija recognized that its strength was not logistics but communication, the ability to fill gaps in technologies and resources with wit and ingenuity.

Moderna galerija's whole exhibition strategy is based on thematizing this clear-eyed understanding of its place in the world and on the ability to see strength in its weaknesses. A large number of its famous projects—from *Body and the East* to *7 Sins* (on which I was lucky enough to work)—are an attempt to understand the specifics of the Eastern European context, not masking but rather emphasizing the antinomy with the Western canon and presenting it less as a shortcoming than as a fruitful resource and source of potentiality. In this, Moderna galerija is again in harmony with the mindset of the Ljubljana art world, which as far back as the "Moscow Declaration" (written and signed at the NSK Embassy), at the beginning of the era of globalization, swore fealty to the historical mission of Eastern Europe. This mindset gave rise to IRWIN's project *East Art Map*, a major international investigation for which they gathered documentation and analytical studies of Eastern European development. Out of this mindset also emerged a collection of new acquisitions, Arteast 2000+, where the museum's priority was art embedded in Ljubljana's system of communications and interests as opposed to examples of the globalized mainstream. As such, the Ljubljana museum has a superb collection of Russian art. And it was procured not through purchases at galleries, art fairs, or auctions but through face-to-face relationships, meetings by Zdenka and me with artists, and as a result of a long period of communication and discussion, i.e. through friendship.

In conclusion, I acknowledge that, as part of the Moscow-Ljubljana Axis, the exhibition *Grammar of Freedom/Five Lessons* is the first example of a museum exchange initiated by Moscow. This is totally natural. Institutional development in Moscow took a different form, ignoring the anthropological dimension that has become such a strong foundation and propulsive force for the Ljubljana museum. In Russia the emphasis was not on personal communications and living knowledge but on public relations strategies and financial investments. Here we were not inclined to keep

(1) Viktor Misiano, "Emergency Ambassadors to a 'State of Emergency': The 'NSK Embassy' and the Moscow Artistic Scene of the 1990s," in *State of Time*, ed. by IRWIN (Ljubljana: Društvo NSK informativni center, 2010), pp. 31–40.

(2) Igor Zabel, "We and the Others" *Moscow Art Magazine*, 22 (1998), 27–35.

(3) "The Institutionalisation of Friendship," in *Transnacionala*, ed. by IRWIN (Ljubljana, 1999), 182–192.

(4) For a fuller and defter analysis of "new internationalism" Alex Farquharson, "Institutional Mores," in *Institutional Attitudes: Instituting Art in a Flat World*, ed. by Pascal Gielen (Amsterdam: Valiz, 2013), 219–228.

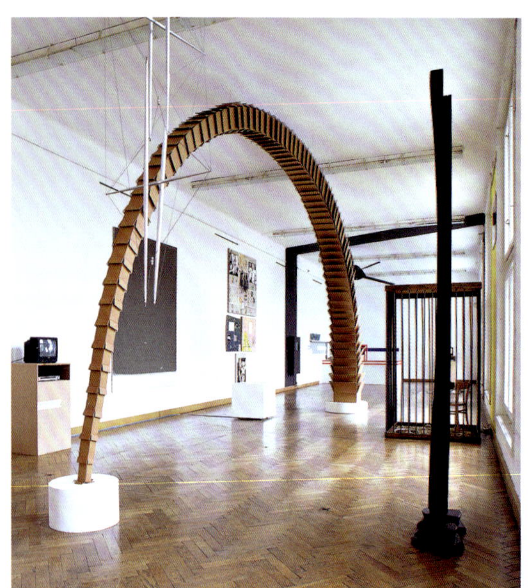
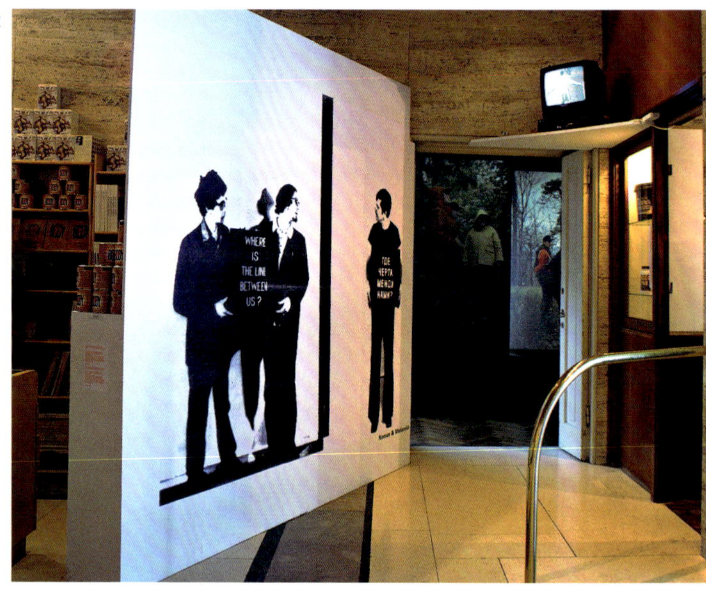
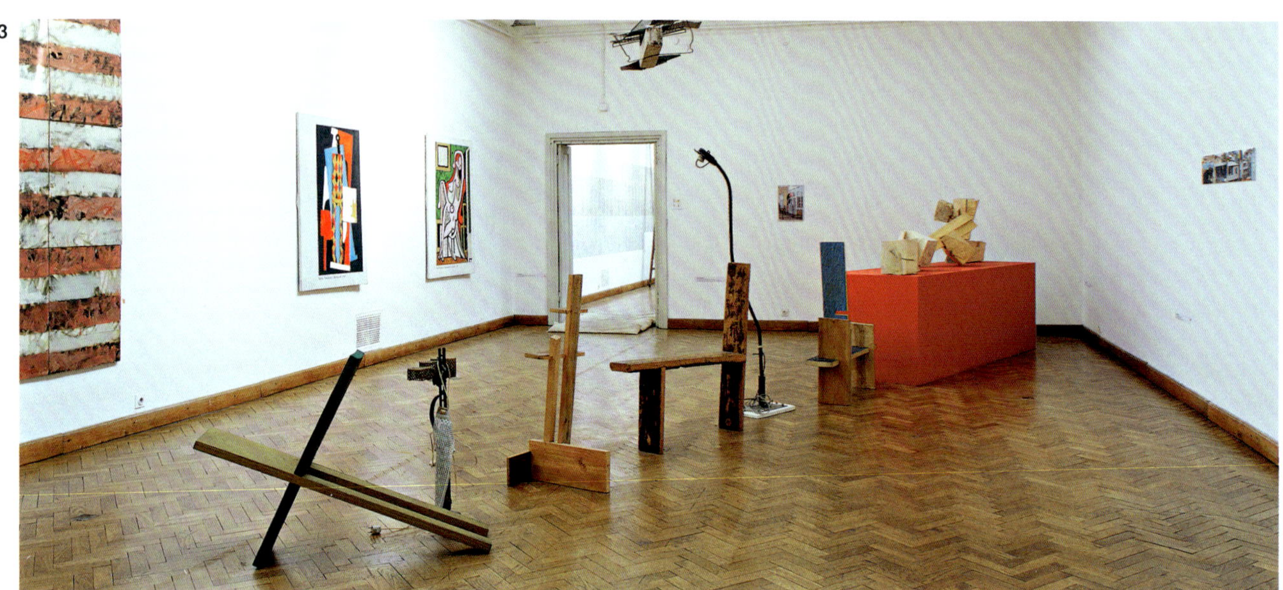
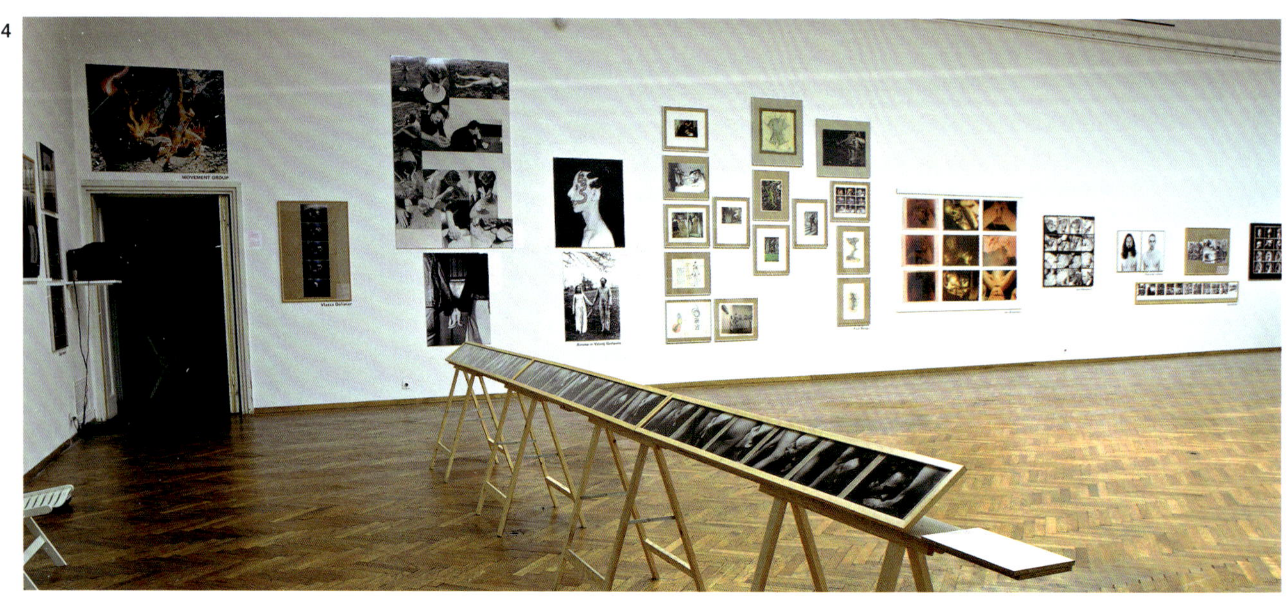

a skeptical distance from the globalized mainstream,
and we followed the cherished dream of finding our
place in it. Heads of Moscow museums believed
in the autonomy of institutional machinery, and as such
were inclined to view artists less as colleagues
and a source of fruitful ideas and more as the raw
materials needed to ensure smooth operations.
Russia's art scene, which throughout the post-Soviet
years vacillated between fears of marginality and
the utopia of the "Russian Breakthrough," turned
out to be largely unable to pinpoint its advantages
and its true place in the world. The fact that Moscow
is finally interested in the Ljubljana experience
is highly significant. Also telling is the fact that it is
happening at this point in time and in this place,
Garage Museum of Contemporary Art. Understanding
why is a fascinating and important issue. But it's
for another essay.

Viktor Misiano
Independent curator and chief editor,
Khudozhestvenny zhurnal
(Moscow Art Magazine)

1. Exhibition: *Body and the East.
From the 1960s to the Present*,
Moderna galerija, Ljubljana, 1998
Photo: Lado Mlekuž,
Matija Pavlovec
© Moderna galerija, Ljubljana

2. Exhibition: *Body and the East:
From the 1960s to the Present*,
Moderna galerija, Ljubljana, 1998
Foreground: Komar and Melamid,
Where Is the Line between Us?,
1975
Photo: Lado Mlekuž,
Matija Pavlovec
© Moderna galerija, Ljubljana

3. Exhibition: *7 Sins: Ljubljana –
Moscow. Arteast exhibition*,
Moderna galerija, Ljubljana, 2004
Photo: Dejan Habicht,
Matija Pavlovec
© Moderna galerija, Ljubljana

4. Exhibition: *7 Sins: Ljubljana –
Moscow. Arteast exhibition*,
Moderna galerija, Ljubljana, 2004
Middle: Taf-Studio, *Through Line*,
2004
Photo: Dejan Habicht,
Matija Pavlovec
© Moderna galerija, Ljubljana

Lesson 1:
The body as a tool for liberation

Negotiating freedom through the physical "self"

The works in this section explore how artists have portrayed the body as representing a space between a "true" self and a "produced" individuality influenced by ideology or capital. In the 1960s and 1970s, artists drew attention to their repressive environments by torturing or disciplining their bodies. In the 1980s, as new political realities emerged, artists treated their bodies as "theater," with personas representing new social constructs. By the 1990s, particularly during the time of the Balkan wars, the body was depicted as physically vulnerable and socially marginalized. Since 2000, with the formation of the European Union and the expansion of capitalism in the region, the body has once again become a powerful tool for drawing attention to new authoritarian forces.

The descriptions on the artists' pages in the following five sections are of works shown at the exhibition *Grammar of Freedom/Five Lessons: Works from the Arteast 2000+ Collection* (Garage Museum of Contemporary Art, Moscow, 2015).

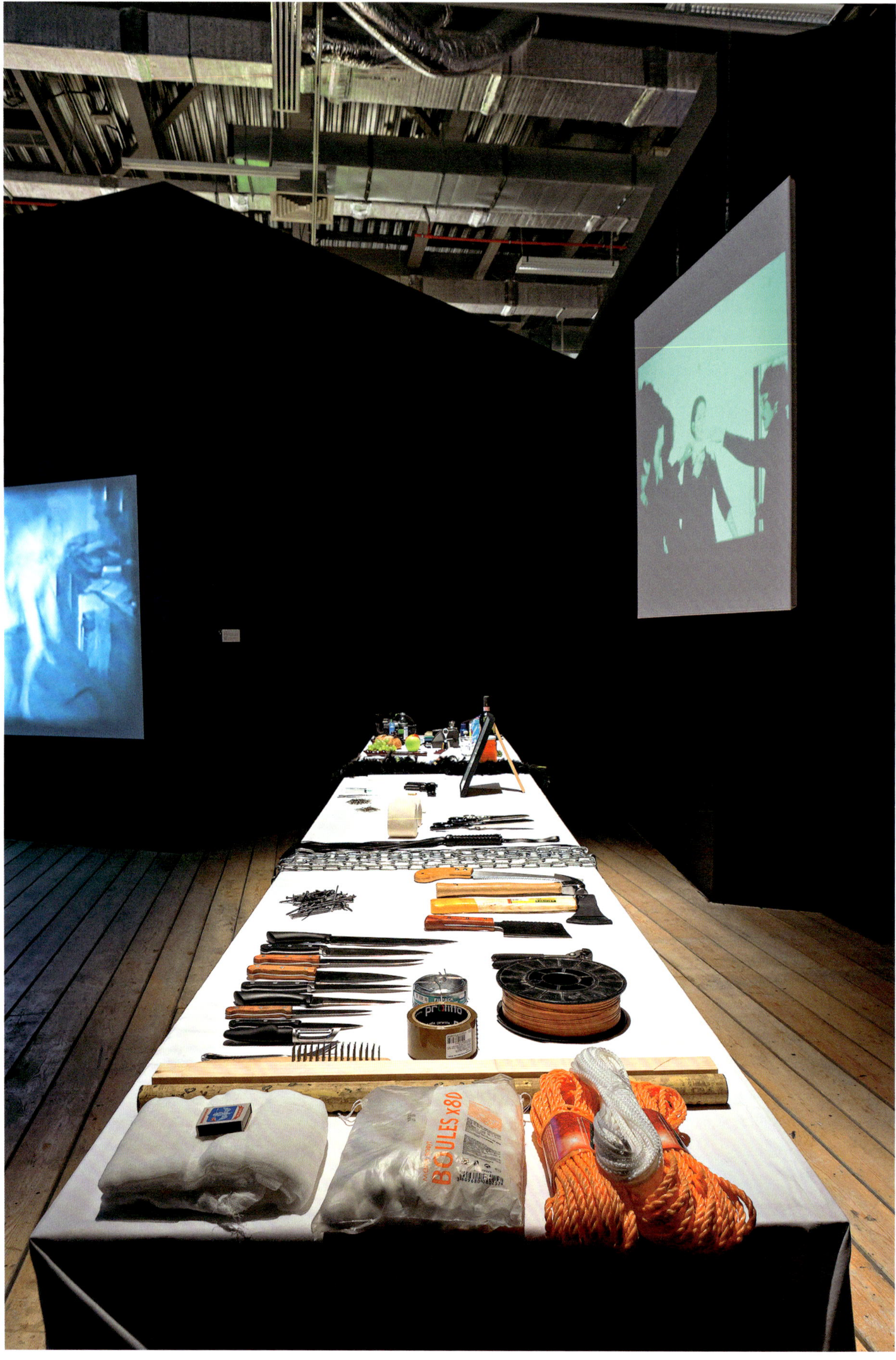

Marina Abramović

(b. 1946, Belgrade, Yugoslavia, now Serbia)

Rhythm 0
1974
Performance, Naples
72 objects, performance instructions, photographic
slides of the performance
Courtesy Moderna galerija, Ljubljana

Rhythm 0 is one of the most challenging in a series of Abramović's early performances that explored the relationship between the performer and the audience and tested the physical and mental limitations of the body and the possibilities of the mind.

In *Rhythm 0* the artist assigned a passive role to herself, with the public being the force that would act on her. She placed upon a table 72 objects that people were allowed to use in any way that they chose— they could give her pleasure or inflict pain, even harm her. The objects included a gun loaded with a single bullet. For six hours the artist sat immobile, allowing audience members to direct the action. At first members of the audience reacted with caution and modesty, but as time passed some people began to act quite aggressively. As Abramović described later, "The experience I learned was that if you leave [the] decision to the public, you can be killed… I felt really violated: they cut my clothes, stuck rose thorns in my stomach, one person aimed the gun at my head and another took it away. It created an aggressive atmosphere. After exactly 6 hours, as planned, I stood up and started walking toward the public. Everyone ran away, escaping an actual confrontation."

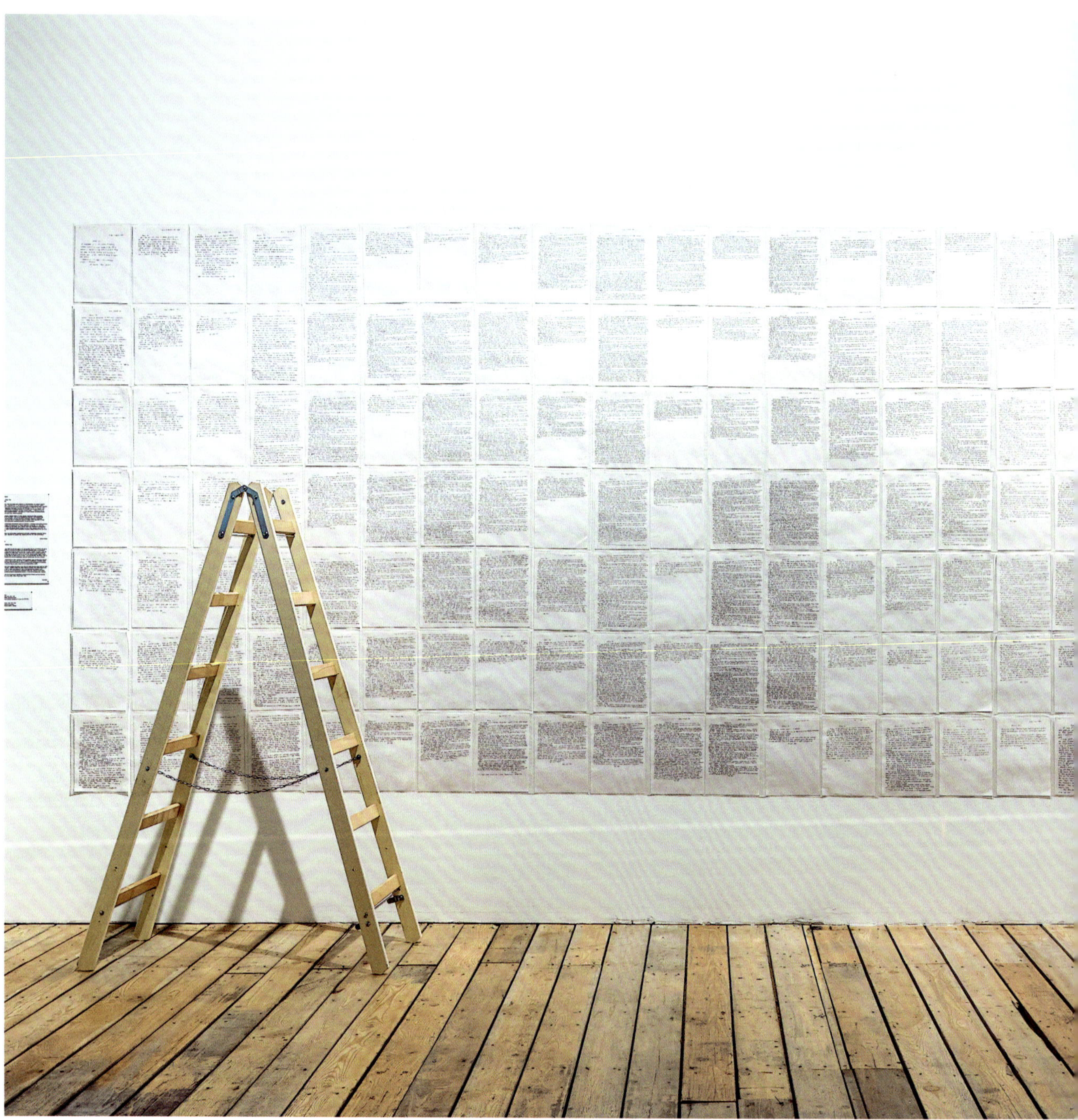

Yuri Albert

(b. 1959, Moscow, USSR, now Russia)

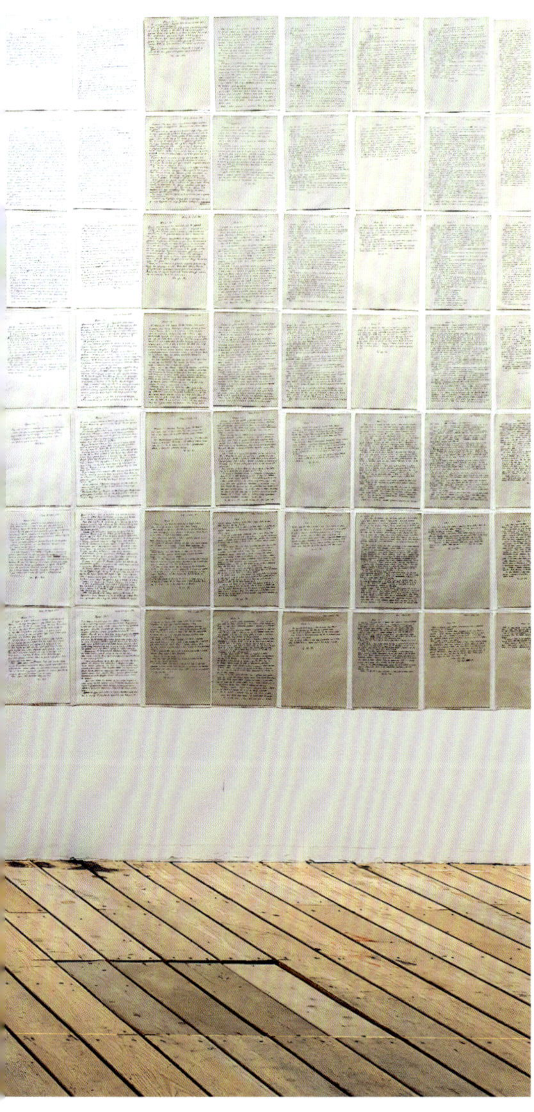

Letters to Brother Theo

1992–1994

Ink and ballpoint pen on paper, 325 sheets, each 29.7×21 cm

Courtesy Moderna galerija, Ljubljana

Yuri Albert is one of the most prominent members of Moscow Conceptualism, whose work poses basic, yet always unanswered, questions about what is art, who is an artist, and what is their role in contemporary society. For his work *Letters to Brother Theo* he copied by hand three hundred letters which Vincent Van Gogh wrote to his brother. The only thing Albert changed was the date of writing and the signature, which he replaced with his own. His reason for doing this was, as he writes, that he had always wanted to be a real artist (like Rembrandt or Van Gogh) but later discovered that he could only make contemporary art, as "real" art no longer exists and will never exist again. His work in the 1990s was based on the assumption that real art is not possible today, as it is a thing of the past. For Albert, the impossibility of going back in time and the inability to reach the real thing and resurrect it into the present was a terrible and sinful irresponsibility that called for repentance and suffering, which can be achieved, as in the past, by copying the holy texts. By analogy, the artist decided to copy the letters that the "real" artist Van Gogh wrote to his brother Theo (meaning "god" in Greek). As in the case of traditional icon painting, this is the closest one can get to the "real thing," which nevertheless always remains out of reach. This is why contemporary artists can exhibit, as Albert writes, "nothing more than memories of the desire to be an artist, evidence that, at least, [they] tried."

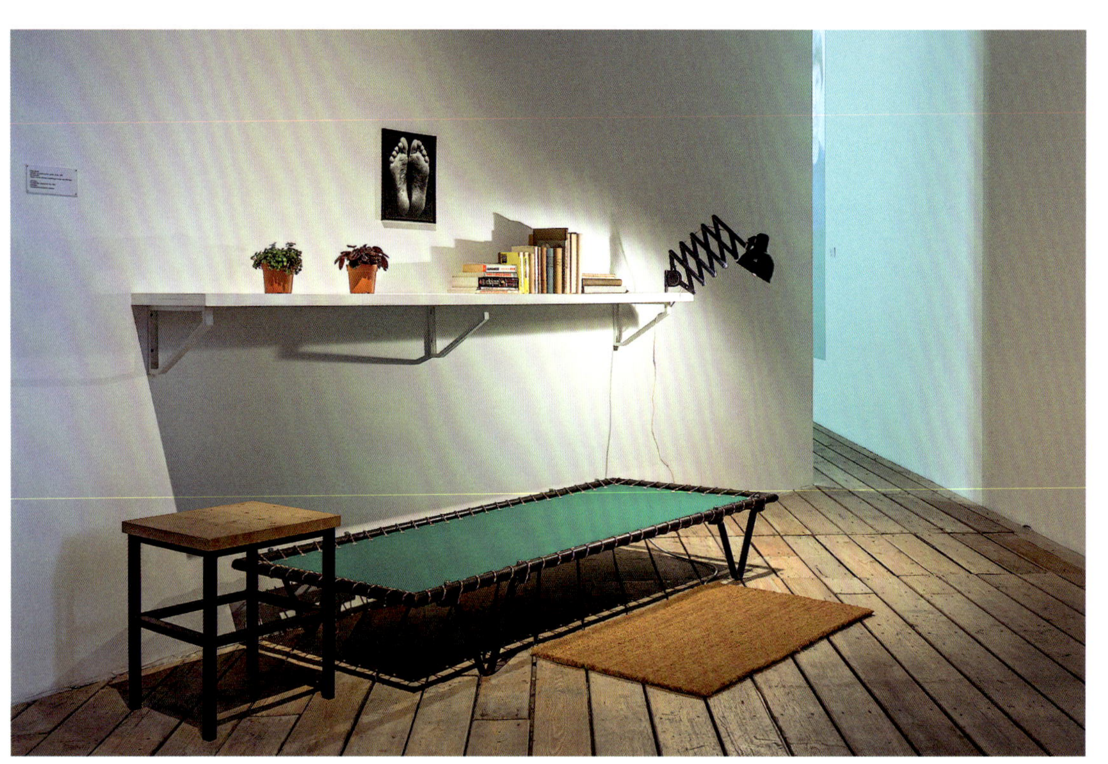

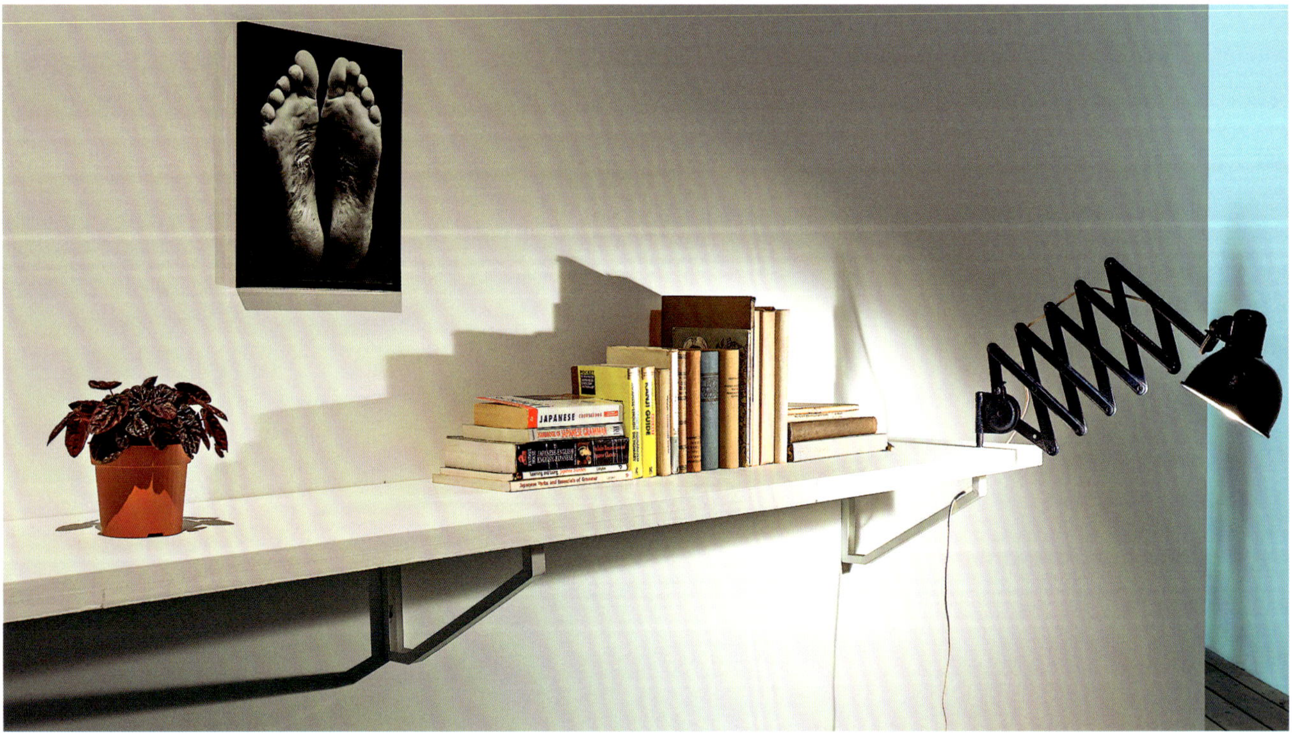

Jože Barši

(b. 1955, Ljubljana, Yugoslavia, now Slovenia)

The Man Who Crossed the Fire
1995
Installation
Courtesy Moderna galerija, Ljubljana

In the mid-1990s, Jože Barši refuted the traditional conceptions and strategies of sculpture making and aimed to deconstruct the sculptural object by focusing on everyday activities and real-life situations. Since the very beginning, his work has been accompanied by an in-depth contemplation of how everyday objects and situations pass into the field of art, and vice versa. The fundamental procedure/effect of his practice is therefore, as Rado Riha said, the "derealization of reality and the desublimation of the sublime," well-illustrated, for instance, by the project *Public Toilet* (1999). The toilet that the artist placed in a public space is not trivial (because it is art), yet at the same time it is nothing more than a trivial object. Movement in this field of minimal differences that enables us to consider, as Riha points out, the world as simultaneously being something other than that which we perceive it to be, is one of the main strategies of Barši's practice.

The Man Who Crossed the Fire is based on a real situation that was not an artistic act in itself but gained new meanings in the context of art. When firewalking, the artist, despite his willpower, suffered severe burns, unlike other participants whose faith seems to have kept them from harm in this ritual of "purification." The event is documented by a photograph of Barši's burnt feet and accompanied by other personal items. The installation can be understood somewhere between its literal and figurative meanings. The photograph proves that somebody (the artist) "crossed the fire," but this event can simultaneously also represent a reflection on the position of the artist and the consequences of his practice, which is no longer based on a belief in the rituals of art.

1   The body as a tool for liberation

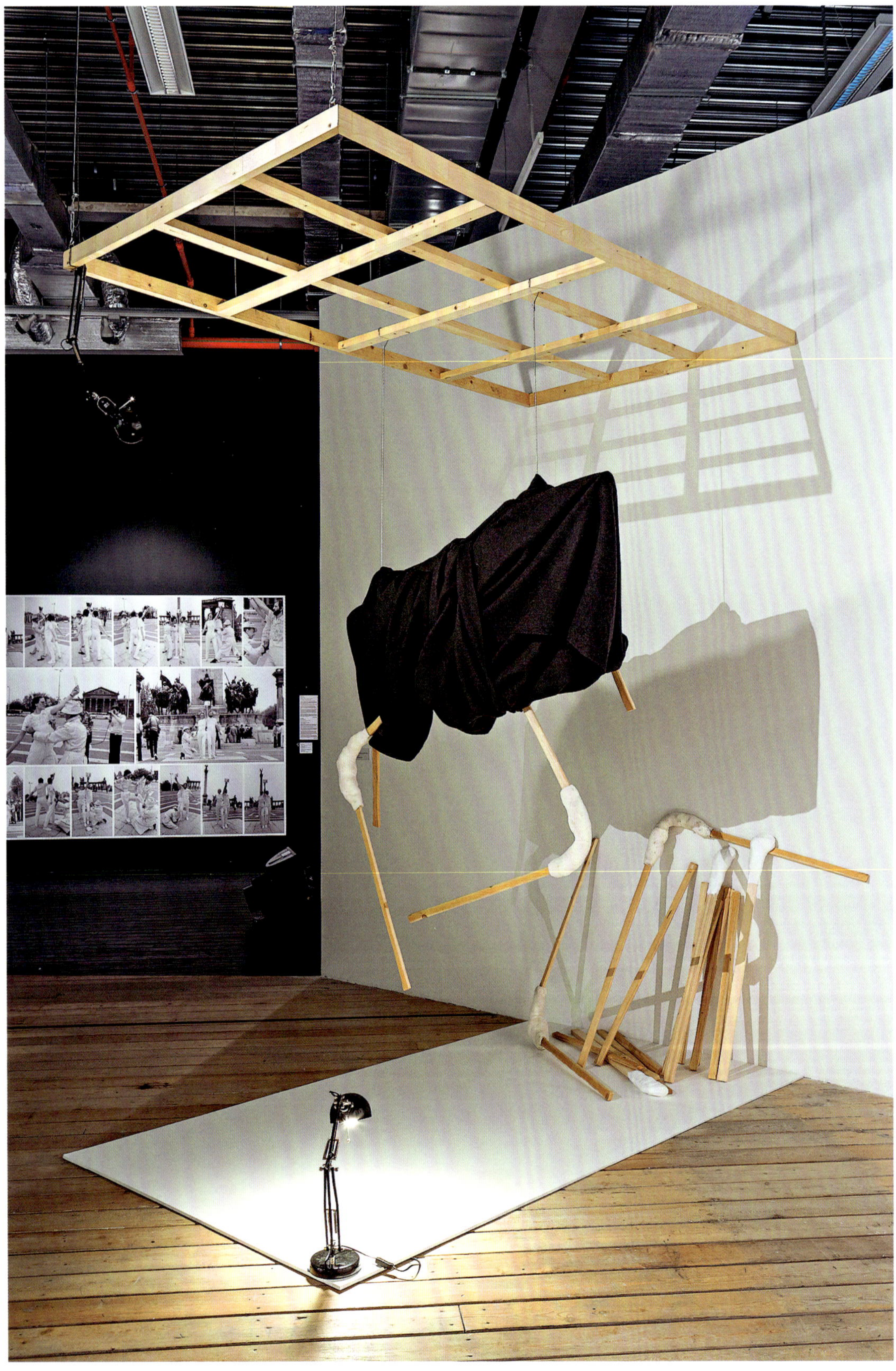

Geta Brătescu

(b. 1926, Ploieşti, Romania)

No to Violence
1974
Installation
Courtesy Moderna galerija, Ljubljana

The allusive shapes of the mural installation and drawings entitled *No to Violence* created by Geta Brătescu in 1974 resemble prostheses needed by a deformed and exhausted body. The body, or better, an experience of the body, is the focus of the more than forty-year career of this unusual Romanian artist.

The series in question is featured in the catalogue of her work, which is divided into the artist's most frequent themes (studio, mythology, classical literature, self-portrait, and drawing with eyes closed). It is described in the chapter *… And Other Artifices*. Brătescu explains her notion of artifices thus: "Culture is an artifice, it is not artificial in its relation to human nature; it is a part of human nature … Man as nature and at the same time, opposed to nature; the spoon versus the hand; the portrait, the mask, the makeup versus the face; the shoe versus the foot; the plane versus the bird…"

In her work, Brătescu uses many elements that speak about female sensitivity: textiles, a theater dress, pins, mirrors. All these elements, whether in her collages, tapestries, objects, or installations, give the impression of imminent and constant danger, the fragility of the body or life in general. The body is presented in relation to everything that threatens or supports it. Every culture and every artifice also represents an act of violence as, to paraphrase to paraphrase Bratescu, we find out that every sculpture is an act of aggression committed against marble and every poem constitutes violence committed against the word.

1 The body as a tool for liberation

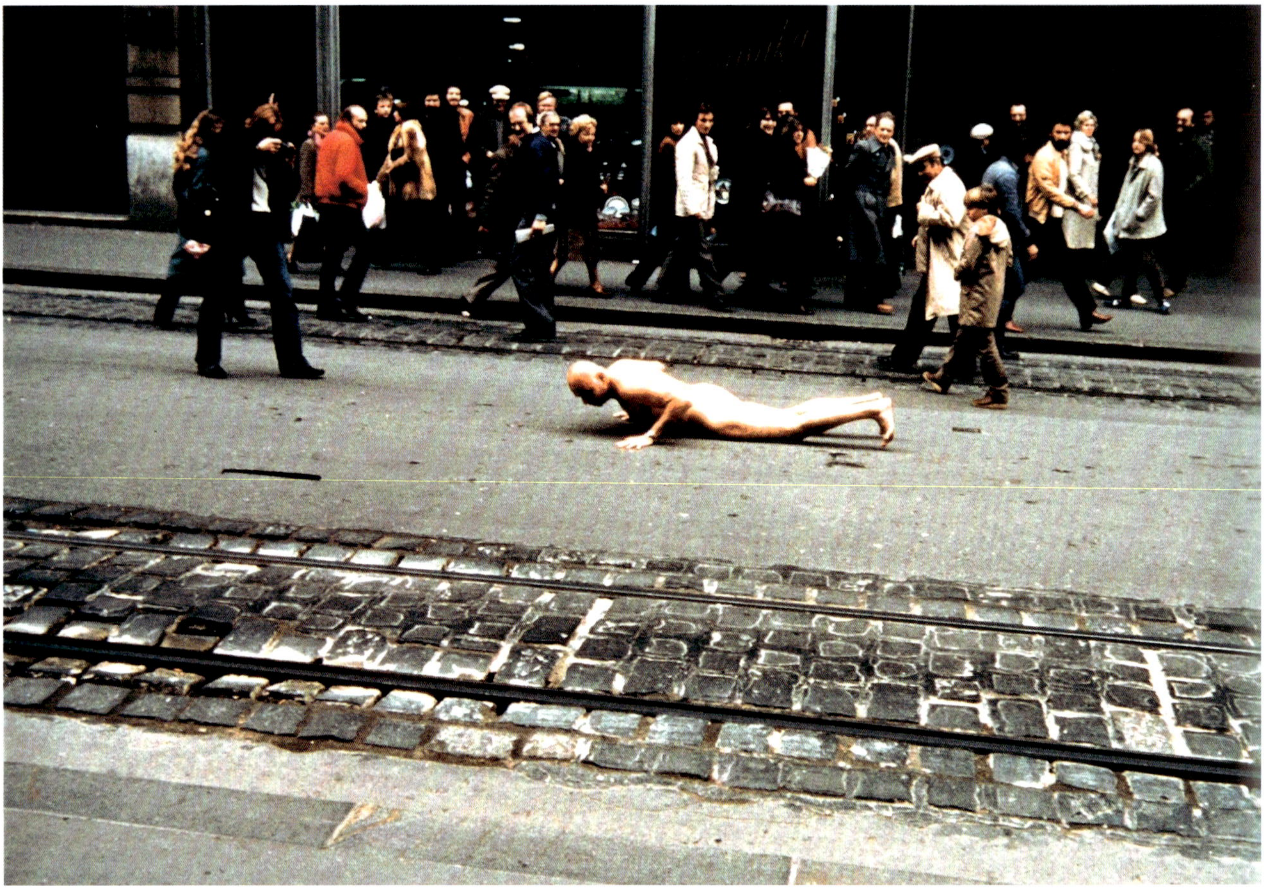

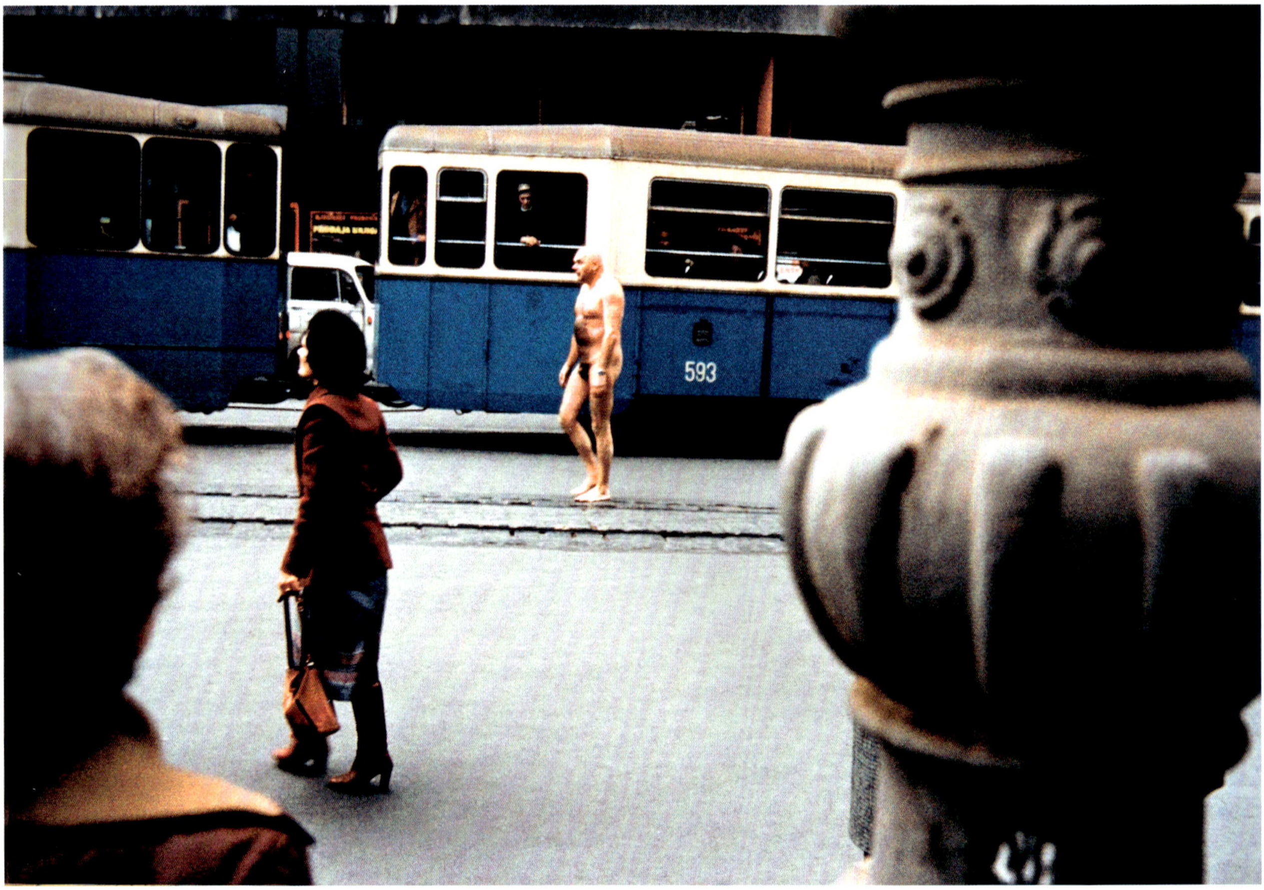

Tomislav Gotovac

(b. 1937, Sombor, Yugoslavia, now Serbia; d. 2010, Zagreb, Croatia)

Zagreb, I Love You!
1981
Action, Zagreb
14 color photographs, each 30×41cm
Photos: Boris Turković
Courtesy Tomislav Gotovac Institute, Zagreb

The practice of Tomislav Gotovac, who is considered a pioneer of performance art in the former Yugoslavia and a key figure of his time, ranged from early photographic works, collages, and avant-garde structuralist films to radical performances. His early actions, such as *Breathing the Air* or *Showing the Elle Magazine* and later *Haircut and Shaves, Watching TV, Listening to the Radio,* explored the politics of the everyday. His work transposed everyday activities into public space, blurring the line between seemingly separate categories of the private and the public.

He did his first streak in Belgrade for Lazar Stojanović's film *Plastic Jesus* (1971), which was later censored, and re-enacted it in Zagreb ten years later in his performance *Zagreb, I Love You!.* Precisely at noon he appeared on Zagreb's main street and ran naked through the city center while screaming, "Zagreb, I love you!" When he reached the main square, he lay on the ground and started kissing the pavement. After 7 minutes the performance was interrupted by the arrival of the police, and Gotovac was arrested. Representing the ultimate freedom of expression, the public exposure of the artist's naked body and his seemingly irrational behavior in *Zagreb, I love you!* were acts in defiance of political repression and the social constraints of the time. "Half of them thought I was completely crazy, and the other half saw this art as mere shit. But in these performances I was actually aiming at the destruction of bourgeois behavior," said Gotovac, whose public actions, by disturbing public order, intervened in the common daily routine of the existing sociopolitical order.

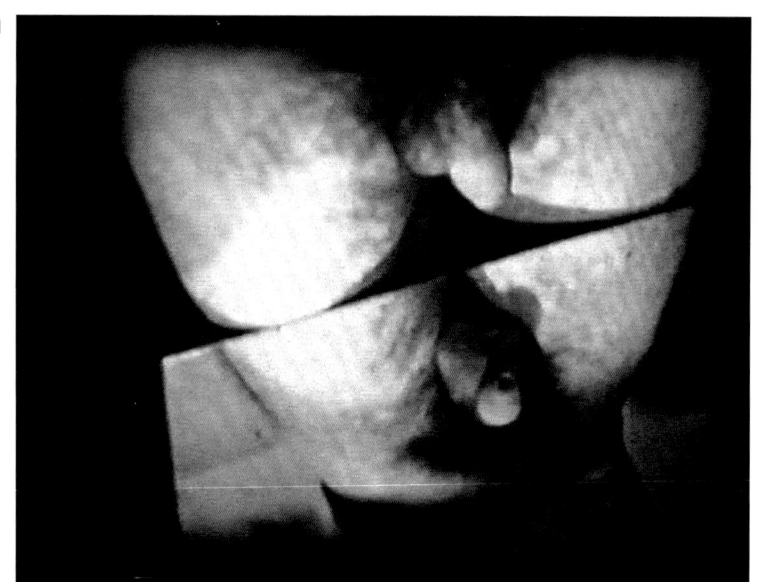

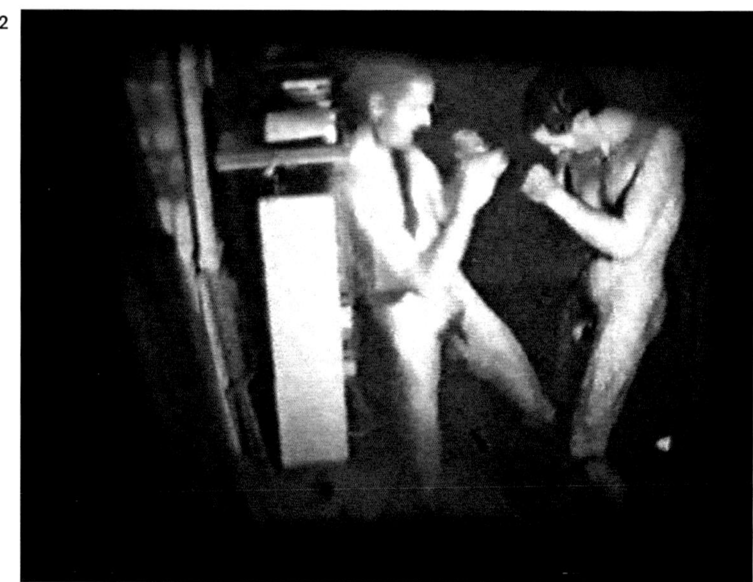

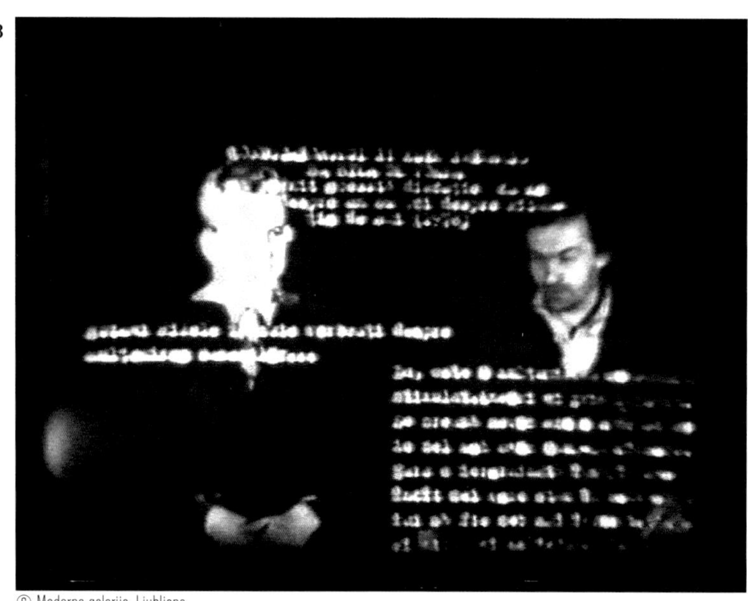

Ion Grigorescu

(b. 1945, Bucharest, Romania)

1

Male, Female (Male as Mask and Penis as Brush)
1976
8 mm film on video, 9'50"

2

Boxing
1977
8 mm film on video, 2'30"

3

Dialogue with Ceausescu (If People Cannot Lead Then They Only Criticize)
1978
8 mm film on video, 7'30"
Courtesy Moderna galerija, Ljubljana

Most of Ion Grigorescu's performances were created in the 1970s, when Romania was ruled by one of the harshest Eastern European regimes, and it was inconceivable that these projects could be presented to the Romanian public. In his performances, where the audience was replaced by cameras, Grigorescu explored the limits of his body, his own intimacy, and the mechanical and psychological dialogue with stills and film cameras. Referencing Katherine Verdery, a US anthropologist specializing in Romanian culture, Kristine Stiles notes that Romanians were experiencing a "social schizophrenia," described as an ability to experience a "real, meaningful and coherent self only in relation to the enemy party." At the same time, they were unable to perceive themselves as anything other than "absolutely dependent upon a government which they could not criticize without being labeled unpatriotic." This paradoxical predicament, which left Romanians feeling conflicted, doubled, and contaminated, characterized Romanian art, wherein the body and its actions are identified as both self and enemy.

In his performances, Ion Grigorescu often used the strategies of doubling and roleplaying and presented himself as filled with anger, guilt, and futility. In *Dialogue with Ceausescu* the artist assumes both roles, the dictator and himself. In *Male, Female* he appears as two genders, while in *Boxing* doubling is employed when the artist fights with himself.

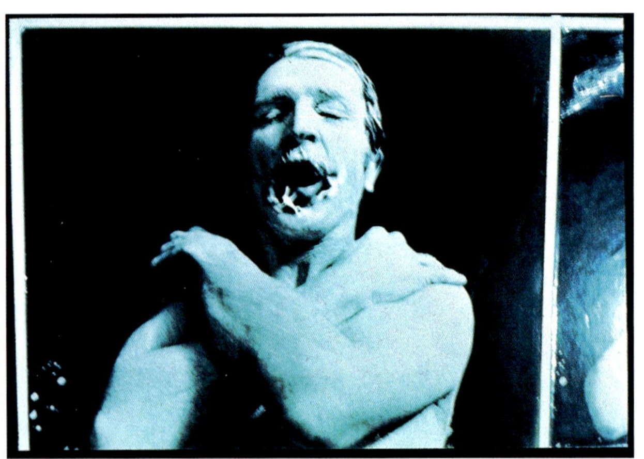
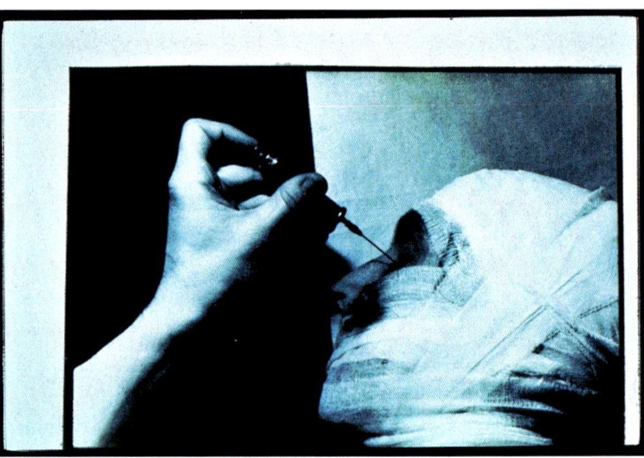
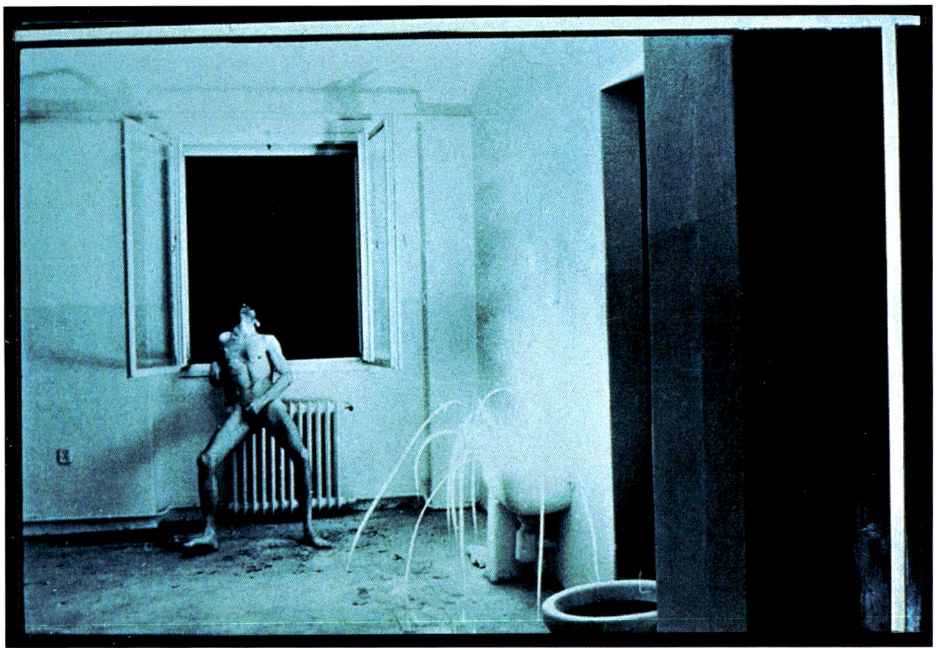
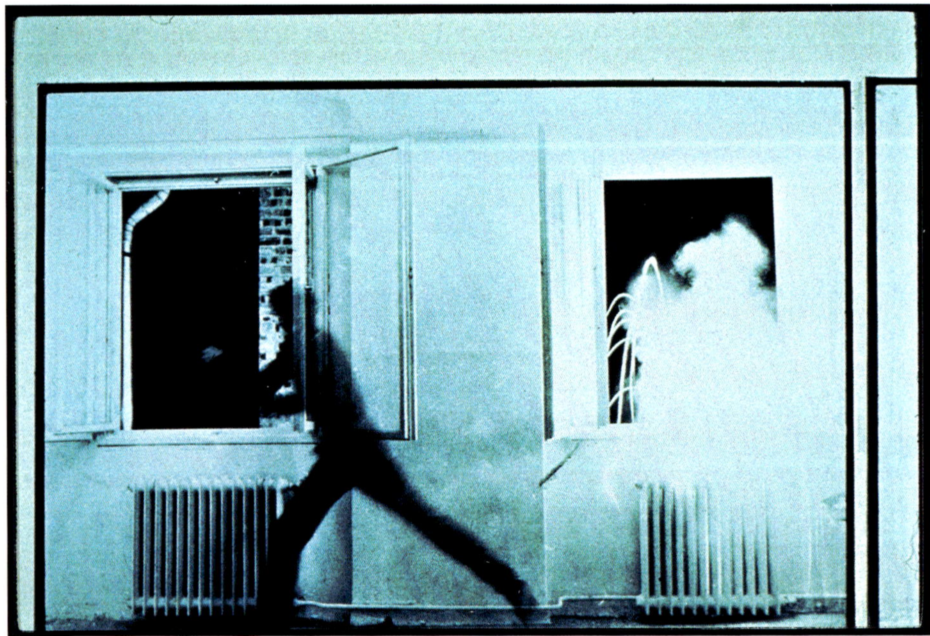

Photos: Janos Vető, © Moderna galerija, Ljubljana

Tibor Hajas

(b. 1946, Budapest, Hungary; d. 1980, Szeged, Hungary)

Flesh Painting II, 1978
Flesh Painting III, 1978
Image Whipping I, 1978
Image Whipping I (detail 1), 1978
Image Whipping I (detail 2), 1978
Image Whipping I (detail 3), 1978
Image Whipping I (detail 4), 1978
Surface Torture I, 1978
Image Whipping III, 1978
Surface Torture III, 1978
Exercises — Tumo I (detail 1), 1979
Exercises — Tumo I (detail 2), 1979
Exercises — Tumo II (detail), 1979
Extinction (detail), 1979
Slides of performances
Courtesy Moderna galerija, Ljubljana

Some argue that Tibor Hajas was the first true Hungarian performance artist. By and large extremely strenuous for the body (hanging upside down blindfolded, being whipped, and featuring elements such as a syringe, a clothes pin, blood, sterile gauze, traces of fire, a light bulb, a flint lamp, and bandages), Hajas's performances could be seen only for a split second, as in the light of a camera flash. Darkness represented Hajas's view of the world and art. "In darkness, I can be alone, one solo picture, undisturbed by any other; it is so sharp and unreal, as if it was the latest one. An image with such qualities cannot be accidental, yet stays motionless, still."

For Hajas, darkness represented much more than nothing, probably even more than a brightly lit room where numerous different images prevent us from truly perceiving. An image that lights up for an instant and immediately disappears into darkness can be fully perceived because of its stillness and isolation. Hajas' performances were as charged with darkness as death, sexuality, and suffering, and a momentarily illuminated image was, among other things, a metaphor for the fragility of life.

Hajas' audiences and critics say that his performances were marked by a kind of fanaticism; he constantly put himself in danger, and this is how his premature death must probably be understood.

1   The body as a tool for liberation

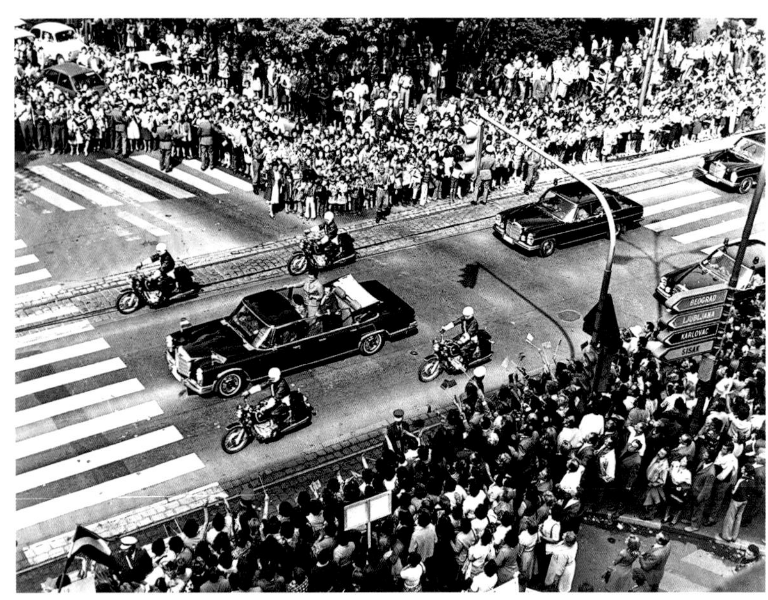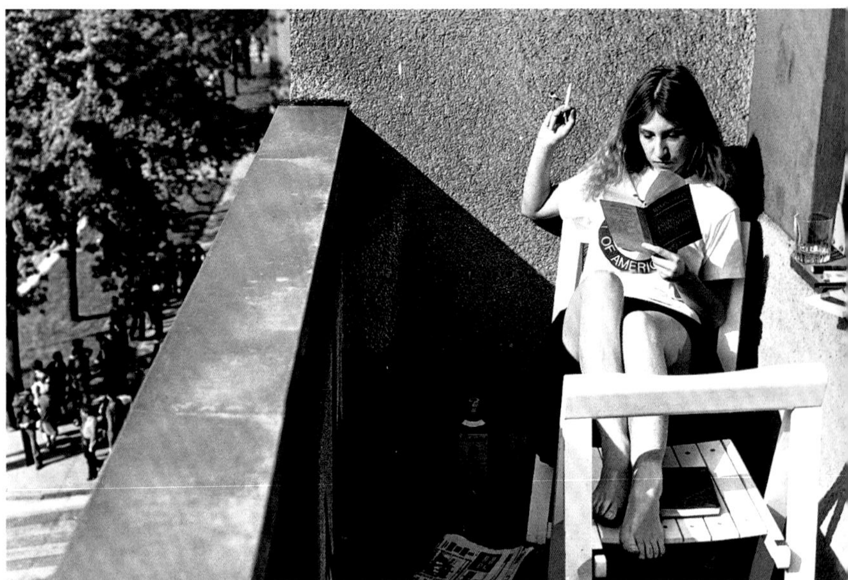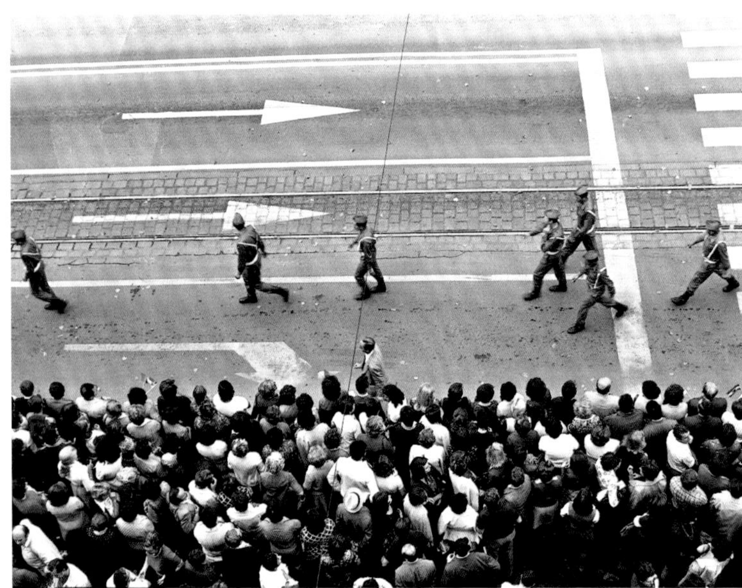

BEOGRAD
LJUBLJANA
KARLOVAC
SISAK

Sanja Iveković

(b. 1949, Zagreb, Yugoslavia, now Croatia)

Triangle 2000+
1979
4 b/w photographs, each 30×40 cm
Courtesy Moderna galerija, Ljubljana

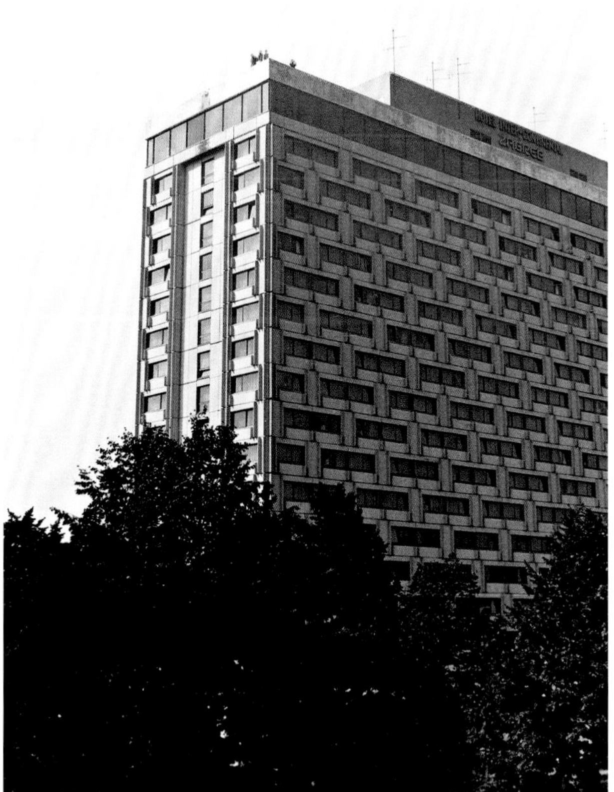

Since the start of her artistic career Sanja Iveković has worked with photography and video. A large part of her work focuses on the social position of women, especially on the strategies of representation of women and their social roles.

The photographs show an action performed by Sanja Iveković on the balcony of her flat in Zagreb on the day Tito visited the city. The depiction of a woman on a balcony is a motif with a long history in Western painting. It speaks both of the external and internal space: women are confined to their homes, they can observe the activity outside from the balcony, but at the same time, they are being observed. The work indirectly speaks about the concept of public space, the geopolitical situation at that time, and the space where only a few women are allowed to participate in political activities. The action may also be understood as a form of civil insubordination. It involved three people:

The person on the roof of the hotel across the street; the policeman in the street in front of the artist's building; the artist on the balcony.

In the artist's words, "Because of the balcony's concrete screen, the action can only be seen and observed by the person on the hotel roof. I assume that he is equipped with binoculars and a walkie-talkie, with which he can contact the policeman in the street. The action begins when I go out onto the balcony. I bring two chairs, a bottle of whisky, cigarettes and some books. I sit, drink, smoke and read. After a while, I lift my skirt and pretend that I'm masturbating. Soon, the doorbell rings and a man introducing himself as an official orders me to 'remove all persons and objects from the balcony.' That was the end of the action."

1   The body as a tool for liberation

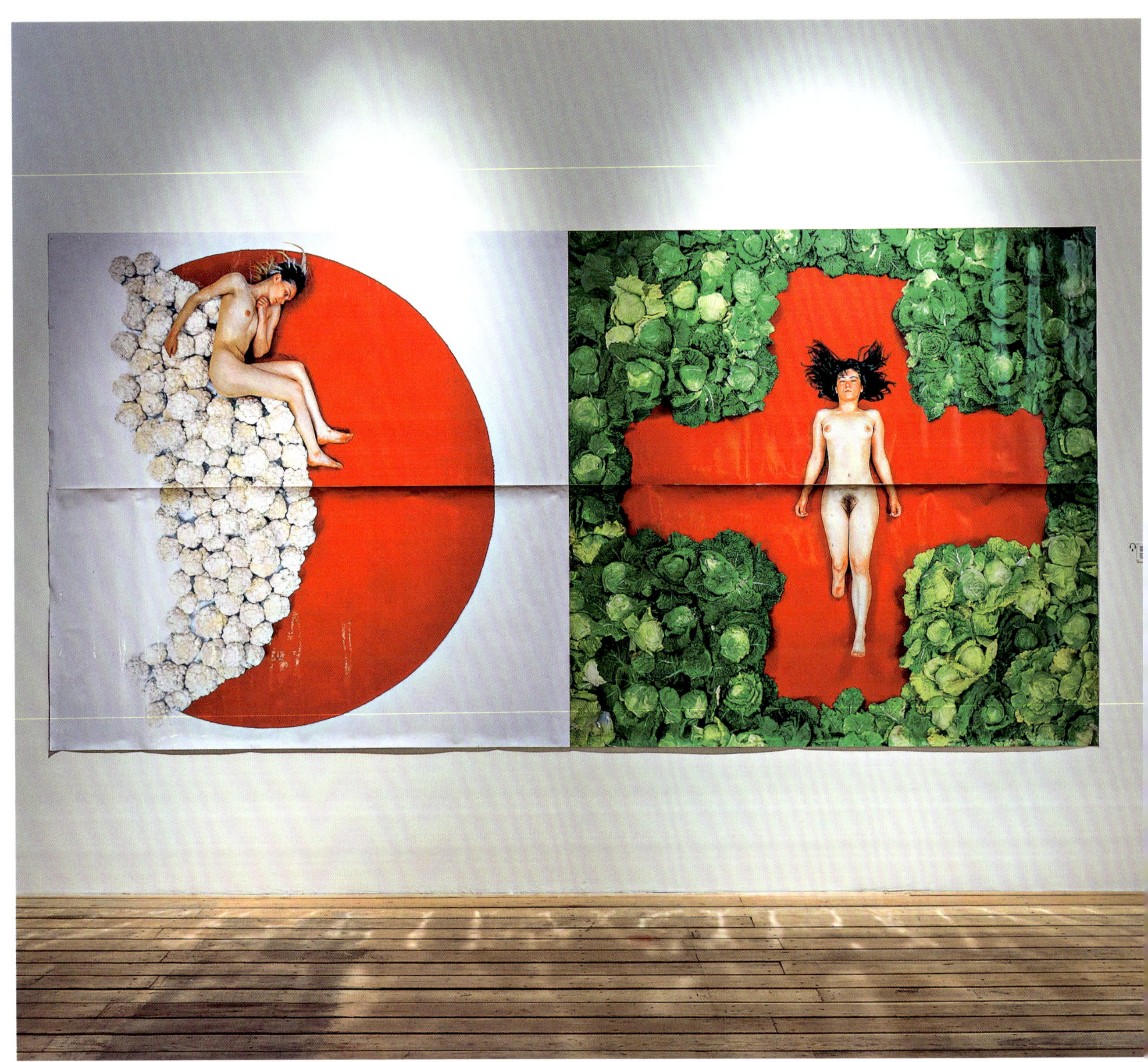

Katarzyna Kozyra

(b. 1963, Warsaw, Poland)

Blood Ties

1995

Color print, 400×200 cm

Courtesy Moderna galerija, Ljubljana

Working within the traditional understanding of body art, Katarzyna Kozyra perceives the artist's body as a medium and object of art. She deals with the significance that the body has for the individual's identity. Her works are both lyrical and critical, dealing with the relationship between personal freedom, individual biography, and communication in society. She places particular emphasis on the female body and how it has been perceived by art and folk culture. Kozyra addresses the spectator with dramatic scenes of her own personal pain, which are metaphors forthe suffering of mankind.

The first version of the *Blood Ties* photograph was presented in 1995 in response to the war in Bosnia. Four years later, *Blood Ties 2* was created. Its message was similar: a commentary on the events in Kosovo; a reproach to the tragedy there, involving major religions and the destiny of women victimized by such conflicts. *Blood Ties 2* was supposed to be displayed in 1999 on 400 billboards in the major towns of Poland. Only a few were displayed and even those had to be removed a few days later due to the negative public response. They were said to denigrate religious symbols—the Christian cross and Muslim crescent—but rather than being iconoclastic or scandalous, the work was actually intended as an anti-war statement.

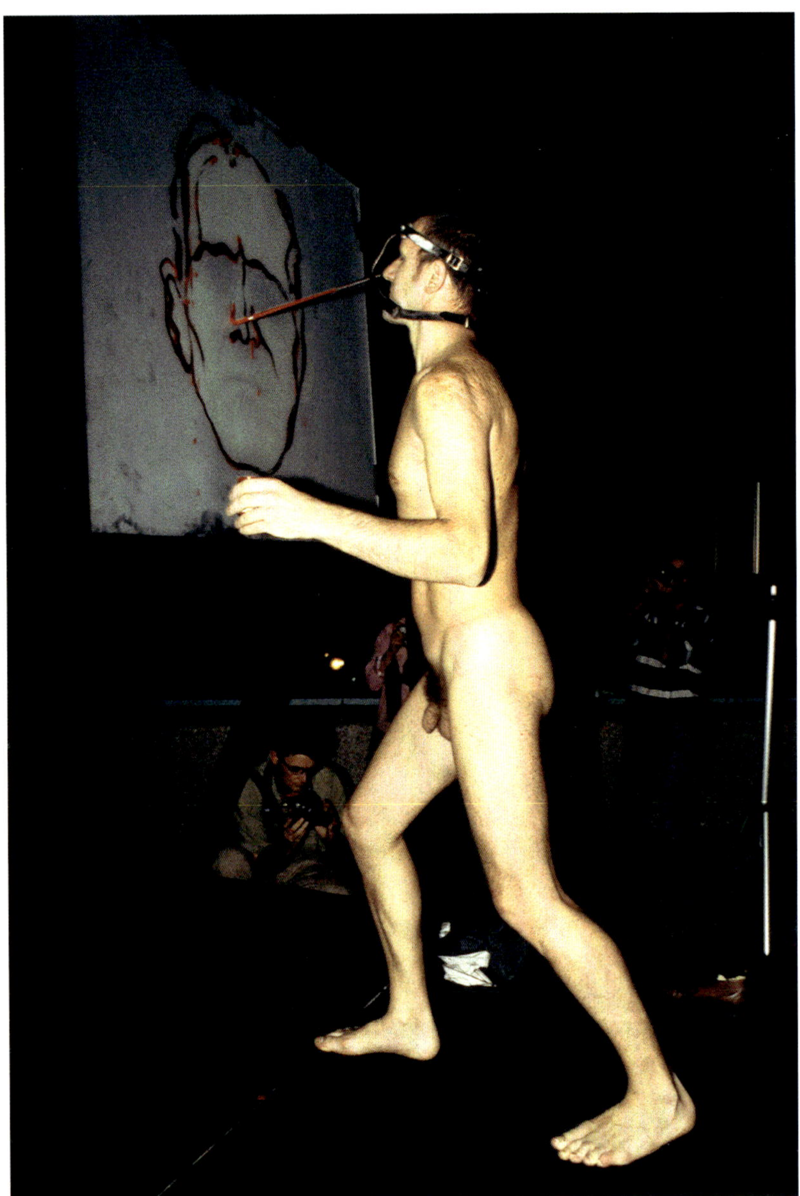

Oleg Kulik

(b. 1961, Kiev, USSR, now Ukraine)

Two Kuliks
1998
Performance
Courtesy of the artist

When Oleg Kulik takes on the persona of a dog and performs his "zoophrenic action"—barking, sniffing, and occasionally biting members of the public—his behavior becomes unpredictable and dangerous. As such, he is no longer the decorative "object of art," but transforms into a "beast" threatening to disrupt the seemingly harmonious relationships of the global art scene. The enjoyment of the (Western) audience is destroyed and the artist is perceived as an enemy as soon as the stereotype of a wild and untamed Eastern neighbor is enacted in a literal and aggressive way.

Kulik's works are based on the idea that communication between the East and the West is impossible due to an inequality between people. Kulik reminds us that communication is never neutral. He exposes the unresolved tensions of the East-West relationship, their inequality in the exchange of ideas, and highlights the constant power struggle that the current ideology tries to conceal while promoting dialogue. It seems that "in a vacuum of democracy," as Viktor Misiano observes, "conflict has become the most effective method of acquiring an identity."

For the exhibition *Body and the East*, held in 1998 in Ljubljana, Kulik performed *Two Kuliks.* Naked and wearing special headgear, he painted a self-portrait on a large sheet of glass onto which his image was projected. The performance represented a dialogue between the two Kuliks—the one painting and the other being painted. The performance ended when Kulik smashed the glass and his image of his head.

1   The body as a tool for liberation

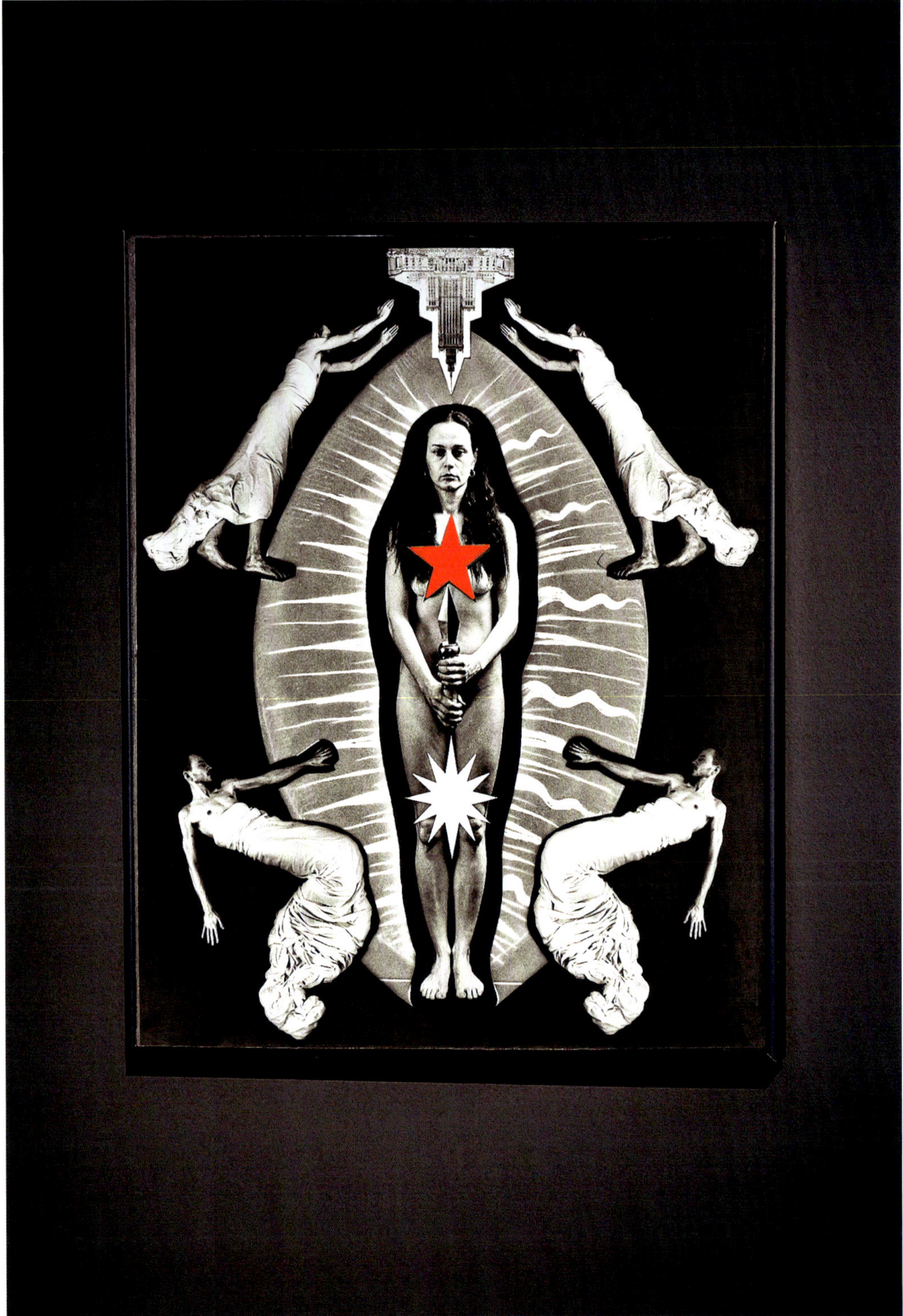

Zofia Kulik

(b. 1947, Wroclaw, Poland)

Self-Portrait with the Palace
1990
Multiple-exposure b/w photo collage, 40×48cm
Courtesy Moderna galerija, Ljubljana

Between 1971 and 1987 Zofia Kulik worked closely with Przemysław Kwiek in a duo named KwieKulik that performed various actions which critically examined the social and political reality of the communist regime in Poland. After the collapse of the socialist state and the duo's separation in 1987, she developed her own artistic language and started to create large-format self-portraits—multiple exposure photo collages, where many different depictions and hundreds of images, organized in ornamental patterns, can be seen. Kulik is a collector of images. "I dress myself in them," she says. Her complex works, full of ornament, allegory, and historical references, comment on the political and ideological reality of the time and are the result of examining issues relating to her identity as an artist and a woman.

In *Self-Portrait with the Palace* the composition is based on a Baroque painting entitled *The Assumption of the Virgin Mary* from a parish church in Pszczew. Kulik is presented enclosed in a shape in the form of a mandorla, holding in her hands the metal top of a banner pole, while photograms of two stars, the upper being red, "veil" her body. For the depiction of a crown she used an upside-down image of the tallest building in Warsaw—the Palace of Culture and Science.

1   The body as a tool for liberation

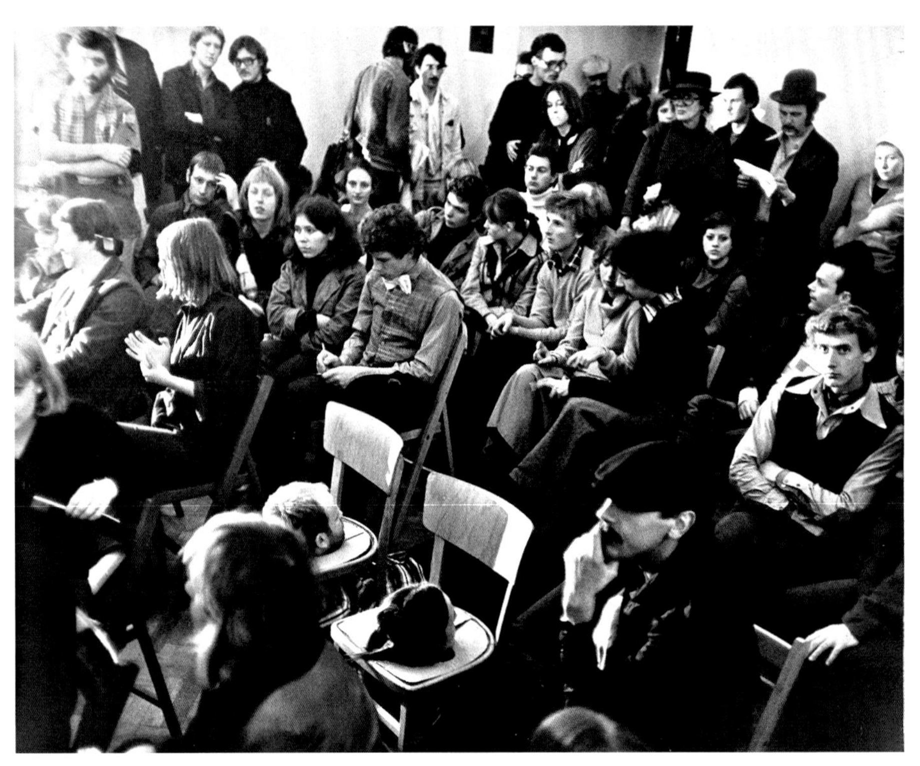

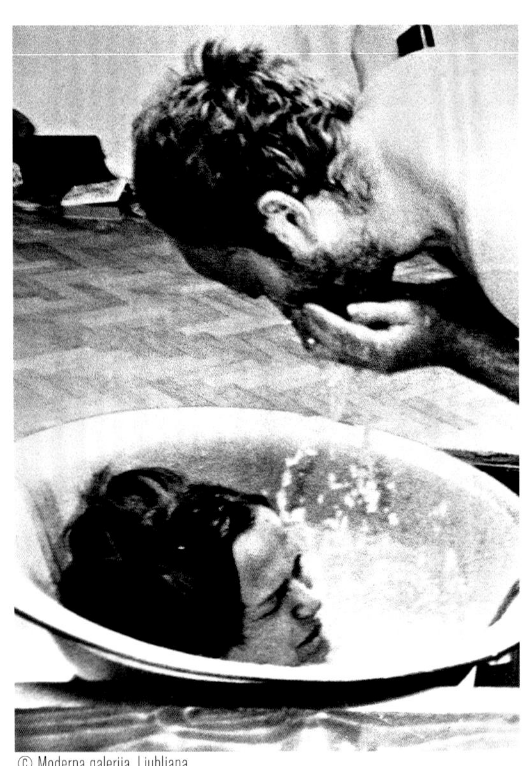

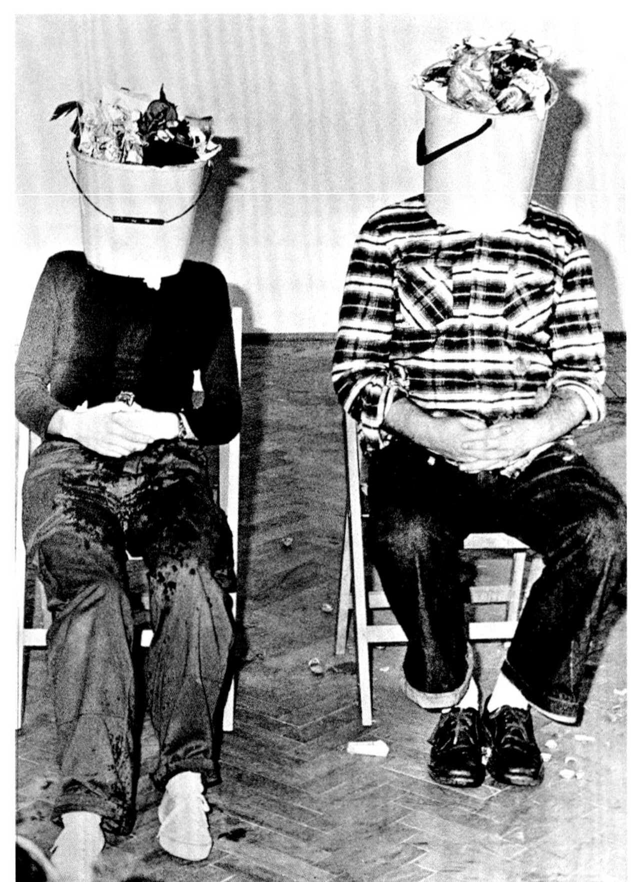

KwieKulik

Activities with the Head
1978
Body performance, Labyrinth Gallery, Lublin
3 b/w photographs, 28×37 cm, 27×37 cm, 35×28 cm
Courtesy Moderna galerija, Ljubljana

The artistic duo KwieKulik (Przemysław Kwiek and Zofia Kulik) is recognized as one of the most important artistic phenomena of postwar Polish art. They opposed official, state-controlled art and instead experimented with new media, developing their practice as a process which crossed the boundaries between art and life. They performed various actions together and produced different forms of archives, films, and object installations. Their works examined the concept of freedom in a society under a communist regime and often used irony, ridiculing national symbols in order to criticize the restrictions of Poland's national politics at that time.

The political context was also referenced in the performance *Activities with the Head*, the title of which is a comment on political indoctrination in communist Poland. Before the performance started visitors were asked to put a small red flag behind their left ear. *Activities with the Head* was carried out in three parts. In the first, the artists lay on the floor facing the audience with their heads coming out of seats. A brown paper curtain opened the second scene, and Kulik could be seen sitting on the floor with her head in a bowl while Kwiek poured water into the bowl until she could breathe only through her nose, then washed his feet, hands, and face while shouting, "Say something you whore, come on, say something!" In the last scene, Kulik and Kwiek were seated on chairs, their heads covered with buckets full of rubbish.

1   The body as a tool for liberation

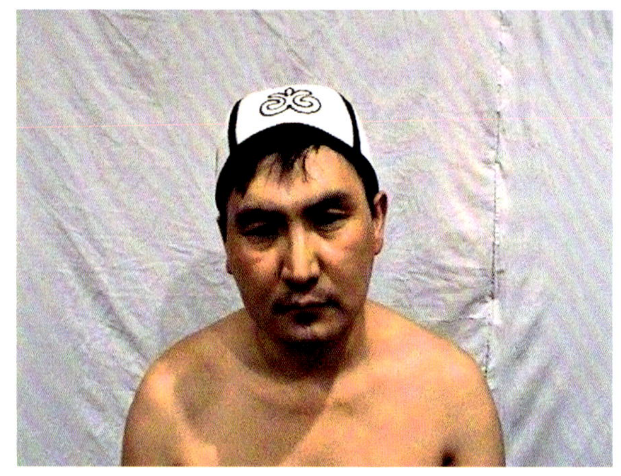
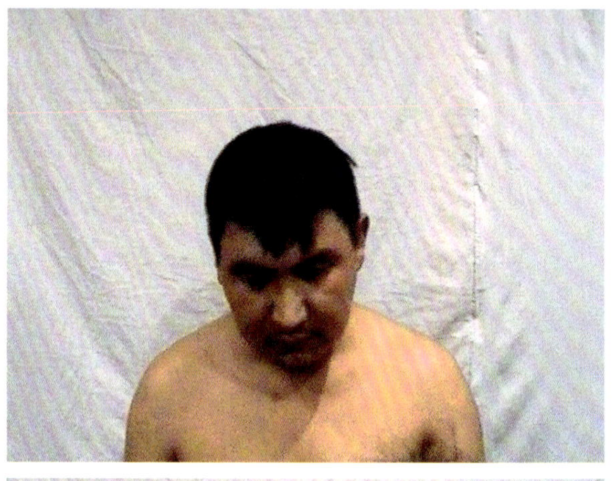
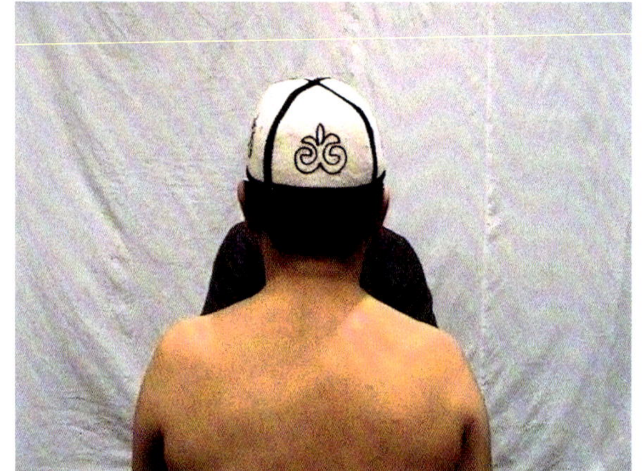
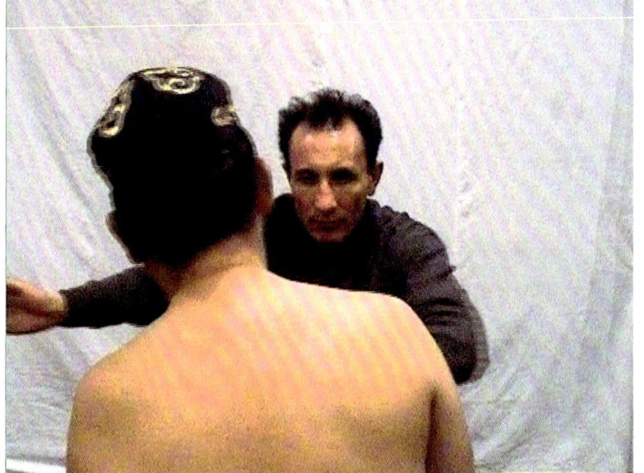
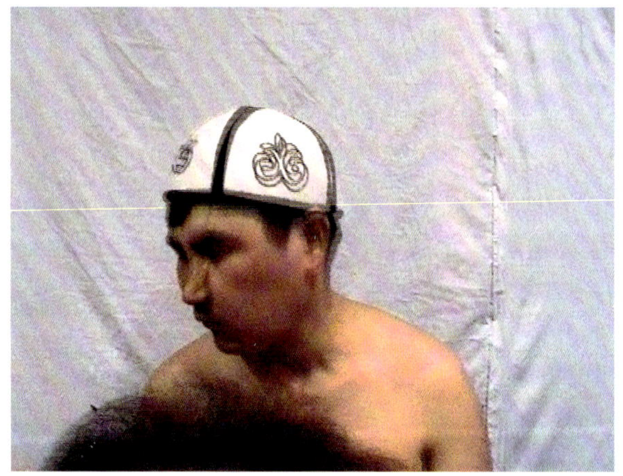
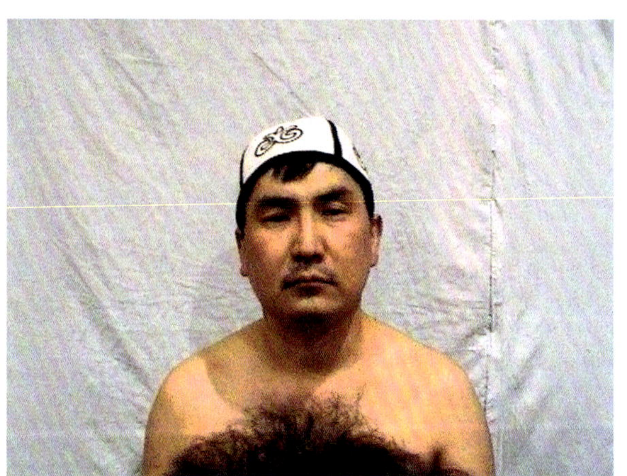
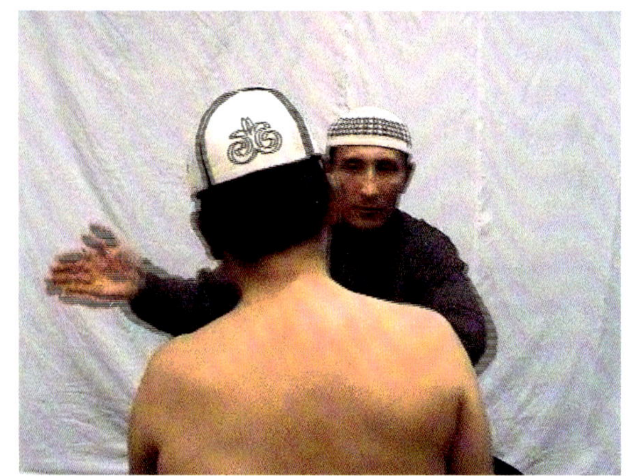
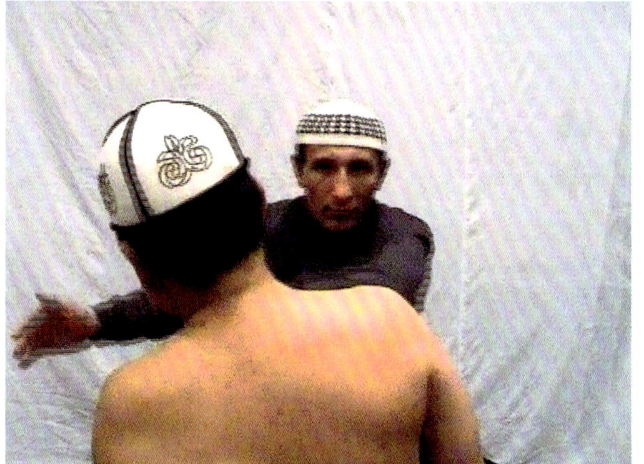

Yerbossyn Meldibekov

(b. 1964, Tyulkubas railway station, USSR, now Kazakhstan)

Pastan
2002
Video, 6'53"
Courtesy of the artist

Yerbossyn Meldibekov was one of the first Kazakhs to choose the life of a contemporary artist. With the collapse of the Soviet Union and national independence Kazakh artists faced a pressing issue: the search for identity. While incorporating and reinterpreting Kazakh folk myths in his artworks, Meldibekov simultaneously creates a personal mythology. In particular the story of his artistic education was transformed into the stuff of legends. One day a relative from Alma-Ata arrived at a small village by the railway station, where the artist was born and lived, intending to buy a cow from his father. He could only afford half an animal, so in exchange he promised to get Meldibekov, who dreamed of becoming a train driver, into university. These connections became apparent only at art school. While serving as a radio engineer during the Afghan war, Meldibekov gained access to information concealed from most people. At that moment he concluded that an artist must study the mechanisms of power on the one hand and reconsider the history of their country on the other. He has described himself as a political artist on numerous occasions. Meldibekov also cultivates in his work the image of the Asian barbarian who behaves forcefully and coarsely. The barbarian lives in a place invented by the artist—the country of Pastan. One of the paths to self-knowledge chosen by the artist is that of flagellation. An unknown person dressed in a robe and Kazakh skullcap strikes the artist in the face while swearing. Only in this way does it seem possible to understand a country with such strict laws and rules.

1   The body as a tool for liberation

1

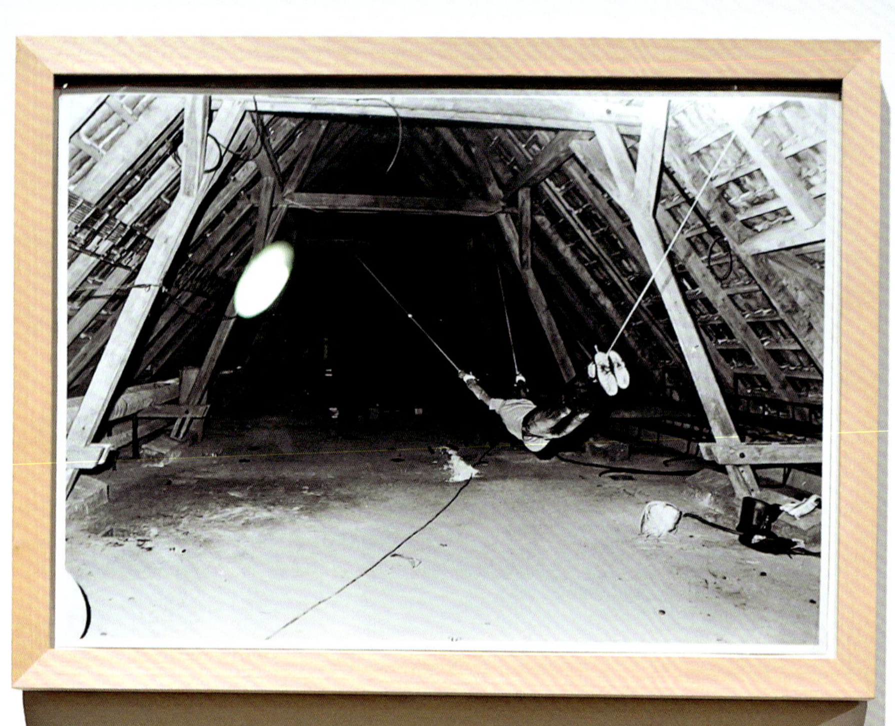

2

Jan Mlčoch

(b. 1953, Prague, Czechoslovakia, now Czech Republic)

1

The Hanging — Big Sleep
1974
Performance, Prague
Performance photograph, 40×30 cm
2

20 Minutes
1975
Performance, Prague
Performance photograph, 40×30 cm
Courtesy Moderna galerija, Ljubljana

Karel Miler, Jan Mlčoch, and Petr Štembera worked closely together until 1979. Even though they performed only for a small circle of friends outside the institutional framework of galleries, they nonetheless attempted to internationalize their practice by exhibiting abroad and establishing connections with foreign action artists. For Mlčoch, performing was a means of "personal confession." We can see two lines in the performances he gave in those years: on the one hand, he infiltrated everyday activities, lending a new context to familiar meanings; and on the other, he was inspired by work with space which he perceived in an ambivalent way. It served him as a place where he could disappear from participants, whereas in other cases, he would oust them from the space in the most diverse ways.

In *20 Minutes* he sat between the basement wall and a knife which was tied to one end of a long iron rod attached to the floor, and asked a member of the audience to move the rod as far as they chose. In *The Hanging — Big Sleep* he covered his eyes with black fabric, plugged his ears with earplugs, and suspended himself by his hands and feet from the ceiling of an attic. As Jiří Ševčík notes, the performance expressed the situation of the time through the paradox of physical action: while the isolation from phenomenological reality allows the performer to fuse with the totality of being, the weight of the human condition, which is expressed through pain, at the same time forces him to descend to everyday reality.

1   The body as a tool for liberation

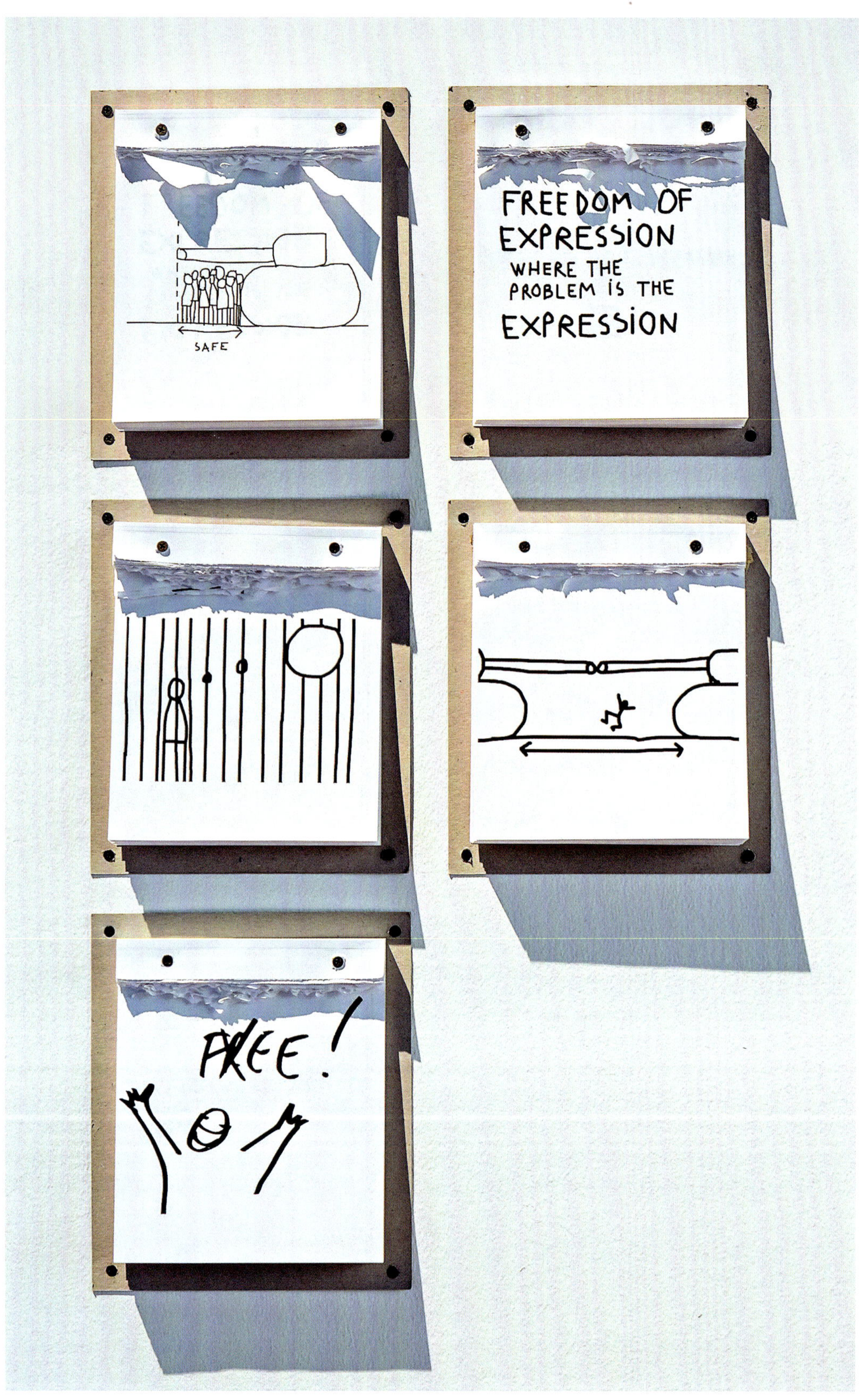
SAFE
FREEDOM OF
EXPRESSION
WHERE THE
PROBLEM IS THE
EXPRESSION
FREE!

Dan Perjovschi

(b. 1961, Sibiu, Romania)

Drawing Freedom
2005–2015
Print on paper
Created specifically for the exhibition *Grammar of Freedom/Five Lessons:*
Works from the Arteast 2000+ Collection
Courtesy of the artist

Dan Perjovschi lives and works in Bucharest. Although he trained as a painter, he works primarily in black-and-white drawings. As he describes it, his desire to create quick sketches instead of paintings emerged in the 1990s, at a moment of radical political transformations, when one of the most important forms of media was newspapers. As a newspaper illustrator Perjovschi was able to freely express his opinions, react quickly to social changes, and convey his message to thousands of readers.

Not only does he publish his own newspaper featuring his drawings, for years he has worked directly with exhibition spaces, on the walls of which he applies images and texts with a black marker. The main subject of his work, as before, is political and cultural reality. But now his gaze reaches far beyond the borders of his own country and into the global space of information. The contradictoriness, absurdity, and cynicism of current affairs are reflected in Perjovschi's spontaneous drawings, which reveal the true meaning of social shifts with a subtle humor. In his works Perjovschi often criticizes the relationship between the European Union and the former socialist states, and he also focuses on tense recent political situations, particularly the Arab Spring and the events in Ukraine. His art practice has a situational aspect, and the content of his drawings varies depending on the context of the place in which he is working. Owing to the fact that Perjovschi's works are influenced by information from the wider world, they not only resonate with the surrounding social space, they also invite an instant response from audiences, who encounter comprehensible subjects and themes that are important to them.

1   The body as a tool for liberation

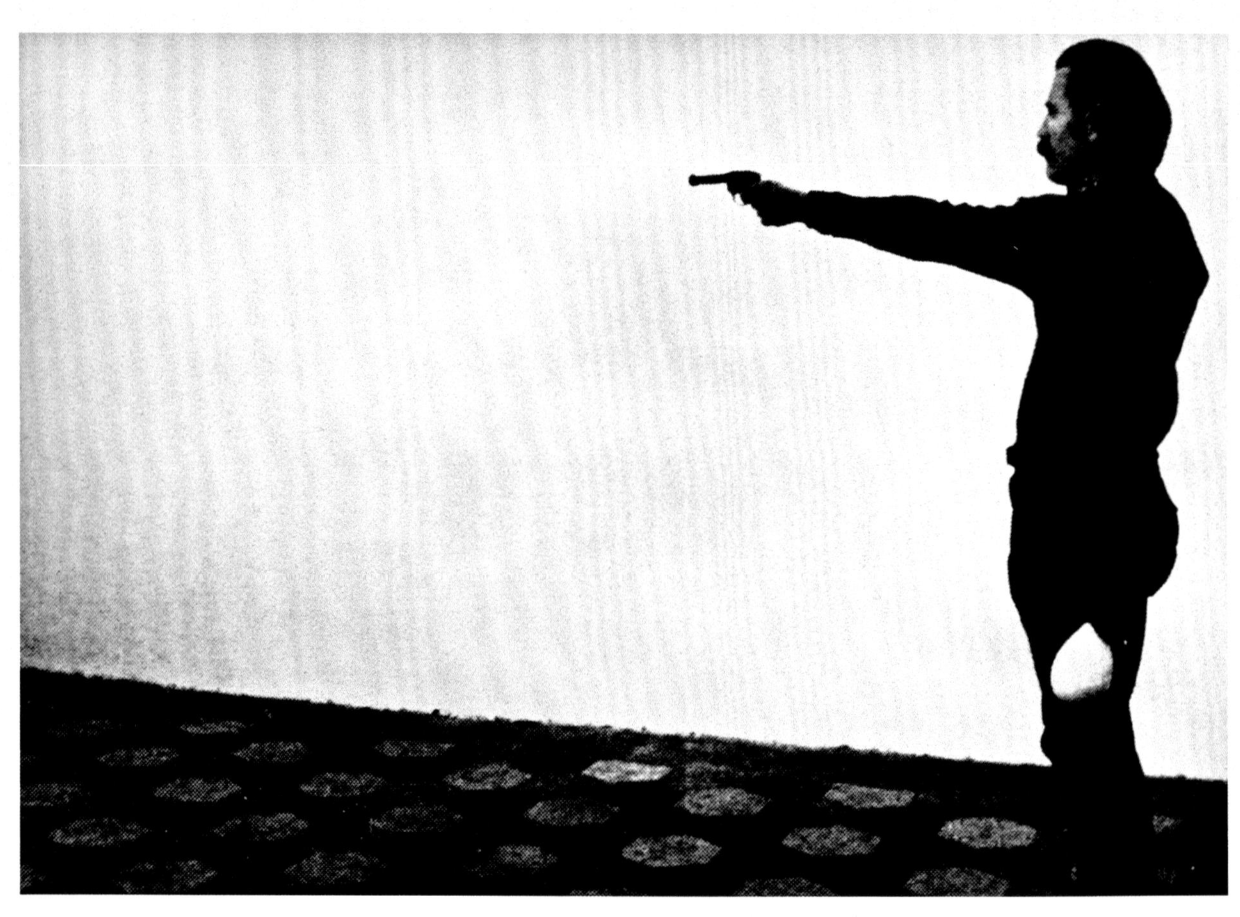

© Moderna galerija, Ljubljana

Ilija Šoškić

(b. 1934, Dečani, Yugoslavia, now Kosovo)

Milk and Silk, Maximum Energy — Minimum Time
1975
Performance, Galleria L'Attico, Rome
B/w photograph, 45×60 cm
Courtesy Moderna galerija, Ljubljana

As an artist and an intellectual Ilja Šoškić was formed in the context of the ideas and artistic practices of 1968, as well as in the context of the international student revolts that were taking place at the time. Šoškić's events, actions, and performances usually express a "militant" attitude towards the institutions of power, be it ideological, political, or art institutions.

In 1975, Ilija Šoškić carried out the performance *Milk and Silk* in L'Attico gallery in Rome. It consisted of four acts which the artist performed at intervals. In the final, most emblematic and widely-known act, entitled *Maximum Energy — Minimum Time*, Šoškić, dressed in a Red Army uniform, holding a bottle of milk in one hand and a revolver in the other, aimed and fired all six shots at the gallery wall.

The performance was dedicated to the Russian futurist poet Vladimir Mayakovsky, who committed suicide by shooting himself in the head, leaving behind a note that said, "This is not the way (I do not recommend it to others), but there is no other way for me." In *Maximum Energy — Minimum Time* the artist, being the active force, is positioned between two "passive" forces, represented by the bottle of milk and the revolver. His artistic performance is thus a sharp and decisive gesture. The shot is the maximum amount of energy concentrated in one bullet that can penetrate the wall of the art gallery and break the border that the gallery represents as a place of the institutionalization of art. *Maximum Energy — Minimum Time* thus exemplifies the possibility of freedom and of breaking the barriers of social normativity. As Petar Čuković writes, Šoškić's shot therefore affirms life, "The evocation of death here is understood as a function of life, of the vital strength of mind and intelligence."

1   The body as a tool for liberation

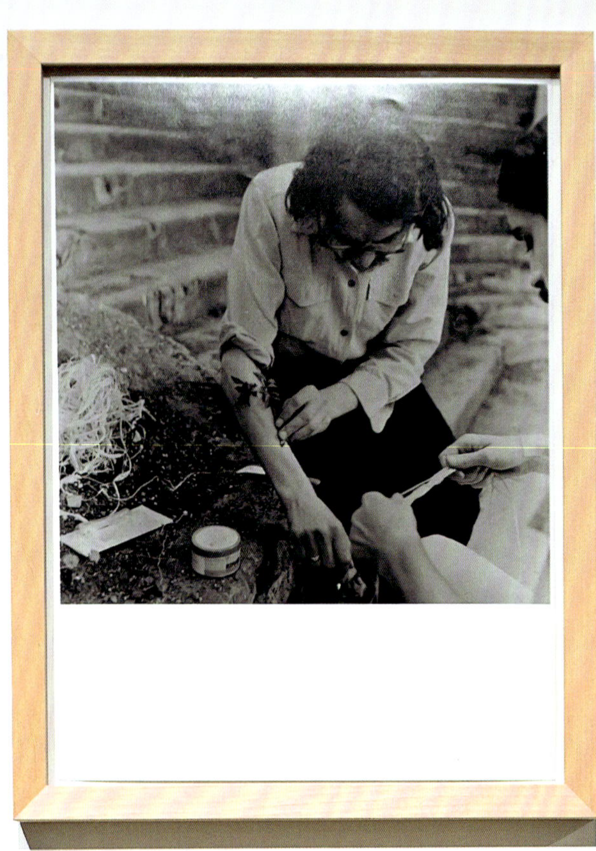

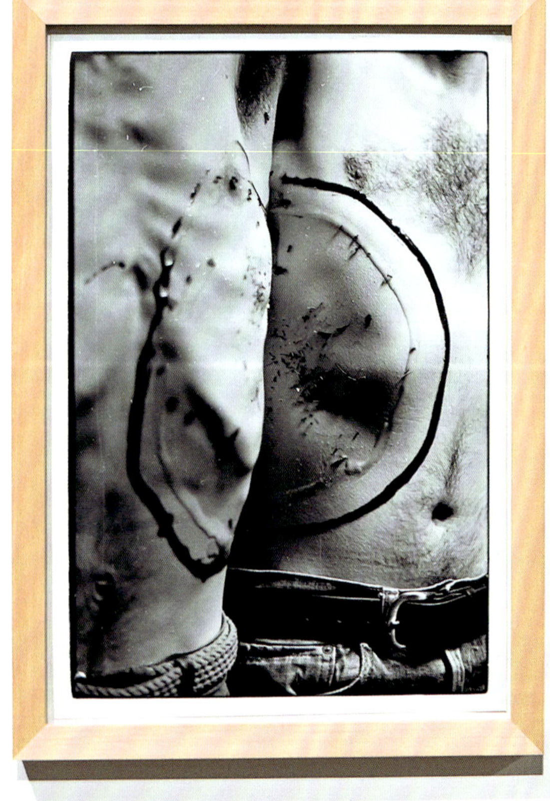

Petr Štembera

(b. 1945, Prague, Czechoslovakia, now Czech Republic)

1
Joining (with Tom Marioni)
Performance photograph, 27×40 cm
2
Grafting
Performance photograph, 40×30 cm
Courtesy Moderna galerija, Ljubljana

The performances of Petr Štembera, one of the pioneers of Czech conceptualism, were a critical response to anxiety, fear, and secrecy— the consequences of living under the tyranny of the Communist regime. Štembera performed (and documented) his pieces first in solitude and later within a small circle of close friends. His performances always included both an inside and an outside threat: he turned on his own body with self-destructive acts (by which he attempted to achieve transcendental experiences), and exposed it to extreme conditions by using dangerous and unpredictable materials such as acid and fire. In his most demanding performances he tested his identity in unbearable situations. His actions acquired the character of sacrifice, questioned "the morals and aesthetics of pain," or referred ironically to the situation of the intellectual sphere within civil society.

In *Joining*, Štembera and Tom Marioni joined their bodies with two circles made from milk and cocoa. Štembera then put some hungry ants in the middle. While some moved towards the edges, other ants remained in the center and began to bite the artists.

In *Grafting*, he wanted "to make contact with the plant, to put it in [his] body to be together with it as long as possible." He therefore grafted a branch taken from a shrub to his arm in a customary fruit farming method that included poisonous materials and left it there until his blood became infected.

1   The body as a tool for liberation

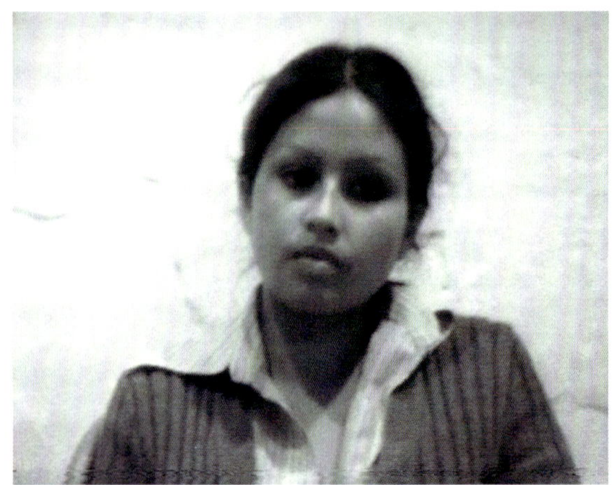

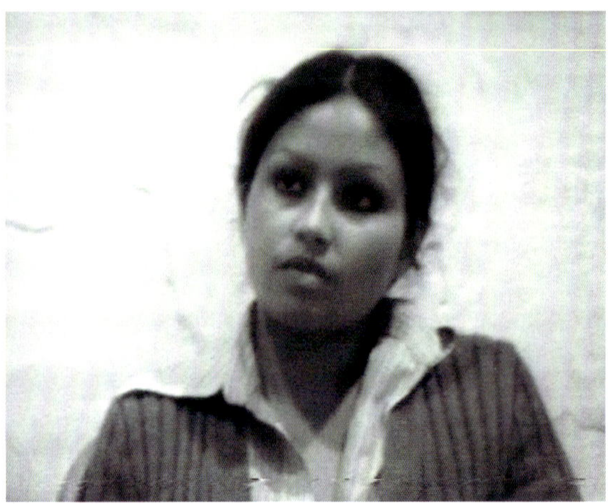

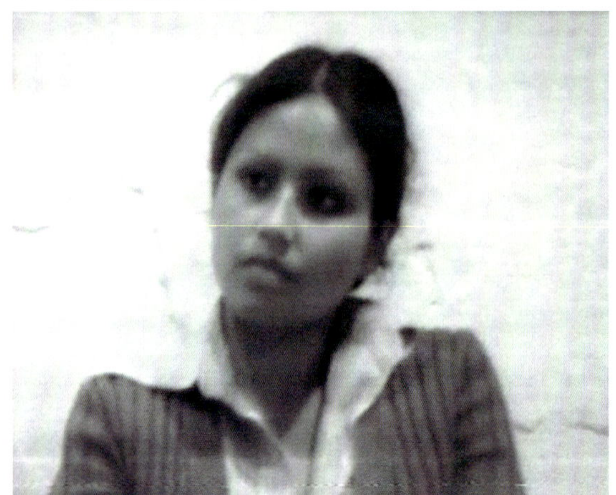

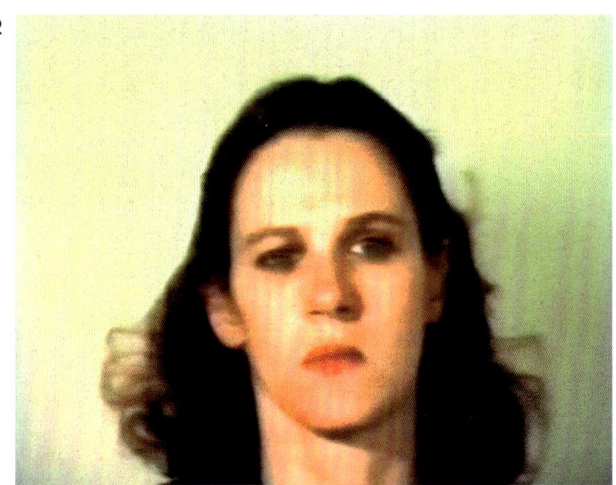

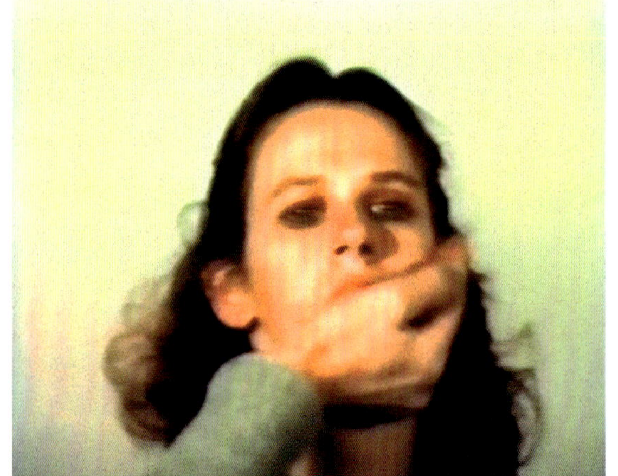

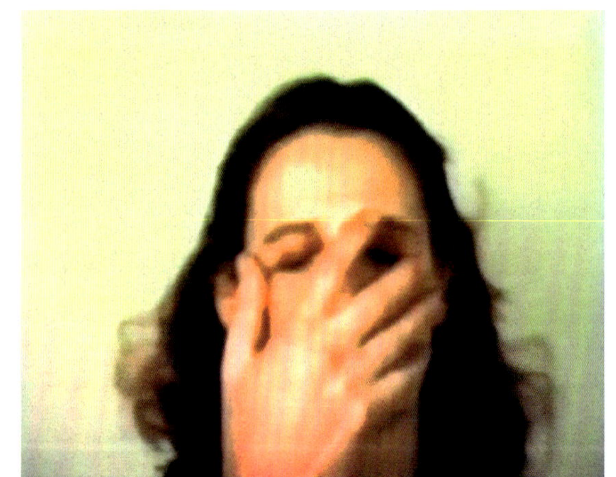

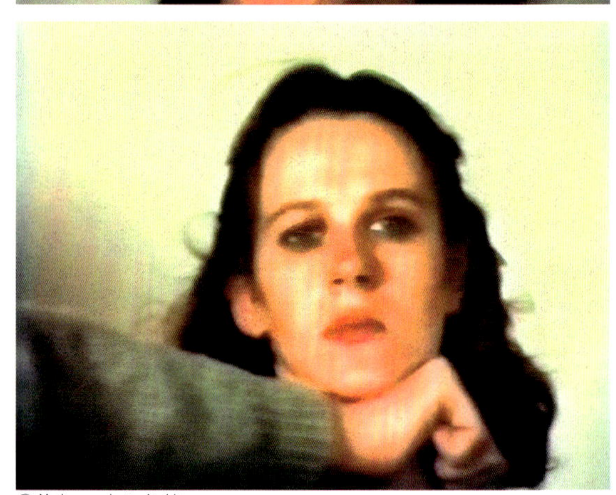

Raša Todosijević

(b. 1945, Belgrade, Yugoslavia, now Serbia)

1

Was ist Kunst, Patricia Hennings?

1976

Video, 30'

2

Was ist Kunst, Marinela Koželj?

1978

Video, 16'20"

Courtesy Moderna galerija, Ljubljana

Raša Todosijević was a member of an informal group of young conceptual artists who in the early 1970s gathered at the Students' Cultural Center in Belgrade. They conceived a new form of practice, later recognized as a part of the "New Artistic Practice" that rejected traditional (modernist) artistic concepts, questioned the dominant structures of art and society of the time, and tested the boundaries of traditional media by using new forms of artistic expression (video, performance, actions, and new media).

In *Was ist Kunst?* (What is art?), the artist shouts the question "What is art?" in German over and over again to a woman silently sitting in front of him and patiently enduring his interrogation. Besides commenting on the relationship between the traditionally male artist and the female model, Todosijević also questions the dialectic between the intention and the interpretation of art. The philosophical and theoretical question "What is art?", when posed in an authoritarian tone, becomes a violent and intrusive search for "truth," demanding an answer that cannot (will not) be given. Todosijević's piece thus exposes the ambivalent nature of the question itself: on the one hand, the indefinite repetition of the same question functions as despotic speech, as a tool of torture, subordination, and control; but on the other hand, the repetition exposes its weakness and impotence since the person questioned stays silent and the performance ends when the "interrogator's" voice fails him, leaving the question unanswered.

1   The body as a tool for liberation

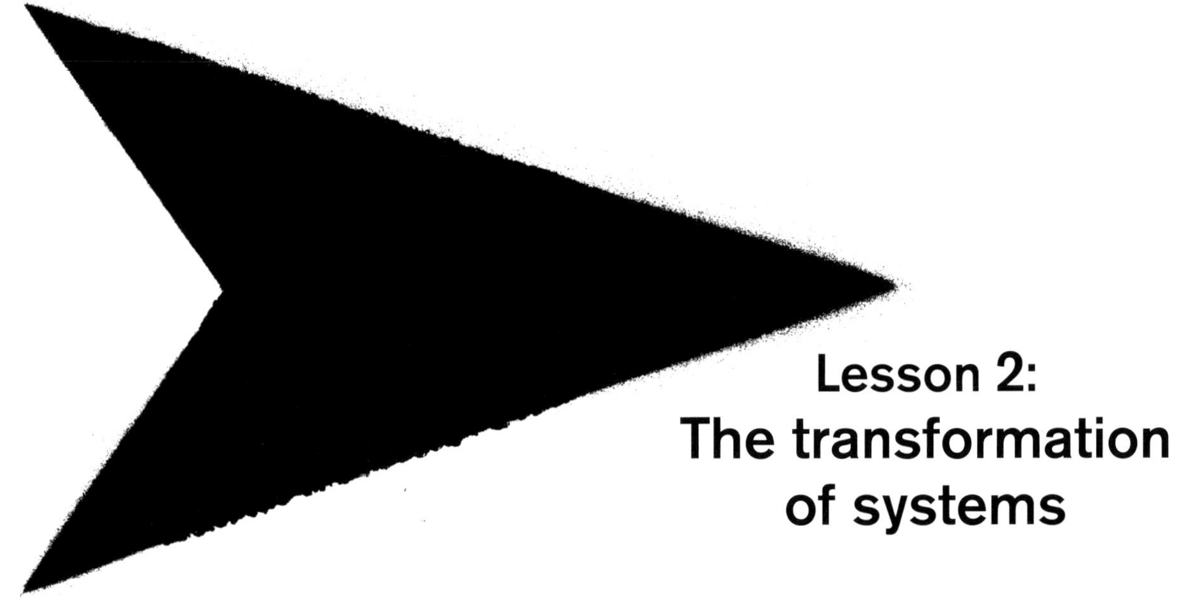

Lesson 2:
The transformation of systems

Revealing the workings of the art world to change inequities in the distribution of art and ideas

Under socialism, when art was controlled by the state, there were minimal systems of support and little international exposure. Now, as multinational capital (or the lack thereof) increasingly controls all art worlds, the circulation of art and knowledge primarily responds to the dictates of the market. Under both systems the amount of exposure art will gain, and where, is impacted. By using their work to critique the art system, artists can draw attention to these paradoxes while also providing under-represented perspectives to the dominant narratives in art.

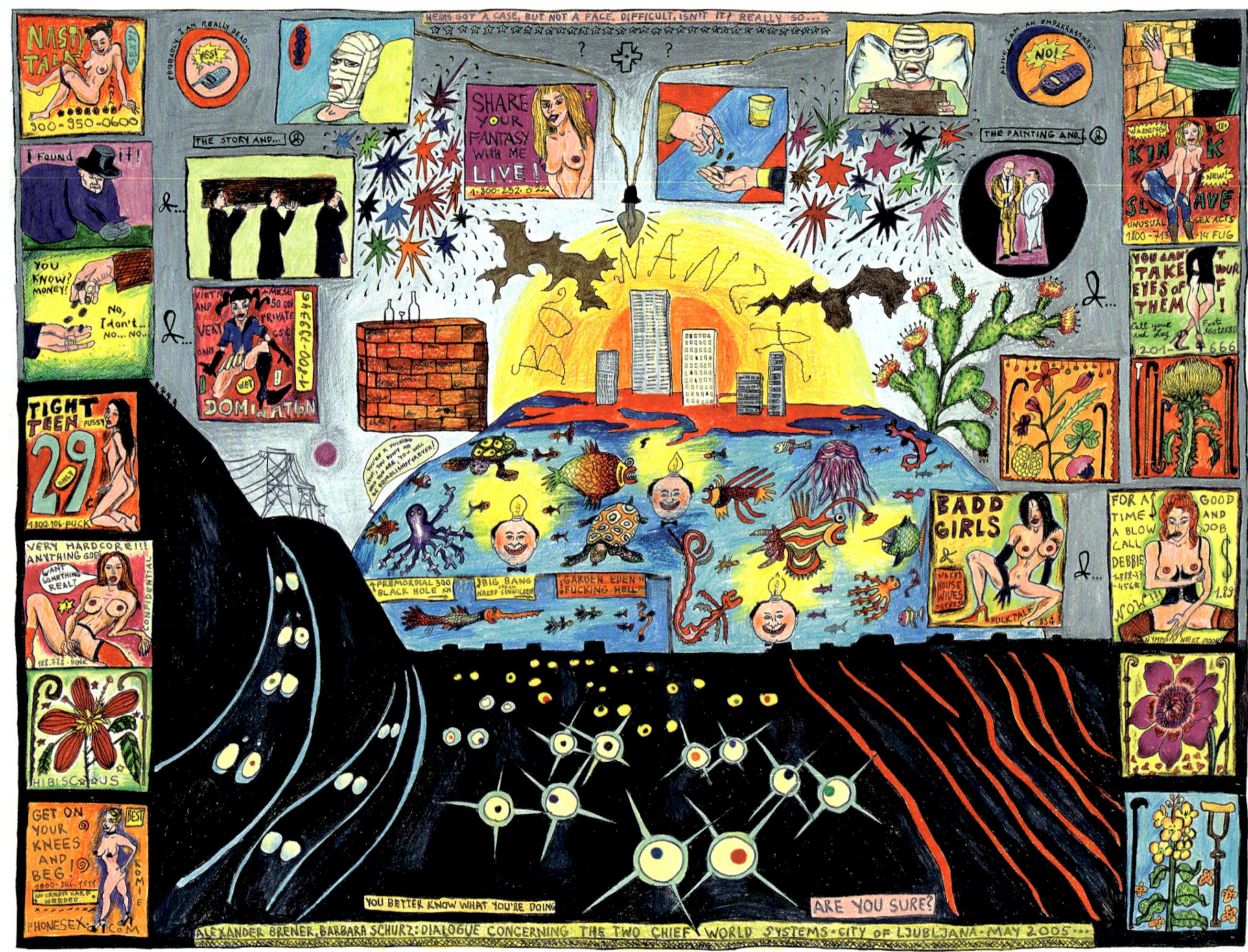

Photo: Dejan Habicht. © Moderna galerija, Ljubljana

Alexander Brener and Barbara Schurz

(b. 1957, Alma Ata, USSR, now Kazakhstan; b. 1973, Klagenfurt, Austria)

Dialog on the Two Dominant Global Systems
2005
Mixed media on paper, 56×76 cm
Courtesy Moderna galerija, Ljubljana

Few know that the poet and performance artist Alexander Brener lived and worked as a journalist in Israel for three years from 1989. He appeared on the Moscow art scene only in 1992 and quickly won acclaim as one of the most scandalous artists of the Moscow Actionism movement. It is important to note that the Moscow Actionists did not consider themselves a cohesive group, but this did not prevent them from sometimes carrying out joint performances. One of the most famous is *The Mad Dog, or the Last Taboo Guarded by a Lone Cerberus* (1994). The mad dog was the artist Oleg Kulik, who, on all fours, pretended to be Cerberus, biting people and pouncing at passing cars. Brener held him on a thick metal chain, not hindering and even encouraging his transgressive behavior. Another famous performance, *First Glove*, took place on Red Square in February 1995. Wearing only boxing gloves, athletic shorts, and sneakers, Brener jumped up onto Lobnoye Mesto (a stone plinth from which the town crier once announced royal decrees). The solitary artist shouted in the direction of the impregnable Kremlin walls: "Yeltsin, come out!" As sports journalists later noted, victory went to the artist inasmuch as his opponent never entered the fray. In 1996, Brener left the Moscow art scene after criminal charges were brought against him. As part of another performance, Brener threw bottles of ketchup at the Belarusian embassy, causing damage to the property of a foreign state, an act that the law enforcement agencies could not ignore. Over the course of the next year, he made a scandalous array of performances in Europe and even ended up in a Dutch prison, after which he stated that he was moving on from the role of artist in order to focus fully on literature. With his colleague Barbara Schurz he travels the world, publishing "samizdat" poetry collections. From time to time they supplement their literary works with illustrations that might be described as a conceptual continuation of their programmatic critique of capitalism and the current world order.

2　The transformation of systems

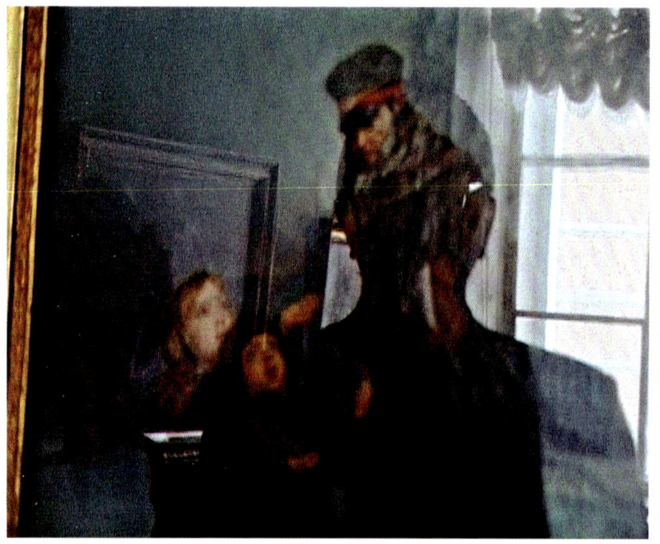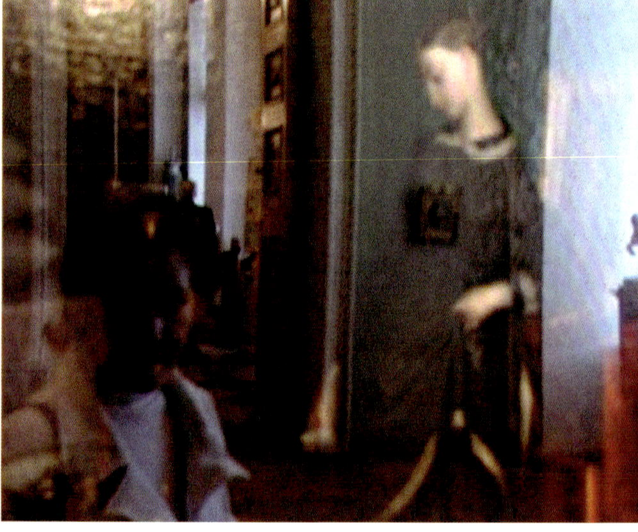
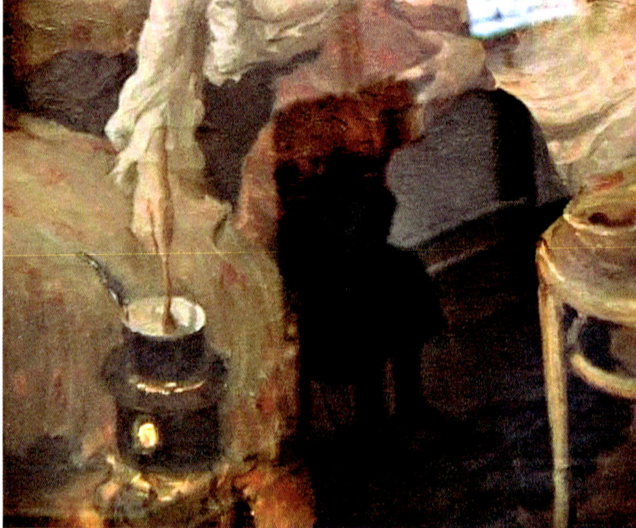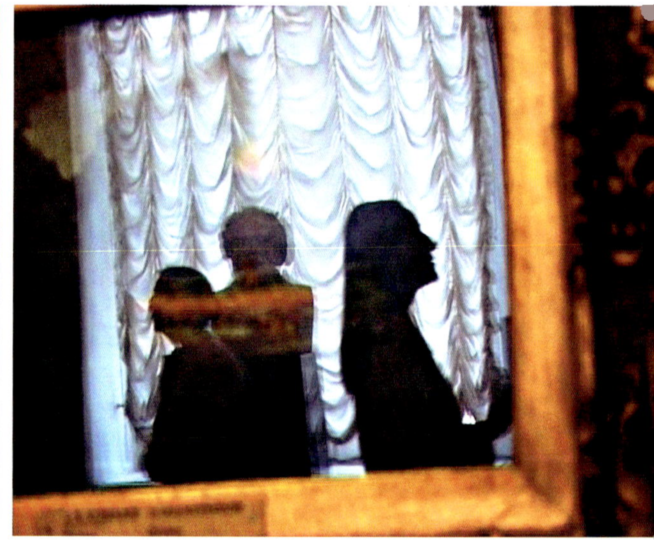

© Olga Chernysheva

Olga Chernysheva

(b. 1962, Moscow, USSR, now Russia)

Russian Museum
2003–2005
Video, 6'11"
Courtesy of the artist

Olga Chernysheva is one of the most subtle and accomplished Russian artists working in video today, but her arsenal also includes painting, objects, and photography. Her work includes unexpected themes which go against the grain of the art market, as well as what might be described as "at a distance from human touch" to use the words of director John Cassavetes. Her ongoing series *Security Guards*, for which she creates unstaged photographic portraits of security guards at art institutions, evinces a particular interest in the problem of observing the "human." But her subjects are not simply sentinels, spending their days and years waiting for something that might never happen. The essence of her work is a philosophical viewing of the world or, more precisely, an observing of it. Security guards are able to contemplate daily life in a mode that is extended and ahistorical. In *Holiday Dream* (2005), Chernysheva takes the viewer into the dream of a homeless person sleeping on a bench. We see a comfortable and carefree Soviet life, with rich borscht and folk festivals. But the sleeper's fragile and endlessly vulnerable dream world tragically disintegrates when he is awoken and sent packing by local hooligans who want to drink beer on the bench.

The video *Russian Museum* is also, to a certain extent, built on various ways of observing people. The action takes place in St. Petersburg's State Russian Museum, where the visitors can be seen as reflections in the glass covering works by classic Russian painters such as Vasily Perov and Aleksei Venetsianov. Chernysheva chooses a literal means of observing people via art, and this magical and sideways moving glance reflects the secret heart of Russian culture. The voice of a guide outside the image repeats: "Sense the space, the endless space of Russia… Still, we do not value what we have…"

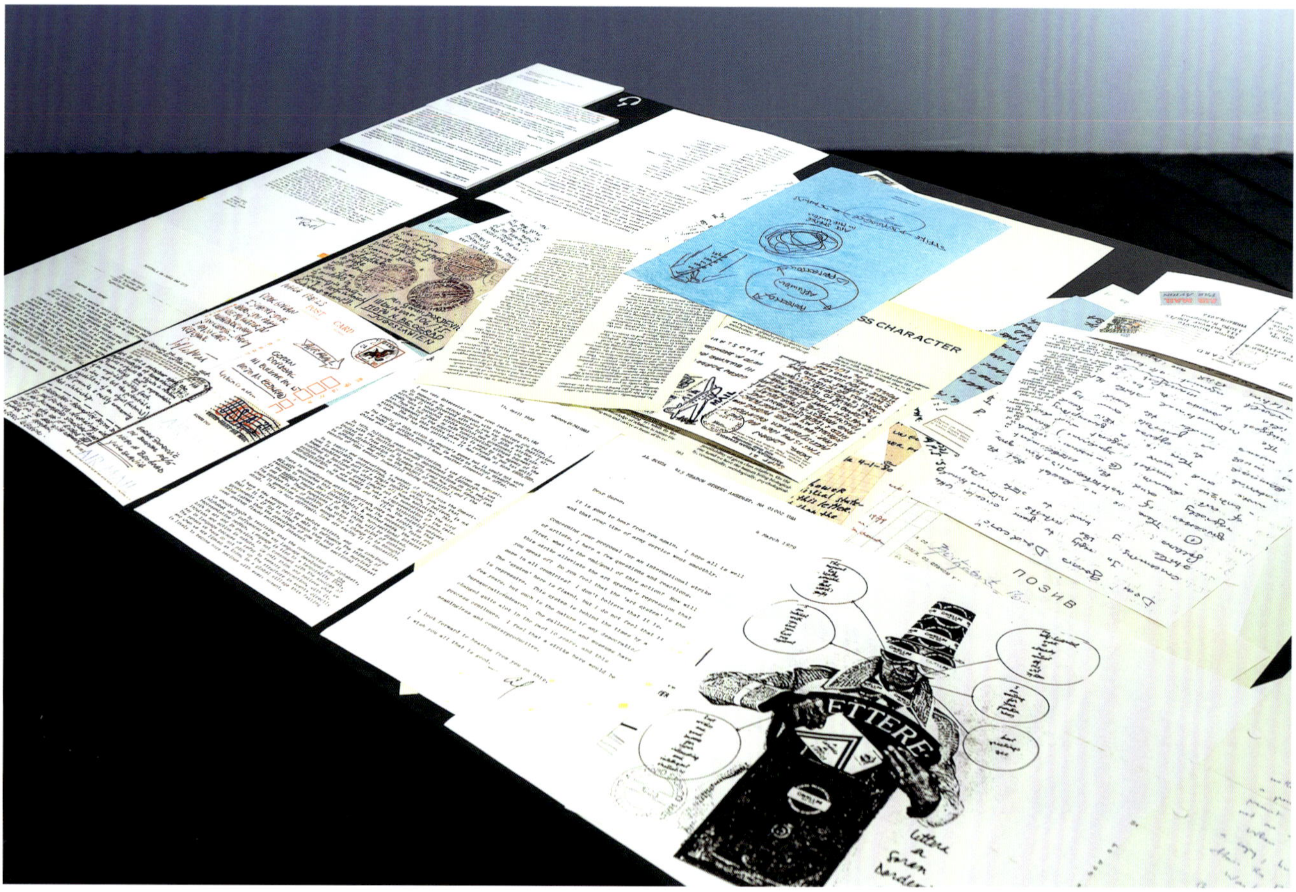
LETTERE

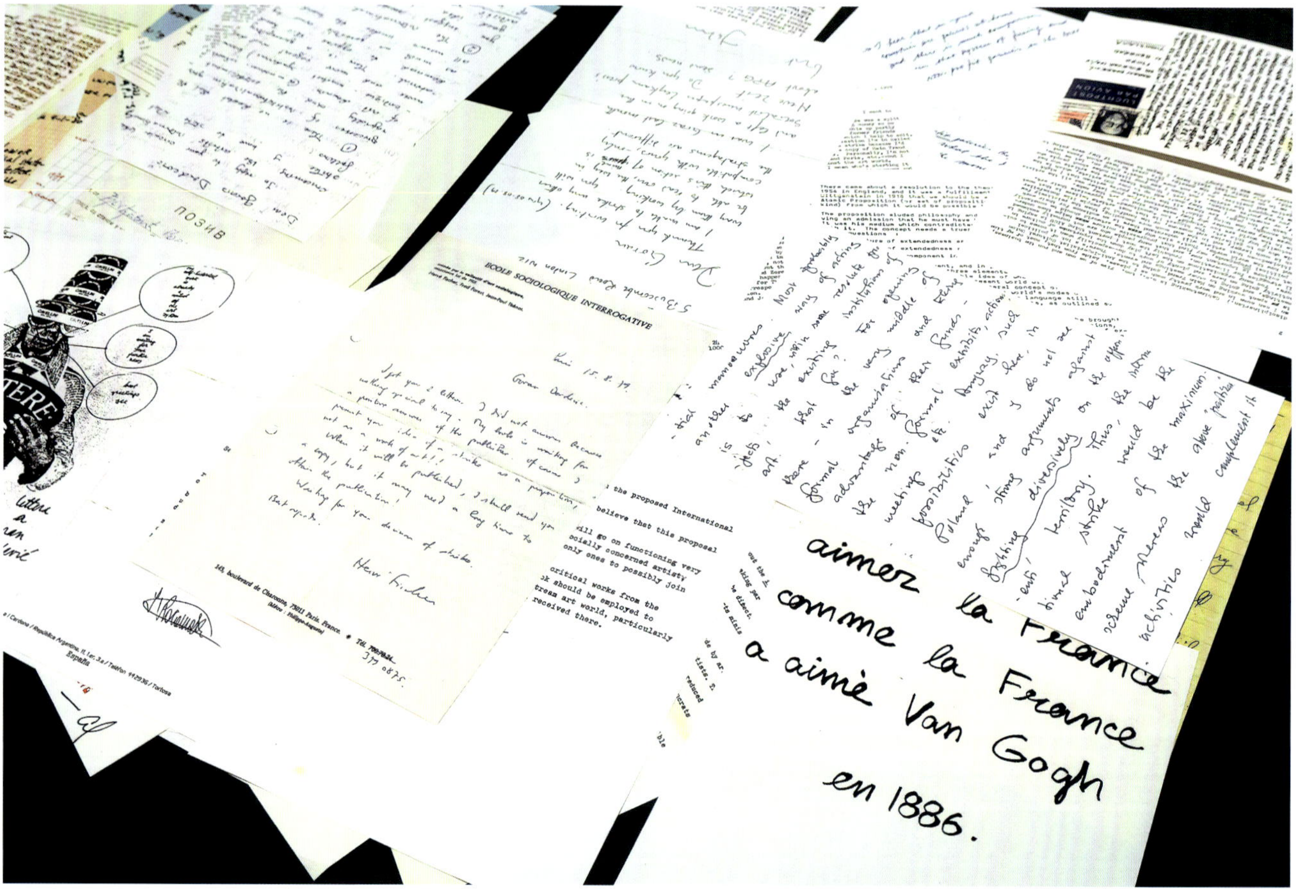
ECOLE SOCIOLOGIQUE INTERROGATIVE
aimez la France
comme la France
a aimé Van Gogh
en 1886.

Goran Đorđević

(b. 1950, Dragaš, Yugoslavia, now Kosovo)

International Strike of Artists

1979

Textual material, prints on paper, 21×29.7 cm

Courtesy Moderna galerija, Ljubljana

Goran Đorđević, one of the protagonists of the so-called "analytic line" of Belgrade conceptualism, started his career in the early 1970s with conceptual works and later, after 1979, focused exclusively on concepts and strategies of copying. In 1979, in protest against, as he wrote himself, "the art system's unbroken repression of the artist and his alienation from the results of his practice," he called upon artists from around the world to go on strike. He received 40 replies to the circular letter in which he proposed stopping the production of art and, by doing so, boycotting the art system. There were some positive replies, but the majority of artists doubted whether such a project could be realized and the proposed strike never took place. Later the artist decided to publish the replies as it occurred to him that, due to the institutionalization of radical artistic practices, there was a possibility that this idea could someday become a real alternative. Although it became evident in 1979 that the idea of an international art strike is utopian, the idea has never been so pertinent as it is today, in the context of a thorough institutionalization of critique, which Đorđević himself cautioned against, and of ever greater exploitation and precarization, the global dimension of which calls for the internationalization of resistance.

2   The transformation of systems

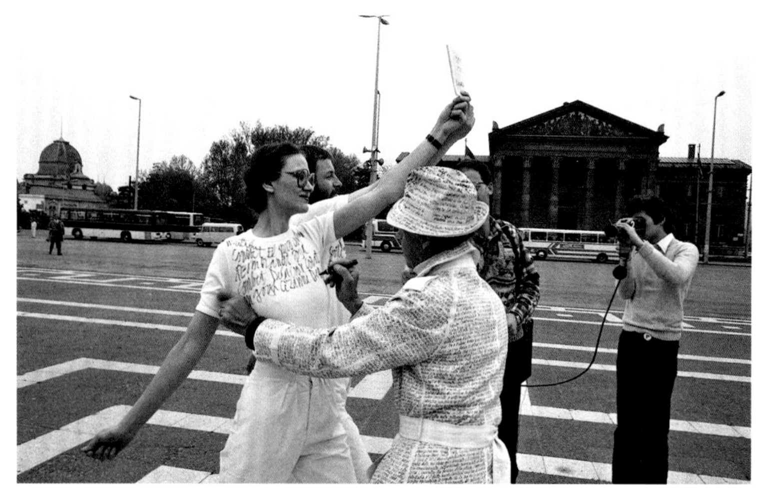
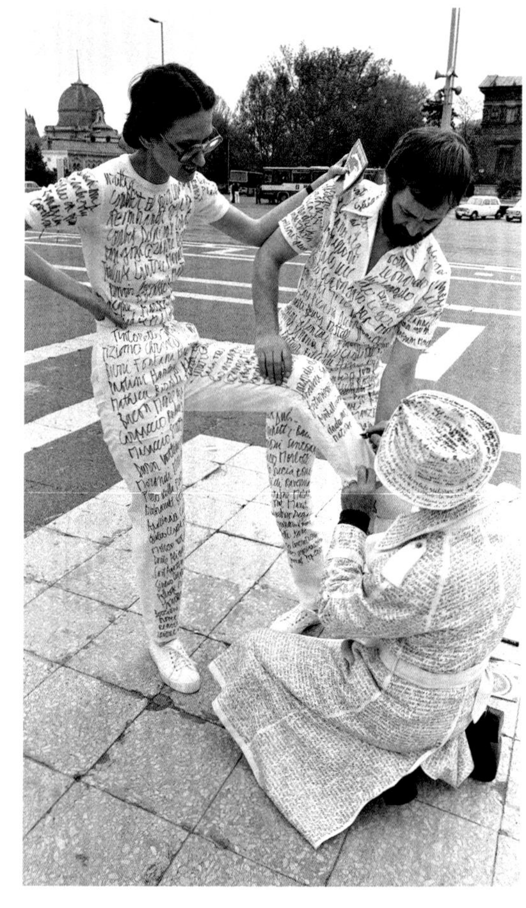

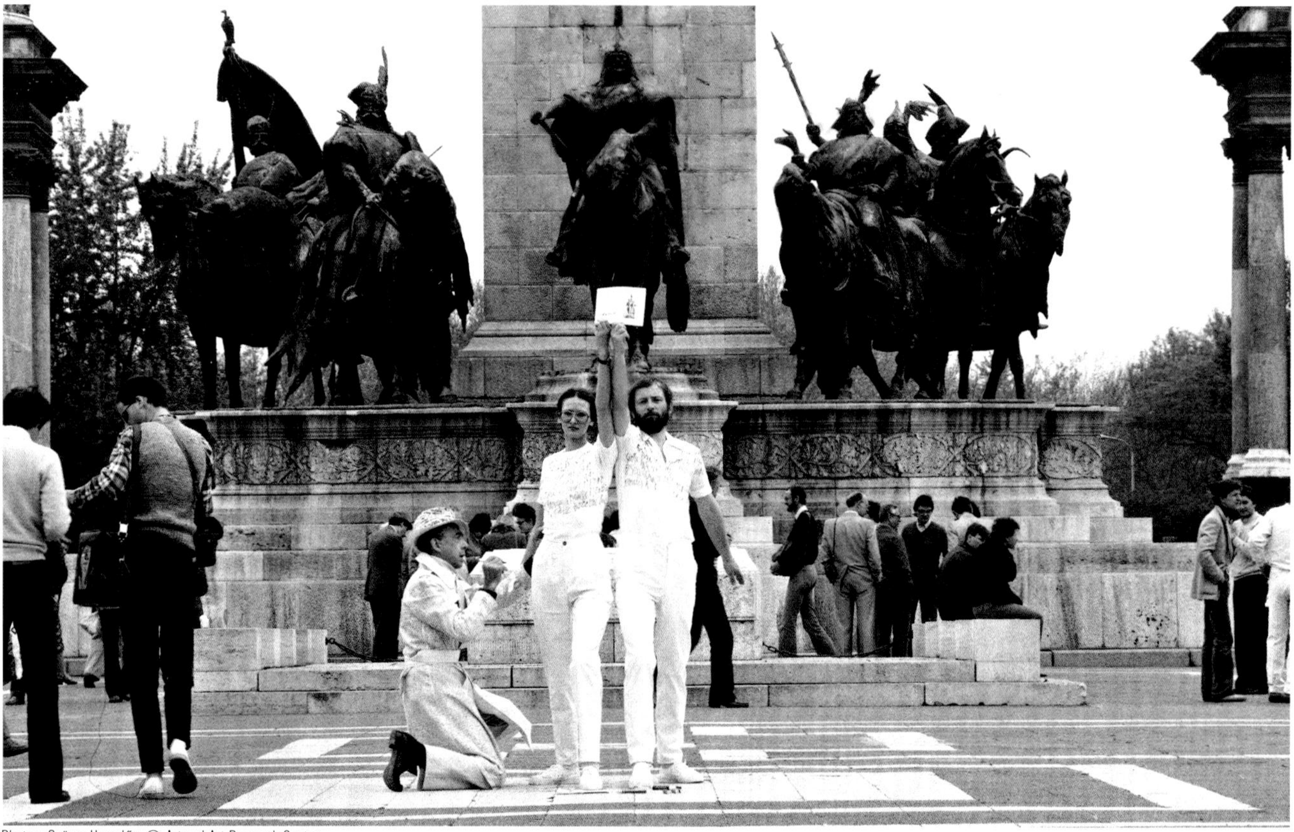

Photos: György Hegedűs. © Artpool Art Research Center

György Galántai

(b. 1941, Bikács, Hungary)

Homage to Vera Mukhina

1980

Performance with the participation of Julia Klaniczay and Guglielmo
Achille Cavellini, Budapest

Performance photographs

Video, 3'20"

Courtesy Artpool Art Research Center, Budapest

György Galántai is a renowned Hungarian artist and member of the Fluxus movement, who spearheaded the launch of several art institutions. At the time of the socialist regime in Hungary, when censorship was strong, Galántai organized a famous series of shows, entitled the *Chapel Exhibitions*. Today we would describe this as a four-year (1970–1973) multimedia marathon of contemporary culture— it included 35 exhibitions, concerts, poetry readings, theater performances, and movie showings, among other events. This flurry of activity drew the attention of the secret police, however, after which Chapel Studio, where the events were held, was closed. The complex situation in Hungarian politics prompted Galántai to turn to mail art in the late 1970s. Correspondence as an artistic practice was one of the few ways to be part of the international context. An archive of this correspondence formed the basis of the Artpool Archive, a Budapest institute engaged in preservation and holding exhibitions which preserved a mass of information about Hungarian artistic life in the form of plans, notes, books, photographs, catalogs, invitations, diagrams, films, and other media. From 1983 to 1985, the institution published 11 issues of a samizdat magazine, *Artpool Letter*, which was essentially the only source of information about contemporary art in Hungary during this difficult period for culture.

In the performance *Homage to Vera Mukhina*, the artist, together with Julia Klaniczay and Guglielmo Achille Cavellini, recreated the composition of Mukhina's sculpture *Worker and Collective-Farm Woman* (1937). Dressed in clothes bearing the names of important figures in world art, the artists stood immobile for three hours in the police-patrolled Heroes' Square in Budapest. This deconstruction of communist symbols, together with the challenge to the city's repressive machine, transformed the status of the artists' bodies, which became living sculptures. In this way the performance proclaimed a set of meanings with a social, political, and artistic genealogy.

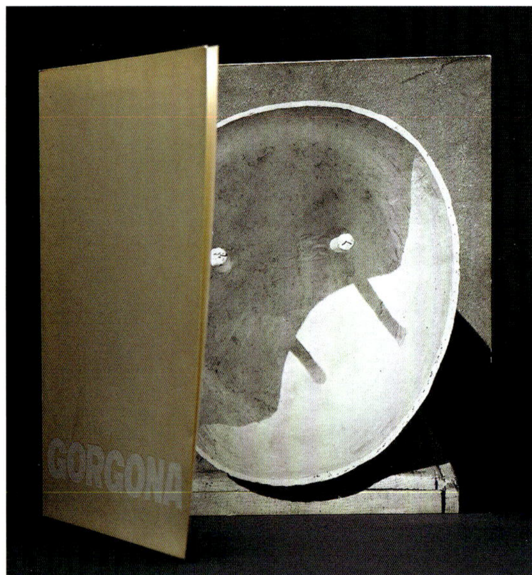

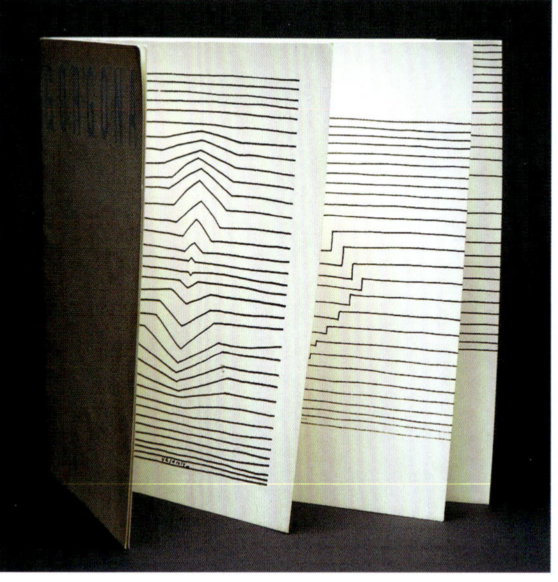

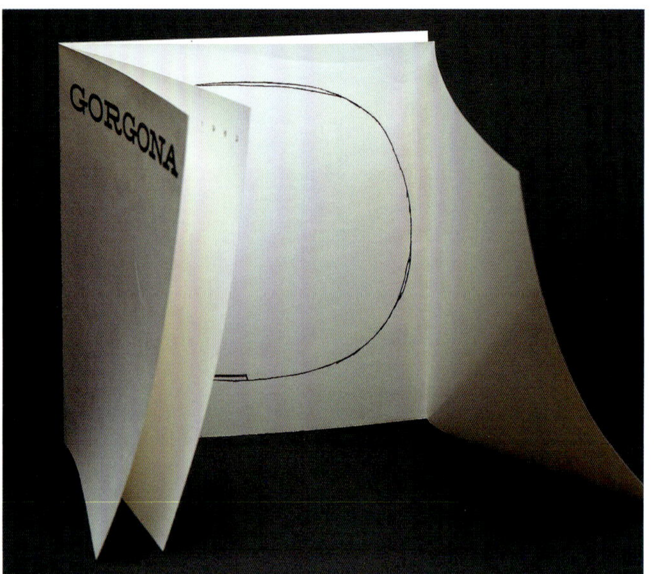

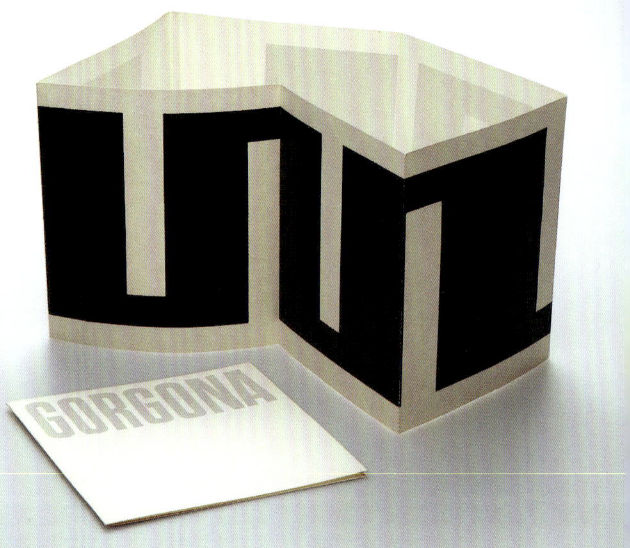

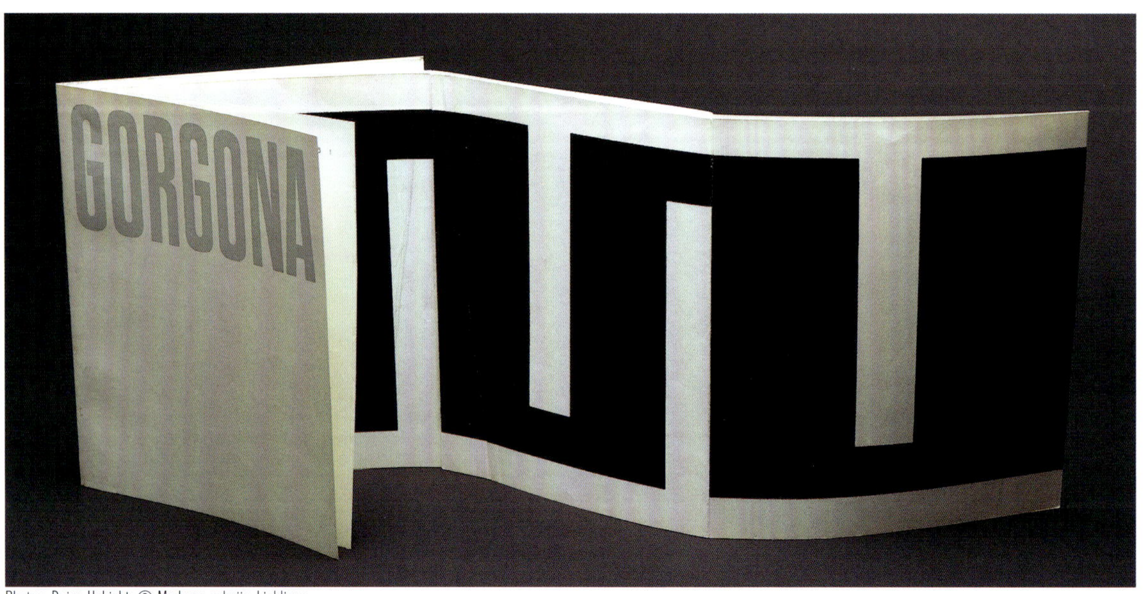

Photos: Dejan Habicht. © Moderna galerija, Ljubljana

Gorgona

(1959–1966, Zagreb, Yugoslavia, now Croatia)

Anti-magazine Gorgona

1961–1966

Silkscreen, offset, photographs/paper, 21×30 cm

Issue (Year) Author

1 (1961) Josip Vaništa

2 (1961) Julije Knifer

3 (1962) Marijan Jevšovar

4 (1961) Victor Vasarely

5 (1961) Ivan Kožarić

6 (1961) Josip Vaništa

7 (1965) Miljenko Horvat

8 (1965) Text by Harold Pinter

9 (1965) Dieter Roth

10 (1966) Josip Vaništa

11 (1966) Josip Vaništa

Courtesy Moderna galerija, Ljubljana

Gorgona was a Zagreb-based group of artists, architects, critics, and art historians. It existed from 1959 to 1966, and its driving force was the painter Josip Vaništa. It was not a tightly-bound group with a defined program and goals, but more an association of creative individuals who were, and still are, highly original and unconventional in their work. Basing their work in absurdity, anti-aestheticism, and confrontation with official and established art forms, Gorgona members' activities included exhibitions, meetings, group walks, and other events. An essential part of their activity was the "antimagazine" *Gorgona*, which was not a proper magazine but rather a series of artists' contributions. A strong tendency in the group was replacing visual and material art objects with proposals, descriptions, and concepts, several of which, from today's perspective, seem quite visionary. In 1964, for example, Vaništa created a painting which existed only in its verbal description. Also deserving of mention are Ivan Kožarić's proposals (for example to cast in plaster the interior spaces of buildings, cars, public spaces, or even the heads of all the group members) and the contributions of Dimitrije Mangelos and Julije Knifer.

2   The transformation of systems

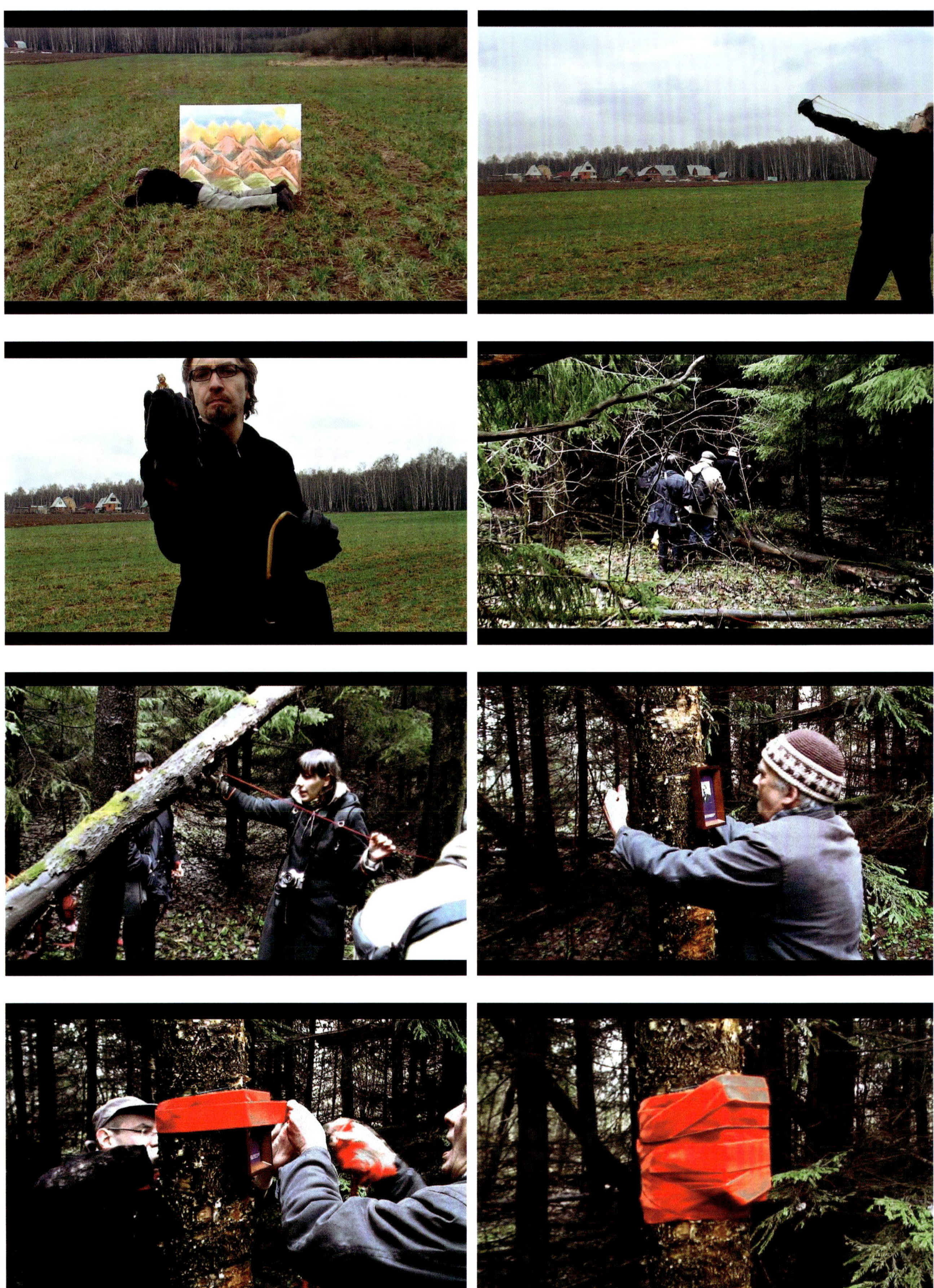

Kapiton

(2008–2009, Russia)

Fourth Meeting. 16 April 2008
2008
Film (DVD), 18'55"
Documentation by Vadim Zakharov
Courtesy of the artists

Kapiton was formed in early 2008 by Yuri Leiderman, Andrei Monastyrsky, and Vadim Zakharov. Over the period of a year the group met ten times. For each meeting, each of the three artists created a work which they then discussed as a group, the meetings being carefully documented. Kapiton's approach mirrors that of Collective Actions, in that the group's work is produced for the participants themselves and without the presence of an audience.

Fourth Meeting. 16 April 2008 documents an action which took place at Kievogorskoe Field, the site of a number of famous group performances by Collective Actions (founded by Monastyrsky in 1976) under the common title *Journeys to the Countryside*. Collective Actions considered Kievogorskoe Field a pure space, free from ideology. Today it has been encroached by country homes for the new elite. Leiderman's action, *Dima Blain's Fifteenth Performance,* imagines an alternative, pure space of hills and volcanoes using a canvas which he places in the field, but the artist subverts this purity by lying down in front of the painting and producing volcano "smoke" from his behind. Zakharov's action, *Uzbeks Will Return To Us What is Rightfully Ours—Kievogorskoe Field* involves firing Uzbek figures, similar in appearance to Japanese netsuke, at the new houses using a catapult, like Jason sowing dragon's teeth. The artist considers the field to be lost to the new inhabitants and, with this action, is demanding its return through the medium of central Asian figures, reflecting the ethnic makeup of the workforce which builds such new houses. Monastyrsky's action, *Journey to the West*, involves fixing to a tree a portrait of little-known Hungarian composer Egon Wellesz, alongside a quote from a little-known novel by Russian writer Yuri Ivanov-Milyukhin and wrapping it in red velvet ribbon. The portrait is then "attached" to the Kievogorskoe Field using a red thread leading to the location of the Collective Actions Library, which is buried there, thus reclaiming the field as a place of artistic reflection.

2   The transformation of systems

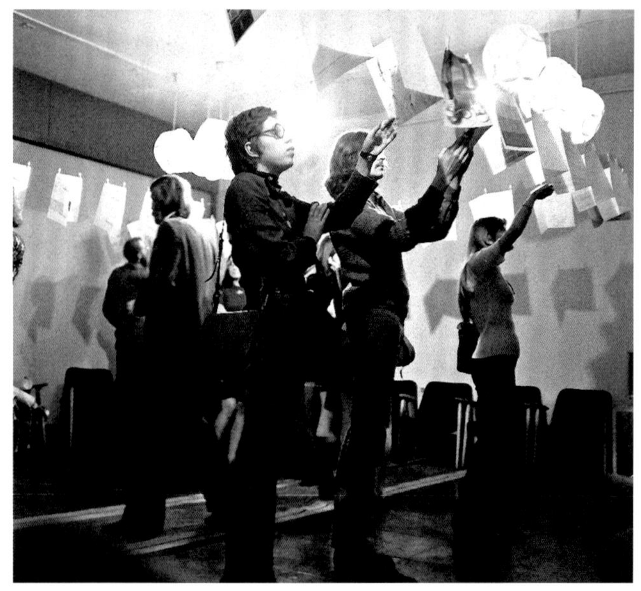
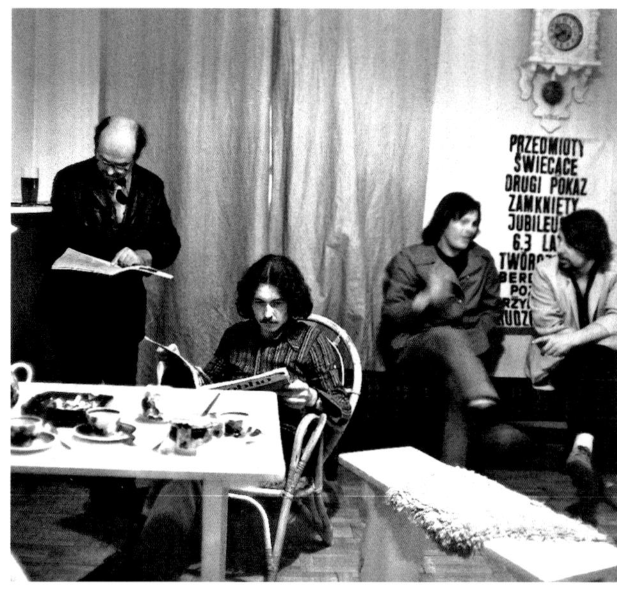

PRZEDMIOTY
ŚWIECĄCE
DRUGI POKAZ
ZAMKNIĘTY
JUBILEU
6.3 LA
TWÓRCZ

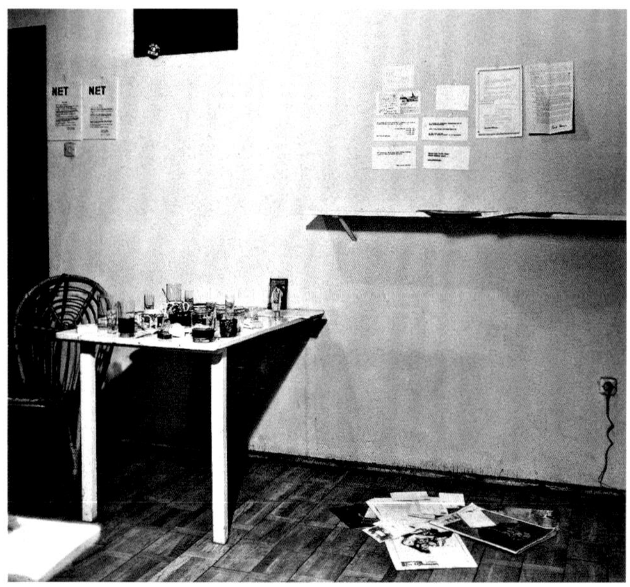

NET   NET

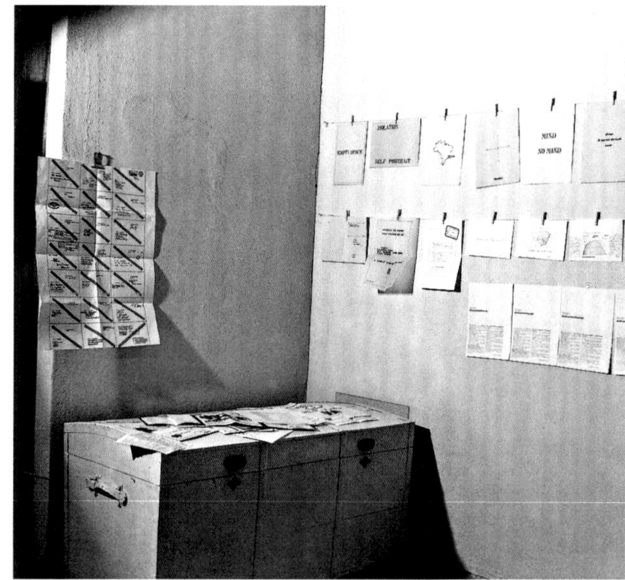

ISOLATION
SELF PORTRAIT
MIND
NO MIND

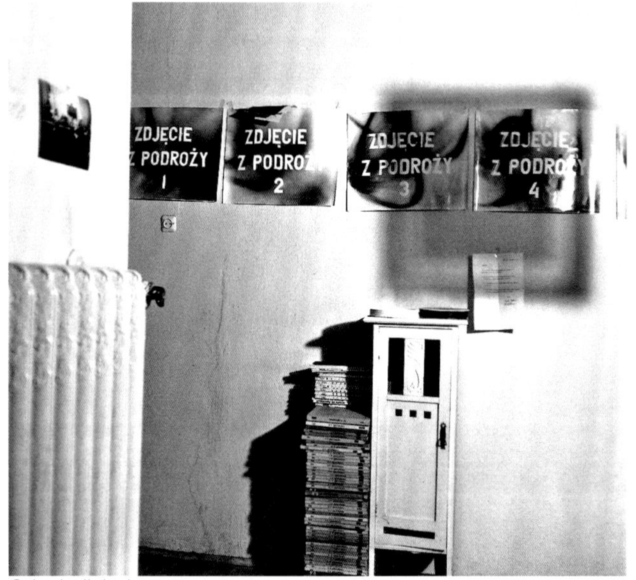

ZDJĘCIE
Z PODRÓŻY
1
ZDJĘCIE
Z PODRÓŻ
2
ZDJĘCIE
Z PODRÓŻY
3
ZDJĘCIE
Z PODRÓŻY
4

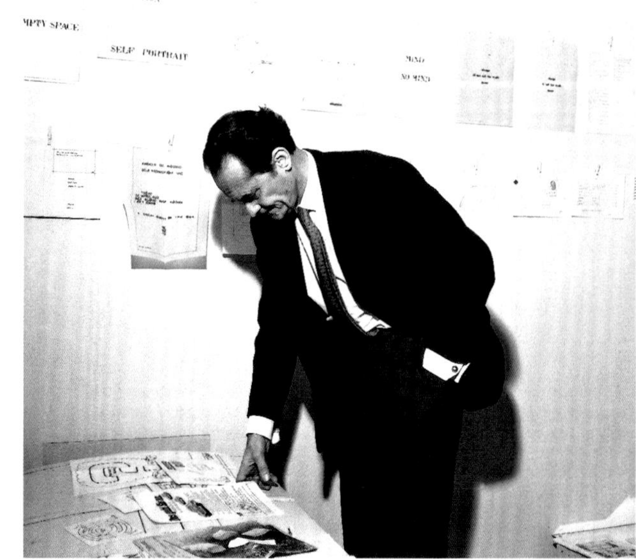

ISOLATION
EMPTY SPACE
SELF PORTRAIT
MIND
NO MIND

Jarosław Kozłowski

(b. 1954, Śrem, Poland)

NET

- a NET is open and uncommercial

- points of the NET are: private homes, studios and any other places, where art propositions are articulated

- these propositions are presented to persons interested in them

- propositions may be accompanied by editions in form of prints, tapes, slides, photographs, books, films, handbills, letters, manuscripts etc.

- NET has no cenntral point and any coordination

- points of the NET can be anywhere

- all points of the NET are in contact among themselves and exchange concepts, propositions, projects and other forms of articulation

- the idea of NET is not new and in this moment it stops to be an authorized idea

- NET can be arbitrarily developed and copied

Jarosław Kozłowski
Andrzej Kostołowski

Persons invited to be co-creators of NET — APPENDIX 1

VITO ACCONCI — 1o2 Christopher St., New York 1oo14, USA
DITRICH ALBRECH — 7 Stuttgart 61, Reichbergstr. 7, W. Germany
ERIC ANDERSEN — Willemoesgade 67/1, Coprnhagen OE, Danmark
KEITH ARMSTRONG — 16 Devenant Road, Oxford, G. Britain
TERRY ATKINSON — 26 West End, Chipping Norton, Oxon, G. Britain
WALTER AUE — 1 Berlin 12, Carmerstr. 2, W. Berlin
DAVID BAINBRIDGE — 26 West End, Chipping Norton, Oxon, G. Briatin
MICHAEL BALDWIN — 26 West End, Chipping Norton, Oxon, G. Brixtain
FREDERIC BARTHELME — 26 West End, chipping Norton, Oxon, G. Britain
MEL BOCHNER — 126 Chamers St., New York, USA
JOSEPH BEUYS — 4 Dusseldorf, Drakeplatz 4, W. Germany
CLAUS BOHMLER — 415 Urdingen, Bahnhofsplatz 3, W. Germany
SLATI BOYADGIEV — 6 September 1, Ploudiv, Bulgaria
JAN BREAKWELL — Top Flat 26 St. John Street, London EC 1, G. Britain
KEITH BROCKLEHURST — 79 Huron Road, Tooting, London SW 1, G. Britain
IAN BURN — 26 West End, Chipping Norton, Oxon, G. Britain
DALIBAR CHATRNY — Brno, Botanicka 8, Chechoslovakia
WALTER DE MARIA — 27 Howard St., P.O. Box 258, New York, USA
G. DENARO — Via Maqueda 165-177, Palermo, Italy
H.J. DITRICH — 4 Dusseldorf, Holbeinstr. 24, W. Germany
WOLFGANG ERNST — Wien 118o, Gersthofer Str. 118-2o, Austria
WOLFGANG FEELISCH — 563 Remscheid 1, Postfach 1oo343, W. Germany
ROBERT FILLIOU — 56, Rue des Rosiers, Paris 4, France
KEN FRIEDMAN — 6361 Elmhurst Drive, San Diego, Calif. 9212o, USA
JOCHEN GERZ — 41 Rue Buffon, Paris 5, France
JORGE GLUSBERG — Cayo, Elpidio Gonzales 4o7o, B. Aires, Argentina
JOHN GOODYEAR — Duglas College, Rutgers Univ. New Brunswick, N.Y. o89B, USA
DAN GRAHAM — 5o1 Lexington Av., New York, 1oo17, USA
AL HANSEN — 22o East 2nd, St., New York, USA

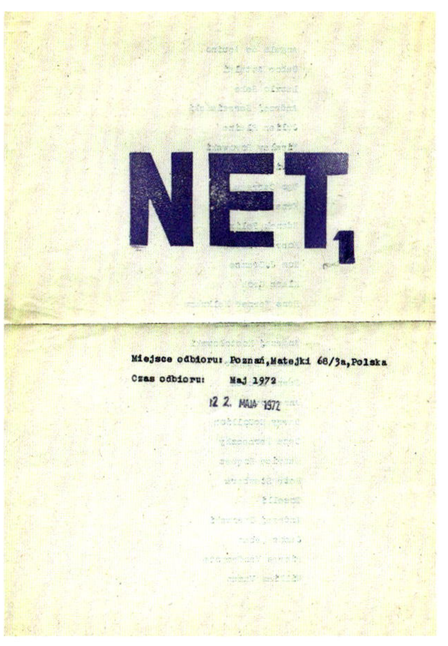

Miejsce odbioru: Poznań, Matejki 66/3a, Polska
Czas odbioru: Maj 1972
12 2. MAJ 1972

Network
1972
Action, Poznań
Paper, printed materials, 14 b/w photographs, each 18×18 cm
Courtesy of the artist

Jarosław Kozłowski is one of the best-known representatives of the Polish conceptual art scene. From 1972 to 1990 he was also the director of the Akumulatory 2 gallery in Poznań. This institution was a platform for the development of contemporary Polish art and for cultural exchange with other countries. In his work, Kozłowski engages the conceptual tradition, creating mostly installations that include drawings, found objects, light, sound, and photography. In 2010, he took part in the exhibition *The New Décor* at Garage, for which he created a new work in his usual style. Over the course of a long period (about three months) Kozłowski, with help from museum staff, gathered old furniture from Moscow apartments. In the exhibition space he erected a construction made of sewn-up parts of the found furniture, with paper from various news publications inserted into the joints between them. In this way he revealed the conflict between two realities—domestic furniture as a symbol of the private dimension, and newspaper clippings as an artefact of the external world or, in other words, the political dimension.

The *Network* project was one of the most important art initiatives in Eastern Europe in the 1970s. The project was formulated by Kozłowski and historian Andrzej Kostołowski. Its goal was to use correspondence as a means to forge international connections between 350 artists and critics in Poland and internationally. Such a large-scale undertaking, which was part of the mail art movement, was based on the principle of the free circulation of information and aimed at overcoming ideological isolation. In 1972, the secret police paid a visit to the first presentation of the project at Kozłowski's apartment.

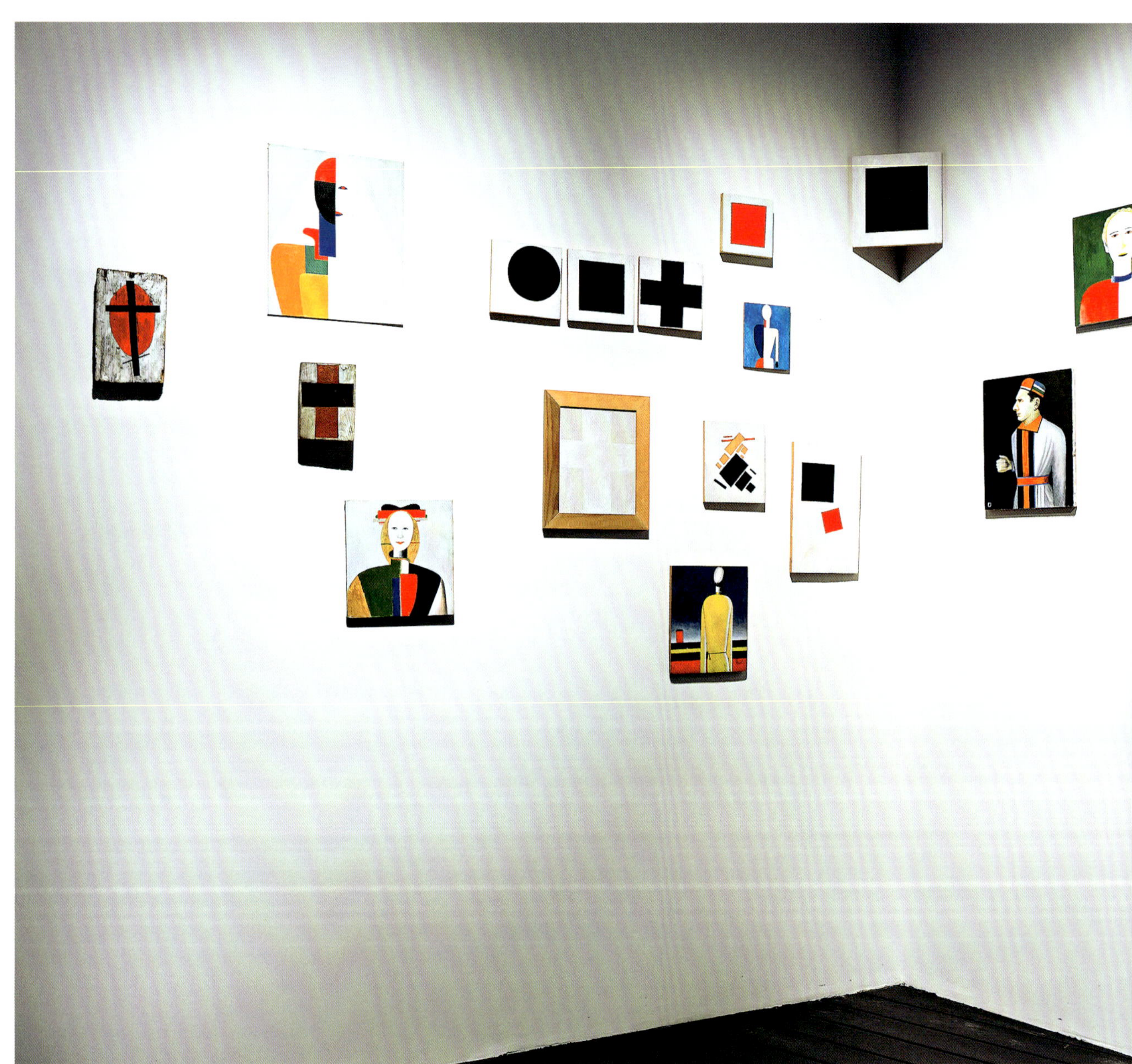

Kazimir Malevich

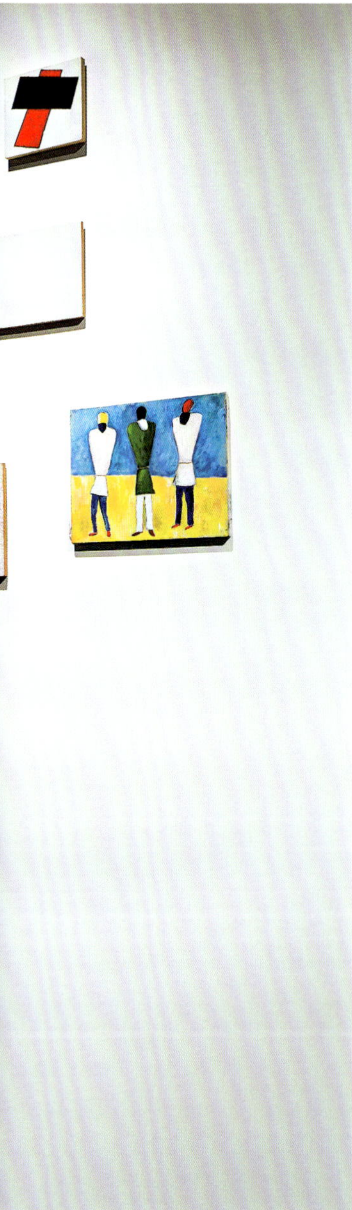

The Last Futurist Exhibition
1985–1986
Installation. 20 paintings, dimensions variable
Courtesy Moderna galerija, Ljubljana

Seventy years after the *Last Futurist Exhibition* (1915), Kazimir Malevich staged a reconstruction of the famous St. Petersburg exhibition in an apartment in Belgrade. The reconstruction was made on the basis of the only existing document, the iconic black–and–white photograph that has been reprinted many times in numerous art history books. In a letter signed "Kazimir Malevich (Belgrade, Yugoslavia)" which was published in *Art in America* magazine in 1986, the artist wrote, "I have an impression that this photo is becoming even more important than my supremacist paintings! This was the major reason I kept on thinking for years to do the same exhibition again. Since, for obvious reasons, it was not possible to do it in Petrograd, I decided to make *The Last Futurist Exhibition* again exactly 70 years later […] in a small apartment in the beautiful town of Belgrade."

The Last Futurist Exhibition focuses on the dialectic between the copy and the original, and highlights the copy as something that, besides the parameters of the original work, also contains the idea and act of copying and, as such, may be far more complex. The copy turns the known (the original) into the unknown, showing ambivalence where there seemed to be clarity, and debunks the originality of the original.

By declaring copying as an attitude to art, the artist subverted the foundations of modern art by renouncing the concepts of authenticity and authorship. His reconstructions do not try to falsify and reaffirm the original. They question its identity and examine the conceptual processes that secured its status in the history of art, deconstructing the established art historical narratives along the way. As Marina Gržinić pointed out, these works "explicate the fact that the original itself is nothing more than a universalized copy."

2   The transformation of systems

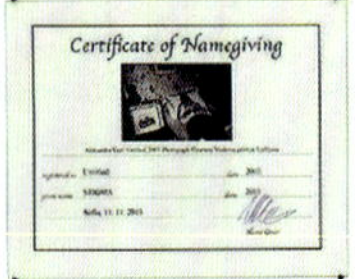

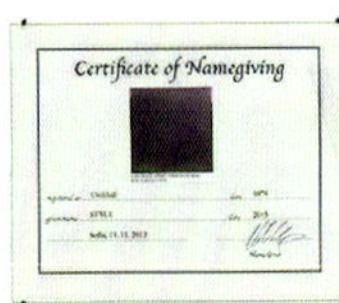

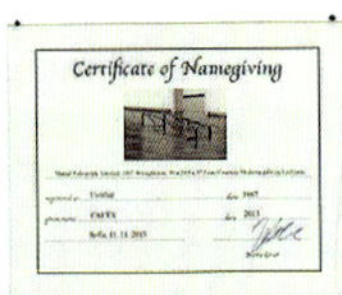

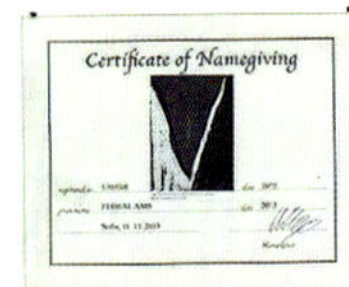

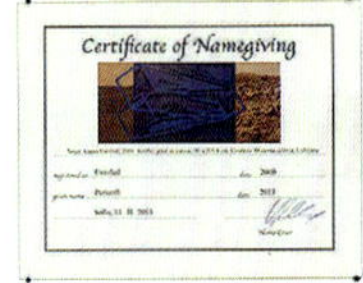

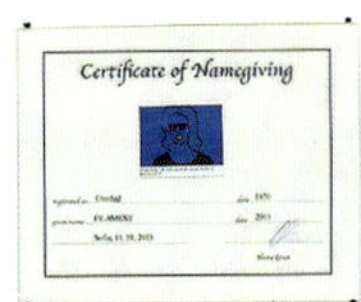

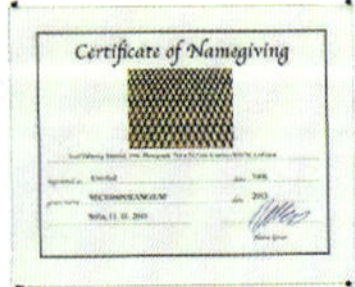

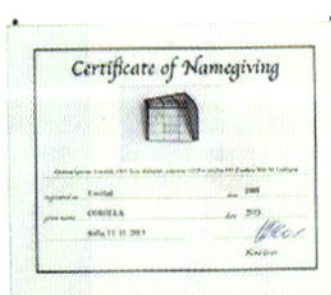

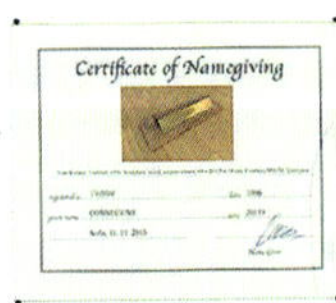

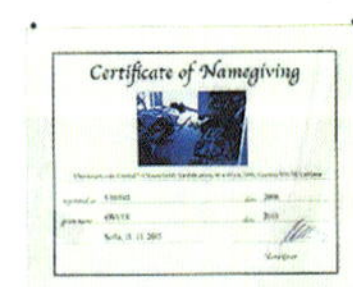

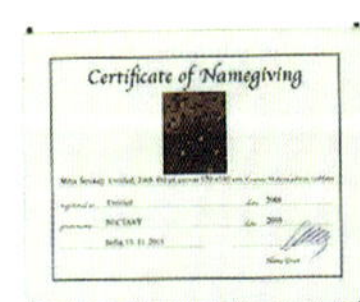

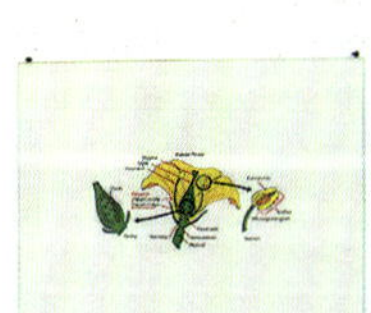

Ivan Moudov

(b. 1975, Sofia, Bulgaria)

Certificate of Namegiving

2013

Series of prints and collages, each 24.7 × 19.7 cm

Courtesy Moderna galerija, Ljubljana

Ivan Moudov is one of the most intriguing Bulgarian artists of his generation and is internationally renowned. He uses post-conceptual tools to analyze the world and the art system. His performance *Traffic Control* (2001/2003) is particularly well-known. Dressed as a traffic policeman, Moudov directed the flow of cars in various European cities. Behind this seemingly mischievous act was a complex game with social and political subtexts. As Moudov himself noted, in his native Bulgaria the police symbolize the unchecked power of the regime, such that when one encounters them it is unclear whose rights they are protecting. Moudov is interested in what it means to be "on their side" but at the same time to remain beyond the law, as his actions were not actually sanctioned by any regulatory authority. His appearance in a Bulgarian police uniform on the streets of other countries gives rise to a whole array of meanings because such symbols of power are not even recognized there.

In the work *Certificate of Namegiving*, Moudov manipulates the art scene rather than society. The series of certificates was created for the artist's exhibition at Berlin's Gregor Podnar gallery, the theme of which was appropriation. When Moudov was a student, the collection at Moderna galerija in Ljubljana made a great impression on him, and he noticed that some of the works did not have a name or, more precisely, were described as "Untitled." He was inspired to give the works names and to unite them conceptually by writing titles appropriated from an illustration reminiscent of an extract from a botany textbook, where the structures of flowers are described in detail. On the one hand this ironically plays up the conceptual abstraction created by a name like *Untitled*, and on the other it raises for discussion the hermetically sealed quality of the contemporary art system as a whole.

Certificate of Namegiving

Miha Štrukelj. Untitled, 2005. Oil on canvas 170 x140 cm. Courtesy Moderna galerija, Ljubljana

registered as	Untitled	*date*	2005
given name	NECTARY	*date*	2013

Sofia, 11. 11. 2013

Name Giver

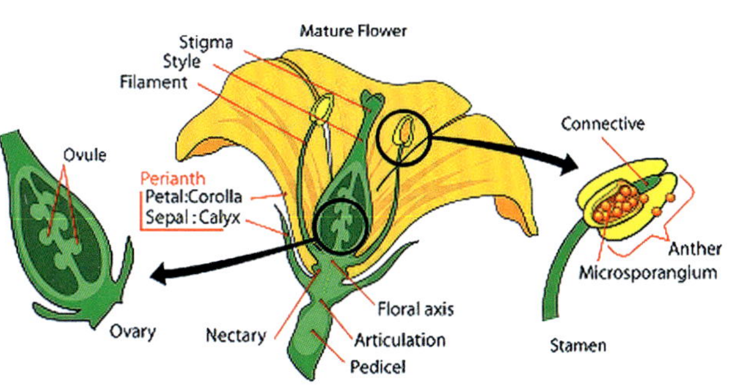

© Moderna galerija, Ljubljana

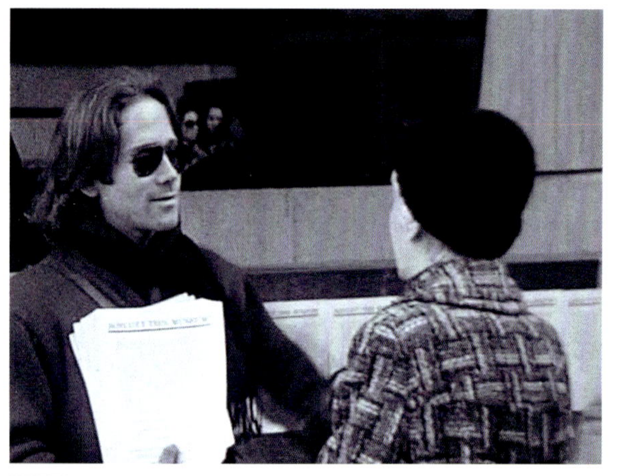

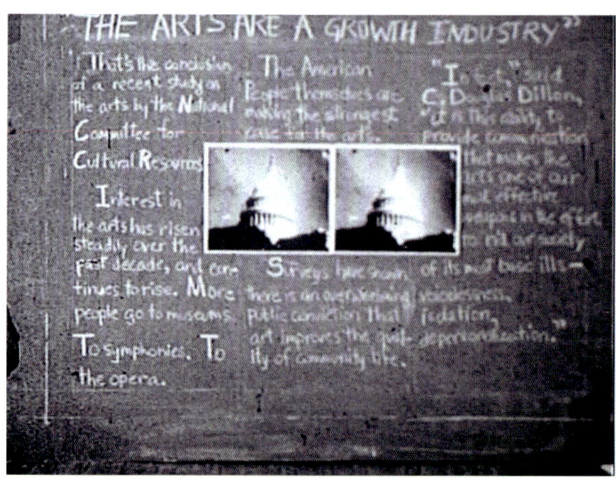
"THE ARTS ARE A GROWTH INDUSTRY"

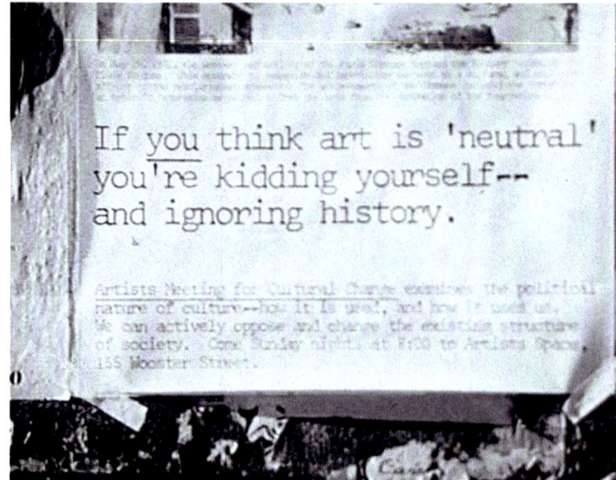
If you think art is 'neutral'
you're kidding yourself--
and ignoring history.

Artists Meeting for Cultural Change examines the political
nature of culture--how it is used, and how it used us.
We can actively oppose and change the existing structure
of society. Come Sunday night at 8:00 to Artists Space,
155 Wooster Street.

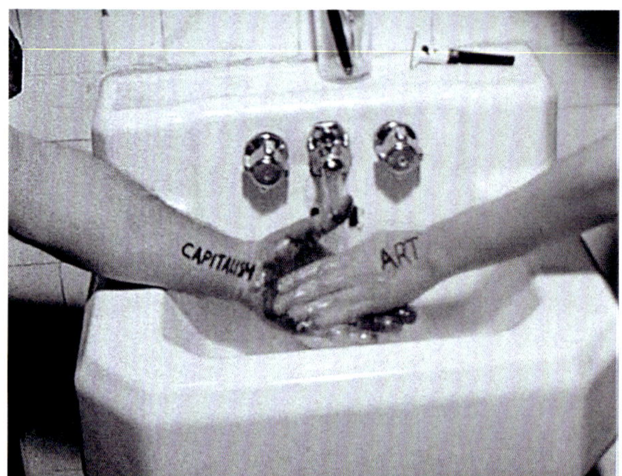
CAPITALISM
ART

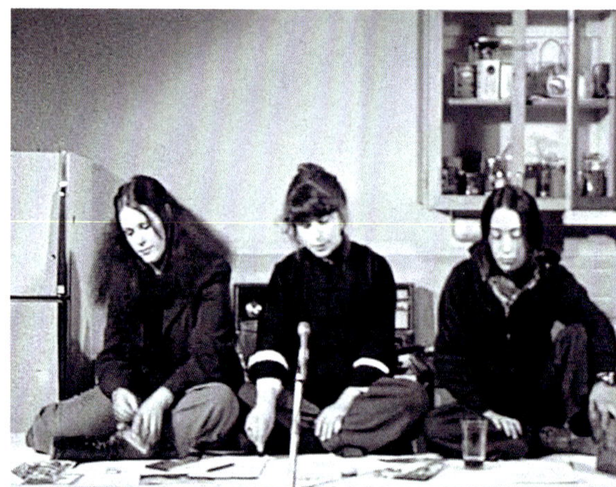

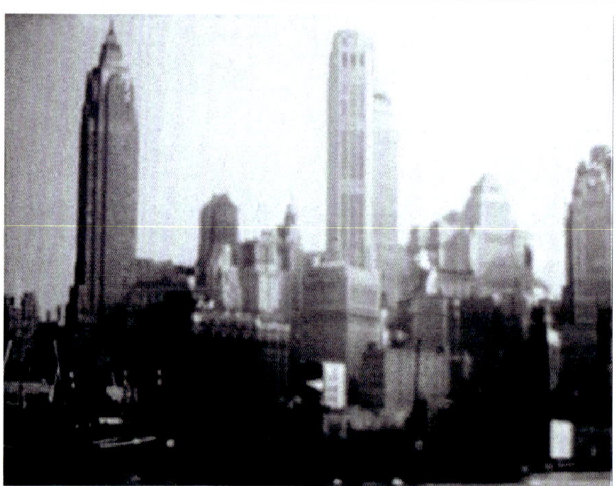

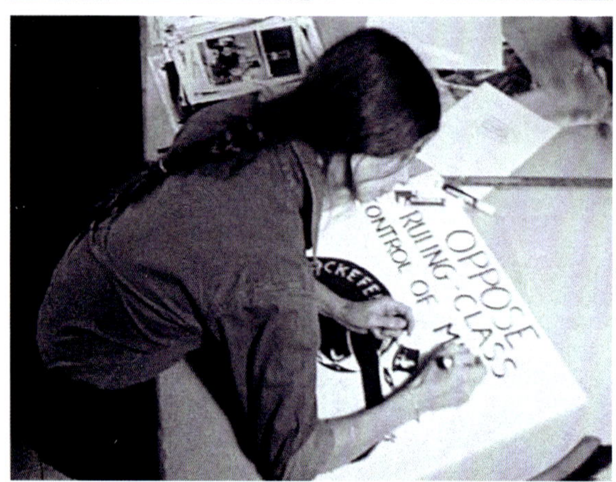
OPPOSE
RULING-CLASS
CONTROL OF

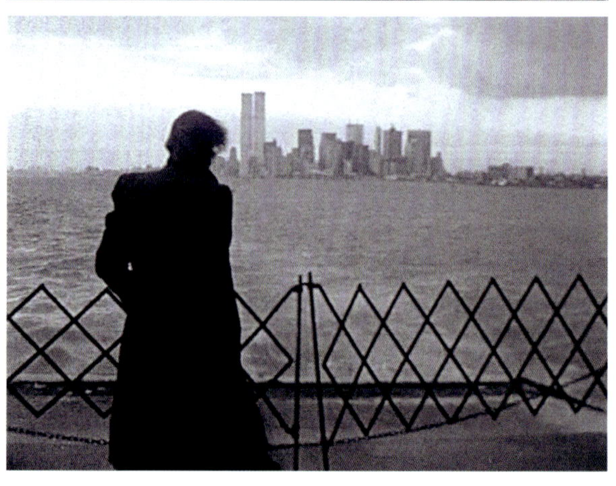

Zoran Popović

(b. 1944, Belgrade, Yugoslavia, now Serbia)

Struggle in New York
1976
16 mm film, b/w, sound, 56'30"
Courtesy Moderna galerija, Ljubljana

Zoran Popović is one of the most typical representatives of Yugoslav independent film and a member of the New Artistic Practice. His films, marked by a high level of conceptualization, represented a deviation from the standardized film production of the 1960s and 1970s.

The film *Struggle in New York* questions its own role (and more broadly the role of art and culture) in the production of social relations. Filmed by Popović in 1976, the film is a collective work of several artists and activists and is composed of ten parts that were designed by participants. In the first part, Sarah Charlesworth, Joseph Kosuth, and Anthony McCall highlight the conditions of production, distribution, and consumption of the film. These define reciprocal relations between participants, the director, and the public. The three authors classify the film as a "social product"—a product of social relations, collaborative and non-collaborative, paid and unpaid work—the production of which is marked not only by division of labor, but also by division of film and distribution rights: by allocation of power. The contribution of the group of activists Artists Meeting for Cultural Change (AMCC), active in New York in the mid-1970s, focuses on the political nature of culture—"how it is used, and how it uses us." In the action *Boycott This Museum*, targeted at racist and sexist policies of the Whitney Museum of American Art, the AMCC took a critical stand against museums as institutions that serve the private interests and values of the ruling class. They rejected the seemingly political neutrality of art, the way institutions deny the social context of art and thus enable its commodification, and called for democratization of museums. Other contributions critically address the aestheticization of social revolution, the role of culture in class displacement and gentrification, and the unequal position of women in art society; oppose the naturalization of gender roles and clichés regarding institutional ways of living and producing; and call for a break with the traditions of the bourgeois world.

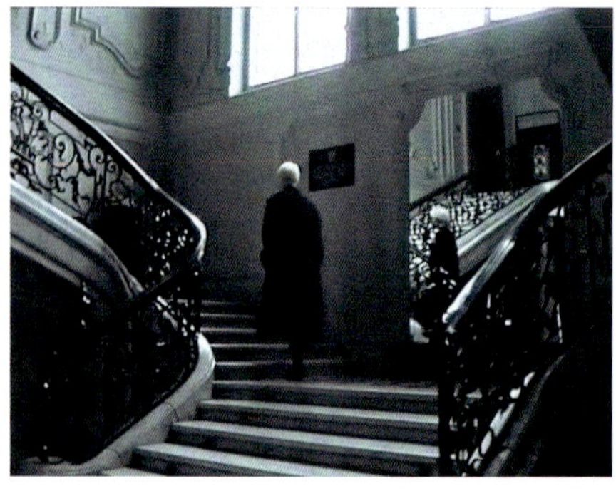
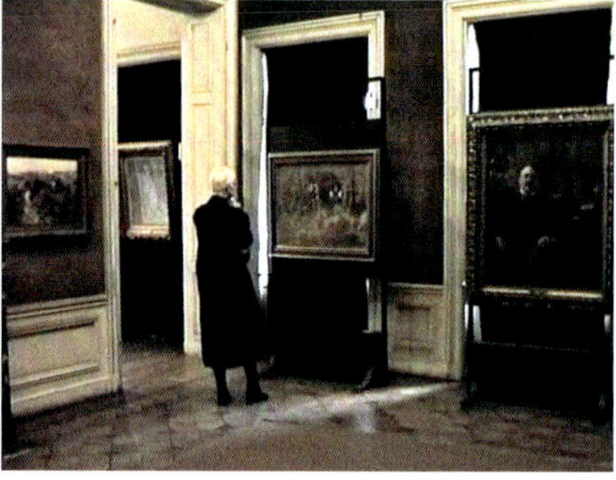
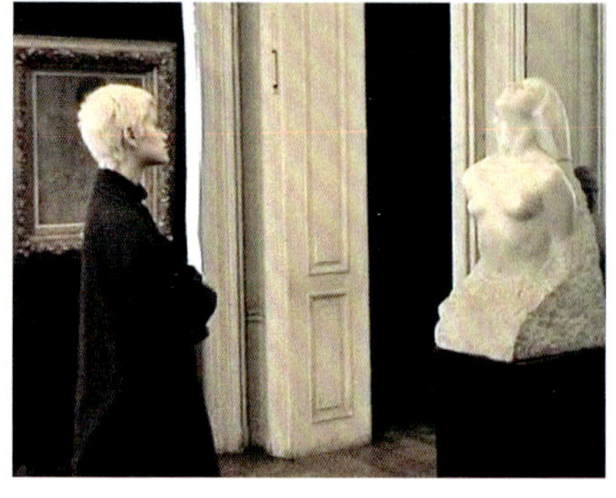

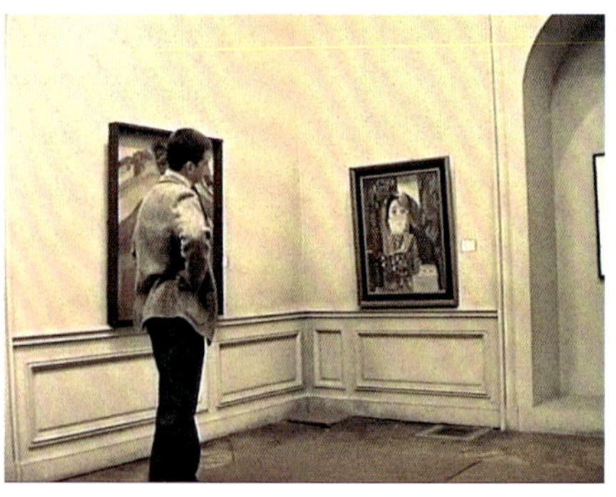
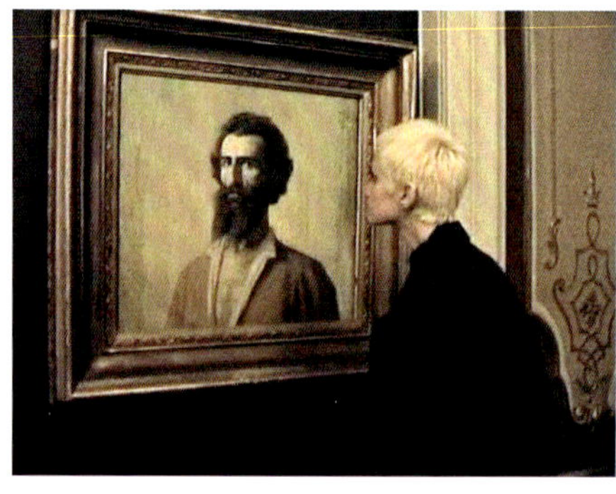
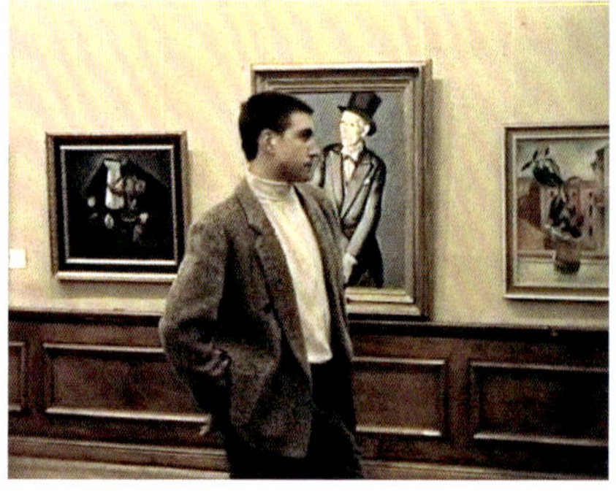

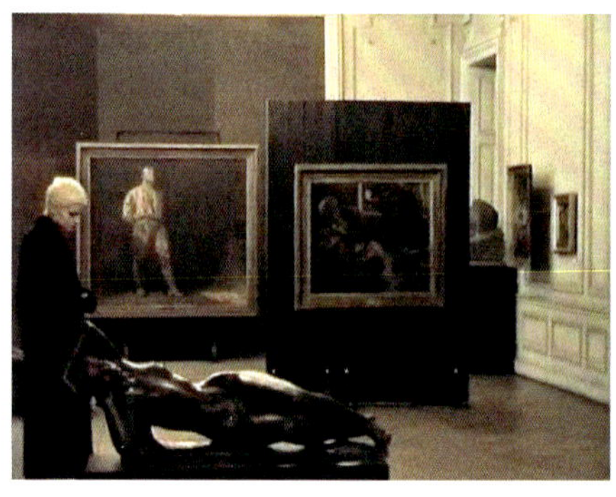
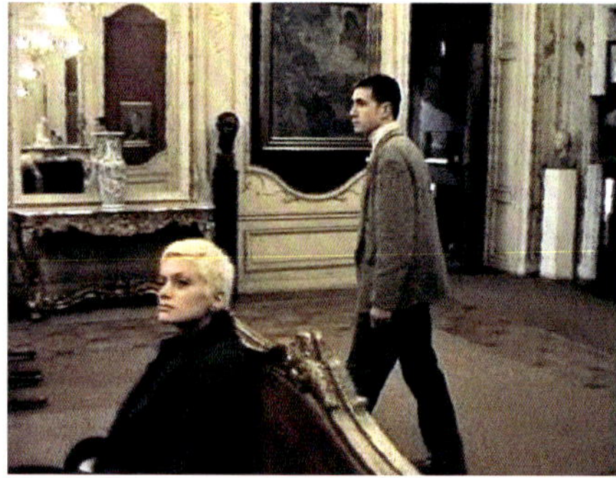
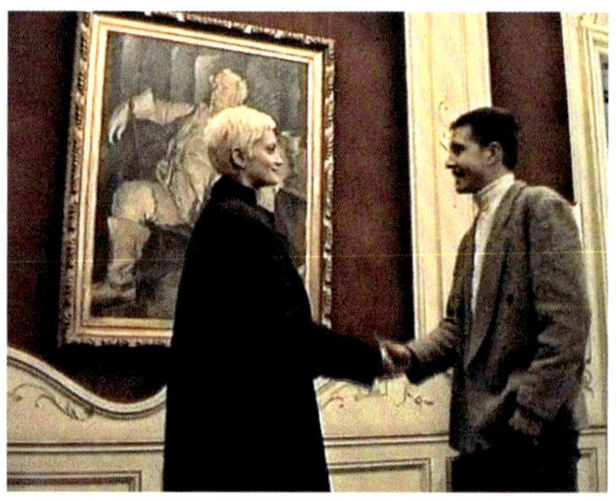

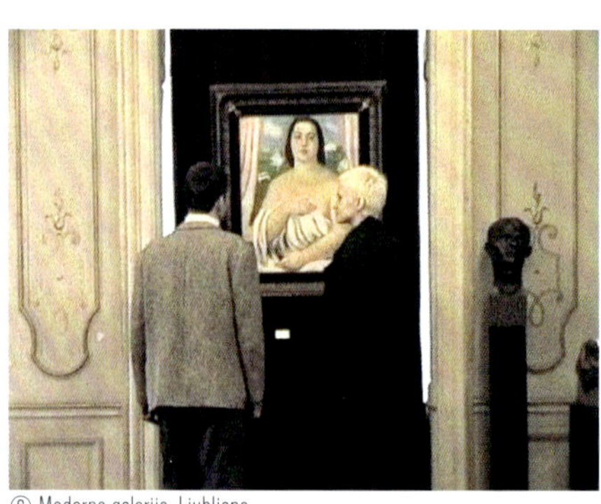
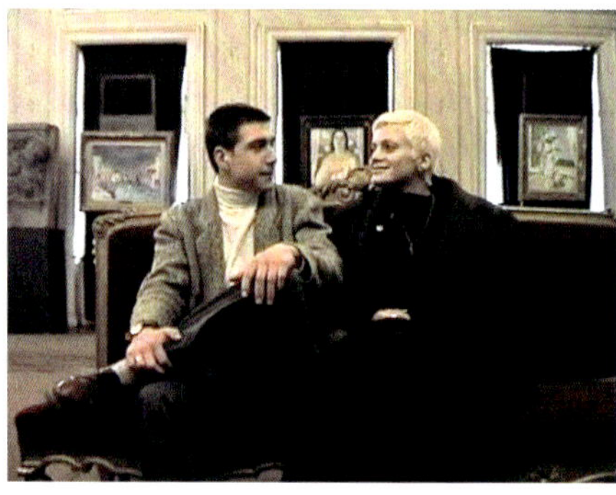
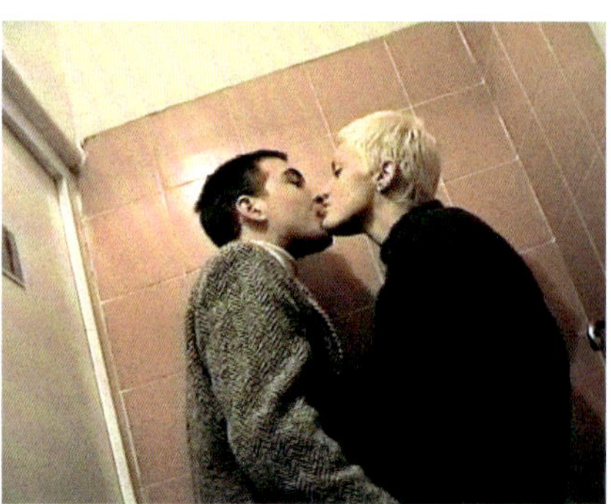

Kalin Serapionov

(b. 1967, Vratsa, Bulgaria)

The Museum – Cause of Meeting and Acquaintance
1997
Film, 21'9"
Courtesy Moderna galerija, Ljubljana

Kalin Serapionov belongs to the generation of artists who began to create art after 1989, in the period of tectonic social shifts when Bulgaria lay at the crossroads of the capitalist and socialist camps. Serapionov was a key participant in the late conceptual art scene of that era. Synthesizing photographs, found objects, text, and spatial experiments, he carefully built and played with the new cultural codes of that time.

The installation *Heating up the Air* (1995) is a fascinating example of his work, with space and the history of place. For this work, Serapionov chose a very special location—the Turkish baths in the town of Plovdiv (Bulgaria's second largest city). Serapionov fitted out one of the rooms with several heaters for a simple, purely artistic reason: "to bring back warmth." In one sense he wished to draw attention to a destroyed building in need of renovation, but in another he wanted to accentuate the universal human wish to revive lost warmth (particularly emotional warmth) from the past.

His short film *The Museum – Cause of Meeting and Acquaintance* is based on an extremely simple story: a woman and a man wander alone through the National Art Gallery in Sofia, and then they meet and rapidly bring their relationship to a culmination—sex. Behind this seemingly trivial facade is a sophisticated clash of ideas. Serapionov methodically juxtaposes different social and artistic dimensions, most obviously the "deadness" of the museum with a vital, transitory passion, and high art with base human lust.

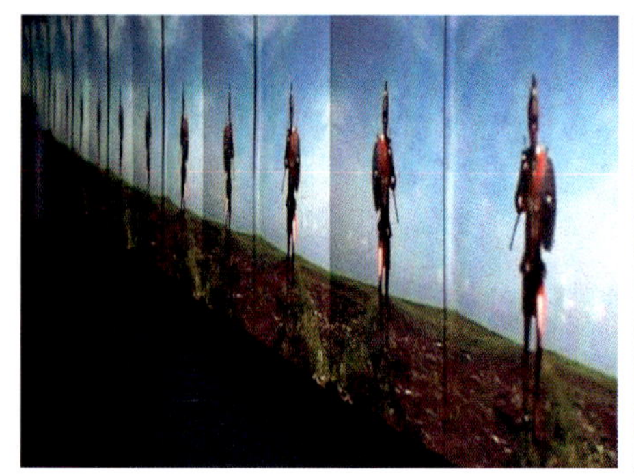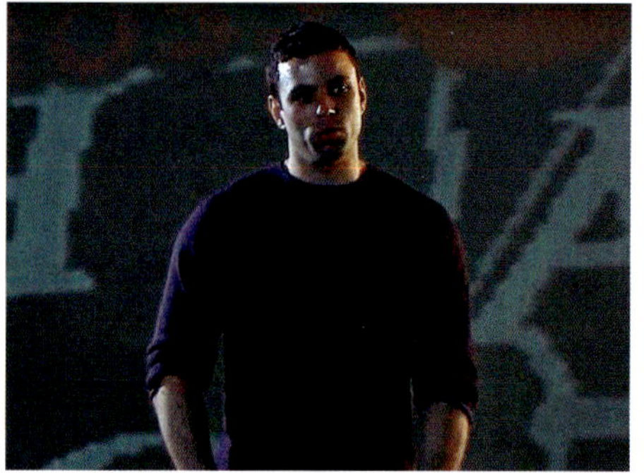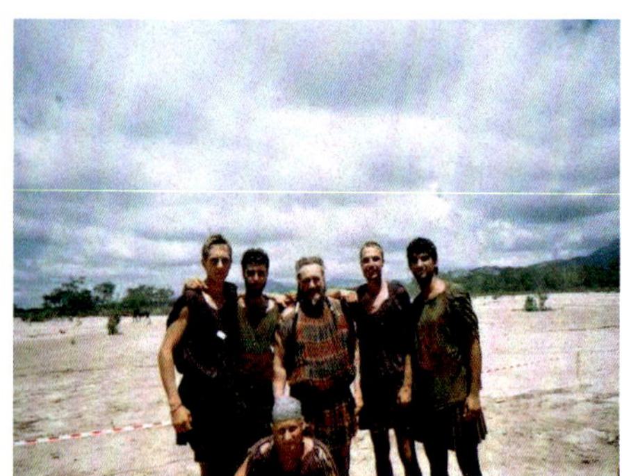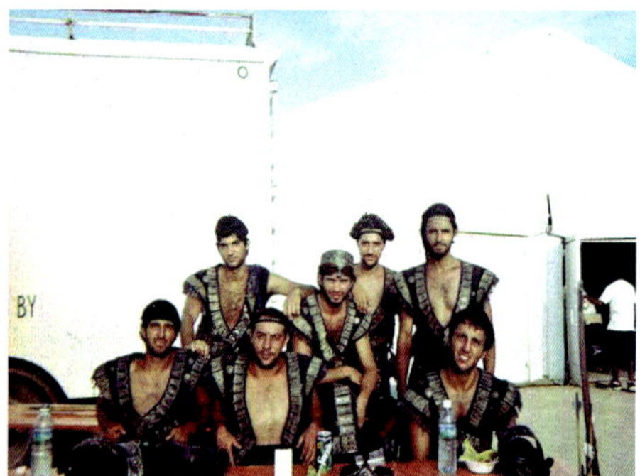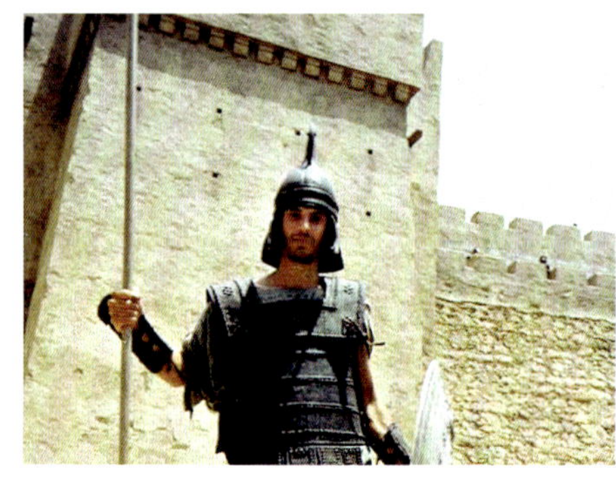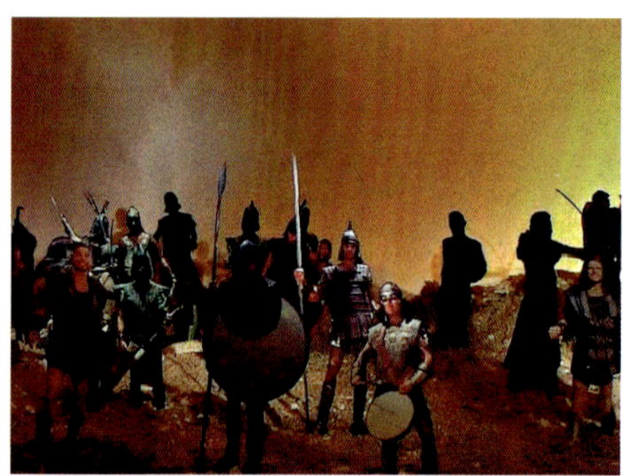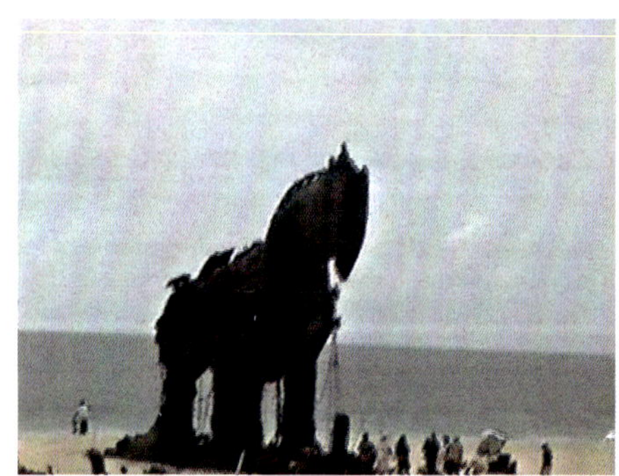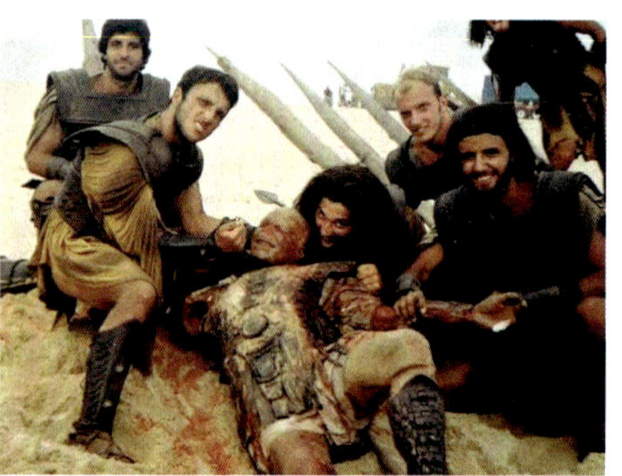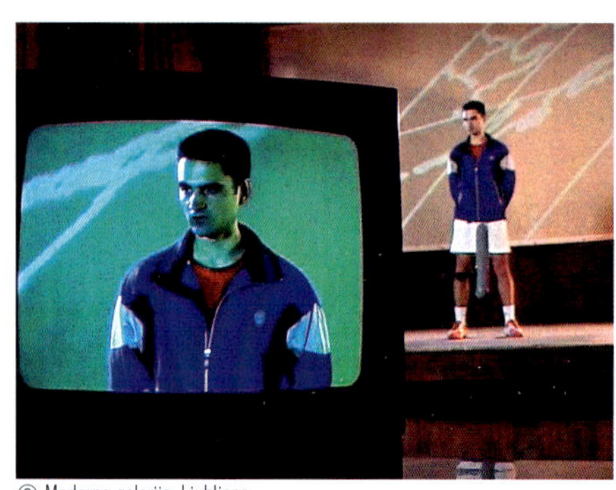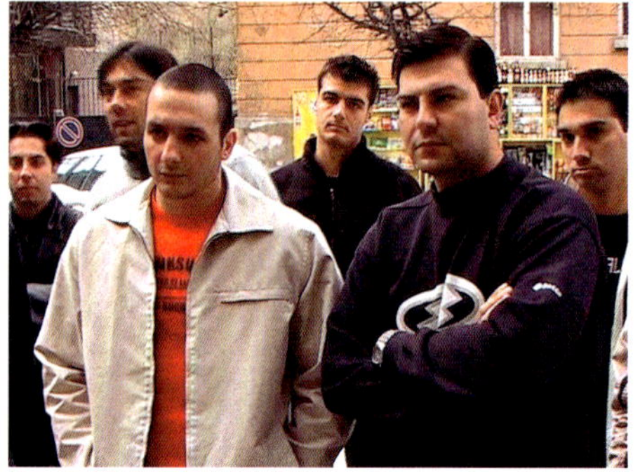

Krassimir Terziev

(b. 1969, Dobrich, Bulgaria)

Battles of Troy
2005
Documentary video, PAL, color, stereo, 51'
Courtesy Moderna galerija, Ljubljana

The documentary video project *Battles of Troy* is a study on the internal economy of contemporary, globalized cinema production, critically and ironically tracing the economic and political interconnections in the film industry. In 2003, Warner Bros. started one of the most expensive motion picture productions ever made, the film *Troy* (2004). For the film, which was shot in the UK, Malta, and Mexico, Warner Bros. hired 300 Bulgarian athletes to be the core of the armies in the movie. The perfect soldiers—large, strong, muscular, "Mediterranean-looking" guys—were recruited from the Sports Academy in Sofia, the capital of Bulgaria. *Battles of Troy* presents the "making of" of the film *Troy* through the viewpoint of the extras: cheap labor, the lowest units in the production hierarchy of a film with a budget of $185 m. *Battles of Troy* is centered on the experience of these Bulgarian men, who spent three months on the Mexican coastline, training and shooting the massive battle scenes of *Troy,* which were nevertheless nothing more than a backdrop to the "real" action performed by movie stars. Why did all these men decide to work on the project if in the final version it is impossible to even distinguish the silhouettes of their bodies, let alone their identities? By shifting its focus to the usually overlooked protagonists of background action, *Battles of Troy* tries to investigate the expectations, hopes, conflicts, and disappointments of those people whose silent bodies create the crowds we see in films.

2   The transformation of systems

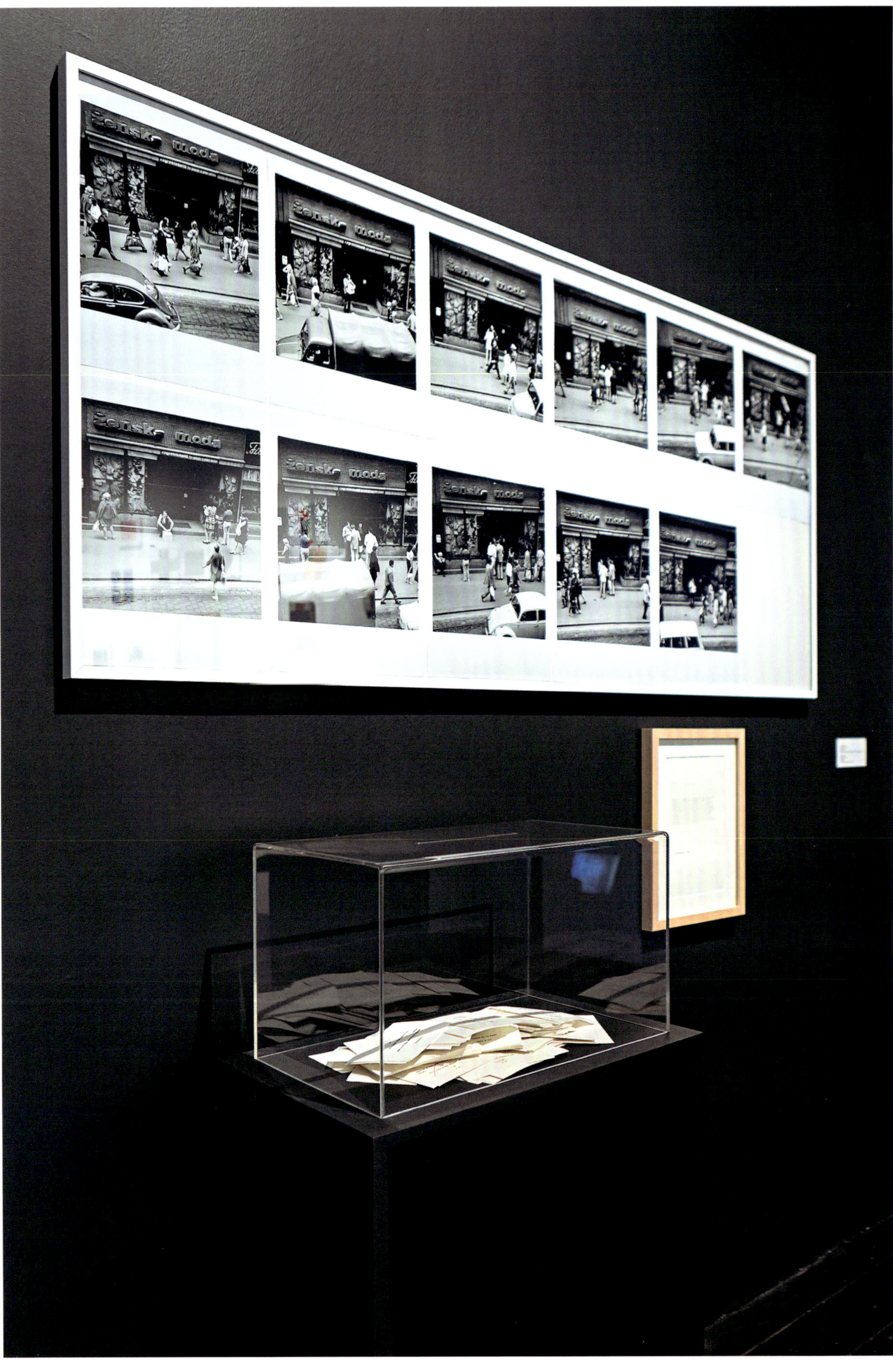

Goran Trbuljak

(b. 1948, Varaždin, Yugoslavia, now Croatia)

Referendum
1972
Installation
Courtesy Moderna galerija, Ljubljana

Goran Trbuljak, who has been active since the late 1960s in the context of conceptual art and the so-called New Art to Artistic Practices, has turned his attention to the position of art in the contemporary world. On the one hand, the traditional art media, such as painting, have become obsolete; it is impossible to paint a traditional image without being laughable. On the other hand, any kind of practice can become art if it is accepted as such by the audience and art institutions. In his playful and ironic works, Trbuljak researches the possibilities of making a painting at a time when such an act seems "impossible," as well as considering the mechanisms by which something is accepted as art. This kind of approach implies a certain moral attitude, a wish to remain independent from the demands of the art system by distancing oneself from it and laying bare its principles and mechanisms. His *Referendum* from 1972 was an attempt to use the most democratic means, public voting, to find out whether he was an artist or not. Since, as he says, an "artist is a person who is given the opportunity to be one by others," other people should determine his status. Trbuljak stood on the street with ballot papers and a box, inviting passersby to vote.

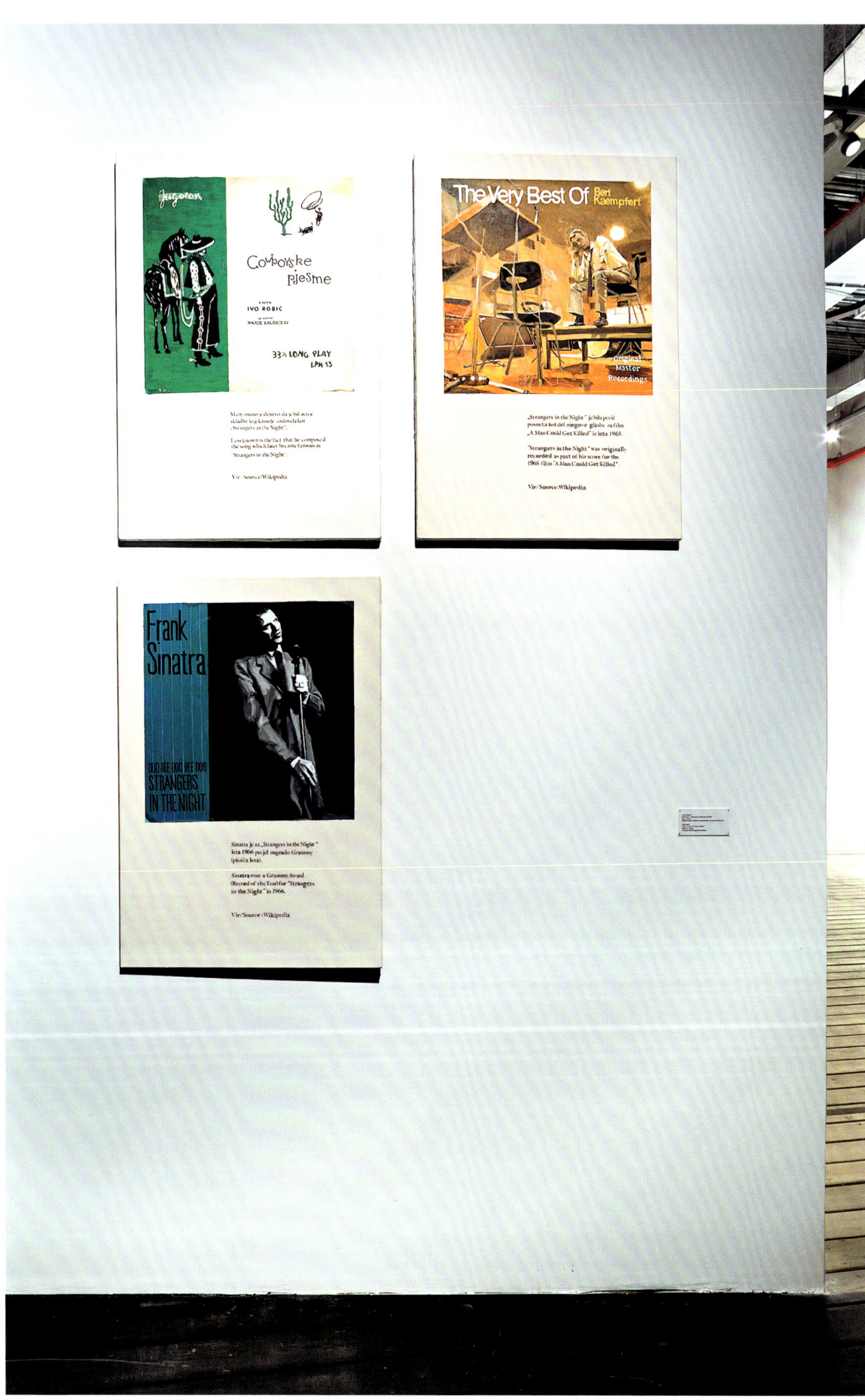

Sašo Vrabič

(b. 1974, Slovenj Gradec, Yugoslavia, now Slovenia)

Covers I-III

2006

3 paintings, acrylic and letter-press on canvas, each 100×70 cm

Courtesy Moderna galerija, Ljubljana

Sašo Vrabič's works are crucially marked by the contemporary context of media-sourced and computer-generated images. One of the main strategies of his practice is the recycling of visual material which Vrabič recontextualizes by placing it in a different medium (often painting). Although projects combining various visual media represent the bulk of his creative activity, Vrabič is also interested in music, which played an important role (alongside other circumstances) in the creation of the series *Covers I-III*.

In *Covers I-III* Vrabič uses the example of the well-known song *Strangers in the Night* to thematize the questions of originality and authorship in the context of East-West relations. Since the East was defined by the lack of a developed art system—its own art institutions and mechanisms of historicization and evaluation—the West is supposedly a space of tradition and authenticity, while the East can only mimic and copy Western concepts and styles. The series of three paintings combines realistically-painted album covers and Wikipedia quotes, giving a different view by pointing out the "unclear" authorship of *Strangers in the Night*. We learn from *Cover I* that the author of the melody is the Yugoslav singer Ivo Robić; *Cover II* tells us that the melody was first recorded as a part of a film score composed by Bert Kaempfer; and *Cover III* that it was Frank Sinatra who received a Grammy Award for the song in 1966.

The word "cover" has many meanings, of which at least three are at play in Vrabič's series. On the one hand, it signifies the motif of the paintings—an album cover—and on the other, the re-arrangement of a well-known melody. However, it can also be understood as a disguise; the procedures of appropriating and copying employed by Vrabič can be seen as a form of concealing one's identity or at least making it somewhat less clear.

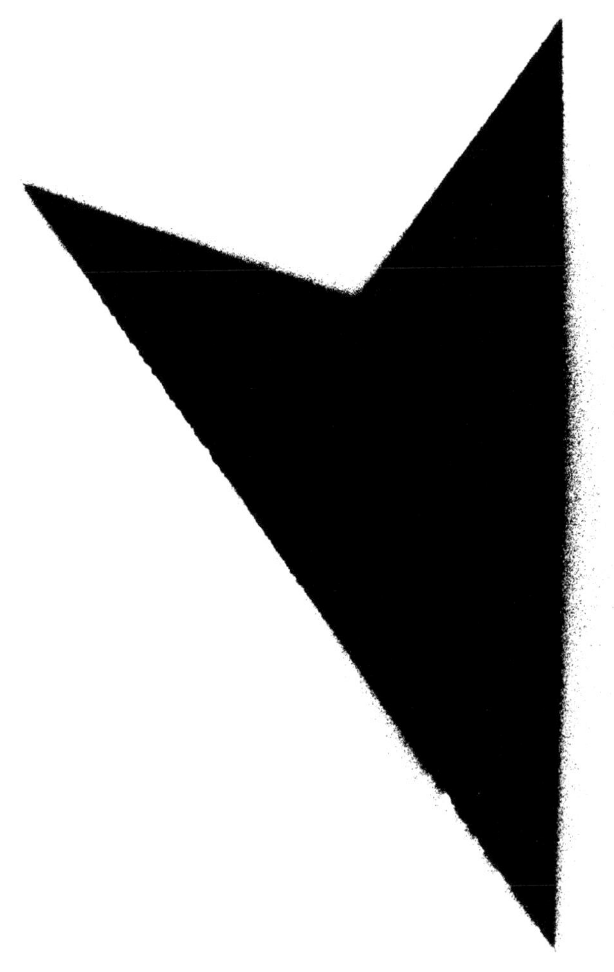

Lesson 3:
The power
of collaboration

Enriching local art traditions while building a shared identity through regional and international cooperation

The works included in this section are the direct outcome of personal and institutional collaboration, as indeed is this exhibition. Particularly during tight state control, but also at times of transition, informal regional networks have enriched local art scenes through shared knowledge. For example, artists from the former Yugoslavia—particularly Slovenia—and the former USSR developed a number of important projects in the early 1990s that charted the radical political transformations as they occurred.

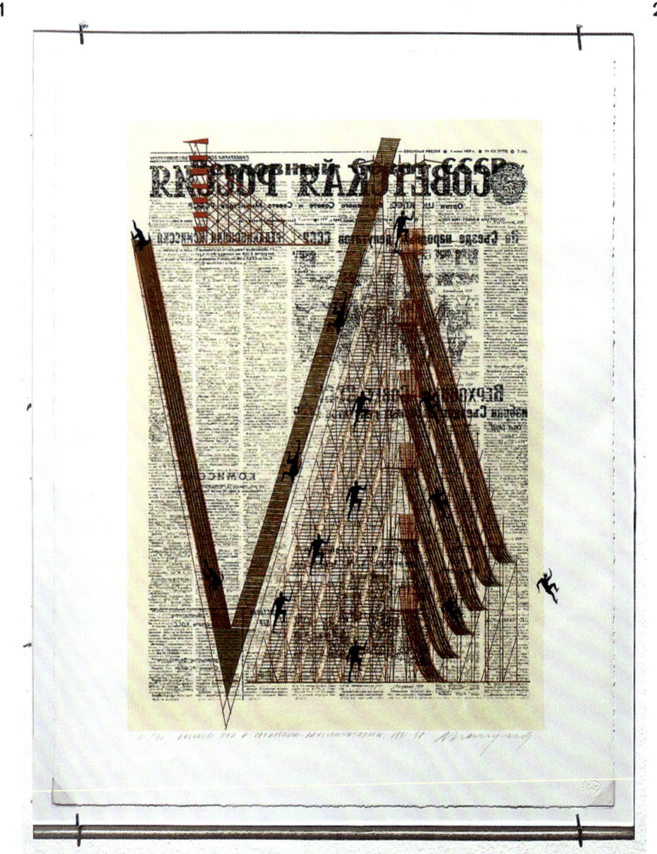

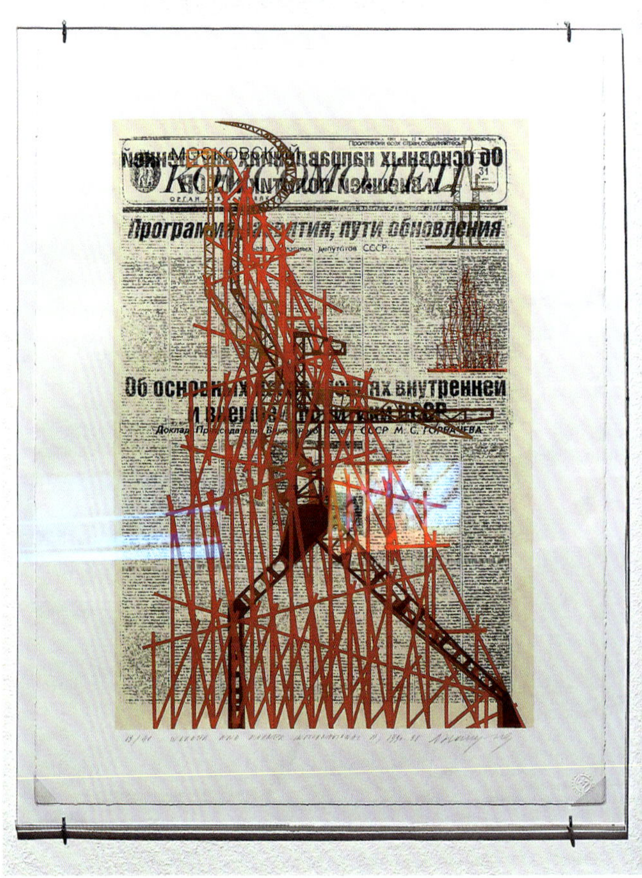

Yuri Avvakumov

(b. 1957, Tiraspol, USSR, now Moldova)

1
Worker & Farmer International
2
Rostrum for a Sportsman/Parliamentarian
1991–1998
Silkscreen on paper
Courtesy Moderna galerija, Ljubljana

Yuri Avvakumov has long been associated with the phenomenon of "paper architecture" in Russia. A movement that emerged in the 1980s, it proclaimed itself an alternative to semi-official Soviet architecture. A group of young Soviet architects (including Yuri Avvakumov, Ilya Utkin, and Alexander Brodsky), understanding that it would be impossible for them to realize their projects, decided to skip the construction part altogether. They chose instead to create architectural fantasies and utopian projects which often had no practical application. Avvakumov not only introduced the term "paper architecture" to Russia, he defined this type of work as a form of conceptual art.

In his series of paired works, comprising architectural models of imagined structures and sketches on newspaper, Avvakumov addresses the legacy of the Russian avant-garde. *Rostrum for a Sportsman/Parliamentarian*, dedicated to El Lissitzky, is a project for a utopian facility—a sports tower with numerous platforms on which several speakers can appear before the public, and from which one can dive into the water. *Worker and Farmer International* is a hybrid of Vera Mukhina's *The Worker and the Collective-Farm Woman* (1937) and Vladimir Tatlin's *Monument to the Third International* (1919–1920), and is intended by the artist to be a literal synthesis of constructivism and socialist realism.

3   The power of collaboration

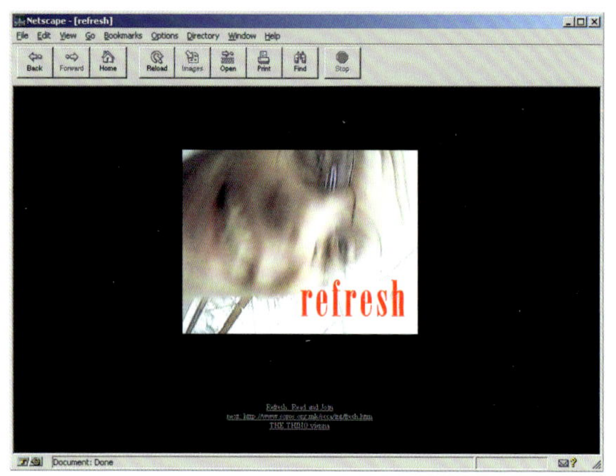

refresh
Refresh Read and Join
next: http://www.cont.org.mk/.../refresh.htm
THE THIRD vuvu

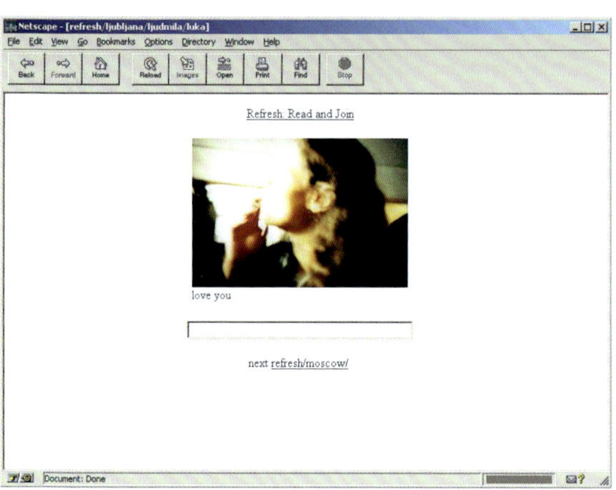

Refresh Read and Join
love you
next refresh/moscow/

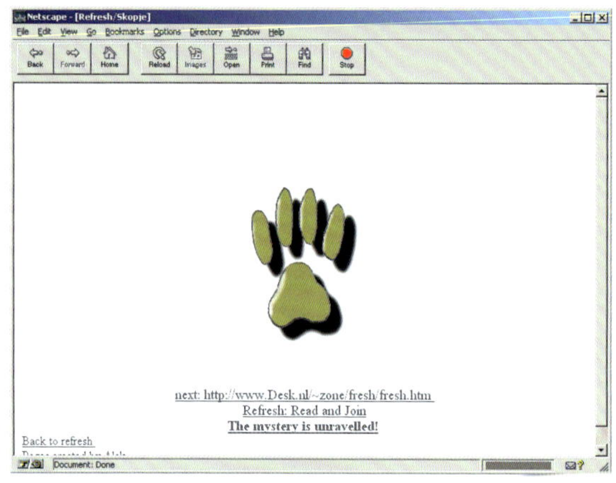

next: http://www.Desk.nl/~zone/fresh/fresh.htm
Refresh: Read and Join
The mystery is unravelled!
Back to refresh

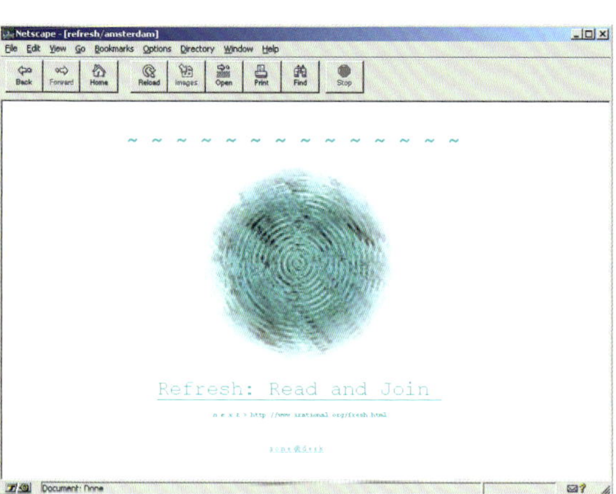

Refresh: Read and Join
n e x t : http://www.irational.org/fresh.html

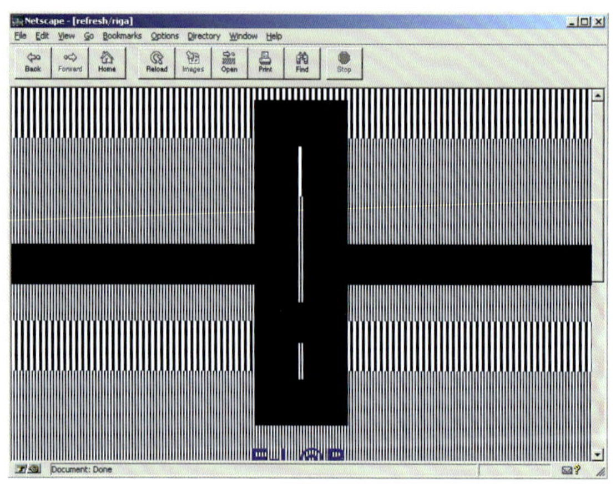

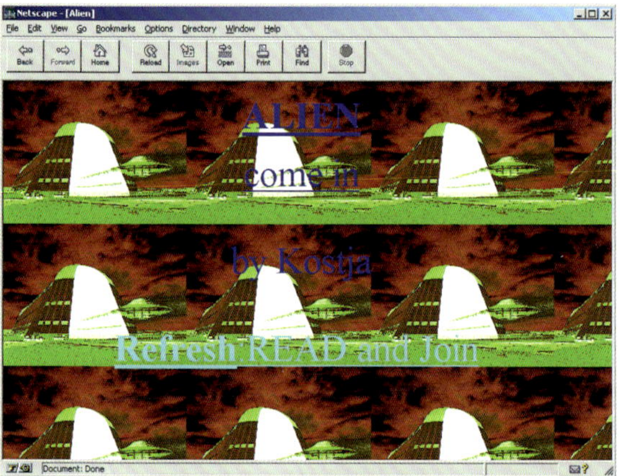

ALIEN
come in
by Kostja
Refresh READ and Join

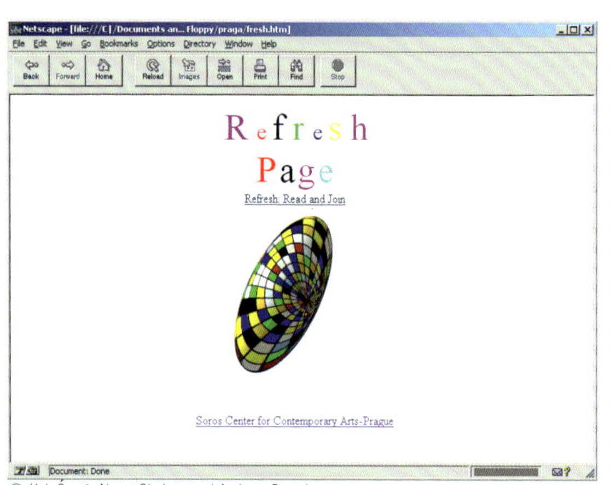

R e f r e s h
P a g e
Refresh: Read and Join
Soros Center for Contemporary Arts-Prague

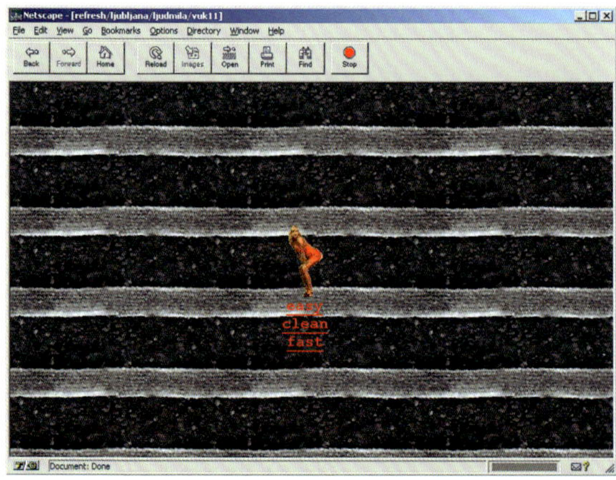

sexy
clean
fast

Vuk Ćosić, Alexei Shulgin, and Andreas Broeckmann

(b. 1966, Belgrade, Yugoslavia, now Serbia; b. 1963, Moscow, USSR, now Russia; b. 1964, Kevelaer, Germany)

Refresh
1996
Paper, color print, video, 11 screenshots
Courtesy of the artists

For the project *Refresh*, which took place on Sunday, October 6, 1996 from 6:00 to 10:00 pm CET, more than twenty web pages located on numerous servers across Europe and the US were linked together in a loop through which the visitor would be "zapped" automatically, the page changing every ten seconds. The project made use of the "Refresh" meta-tag, a command within HTML, the language that is used to design web pages. The command tells the browser software on the personal computer of the user to automatically go to a particular page after a certain time. By making sure that all these links created a loop, *Refresh* would take you through all the pages over and over again.

The project was exciting for those immediately involved as they could experience how the loop grew page by page, while they were simultaneously communicating and negotiating via an IRC chat channel how to solve certain problems. More generally, the *Refresh* loop was designed to employ the interconnectivity of the computer and software infrastructure to create a single project happening simultaneously at more than twenty different locations, a genuinely distributed artwork whose experiential effect both depended on and transgressed the physical distance between the participants.

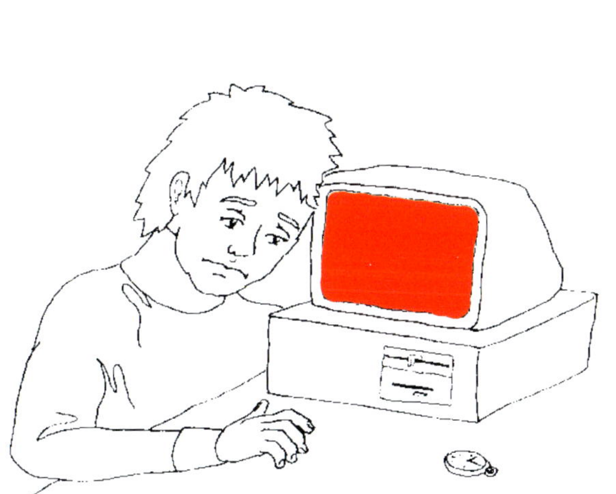

3　The power of collaboration

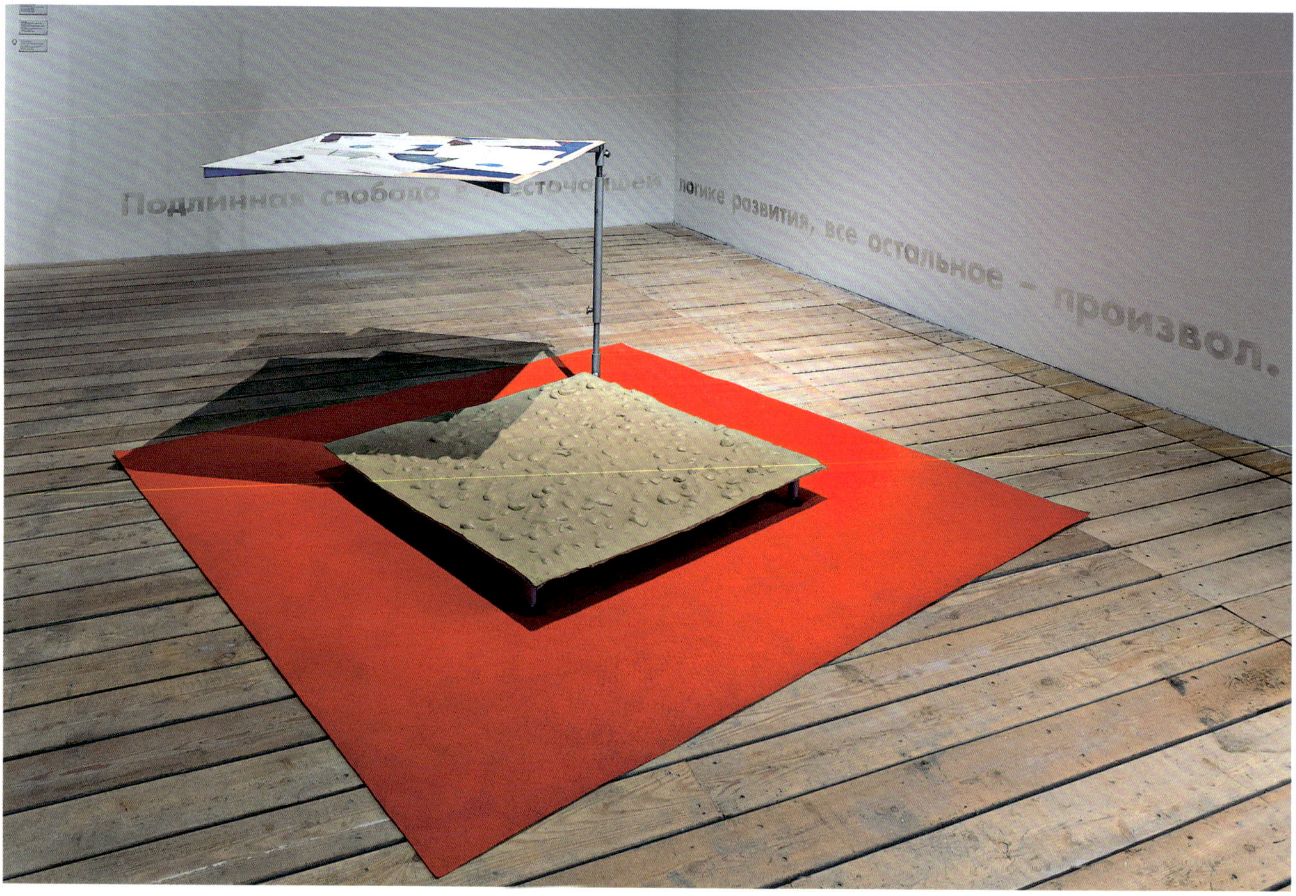
Подлинная свобода
логике развития, все остальное – произвол.

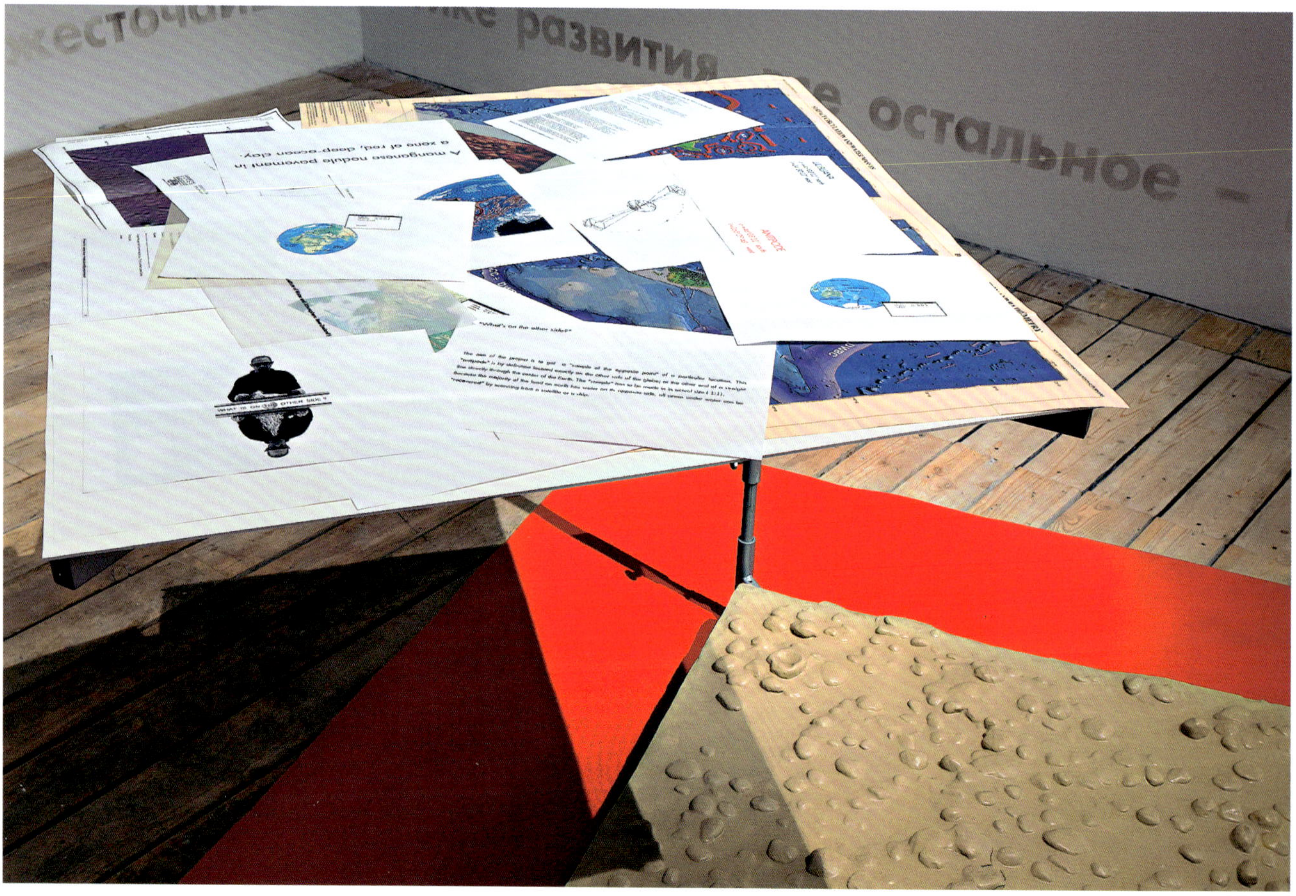
развития
остальное –

Vadim Fishkin

(b. 1965, Penza, USSR, now Russia)

What's on the Other Side? Ljubljana, Latitude 14°25'12"E, Longitude 46°03'11"N

2000

Installation

Courtesy Moderna galerija, Ljubljana

The creative debut of Vadim Fishkin took place in Moscow in the late 1980s as a member of the World Champions group. His subsequent works retained only one feature from that period of "championship," namely his connection with avant-garde projects. All his activity is an attempt to preserve and defend his conception of the constructive and life-enhancing potential of artistic creativity. Hence Fishkin's interest in the spiritual roots of Russian avant-gardism—the visionary cosmogony of Tsiolkovsky and Chizhevsky. Therefore it seems natural that he belongs to both the Moscow and Ljubljana artistic scenes, as the themes of Utopia, cosmogony, and aeronautics are inherent to the work of many Slovene artists and producers.

What's on the Other Side? is one of Fishkin's most programmatic works. The idea of reconstructing within an exhibition space the relief of a place located precisely on the opposite side of the globe exemplifies Fishkin's practice. This project also has a constructional inventiveness, a cosmic way of thinking, and, most typically, a palpable connection with actual scientific research. After all, the artefact being reconstructed by the artist is not just a product of his untrammeled imagination; its creation is based on a real scientific reconstruction.

3   The power of collaboration

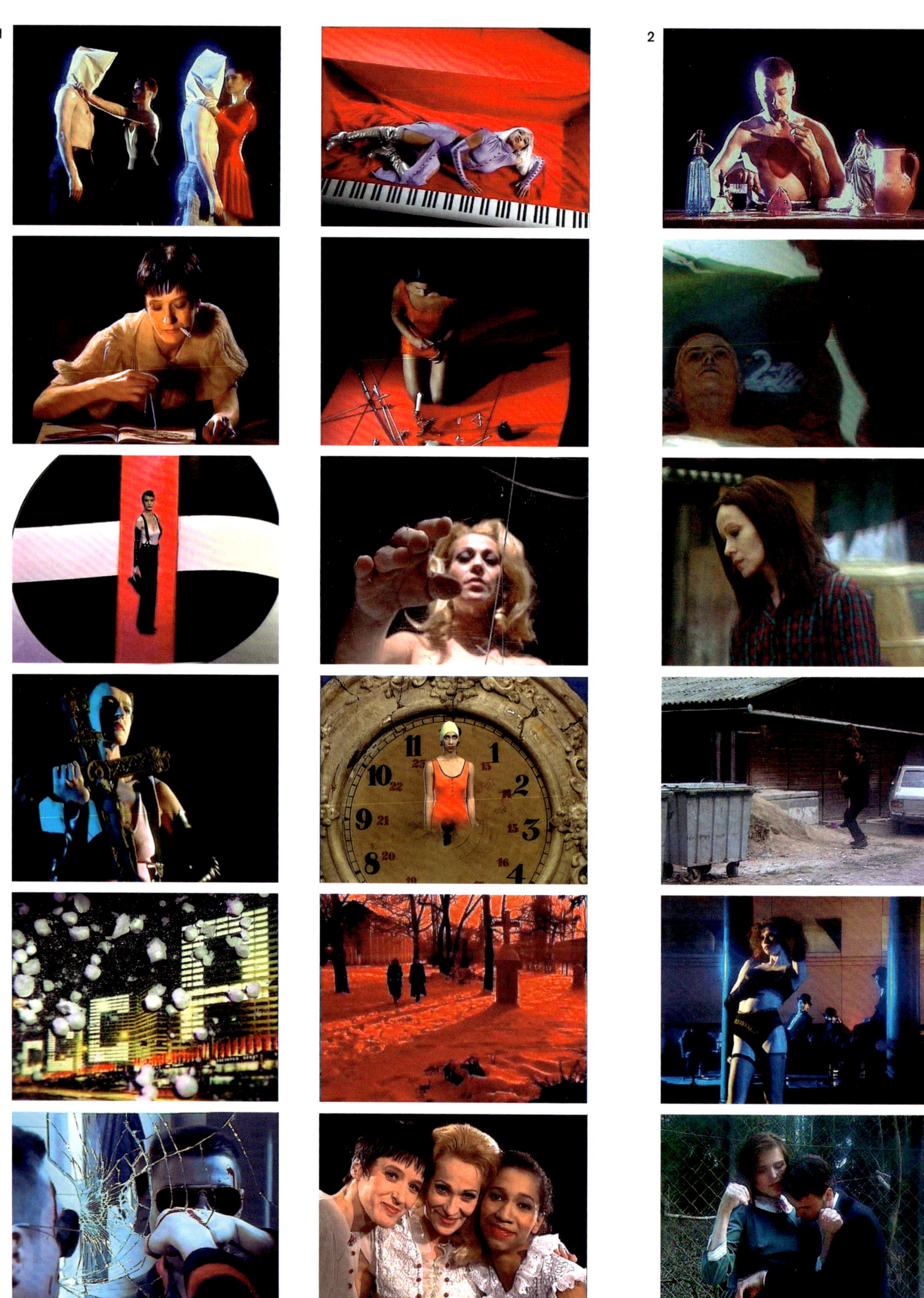

Marina Gržinić and Aina Šmid

(b. 1958, Rijeka, Yugoslavia, now Croatia; b. 1957, Ljubljana, Yugoslavia, now Slovenia)

1
Labirint (Labyrinth)
1993
Video, Betacam SP PAL, color, stereo, 11' 45"
Produced by TV Slovenia
2
Tri sestre (Three Sisters)
1992
Video, color, Betacam SP PAL, 28'
Produced by Slovensko Mladinsko Gledališče Ljubljana and TV Slovenia
Courtesy Moderna galerija, Ljubljana

The work of Marina Gržinić and Aina Šmid explores the position of the body, identities, and theory in relation to specific sociopolitical histories (especially the breakup of Yugoslavia and the war that followed). In the 1980s the two artists questioned socialist ideology and then focused on subverting the Western system of aesthetics/ethics/visuality in the 1990s. Today, as they say themselves, they are obsessed with the turbo capitalist system, processuality, and the politics of performativity.

Quotations, reappropriation, mixing different styles, histories, and cultures, and recurrent use of video effects are the key features of their work, where they primarily try to develop the political and conceptual prerogatives of the video medium, dismantling aesthetics, languages, and discourses that renaturalize inequalities, capital exploitation, dispossession, racism, and discrimination.

Three Sisters is an attempt to discuss the disintegration of communism, but it also discusses racism, nationalism, and the new political machinery of free market capitalism. Furthermore, it explores issues related to the position of women, the division of roles between men and women, and religious racism. The video visualizes the classic play by Anton Chekhov in a radically altered political and artistic context. Sequences from documentaries about the war in Croatia are used and integrated in an imaginary video story about wars, history, love, and hate.

Labyrinth offers a poetical and cynical look at the situation in the ex-Yugoslav territory by juxtaposing surrealist imagery referencing René Magritte's work, documentary footage from the camps for Bosnian refugees in Ljubljana, and the hectic movements of dancers. The placement of the body in traumatic places of the outer and inner world—the architecture of misery and deprivation—forms a specific territory that forces the body, the psyche, and memory (of the dancers) to seek final solutions.

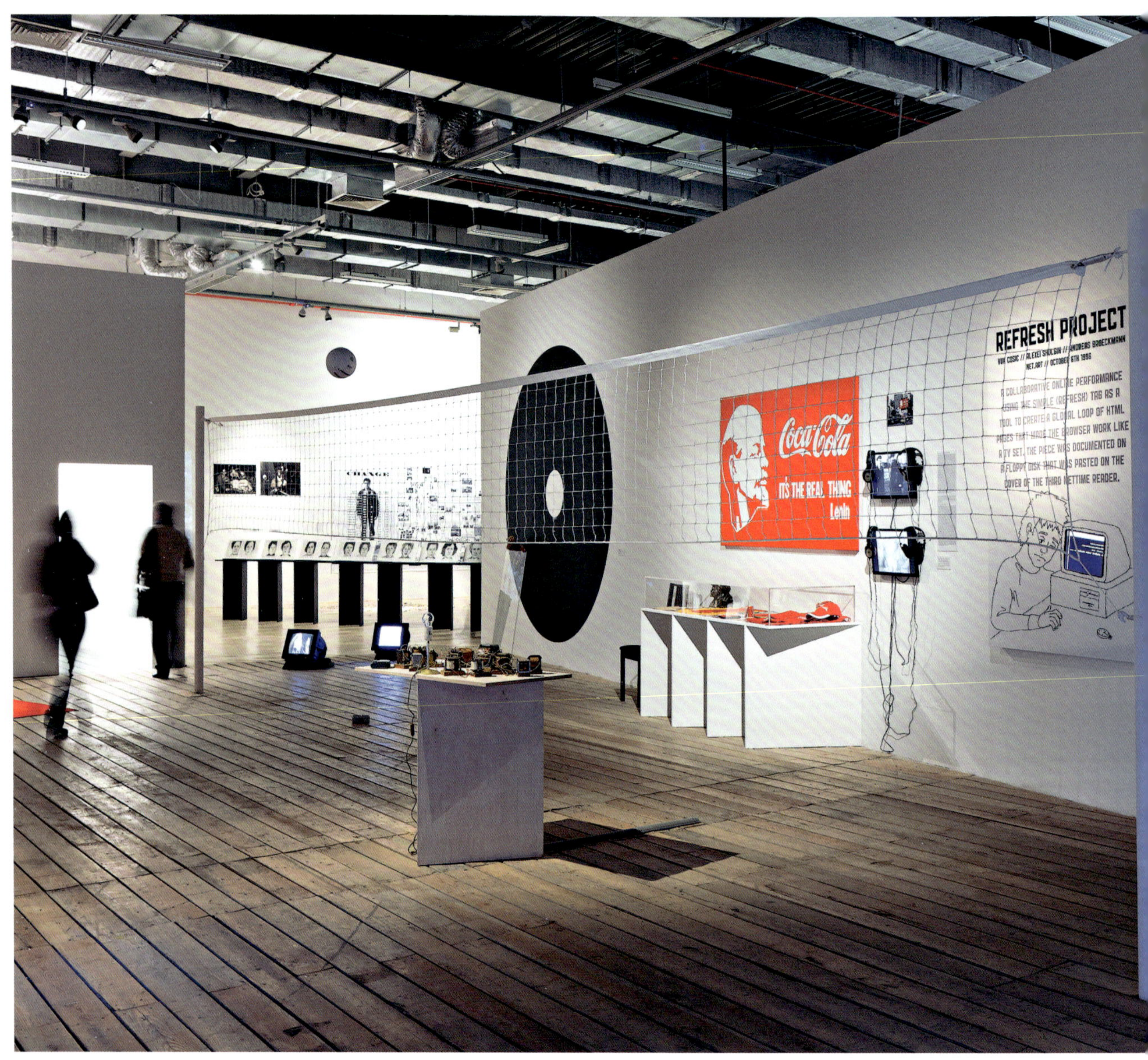
REFRESH PROJECT
VUK COSIC // ALEXEI SHULGIN // ANDREAS BROECKMANN
NET.ART // OCTOBER 6TH 1996

A COLLABORATIVE ONLINE PERFORMANCE
USING THE SIMPLE (REFRESH) TAG AS A
TOOL TO CREATE A GLOBAL LOOP OF HTML
PAGES THAT MADE THE BROWSER WORK LIKE
A TV SET. THE PIECE WAS DOCUMENTED ON
A FLOPPY DISK THAT WAS PASTED ON THE
COVER OF THE THIRD NETTIME READER.
CHANGE
Coca-Cola
ITS THE REAL THING
Lenin

Dmitry Gutov
(in collaboration with
Konstantin Bokhorov)

(b. 1960, Moscow, USSR, now Russia)

Smash!
1992
Installation
Courtesy Moderna galerija, Ljubljana

Dmitry Gutov's professional arsenal includes an academic knowledge of psychology and a specialist artistic education, and he works with almost every medium: installations, objects, paintings, films, drawings, and texts. His works are full of associations and references to the most unexpected, and sometimes even apparently forgotten subjects and figures. For instance, the installation *Above Black Mud* gestures to Yuri Pimenov's *Wedding on Tomorrow Street*, and there are entire series of works where he uses graphic design from Soviet magazines of the 1950s and 1960s, or images from ancient Greek vases. As well as devoting a significant amount of attention to left-wing intellectual discourse, which attracts many contemporary artists, Gutov also insists on working with the theoretical legacy of the Soviet Union. He rediscovered the Marxist philosopher Mikhail Lifschitz and, together with Konstantin Borokhov, founded the Lifschitz Institute with the goal of reviving the thinker's ideas, which had become stale during the Soviet era and were forgotten. Gutov created his series of "aerial works" (*Amphibian Man*, *Hammock,* and *Smash!*) in 1991 and 1992. These works could only have emerged in this historical gap. Atthe point of rupture between two states, two temporal and sociocultural realities, Gutov found a vacuum inside of which it was possible to construct something that would dispassionately juxtapose past and future. The installation is based on a volleyball match, frozen at the moment of its culmination, when the player needs to make a powerful shot. For Gutov, space must possess the quality of a structure that, like a net, is pulled taut in different directions, and which, in his view, embodies the Soviet, with the "multifacetedness" of its architecture and cinema. The ball suspended in the air symbolizes less the idea of an abstract, empty space and more that which appeared after the collapse of an enormous state and big ideas.

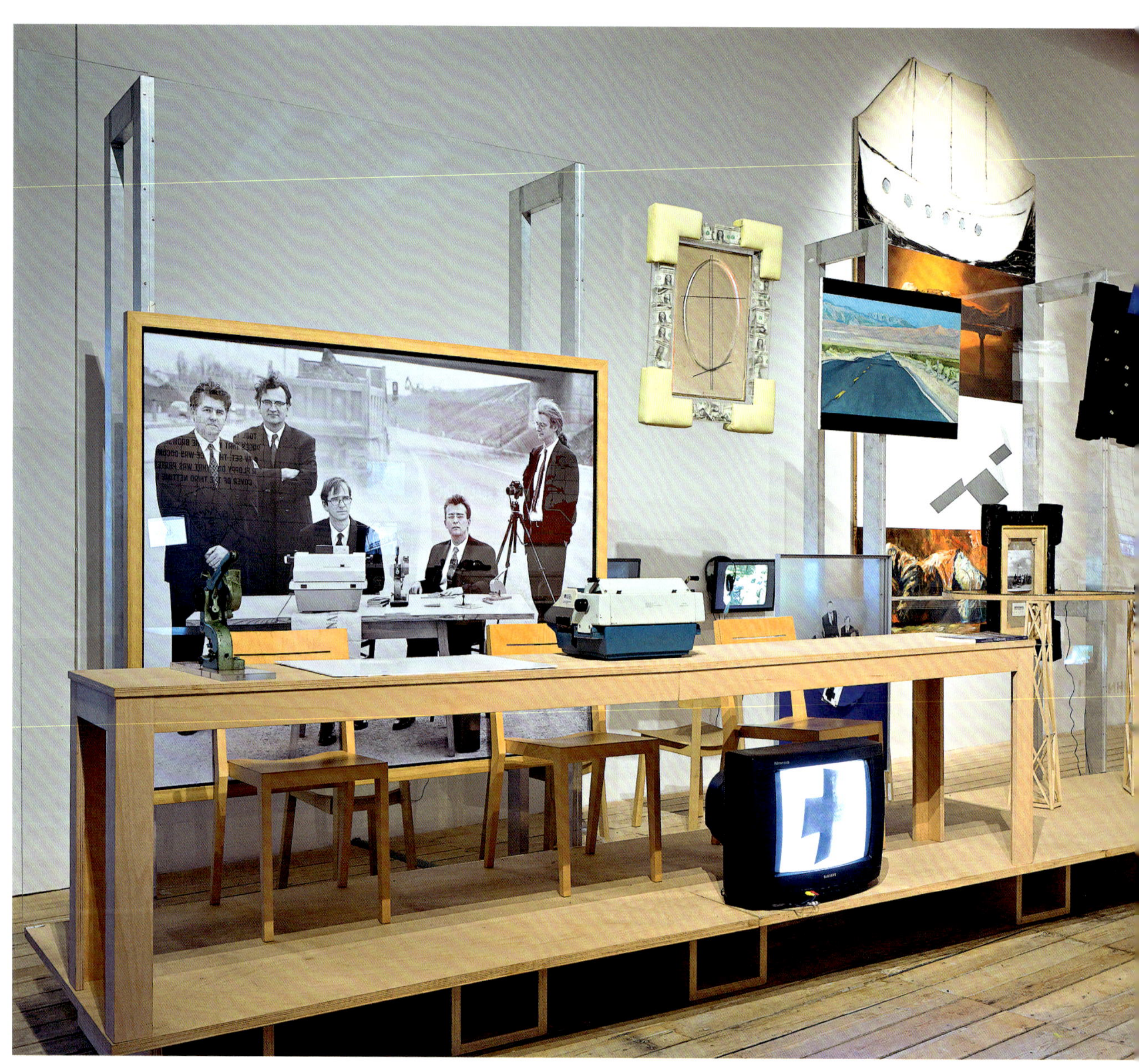

IRWIN

(1983, Ljubljana, Yugoslavia, now Slovenia)

Transnacionala
1998
Installation, mixed media, 260×520×120 cm
Courtesy of the artists

IRWIN (Dušan Mandič, Miran Mohar, Andrej Savski, Roman Uranjek, and Borut Vogelnik) is one of the core groups of the Neue Slowenische Kunst (NSK) collective. Its work is concerned with the art history of Europe and especially the dialectic of the avant-garde and totalitarianism. Since the 1990s, following its early predominantly painting projects, the group has focused on a critical examination of the art history of "Western modernism," which it counters with the "retro-avant-garde" of a fictitious "Eastern modernism," which, in its own obvious artificiality, points to the artificiality of the historical structures and norms of Western art.

In 1996, IRWIN and an international group of artists (Alexander Brener, Vadim Fishkin, Yuri Leiderman, Goran Đorđević, Michael Benson, and Eda Čufer) set out on a month-long journey across the United States in two recreational vehicles. Their artistic trip, *Transnacionala,* began in Atlanta and ended on the West Coast. Its aim was to discuss various issues concerning art, politics, and existence in the contemporary world. The discussions focused on three interconnected questions: the nature of East–West relations and the trauma of East–West division; the functioning of the global art system and its problems; and the possibilities that entities from different cultural, social, and political backgrounds have for communicating among themselves. Although it might seem, as Eda Čufer writes, that *Transnacionala* "attempted to reaffirm the idea that despite cultural, political, economic, and individual differences the contemporary art community could speak the same language," it was not directed towards the agreement of the participants. Rather, it deliberately provoked "communication noise" and enabled a disconsensual dynamic of debate. The installation *Transnacionala* was developed as a result of several exhibitions in the year following the journey.

3   The power of collaboration

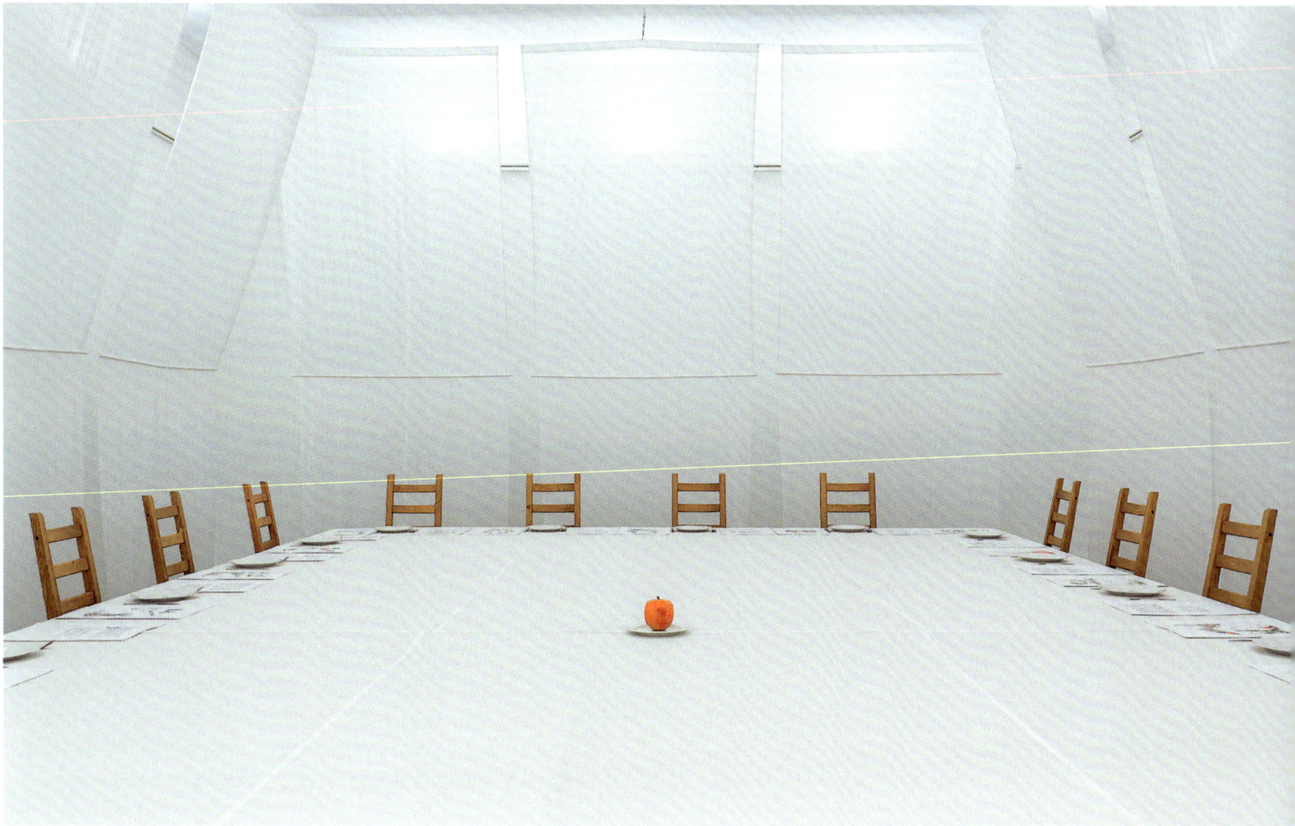

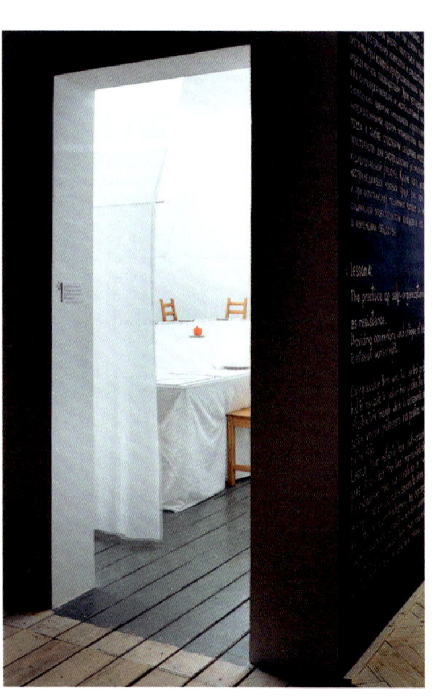

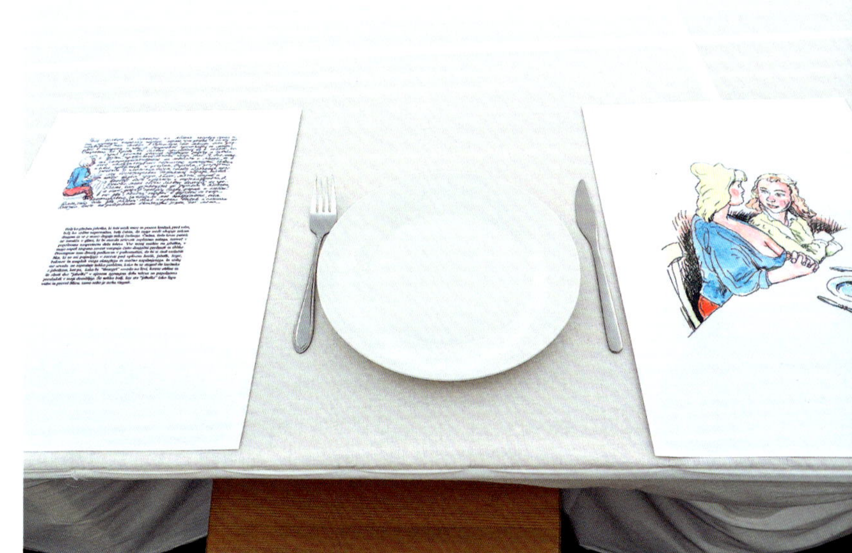

Ilya and Emilia Kabakov

(b. 1933 and 1945, Dnipropetrovsk, USSR, now Ukraine)

Twenty Ways to Get an Apple Listening
to the Music of Mozart

1997

Installation

Courtesy Moderna galerija, Ljubljana

In an interview with Boris Groys, Ilya Kabakov described his installation in the Russian Pavilion at the 1993 Venice Biennale thus: "The basic ideological standpoint is that socialism is good. Even more than that: it is a celebration of life, but we must not touch it. It's 'untouchable', like the view from the balcony of the Russian Pavilion. Socialism is wonderful, but it should stay in Iofan's and Mayakovsky's utopias, and not be put into practice. It is beautiful, but from a distance. It will shine above us as an eternal utopia, evading us like the carrot dangled in front of the donkey. The experiences of the 20th century have made it manifest that it is better not to come too close to utopias. We cannot give them up, but we had better not even try to realize them." The job of modern art is precisely to deconstruct the tricks which make us enjoy illusions.

The installation *Twenty Ways to Get an Apple Listening to the Music of Mozart* consists of twenty drawings and stories explaining the various tricks by which one can reach an apple in the middle of an enormous table, two or three arms' lengths away.

The hero of the installation is not very successful in real life. Everything he accomplishes, he accomplishes in his imagination. But this is not the kind of failure we are familiar with from everyday life; rather, it is a certain tension between the attainable and the non-attainable, between reality and illusion that can never be resolved.

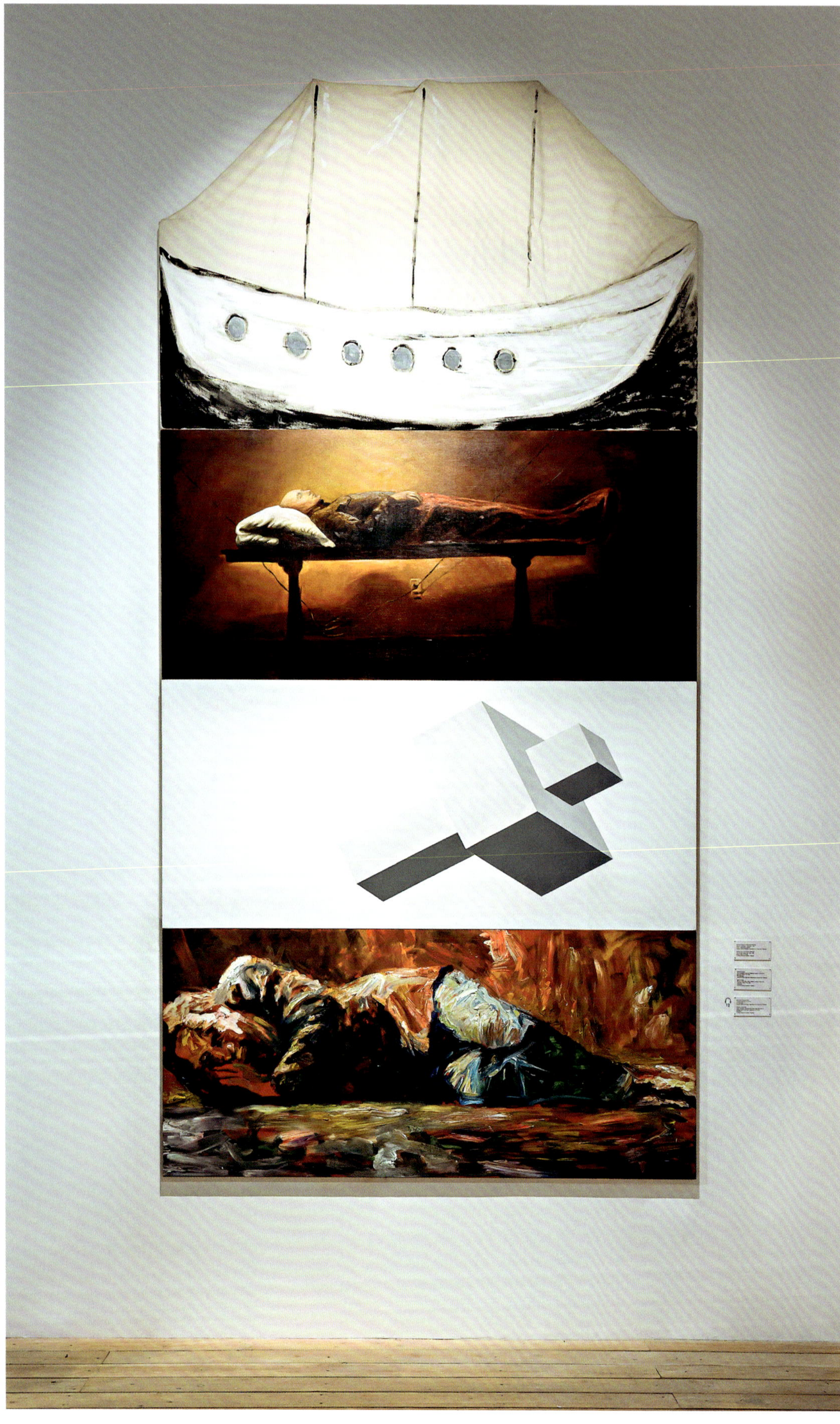

Komar and Melamid

(b. 1943 and 1945, Moscow, USSR, now Russia)

Smooth Sailing with Lenin
1985
Mixed media, 203.5×128 cm
Courtesy Moderna galerija, Ljubljana

In the early 1970s the artistic duo Komar and Melamid founded the Sots Art movement as a reaction against Socialist Realism, the official aesthetic doctrine of the state. Sots Art, usually described as a sort of conceptual Pop Art appropriating the visual language of socialist mass culture, was a form of nonconformist art based on combining apparently disparate styles, images, and cultures, resulting in an ironical pastiche that deconstructed the authoritarian language of the propaganda industry and debunked the ideologies that works of official Soviet art were meant to embody and promote. It examined the role of images and image-making in constructing and validating the dominant systems of power and beliefs through many different projects and series.

Smooth Sailing with Lenin was created as a part of the *Nostalgic Socialist Realism* series (1982–1983). The two artists employed the language of traditional Socialist Realism and blended it with contextual and aesthetic features as expressed in old painting styles. The paintings, closely connected with the artists' ironic and nostalgic memories of their own childhood in Stalinist Moscow, depict scenes from the history of the Soviet Union: they begin with Lenin's revolution, touch upon Stalin, and end with Khrushchev.

In the painting *Smooth Sailing with Lenin* different scenes and styles—an expressionistically painted sleeping homeless person, a "suprematist" image, a realistically depicted Lenin, and a collaged boat— are vertically juxtaposed in order to create/show their similarities and contradictions and question the ideology of socialist progress that most official Soviet art depicted and glorified.

3   The power of collaboration

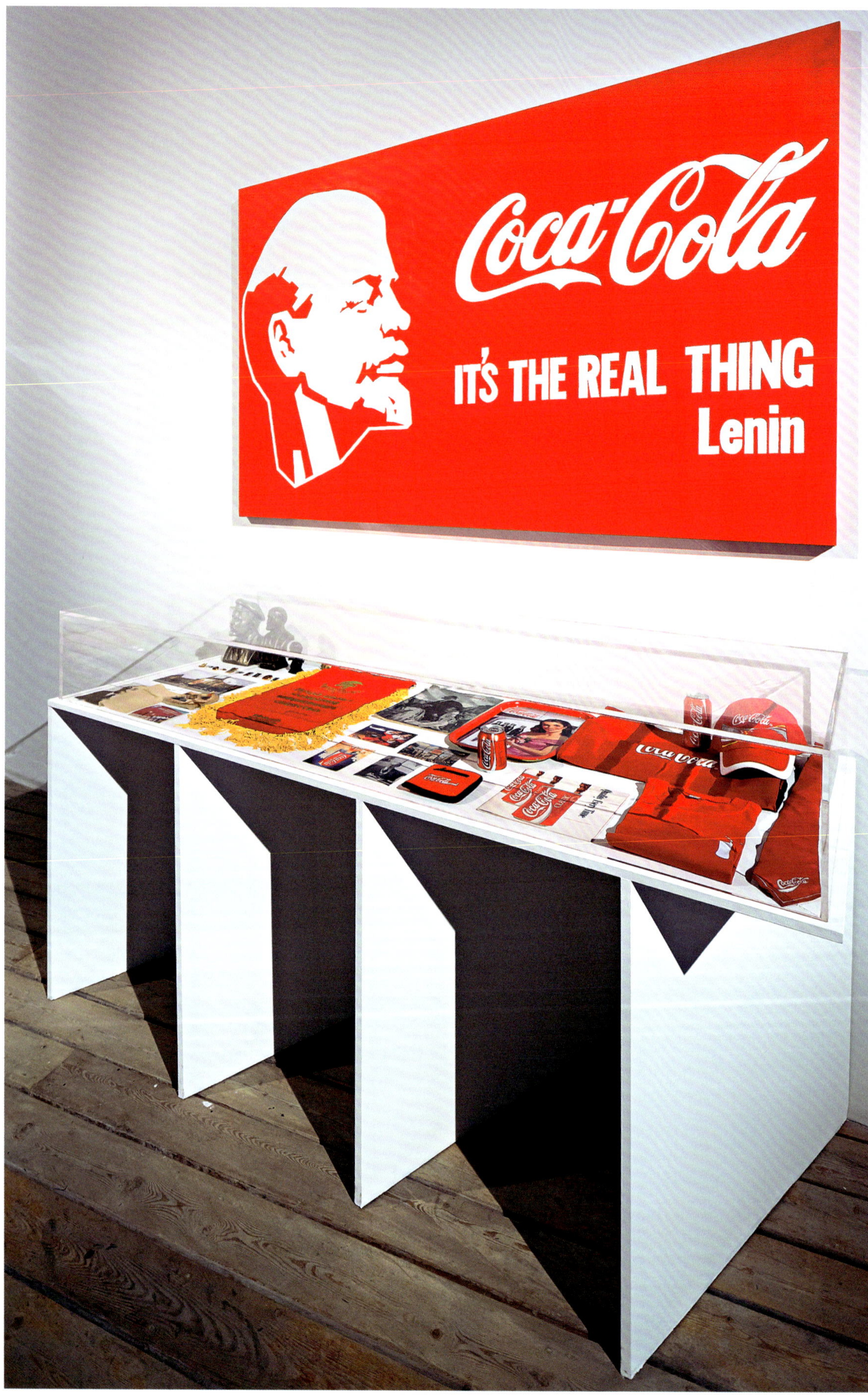
Coca-Cola
IT'S THE REAL THING
Lenin

Alexander Kosolapov

(b. 1943, Moscow, USSR, now Russia)

Lenin–Coca-Cola and related artefacts

1980–2000

Oil on canvas, 120×200 cm

Objects, publications, film footage, 2011

Courtesy Moderna galerija, Ljubljana

Alexander Kosolapov's painting *Lenin–Coca-Cola* (1980) is part of the collection of Moderna galerija in Ljubljana. Its iconography is recognizable for many viewers as it combines two well-known and contrasting images of 20th century mass culture. One is the portrait of Lenin (Vladimir Ilyich), leader of the revolution from which the USSR emerged in 1917. Until its demise in 1991, this new country had a huge influence on the history of the 20th century. Since his death in 1924, Lenin's image, often portrayed on red banners, has become one of the most recognizable symbols of the international communist movement. Another globally-recognized symbol is the Coca-Cola logo, perhaps the most popular soft drink in the world today. First introduced in 1886 in the United States, it is now sold in more than 200 countries, and its white letters on a red background have become a key symbol of globalization and consumerism, one of the ultimate achievements of liberal capitalism.

The painting is exhibited here primarily as an artefact. Alongside it are displayed various randomly-selected objects and film footage, related either to Lenin or Coca-Cola. They aim to provide information on the broader political and cultural context to facilitate a better understanding of the iconography behind the painting, the symbolism of each image, and the contradiction and irony of merging them into a single work (Walter Benjamin, Berlin, 2011).

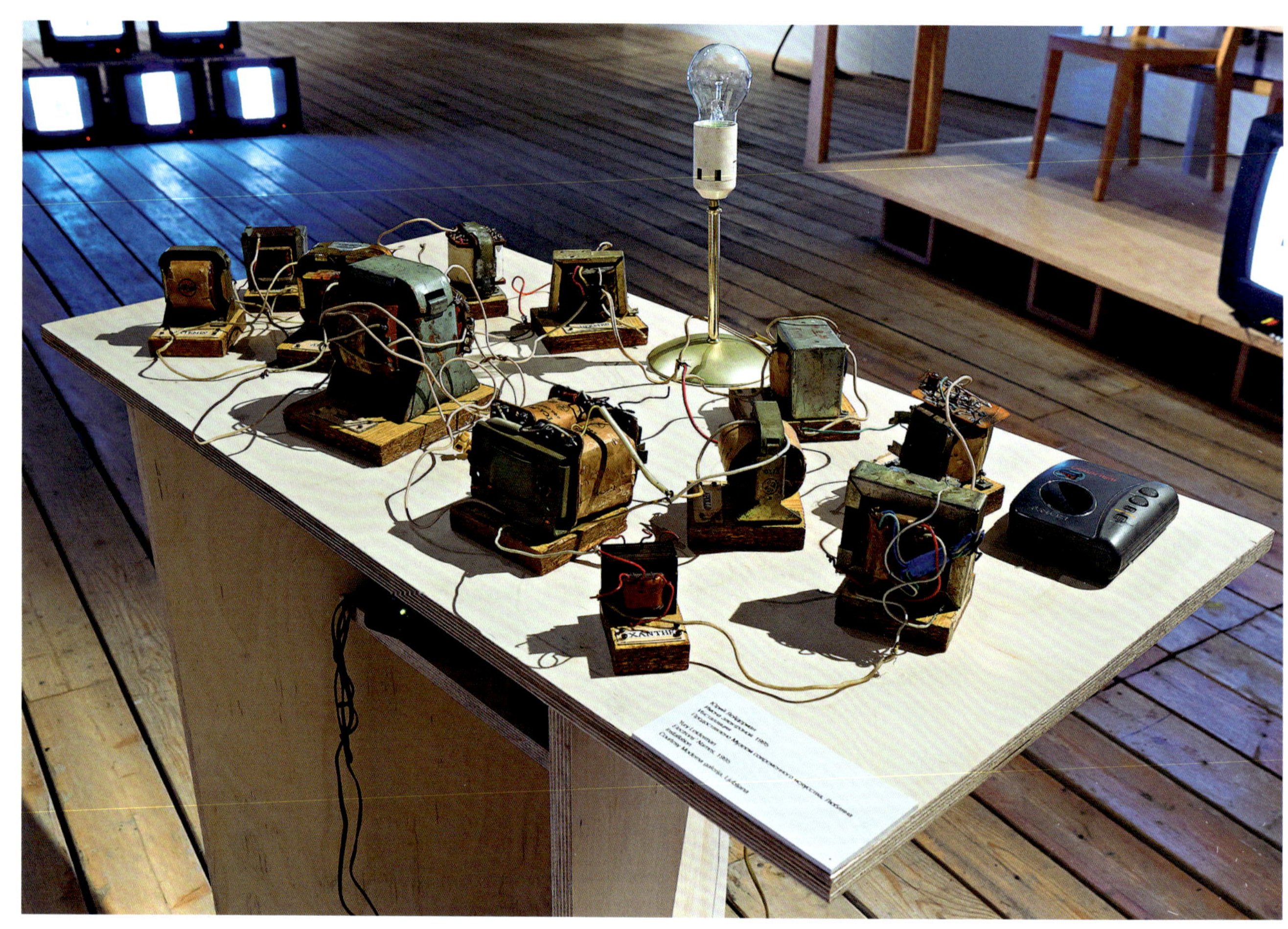

Yuri Leiderman

(b. 1963, Odessa, USSR, now Ukraine)

Electrons' Names
1995
Installation
Courtesy Moderna galerija, Ljubljana

The creative evolution of Yuri Leiderman began in the mid-1980s, when Moscow Conceptualism occupied the mainstream. At the time, he was profoundly influenced by Andrei Monastyrsky, the leader of the Collective Actions group, who proposed a chamber aesthetics of conceptualism as opposed to a theoretical and representative version. Inspection Medical Hermeneutics, the group that Leiderman established together with Pavel Pepperstein and Sergei Anufriev, was dedicated to the development of conceptual reflection. The emerging artists busied themselves with textual pieces of conceptualism, the history and mythology of this orthodoxy, and the canon of conceptualism. Leiderman left Medical Hermeneutics in 1990. His sense of the new decade convinced him of the predominance of subjectivity over text. Since then, his art has focused on the inner layers of subjectivity and eschewed any conventional communication models, becoming increasingly self-contained and avoiding external comprehension.

Leiderman always invokes the traditional fables of different civilizations, ranging from Russian religious philosophy to Scandinavian and Greek mythology, since he is interested in the possibility of creating a subjective ontology rather than in subjectivity as such. And given his bent towards structure rather than chaos, many of his creations take the form of machines which operate with the use of natural processes. Since the main function of any ontology is to identify and name phenomena—naming elementary particles is at its very core—many of Leiderman's projects are designed to do exactly that. *Electrons' Names* is not only the title of the work, but also of the book that comprises the artist's main texts (St. Petersburg, 1997).

3   The power of collaboration

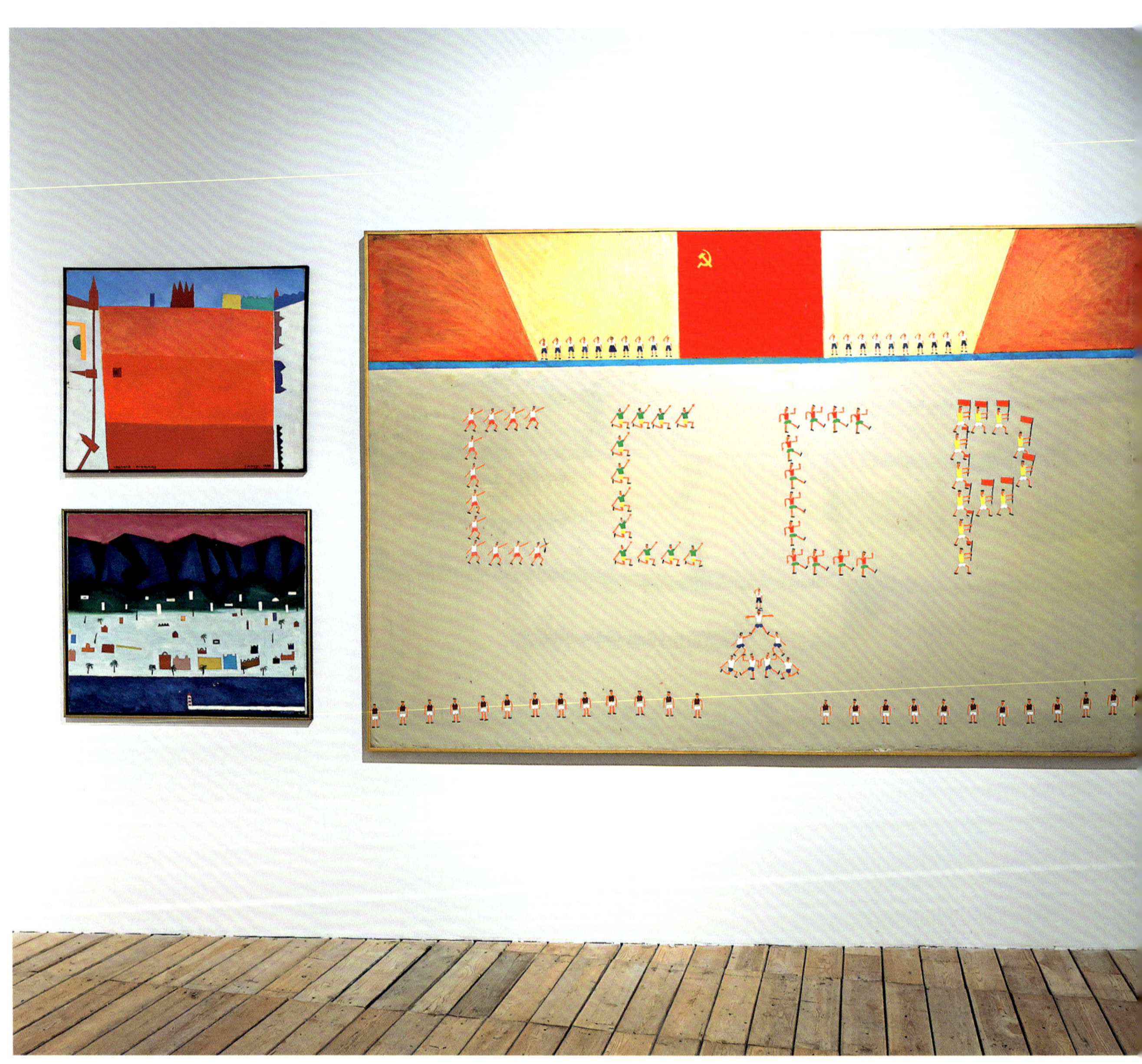

Timur Novikov

(1958, Leningrad, USSR, now Russia—2002, St. Petersburg, Russia)

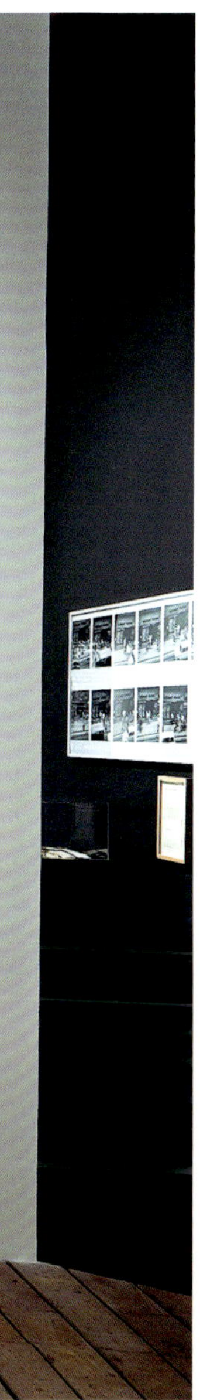

1

Red Square

1986

Oil on canvas, 80×100 cm

2

Yalta in Winter

1987

Oil on canvas, 80×100 cm

3

USSR

Mid-1980s

Oil on canvas, 202×308 cm

Vladimir Antonichuk Collection, Moscow

Timur Novikov is the best-known artist from the St. Petersburg (Leningrad) scene. In the early 1990s he became the leader of the New Artists group, which advocated the principles of the international New Wave movement—mixing various genres in an artwork, borrowing art languages of the past, and using images from pop culture. The New Artists regarded themselves as the inheritors of the idea of "everythingness," which was posited by the Russian futurists Mikhail Larionov and Ilya Zdanevich. Everythingness is the notion that the art of the past is an endless resource of different styles which can be used in the art of the present. In the mid-1980s Novikov turned his attention to the Russian avant-garde, interpreting its themes and techniques in a postmodern way. For example, Kazimir Malevich's spatial concepts can be seen in his textile works. Novikov called the works "horizons," the role of which was played by pieces of stitched fabric. Images of the sun and other entities were placed in the center of the fabric and were drawn or cut using a stencil. Novikov borrowed this stencil technique from another leader of the avant-garde, Vladimir Mayakovsky. In this way, pieces of cheap, universally recognizable cloth obtain a symbolic meaning and transform into landscapes depicting the sunrise. In Novikov's work the entry to a new dimension took place via a focus on the quotidian, through the use of everyday materials which seem to pull the viewer from the earth and allow their gaze to float above the infinite surrounding space.

3   The power of collaboration

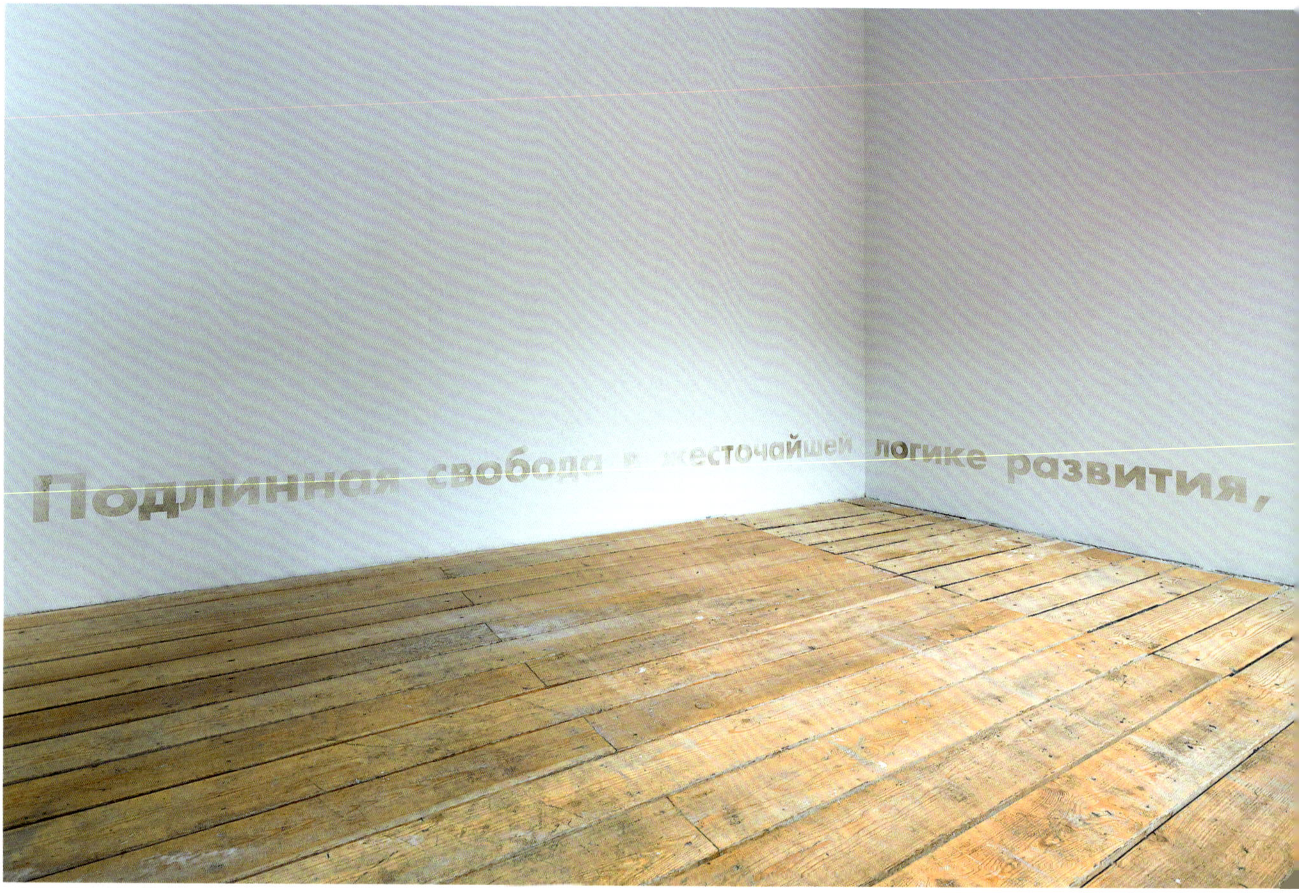

Подлинная свобода в жесточайшей логике развития,

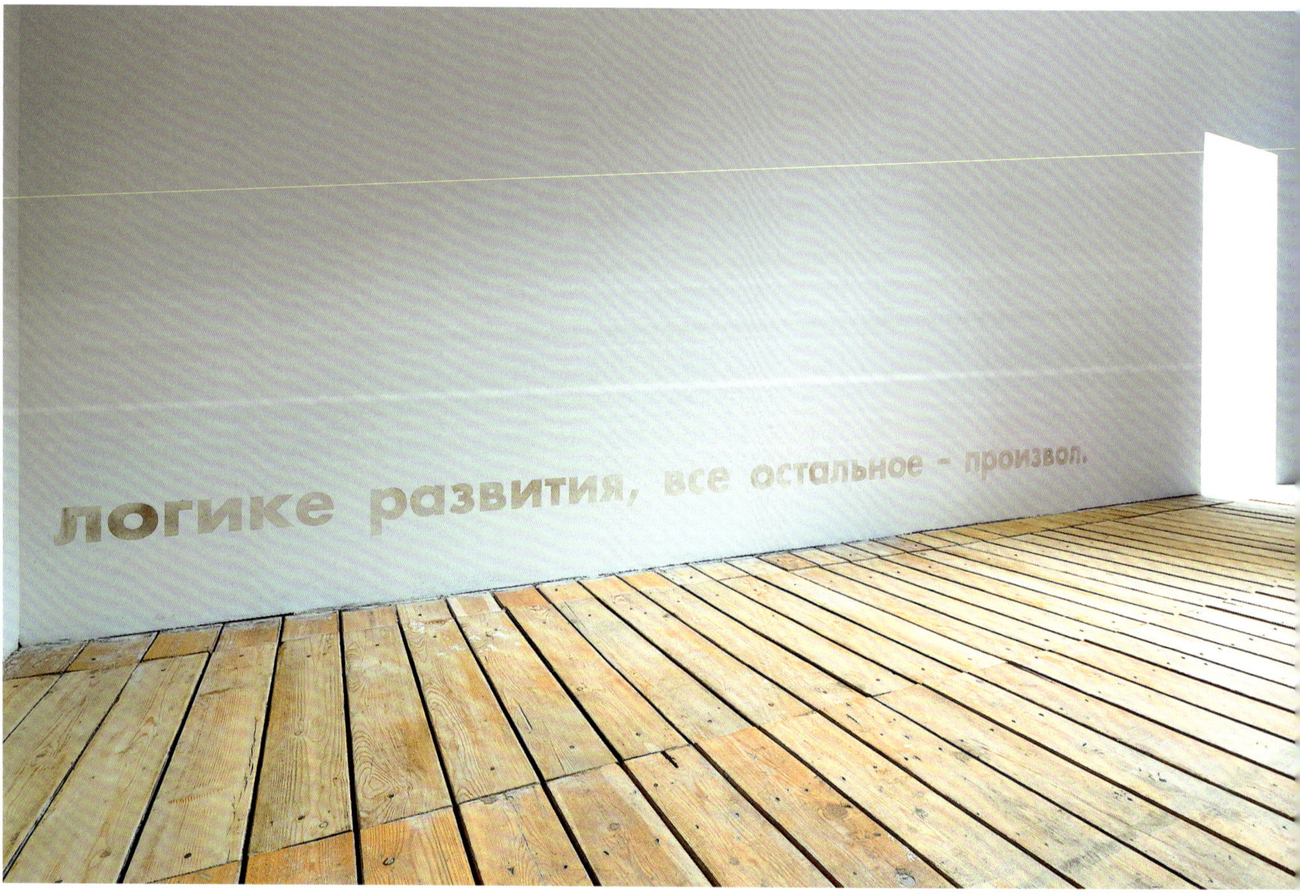

логике развития, все остальное - произвол.

Anatoly Osmolovsky

(b. 1969, Moscow, USSR, now Russia)

Dusty Thoughts
2015
Installation
Courtesy of the artist

Artist, theorist, and curator Anatoly Osmolovsky is a leading figure in Russian art. In the late 1980s and 1990s, he was among the progenitors of some of the most notable art groups (E. T. I. and Netsezyudik). In addition, Osmolovsky's many performances made him one of the most notable representatives of Moscow actionism, a 1990s movement characterized by the artists' provocative and transgressive interaction with the world. For the action *Netsezyudik's Journey to the Land of Brobdingnag* (1993), Osmolovsky rented a crane that hoisted him onto a statue of Vladimir Mayakovsky in central Moscow. The artist sat on the poet's shoulder and smoked a cigarette, after which the crane lowered him to the ground and the performance ended. Alongside the performance's artistic and poetic meanings, such as the notion of continuity with the Russian avant-garde, perceiving oneself as a dwarf on the shoulder of a giant, or the idea of finding a "place," a prominent location on a podium, it is important to remember the political and historical context. The action exposed the total disarray that reigned in the country in the early post-Soviet years, when anyone who so wished could enter a central square in the capital on a crane and then leave peacefully a little while later. Over time, Osmolovsky's work began to appear in museums more frequently. The *Dusty Thoughts* series is made of an unusual material—dust which the artist extracted from a vacuum cleaner. It was first shown in 2003 at Antwerp's M HKA museum. At that time, Osmolovsky was working intensively as a theorist and so, as he notes, it was important for him to use a text that he could stretch across several of the museum's rooms. He placed the phrases at the height of visitors' shins, as if to emphasize the effect of randomness, of the chance appearance of lines made of dust kicked up by visitors as they traversed the space. The slogans range from purely political statements to critical comments directed at the art system.

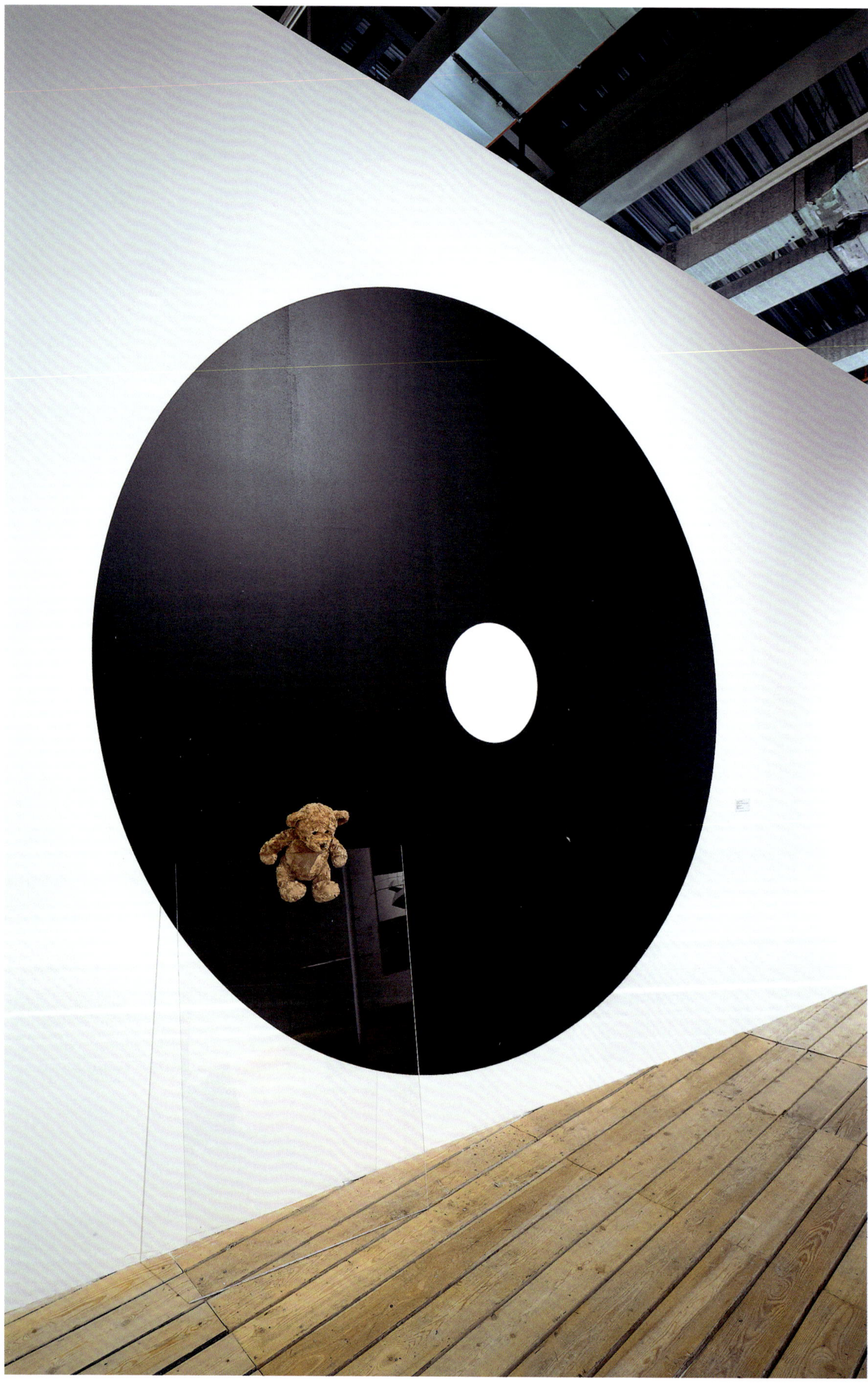

Dmitri Prigov

(1940, Moscow, USSR, now Russia—2007, Moscow, Russia)

Pulsing Black

1998

Installation

Courtesy Moderna galerija, Ljubljana

Dmitri Prigov, who is best known as a writer but acknowledged also as a poet, artist, and the author of performance events, is inseparable from Moscow Conceptualism, being one of its most prominent representatives. It is conceptualism's detached and analytical attitude towards language which allows Prigov to move freely from visual images to their linguistic expressions, since for him they are twinned aspects of a single work rather than distinct creative endeavors. His early works were in the thrall of conceptual objects, visual poetry, and performance events. His installations, usually a combination of a dramatic set and literary drama, appeared only at the end of the 1980s.

Pulsing Black is part of a collection of sketches of potential installations (only a small number of which were destined to materialize) from a large sequential project called *Metaphysics of the Russian Visual Space*. According to the artist, each element of this work bears a symbolic meaning: the colors (white, black, and red) are the basic colors of the Russian avant-garde and icon painting; the teddy bear replicated in different installations expresses tenderness, vulnerability, childhood, and paganism (totemic associations); the black circle is the minimal and contemplative image of metaphysical and transcendental phenomena; and the piece of glass with which the teddy bear is pressed to the circle symbolizes implacability, predestination, and providence. The entire ensemble can be construed as a profound metaphysical message, and at the same time as a staged image which reflects art's striving towards magic and quasi-religiosity.

3   The power of collaboration

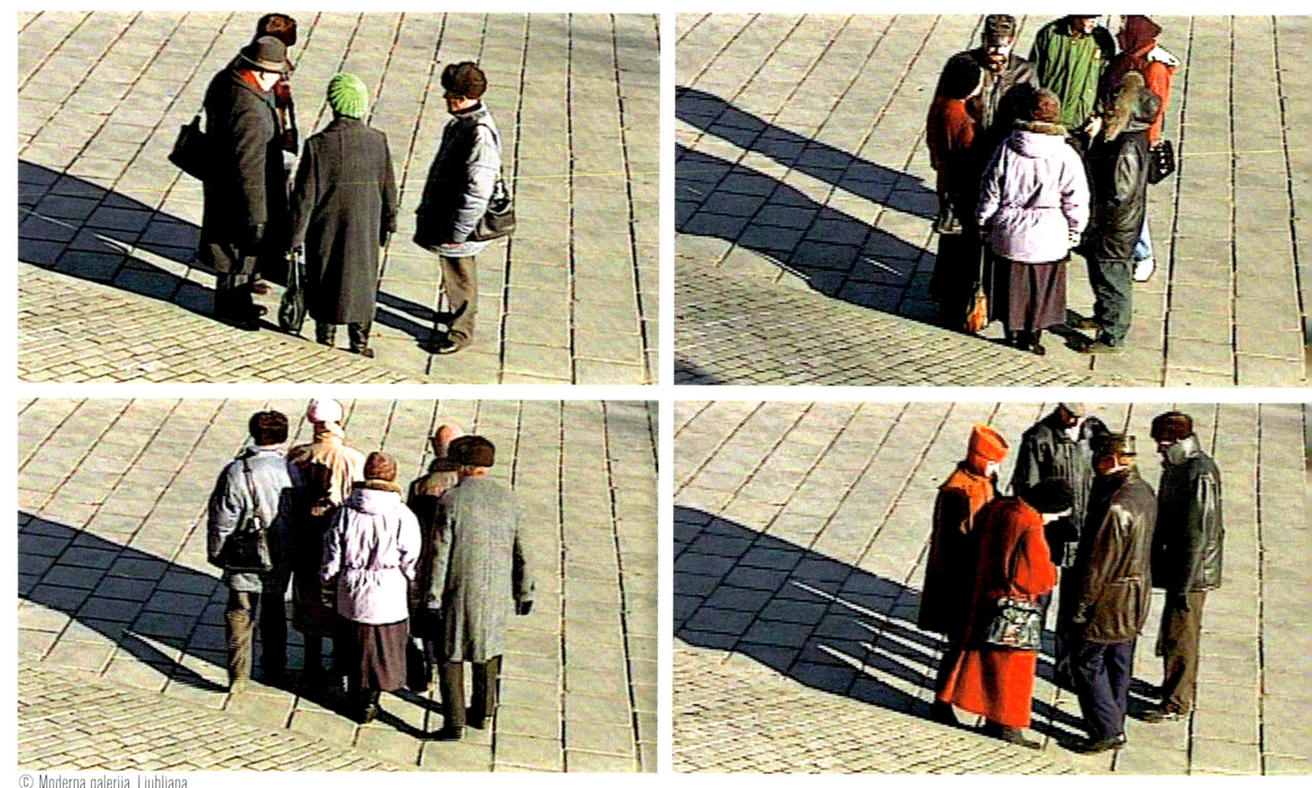

Guia Rigvava

(b.1957, Tbilisi, USSR, now Georgia)

This World Will Be
1995
5 color videos
Courtesy Moderna galerija, Ljubljana

The work of Guia Rigvava, who emerged on the Moscow art scene in 1987 and disappeared unexpectedly in 1996, typically involves the television industry. However, this should not be understood in the literal sense; Rigvava merely utilizes the logic and mechanisms of the media machine, turning society's attention to the danger and ambiguity of this phenomenon. More broadly, Rigvava can be described as one of the first artists in Russia to start working with new media and technologies. But in addition to using them for technological means, he also organically incorporated them into his artistic voice. His video performance *Original Statement* (1993) won him fame; on the screen he repeated one statement, "Don't believe them, they all lie." This curt but also pure gesture suggested a precise and prescient artistic intuition regarding the sociopolitical context of Russia in 1993. His work *You're Powerless, Or It's Not All So Bad* (1993) was also about the regime and the totality of the media. Rigvava created this work at Moscow Center for Contemporary Art, to which he invited a professional camera crew that reported live on the event. The signal was broadcast, however, only to screens inside the Center. In this way, Rigvava meant to expose, or deconstruct, the means by which consciousness is manipulated. To a large extent, *This World Will Be* continues the theme of criticizing the repressive machinery, though this time the artist changes perspective. Five screens show a simple story unfolding, and they all feature a robotic off-screen voice (the first allusion that comes to mind is, of course, Orwell's Big Brother) who, with a peremptory and authoritative tone, tells an anonymous crowd: "Go!" With time this phrase takes on a permissive intonation, and the voice, still ominous, says: "You can go!" And the people always go.

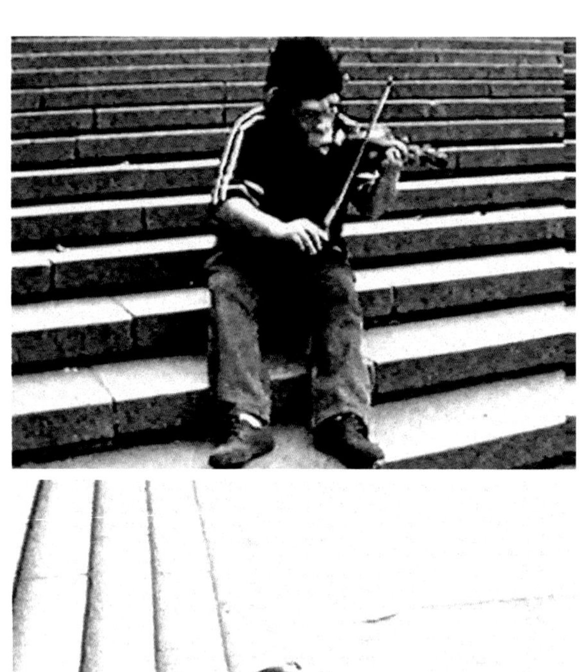

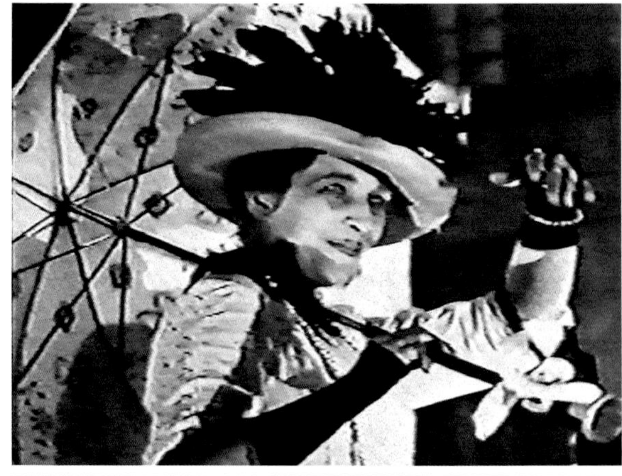

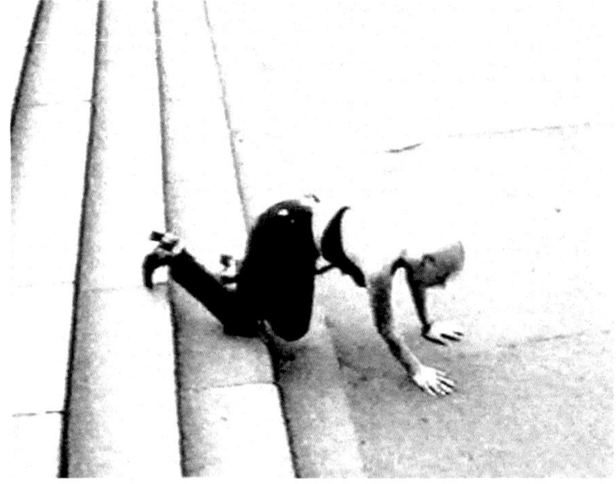

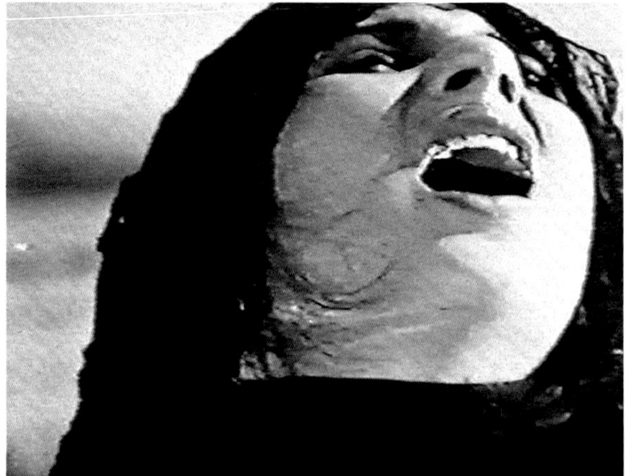

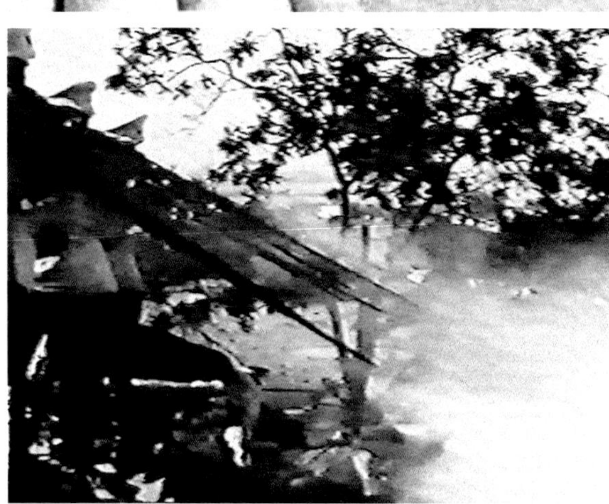

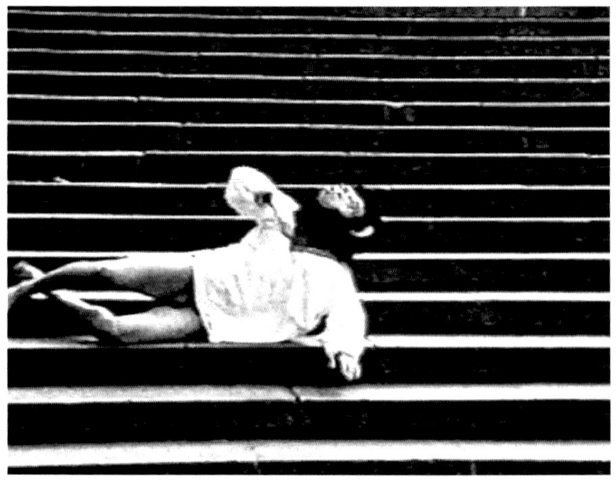

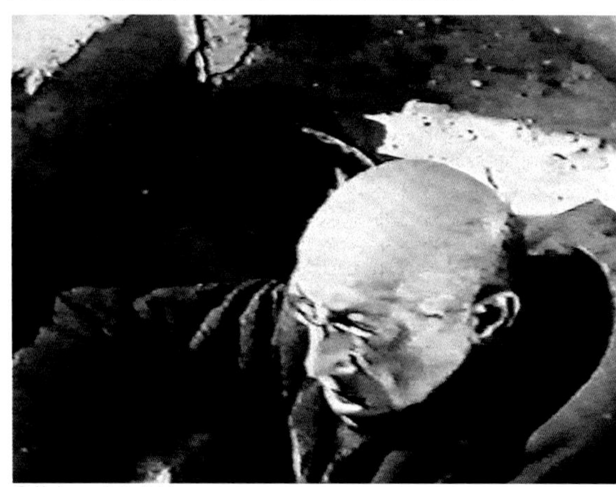

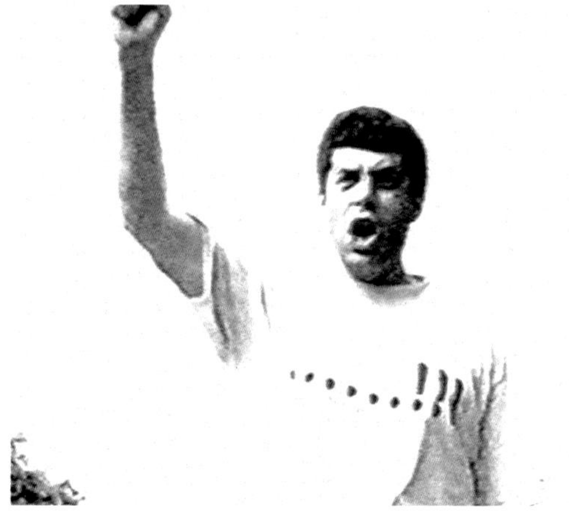

Alexander Roitburd

(b. 1961, Odessa, USSR, now Ukraine)

The Battleship Potemkin's Psychedelic Invasion
of Sergei Eisenstein's Tautological Hallucinosis
1998
B/w video, 54'14"
Courtesy Moderna galerija, Ljubljana

The Ukrainian art scene in the 1990s developed most quickly in the cities Kiev, Kharkov, and Odessa. If, at the beginning of the decade, the first two had the initiative, by its end critics noted an artistic boom in Odessa connected with the activities of two art institutions: the Tirs Contemporary Art Center and the New Art Association, of which Alexander Roitburd became the head. Roitburd can rightly be called the fulcrum of Ukrainian artistic life in that period. Working with various technologies and genres, he tried to sidestep attributing his art to any particular movement. He wisely noted that "postmodern is a temporal diagnosis," and therefore calling him a classic artist is as absurd as being, for instance, a "classic of the late-feudal era."

Roitburd's *The Battleship Potemkin's Psychedelic Invasion of Sergei Eisenstein's Tautological Hallucinosis* was selected by the legendary Harald Szeemann for the *Plateau of Mankind* main project at the 49th Venice Biennale. But it is notable not only for this reason. It is based on the epic *Battleship Potemkin* (1925) by Sergei Eisenstein who, with his film about the 1905 Revolution, fomented a revolution in the movie industry of his era. For Roitburd it was noteworthy that the famous director filmed part of the movie in Odessa and featured certain urban characters based on real people (the legless man on the stairs is the shoe shiner Uncle Vanya, famous throughout Odessa). Roitburd recut several fragments relating to his native city into a multilayered surrealist tale. Over the course of the film, shots from *Battleship* repeat and are often mixed with dramatizations filmed by Roitburd together with a group of artists from the Odessa scene of the 1990s. In this way, he brings together the past and present, the classic and the contemporary, creating an enormous, suggestive artwork.

3   The power of collaboration

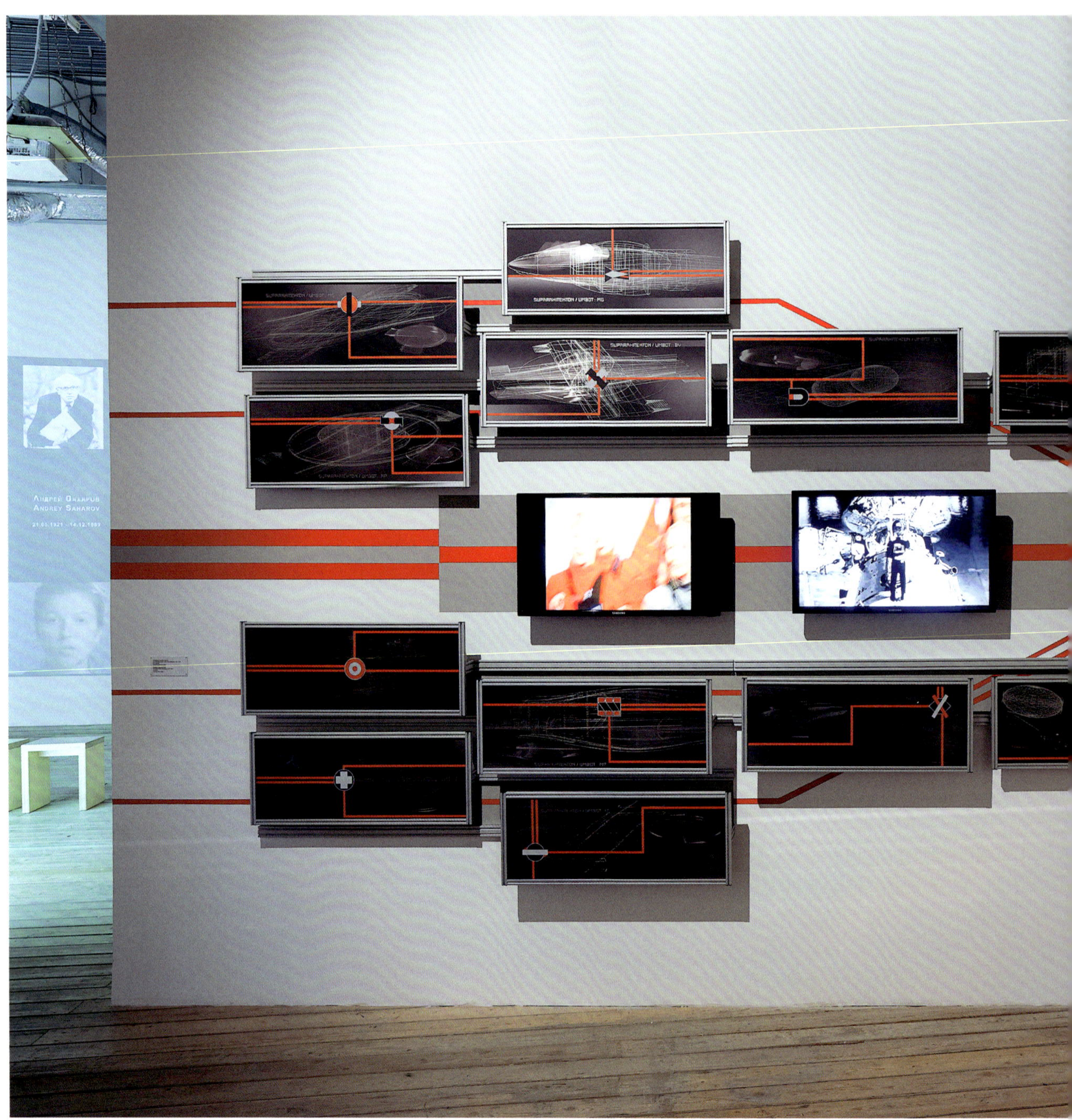

Živadinov::Zupančič::Turšič

(b. 1960, Ilirska Bistrica; b. 1963, Ljubljana; b. 1975, Ljubljana, all Yugoslavia, now Slovenia)

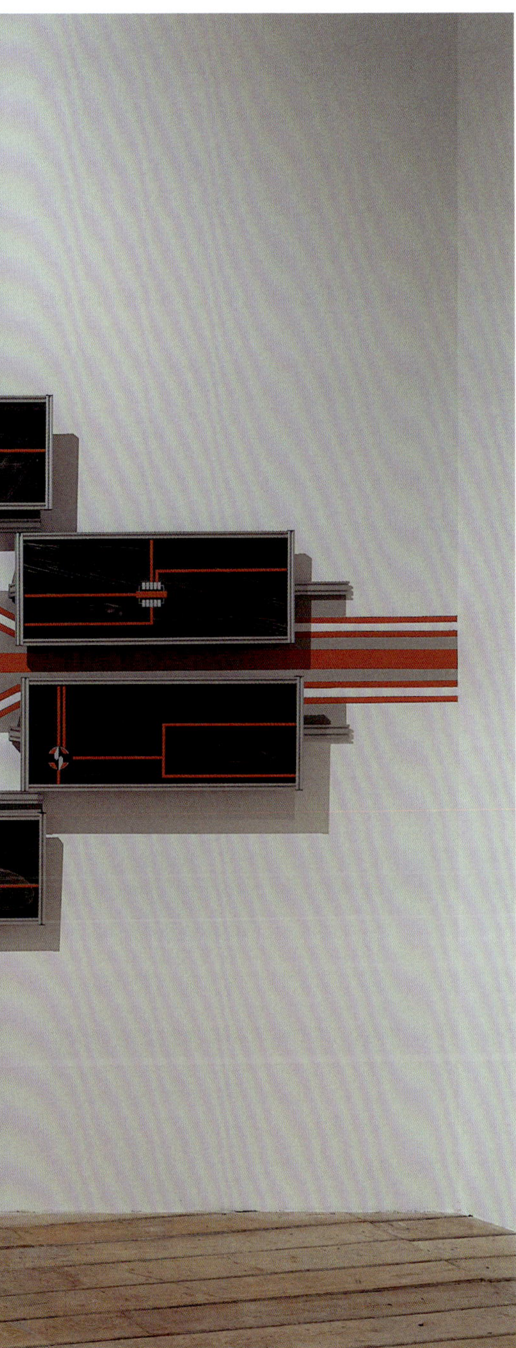

Postgravity Art: NOORDUNG

1995–2045
Installation
Courtesy of the artists

Theater director Dragan Živadinov, visual artist Dunja Zupančič, and designer of zero-gravity environments Miha Turšič are engaged in research into postgravity art. Postgravity art is, as Zupančič explains, an evolutionary art, ontologically conceptual and processual at its base, only possible in zero-gravity conditions where our sense of orientation is lost. The artists' practice aims at the culturalization of the cosmos, adding the cultural to the scientific, commercial, and military logic which controls space exploration and research. In their practice Živadinov::Zupančič::Turšič use high-technology tools and employ the logic of suprematism and constructivism in order to make cosmokinetic, blank-body directing and teleological, mechatronic machines, biomechatronics, and satellites-umbots.

Their 50-year theater project *Postgravity art: NOORDUNG* started in 1995 with a premiere featuring 14 actors. Five repeat performances are planned over the next 50 years. Should one of the actors die, he or she will be replaced by a remote-controlled sign; male actors and their speech will be substituted by rhythm, while female actors and their speech will be substituted by melody. The first repeat performance took place at 10pm on April 20, 2005 inside the model of the International Space Station (MSK-ISS) in the hydro-laboratory at Star City in Moscow. During the fifth and final performance, scheduled for April 20, 2045, Dragan Živadinov, a candidate cosmonaut of the Yuri Gagarin Cosmonauts' Training Center in Star City since 1988, will use a spacecraft to launch 14 satellites-umbots into geostatic orbit, from where they will transmit to Earth signals representing the roles played by deceased actors, while at the same time sending high-resolution 3D syntapiens (synthetic homo sapiens) projections of their faces into deep space.

Archive of various Arteast manifestations and collaborations between Moscow and Ljubljana

Arteast 2000+ Collection

Vadim Fiškin: One-Man Show, exhibition, Mala galerija Ljubljana, December 5, 1995–January 3, 1996

Living with Genocide, conference, Moderna galerija, Ljubljana, 1996

Body and the East: From the 1960s to the Present, travelling exhibition, 1998

7 Sins: Ljubljana—Moscow, exhibition, Moderna galerija, Ljubljana, December 20, 2004–February 2, 2005

Since the 1990s, Moderna galerija has been developing strategies to empower Eastern European art so that it could become a more equal partner in the international cultural space. The key to achieving this goal is the creation of the Arteast 2000+ Collection, which is bound to a specific time and space: in the context of radical geopolitical changes and processes of globalization it was designed as a tool to overcome the isolation of Eastern European art by establishing a dialogue with the Western art system, which continues to maintain its position of power despite the (supposed) dissolution of opposition between the center and the periphery. It is also important to develop the collection's concept as a tool to link and search for experiences and urgencies that can be labeled as "the South," which exceeds mere geopolitical designations.

The mission of the Arteast 2000+ Collection is to systematically collect and research works of Eastern European postwar avant-garde art from the 1960s onwards that were important yet overlooked in the past, and to compare them to corresponding Western trends and non-Western aesthetic concepts. Its numerous manifestations also enable this production to be more visible in the international context. But such mapping of the formerly unknown space that highlights "the art of the Other" and by doing so changes the dominant system, is in danger of stereotyping it in accordance with the image and interests of the one that places it into the spotlight. That is why processes of self-historicization, self-definition, establishment of one's own system of interpretation, and different models of cultural production are key to the practice of Moderna galerija. They allow for the creation of narratives that are parallel to the Western-centric art discourse while giving Eastern European art the role of an active participant in the processes of redefining European history of the 20th century.

Since the 1990s, Moderna galerija and its colleagues initiated several projects in which they acted as subjects (rather than objects) in both defining the identity of local artistic practices and its contextualization in the broader Eastern European situation. The first such project was the exhibition *Body and the East* (1998), which focused on the body as a link with the real and introduced over 80 artists from former socialist countries. Its purpose was to make the international audience aware of the then still relatively unknown postwar art of Eastern Europe and to detect the differences in formation and perception that mark the specificity of Eastern European art. By doing so, it also represented the starting point in concretizing the mission of the Arteast 2000+ Collection, first made available to the public in 2000 through the exhibition *Art of Eastern Europe in Dialogue with the West* (*Umetnost Vzhodne Evrope v dialogu z Zahodom*).

The Arteast 2000+ Collection and its manifestations also play a key role in communications with the wider Eastern European and other international spaces (e.g. Latin America) that to this day are joined and connected by common urgencies and similar conditions of production, musealization, historicization, and distribution. The history of cooperation between Moscow and Ljubljana dates back to the 1992, when the IRWIN group set up an embassy in Moscow for its NSK State, followed by the exhibition *7 Sins: Ljubljana—Moscow* (2004), curated by Zdenka Badovinac, Igor Zabel, and Viktor Misiano, which focused precisely on different dimensions of the links between the two cities. The exhibition tried to emphasize the continuity of cooperation and the interest in similar aesthetic concepts. Even though both cities and cultures fall under the common post-socialist context of the so-called "Eastern European culture" and even though they are joined by similar conditions of production, we must not forget their differences: in the context of European socialist states, the Soviet Union, with its political and economic system of "real socialism" and the model of ideology-controlled and functional cultural production, and the Socialist Federal Republic of Yugoslavia (which comprised Slovenia as well), with its model of self-management and, from the cultural point of view, orientation towards the West, represented two extremes in the political and cultural sense. That is why the focus of the exhibition was not to show an objective history, but to delineate it through numerous narratives, related to the problems of identity, difference, and transformation. The exhibition reacted to the prevalent political correctness in the discourse about the Other and comprised seven chapters that focused on seven Eastern European characteristics which can

[...] Sins: [L]jubljana-[M]oscow [A]rteast [E]xhibition

Coca-Cola
This is my bloo[d]

Kosolapov: This is my blood

[M]useum of Modern Art (Moderna Galerija Ljubljana) set the goal to present the contemporary art of Eastern [Europ]e, which has been until recently hidden from the [Weste]rn public due to historical reasons, as thoroughly as [possib]le with its programme Arteast.

[On thi]s occasion the curators Igor Zabel, Zdenka Badovinac [and V]iktor Misiano wanted to show how and why the [conte]mporary art of Eastern Europe (from approximately [the six]ties to the present day) was and still is different from [the a]rt of the West. The curators have defined these [chara]cteristics as "sins" that prevented the art of Eastern [Europ]e from entering the paradise of Western art. These [sins] are not art styles or movements, they are artists' [reacti]ons and adaptations to the society they lived in.

beyond the Iron Curtain, and b[oth of them got rid of] communism. But Slovenia was c[loser and more open to] Western Europe and hence mo[re eager to accept its] influences, so the similar prob[lems were reflected in] different ways.

The seven sins of Eastern Euro[pean art that the artist] **Constantin Zvezdochetov** pre[sented so well in his] "Apotheosis", made especially [for this exhibition, are:] Collectivism, Utopianism, Masoch[ism, Cynicism, Laziness,] Unprofessionalism, and Love of th[e West.]

But when we inspect these "sins" f[rom a closer point of view,] we realize these "sins" are a[ctually "virtues", which] contribute to the diversity of the [European culture. And we] should be proud of them. This [exhibition is certainly a] wittiful answer to the question: "W[hat is Eastern European] culture?"

Nika Špan: State of air

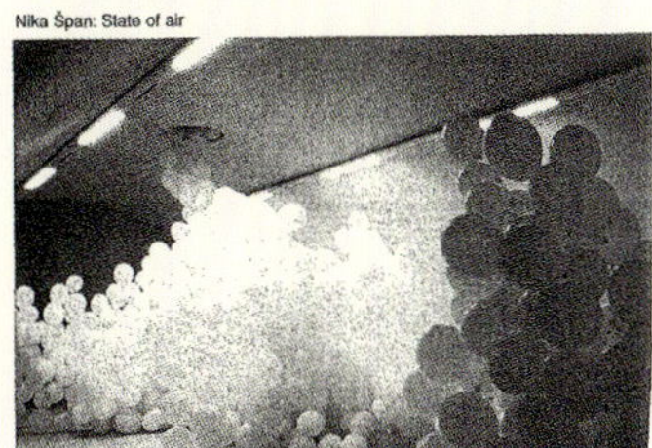

Politično uglajene diskusije o novi Evropi

DELO, 26.6.2000 / leto XLII, št. 146, / str. 5

Pogovora o sodobni vizualni umetnosti in predstavitve spletnih strani in knjig
Otvoritev novih prostorov Moderne galerije in zbirke Arteast 2000+ na Metelkovi

Diskusiji v programu Manifeste 3 na petkovem srečanju mednarodnega združenja umetnostnih kritikov Aica in sobotnem opoldanskem pogovoru s kuratorji Manifeste 3 sta bili zastavljeni kot uglajeno, politično korektno razglabljanje o prepoznavanju evropskih meja in njihovem preseganju skozi umetnost in kulturo.

Po dobri uri se je diskusija na srečanju združenja Aica, ki jo je frazeološko in anekdotično moderiral Branislav Dimitrijević iz beograjskega Centra za sodobne umetnosti, še vedno vrtela okoli vljudnostnih fraz in prigod. A tudi pozneje se je ob temi *Neprevedljive razdalje* pokazalo, da je med drugim težava v prevajanju razdalj, ki naj bi po trditvi Christiana Chamberta, podpredsednika Aice, »izginjalo, saj lahko virtualno obiščemo veliko krajev«, v mešanju različnih ravni diskurzov – od teoretskih artikulacij razlike med Vzhodom in Zahodom Marine Gržinić do splošnih mnenj in prigod, ki jih piše življenje. Pokazalo se je, da je zastavljena tema ideološki zastavek, ki je bil ključno gonilo tudi dan pozneje na pogovoru s kuratorji. Tega se ni udeležil celoten štiričlanski kuratorij, ampak le Francesco Bonami in Ole Bouman, in šele na intervencijo občinstva se je prikazala Mária Hlavajová, ena od kuratork, s čimer se je pokazala utrujenost kuratorija ne le zaradi končnih priprav, ampak tudi medsebojnih nesoglasij.

Niti v petek niti v soboto pa se udeleženci niso lotili oziroma so se občasno zgolj dotaknili ključnih meja, ki so tako v strukturiranosti te prireditve kot tudi v načinu organizacije in ki jih še zdaleč ni mogoče enostavno preskočiti, kakor je to v soboto izjavila Hlavajová. In teh meja je nemalo: najprej razlika v pripravi Manifeste v zahodnoevropskih državah in drugih evropskih državah, tokrat v Sloveniji, ki kot nečlanica EU ni mogla neposredno zaprositi za sredstva kulturnih programov EU in Sveta Evrope. Potem je tu razlika med organizacijskimi modeli na Zahodu in Vzhodu, kjer je infrastruktura skrajno pomanjkljiva, pa dejstvo, da umetniki in obiskovalci iz velike vzhodnoevropskih držav za vstop v Slovenijo potrebujejo vizume oziroma uradna povabila, in da je denimo za Romune, kjer je povprečna plača 150 dolarjev na mesec, obisk ljubljanske Manifeste neprimerno večji finančni podvig kakor za obiskovalce iz Belgije. Z izjemo redkih posegov občinstva sta bili diskusiji naravnani na to, da umetnost in kulturo utrdita kot platformo za detekcijo ran na fantazmatskem telesu Evrope, in hkrati pokažeta na njuno zmožnost te rane zaceliti. To je bil tudi razlog, da kuratorji niti v petek niti v soboto niso hoteli komentirati intervencije Alexandra Brenerja na četrtkovi tiskovni konferenci, ko je Manifesto označil za »eno od prireditev, kjer je selekcija umetnikov diktirana s korupcijskimi interesi kuratorjev, trgovcev in birokratov, medtem ko ostajajo informacije o dogajanju v številnih državah po svetu«.

Da se bo pomote: na petkovi otvoritvi Manifeste 3 v Mednarodnem grafičnem likovnem centru je – po govorih zdajšnjega ministra za kulturo Rudija Šeliga in nekdanjega ministra in predsednika nacionalnega komiteja Manifeste 3 Jožeta Školča – predsednik mednarodnega odbora Manifeste Henry Meyrick Hughes poudaril, da na prireditvi sodeluje 59 in ne 60 umetnikov. Alexander Brener, ki bo moral po petkovi obravnavi na sodišču za uničeno platno poravnati škodo v višini 7000 mark, nikakor ni vključen v izbor sodelujočih umetnikov Manifeste 3.

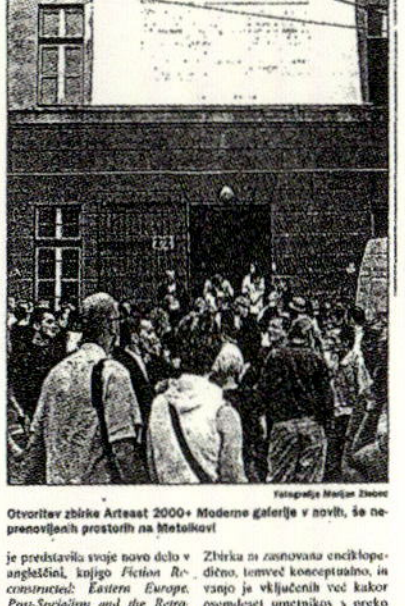

2000+
ARTEAST COLLECTION

Otvoritev zbirke Arteast 2000+ Moderne galerije v novih, še neprenovljenih prostorih na Metelkovi

Predstavitve knjig

V soboto popoldne je International Contemporary Arts Network Association (ali okrajšano i_can) v Cankarjevem domu predstavila dostop do spletnih strani umetnikov, umetniških projektov, muzejev, galerij in elektronskih časopisov iz Vzhodne in Srednje Evrope. i_can je odprta mednarodna mreža oz. platforma za medkulturno izmenjavo [...] je predstavila svoje novo delo v angleščini, knjigo *Fiction Reconstructed: Eastern Europe, Post-Socialism and the Retro-Avant-Garde*, sintezo avtoričinega petnajstletnega dela na področju teorije umetnosti; v njej se izpisuje nova zgodba postsocialistične umetnosti in medijskih strategij. Delo je izšlo pri založbi Edition selene na Duna[ju].

Prva zbirka sodobne vzhodnoevropske umetnosti

Osrednji sobotni dogodek je bila zagotovo otvoritev zbirke Arteast 2000+ v novih muzejskih prostorih Moderne galerije na Metelkovi [...]

Zbirka ni zasnovana enciklopedično, temveč konceptualno, in vanjo je vključenih več kakor osemdeset umetnikov s preko dvestodesetimi deli. Ustanovitelji zbirke so ministrstvo za kulturo, MO Ljubljana, podjetja Pristop, Pro Plus in Mobitel, pri njenem nastajanju pa sodelujejo tudi številni meceni, pokrovitelji in podporniki. [...]

Mojca Kumerdej
Blaž Lukan

Prizor iz videoinstalacije Milice Tomić, 1998, v zbirki Arteast 2000+

Drive-in Camillo v režiji **Emila Hrvatina** je predstava, ki jo opazujemo iz avtomobilov. Sicer lahko tudi stopimo iz vozila in gledamo ter poslušamo predstavo »v živo«, vendar je bil režiserjev namen izolacija gledalcev v njihovih gledalnih komorah, kjer vetrobransko steklo deluje kot rampa med gledalnim in igralnim prostorom, radijski prenos zvočnega dogajanja pa igra vlogo vmesnika. Dejanje se na ta način odmakne od gledalca (ki je morda zaposlen še z dogajanjem v avtomobilu) in se prebije samo do njegove oddaljene površine. Ta je – skupaj z glasbeno spremljavo – emocionalno hladna, linearna in ploskovita, čeprav sestavljena v čvrsto večdelno strukturo. Plesalci na platoju, pritisnjenem ob tla monumentalnega trga za Ravnikarjevimi »ljubljanskimi vrati«, so pravzaprav šibko integrirali v okolje, njihovo gibanje je minimalistično, čeprav bi dimenzije prostora zahtevale »velike« geste, kakršne je denimo poznalo sovjetsko postrevolucijsko gledališče. Dogajanje na trgu je z njim kratko malo v neravnovesju, gledalčev pogled pa sega nekam čez glave plesalcev (obrazov ne vidi, razen če ima avto parkiran v prvih dveh, treh vrstah), v lapanje med obema stolpnicama. Najvišja točka predstave je prizor v pajkovi mreži, ki pa deluje zgolj dekorativno, saj plezalec v njej ne počne drugega, kot da mrežo potresa. Najnižja točka pa je njen govorni del z afektirano, pootročeno in tehnično nezadostno interpretacijo replik na temo: kaj bi bilo, če bi ... Vse filozofske oziroma fenomenološke evokacije spomina, Camilla in še česa se v predstavi nepovratno izgubijo v premoči ambienta, morebitna interaktivnost med dogajanjem na odru in predvajanim plesom na ozadju pa je onemogočena zaradi slabih projekcij in nerazberljivih besedil. *Drive-in Camillo* je anti-spektakel, ki se iz mnogopomenskega historičnega križišča, v katero je postavljen, iztika in navezuje zgolj nase in na svojo konceptualistično naravo; skratka: predstava o spominu, ki ne pušča spominov. *B. L.*

* * *

Nekdanji član skupine Laibach, lastnik nekaj zanimivih eksperimentalnih skupin (Data Error in druge), levoroki kitarist in skladatelj odrske glasbe **Borut Križišnik**, piše zanimivo odrsko glasbo še posebno takrat, kadar svoje ustvarjanje moči združi z Emilom Hrvatinom. Za *Drive-in Camillo* je napisal 11-stavčno partituro, v kateri je svojo postmoderno govorico dodatno izpopolnil, pri tem pa z brijanino inteligenco pometal vzorce klasične simfonične in godalne komorne glasbe s sintetiziranimi digitalnimi zvoki in mehanskimi, monotonimi ritmičnimi obrazci. Poigrava se z modaliteto in ostinatnim igranjem godalnih sekcij ali nežnim solističnim igranjem godal v stavkih, v katerih še vedno prevladujejo elektronika oziroma skoraj punkerski rifi, kar je idealna zvočna podlaga za pripoved o renesančnem geniju Camillu. *Ognjen Tvrtković*

Coca-Cola
IT'S THE REAL THING
Lenin

Akril na platnu Aleksandra Kosolapova Lenin-Coca-Cola, 1980, delo iz nove zbirke Arteast 2000+

DELO 26.6.2000, št. 146, str. 5

THE ART OF EASTERN EUROPE
A Selection of Works for the International and National Collections of Moderna galerija Ljubljana

2000+
ARTEAST COLLECTION

2000+ – 1. kar sega v tretje tisočletje, tudi tretje tisočletje; preneseno: nekaj, kar je odprto in usmerjeno v prihodnost; 2. v ožjem pomenu zbirka sodobne mednarodne umetnosti Moderne galerije v ljubljani kolektiv – zbirka, zlasti umetniška arteast – premik v perspektivi pri oblikovanju zbirke 2000+ (gl.), upoštevanje umetnosti z vseh strani neba, vendar s posebnim poudarkom na delih iz Vzhodne Evropa 2000+ – 1. reaching into the third thousand, also the third millennium; metaphorically, something open and oriented towards the future; 2. in a narrow sense, a collection of modern international art at the Museum of Modern Art in Ljubljana collection – a set of artistic works arteast – a movement in perspective used when assembling the 2000+ art collection – taking the art of all countries into consideration but with emphasis on the countries of Eastern Europe

Orangerie Congress – Innsbruck   *Exhibition Curators* Zdenka Badovinac / Peter Weibel

---

BODY AND THE EAST
MUSEUM OF MODERN ART, LJUBLJANA

"Body and the East," no doubt a provocative topic for the New Europe which tries to put everything together without any distinctions, or rather, to quickly pass over the specific history of modern art under Communism or Socialism in Europe.

"Body and the East," no doubt an appealing title. But as far as we take a serious and friendly look at the exhibition, it shows clearly that it is not as much about the body, nor about history (as it is possible perhaps to judge from the subtitle of the project: "from the 1960s to the present"), as it is about displaying or recollecting the documentation of projects dealing with performance or body art in the East in one gallery space. The exhibition, for the most part, is comprised of photographs (mostly documentary photographs), of few (real) works; also of some pages from catalogues, and, last but not least, video and video documentation. The juxtaposition between the photos is too simple, a rigorous conceptual approach is lacking, and hence, in most cases, we encounter the mere decoration of facts and stories. The result is a documentary index (or, better to say, just a Xerox) of the recognition of the brutal power of the body in the East.

In one of the numerous reviews of the exhibition published in Slovenia and Croatia, in one of the local newspapers of Maribor (100 km from Ljubljana, the capital), I found a statement precisely describing and critiquing the project: "Body and the East — Body Fast." This is the principal problem with the exhibition, after all: it is too much fast food to be tasty enough. Although if we are hungry, and we do not want to risk total starvation, fast food is still better and less dangerous than, metaphorically speaking, that which is truly impregnated with blood and mud: that which is possible to read and perceive in the backgrounds of the works, implying civic discourse, ideology, and a strong concept.

Questions such as: What is hidden behind a fusion of body and the East? Will the addition of the (word? paradigm? password?) "body" — give the East a possibility for new content and challenges? These queries are yet to be answered.

But if we deal, nevertheless, simply with documentation of body art in Eastern Europe, as is the case in this exhibition, then why are these materials not given a real position, or better to say, the position of the traumatic Real of documentation? The body in the East, as is shown in one of the best works of the exhibition, by Polish artist Katarzyna Kozira, was always brutal, cruel — not sterilized and ornamental.

What we need today, as we approach 2000, is not only to assemble together names and papers, but an interpretation of facts and periods, names and struggles. Above all we need their detailed historical, political, and aesthetical articulation in the exhibition. The body in the New Europe of McDonald's easy-going with differences, is to try to establish Eastern Europe and the body as an archaeological discovery.

In short, we have got an abundant catalogue with precious international texts, a symposium, interesting opening and closing performances, and a solid documentary (pre)face to the topic: Let us go now to find the identity of this face and as well that of Eastern Europe.
(Marina Gržinić)
(Translated from Slovene by Adele Eisenstein)

ARTPROSPECT P.O.P., Daring, 1981.

JANUARY FEBRUARY 1999 Flash Art 59

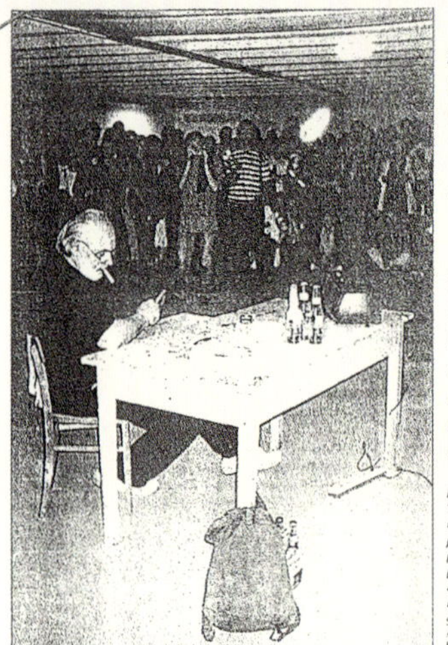

Intrigantne poruke tijela

Izložba "Tijelo i Istok" zaokružena je do kraja. Osim što je dala primjer, potaknula je i raspravu zbivanja koja joj produljuju trajanje izvan samog postava

Izložbom *Body and the East/Tijelo i Istok* ljubljanska je Moderna galerija otvorila novo poglavlje predstavljanja umjetnosti istočne Europe. Izložba obuhvaća pregled rada najznačajnijih umjetnika od šezdesetih godina do danas. Većina od 77 autora predstavlja samu povijest suvremene umjetnosti u istočnim zemljama te stalnu prisutnost na internacionalnoj sceni.

Tu međunarodnu izložbu koncipirala je ljubljanska povjesničarka umjetnosti i direktorica Moderne galerije Zdenka Badovinac. Ono što izdvaja "Tijelo i Istok" od izložbi sličnih tematika nakon pada Berlinskog zida je samosvijest konteksta i kontinuiteta istočnoeuropske produkcije. Izložba s temom body arta, umjetnika koji su u svom radu koristili tijelo kao oblik performansa, akcije ili načina govora, postavlja nove kanone kojima se Istok prvi put osobno predstavlja rekonstrukcijom vlastite povijesti i naslijeda.

Napuštajući stanje objekta, umjetnici istočne Europe primjerom slovenske izložbe grade svoje kriterije prepoznavanja, prestaju biti izdvojeni fenomeni u definiranju umjetnosti 20. stoljeća. Da su granice izmedu Zapada i Istoka još uvijek osjetne, može se naslutiti iz pomalo jednosmjernog dijaloga u kojem se umjetnost zemalja bivšeg Istoka

svodi na slučajnost pojedinca. Smjernice i problematike dekada još se uvijek bilježe iz pozicija zapadne umjetnosti, čiju zaokruženosti i djelotvornosti pridonosi tržišni sustav umjetnosti.

Gotovčeva ideja paranoje

Na ljubljanskoj izložbi koja je otvorena od 7. srpnja do 27. rujna '98. na uvidu je intrigantna povijest istočnih zemalja, koje su to ime naslijedile više političkom nego kulturno-socijalnom određenosti. Tako svoje predstavnike body arta imaju Bugarska, Rumunjska, Slovačka, Slovenija, Mađarska, Njemačka, Poljska, Jugoslavija, Moldavija, Bosna i Hercegovina, Češka, Hrvatska, Litva i Rusija.

Iz Hrvatske na izložbi su videoradovi i dokumentacija Sanje Iveković, Dalibora Martinisa, Tomislava Gotovca, Vlaste Delimar, Slavena Tolja, Božidara Jurjevića i Nenada Dančua. Za vrijeme trajanja izložbe prikazuje se i recentna slajd projekcija Aleksandra Ilića "Weekend Art - Hallelujah the Hill", nastala u protekle tri godine. Samo otvorenje izložbe bilo je obilježeno performancom "Bez naziva (No drugs, no death)" Tomislava Gotovca, rijetkim umjetnikom duge kontinuirane, radikalne, umjetničke prakse tijela kao medija. Gotovac je na ovom otvorenju u desetak minuta ispunio prostor prisutne medunarodne publike svojim performance, slijedeći svoju ideju paranoje kao nezaobilazne činjenice u režiranju i uspostavljanju svjetskog poretka. Spektar ovisnosti, bluza, alkohola, dima, šećera i opisati na umjetnikovu stolu, u dvoboj, a zatim u agoniji konzumirana, metaforički je potkrijepio Gotovčevu parafrazu lošeg zdravlja kao posljedice dobrog života.

Statistika bez sistematike

Rječitosti same izložbe iste je večeri pridonio sarajevski performer Jusuf Hazitejzović, koji živi i radi u Belgiji. Izložbu "Tijelo i Istok" zanimljiva je to više što je osim

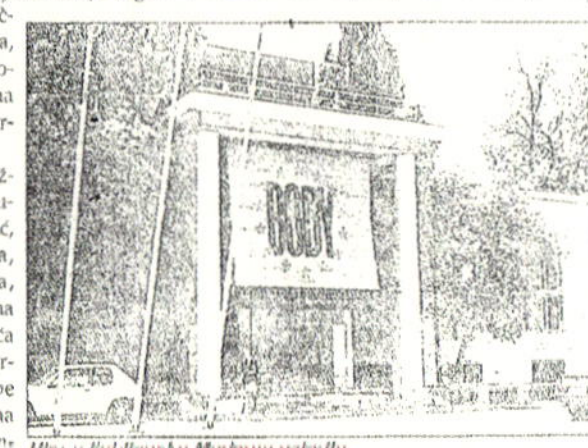
Ulaz u ljubljansku Modernu galeriju

ZBIRKA, KI P...
HUMANITA...

Pretekli petek je bila v Sarajevu svečana otvoritev mednarodne zbirke Muzeja sodobne umetnosti ARS AEVI, katere del je prispevala tudi Moderna galerija Ljubljana.

Leta 1996 je bil v Moderni galeriji predstavljen projekt z naslovom Moderna galerija Ljubljana za muzej sodobne umetnosti Sarajevo 2000.

Sodelujoči umetniki so s posredovanjem Moderne galerije podarili bodoči stalni zbirki Muzeja sodobne umetnosti v Sarajevu svoja dela, to so bili: *Marina Abramovič, Miroslaw Balka, Günter Brus, Sophie Calle, Richard Deacon, Irwin in Bogoslav Kalaš, Anish Kapoor, Marjetica Potrč, "Reason in something the World Must Obtain, Whether it Wants to or Not..." (Evgenij As, Vladim Fiškin, Dimitrij Gutov, Viktor Misiano), Thomas Schütte, Andres Serrano, Bill Viola, V.S.S.D.*

Zbirka Moderne galerije predstavlja segment celotne zbirke in je tudi posebej označena. Ob tej priložnosti je bila v nedeljo 27. junija konferenca z naslovom *The future museum/the museum of the future* in okrogla miza, ki jo je organizirala AICA - mednarodno združenje umetnostnih kritikov, ki je razpravljala o vlogi umetnosti in kritike med vojno in v miru; na

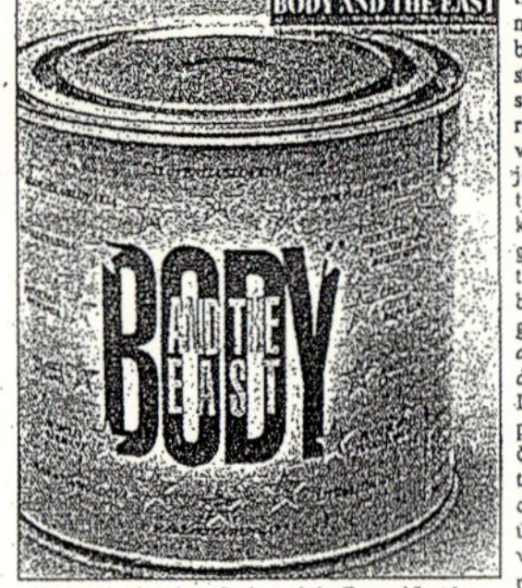

Naslovnica kataloga Body and the East od šestdesetih let do danes/From the 1960s to the Present.

rîjej je sodelovale iz Moderne galerije Ljubljana *Igor Zabel.*

Kratka zgodovina nastale Zbirke 1996

Med trajanjem vojne v Bosni so se v Moderni galeriji ves čas spraševali, kako bi se lahko odzvali na [...]

di s strani nekaterih m... umetnikov, s katerim... galerija sodeljuje nekaj... saj so se ti spraševali k... gati Sarajevu in Bosni... ku jim je bilo jasno, da...

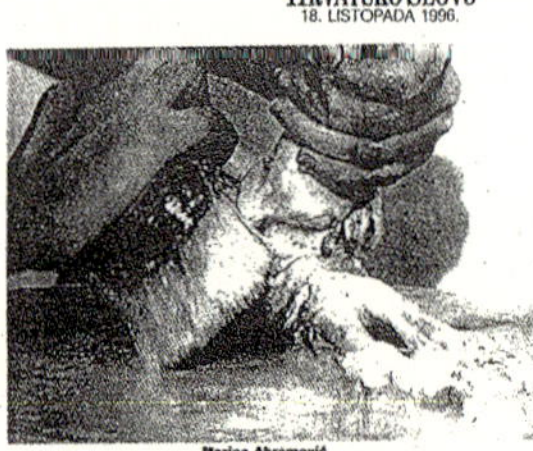
Marina Abramović

ČIŠĆENJE KOSTURA ZA SARAJEVO

Izložba »Zbirka 1996 — Moderna galerija Ljubljana« u sklopu Međunarodnoga kulturnog projekta »Muzej suvremene umjetnosti Sarajevo 2000«

Günther Brus

Marjetica Potrč

Ivica ŽUPAN

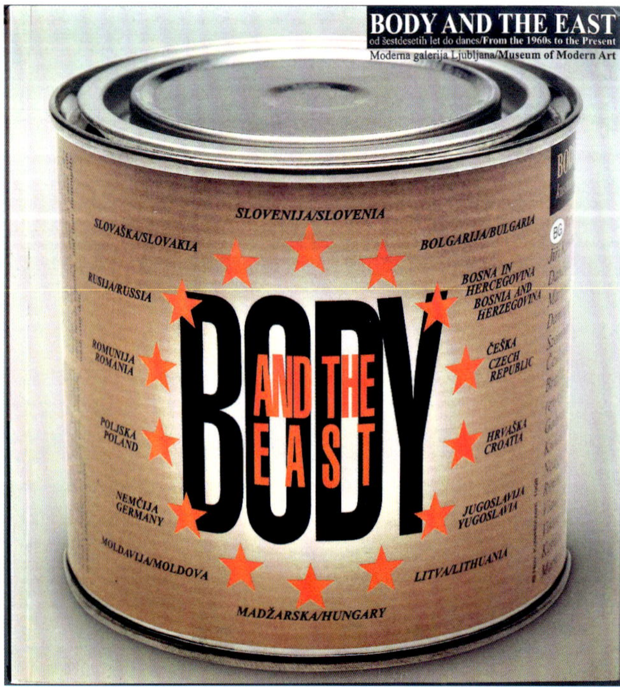

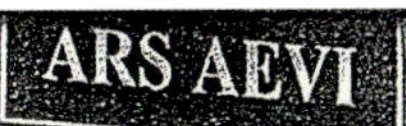

be—from an outside, presumably Western point of view—understood as weaknesses and imperfections, as "sins." Yet in the context of the exhibition, cynicism, collectivism, masochism, unprofessionalism, love of the West, laziness, and utopianism were presented as virtues, shared positive experiences that could also prove beneficial for improving the Western way of life.

When it comes to linking Ljubljana and Moscow and their collaboration, one of the key actors is Viktor Misiano. He set up the exhibition *One-Man Show* featuring the Russian artist Vadim Fishkin in 1995 in Ljubljana, he was a consultant for the Arteast 2000+ Collection and a participant in its later manifestations, and he also participated in the symposium *Living With Genocide*, organized by Moderna galerija in 1996 to encourage reflection on the questions and dilemmas that arise when art and the art system face the reality of war. The symposium took place two years after the establishment of the *Museum for Sarajevo* (*Muzej za Sarajevo*) project, the goal of which was to create an important international art collection and donate it for a future museum of contemporary art in Sarajevo. Twelve artists from different countries, as well as the artists featured in the exhibition…*Reason is Something the World Must Obtain, Whether it Wants To or Not…*, which Misiano curated for the Russian Pavilion at the Venice Biennale in 1995, contributed their works. The project *Museum for Sarajevo*, initiated and carried out by Moderna galerija in cooperation with artists from Ljubljana (especially IRWIN and Jadran Adamović) and the Sarajevo cultural scene, represents an attempt to transcend the declarative condemnations of war and tries to use an art collection—as symbolic and real capital—as a tool to confer economic and cultural power, to make a concrete intervention into the cultural and socio–political reality of Bosnia.

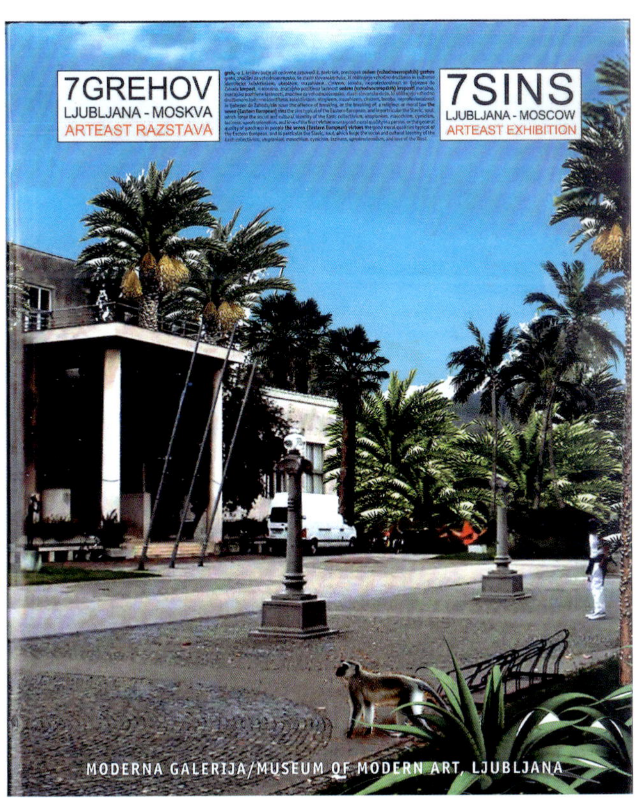

3   The power of collaboration

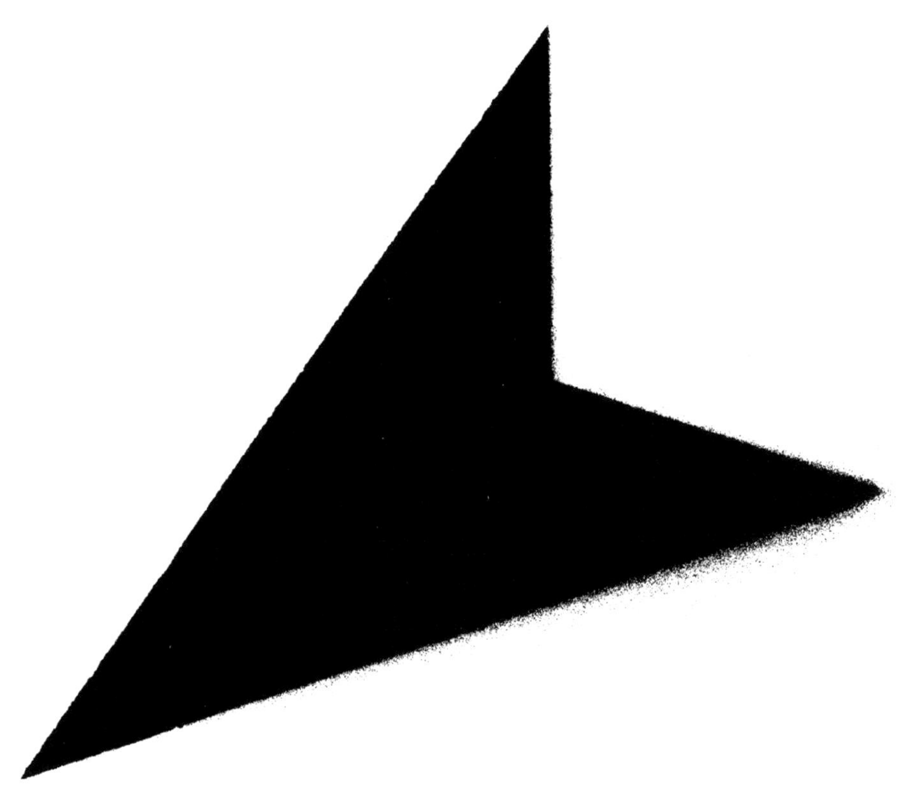

Providing commentary and critique of labor conditions to establish workers' rights

During socialism there were two central problems artists had to navigate to sustain their practice: the lack of infrastructure through which to disseminate art, and the system wherein professions and positions were determined by the state. Lesson four reflects how self-organization and uses of so-called "free time" represented strategies against the established rules and conditions of "work," as well as a way to create alternative spaces to share the outcomes of their private labor. Furthermore, by exposing inequities in working conditions for artists—whether under socialism or capitalism—people question their own responsibilities towards society and their role in effecting change.

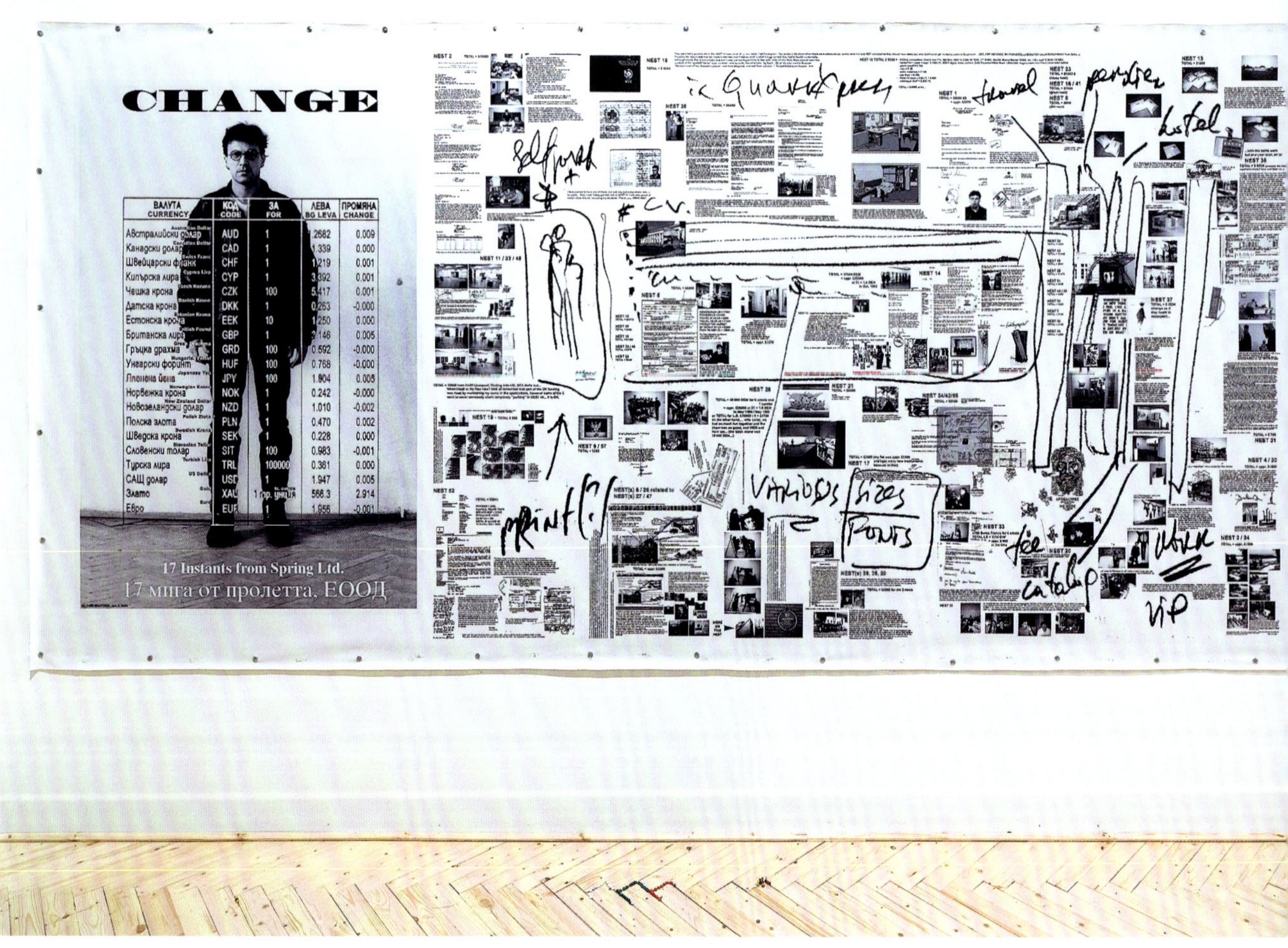
CHANGE
17 Instants from Spring Ltd.
17 мига от пролетта. ЕООД

Luchezar Boyadjiev

(b. 1957, Sofia, Bulgaria)

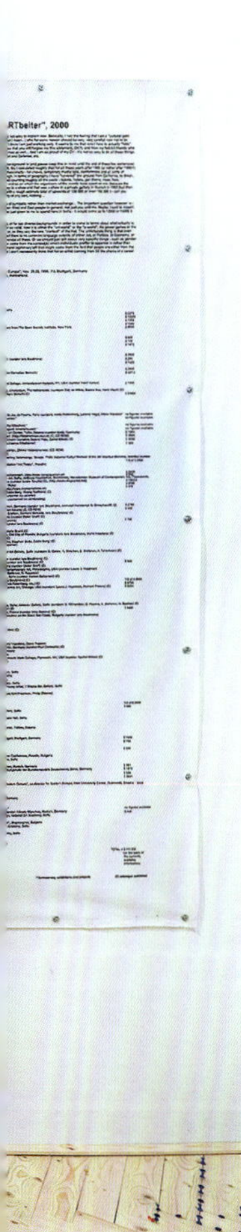

GastARTbeiter

2000–2007

Digital print on fine grain vinyl, 210×510 cm

Courtesy Moderna galerija, Ljubljana

Luchezar Boyadjiev examines the relationship between art, economy, and everyday life by investigating the processes of creation and transfer of cultural and economic capital. In the capitalist operating system of art Boyadjiev is a valuable commodity, as he has received more than $100,000 in grants and other forms of "charitable" support for artists. Since none of this money ended up in the artist's own pocket, benefiting his family for instance, he started to wonder who was actually benefiting from his work and whether the spending was justified.

GastARTbeiter is a type of personal chronicle which presents the monetary aspects of the life and work of Boyadjiev as an internationally recognized artist traveling all over the world, working on various shows and projects. It maps his career not in terms of exhibitions and solo projects at certain institutions, but rather through tracing the amount of money Western institutions and funding programs were prepared to spend on him and his career over a ten-year period. The work consists of various documentation—hotel bills, restaurant receipts, contracts, exhibition budgets—and includes fragments of his correspondence, photographs, and commentaries. By combining the German word "Gastarbeiter" (migrant worker) with the word "art" in the title of the work, Boyadjiev associates the status of a migrant worker with that of an artist: while the first is selling his ability to work to a foreign economy, the second is investing time and effort in creating cultural value in return for inadequate monetary reward. Boyadjiev thus points out that the capitalization of cultural value by the art institutions is based on the artist's self-exploitation.

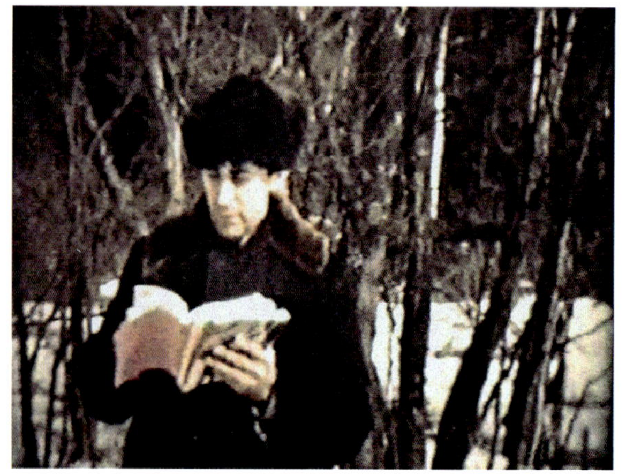

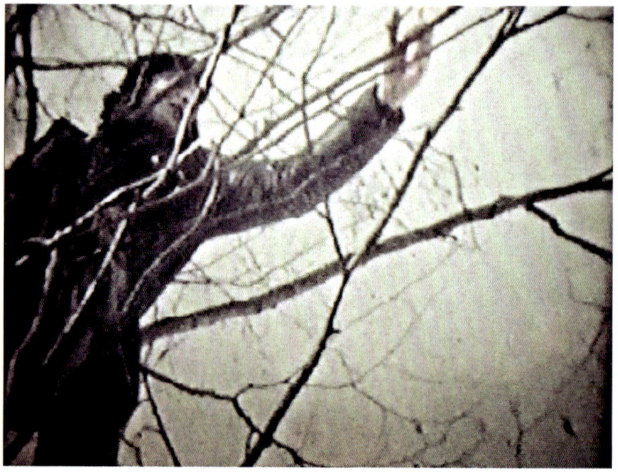

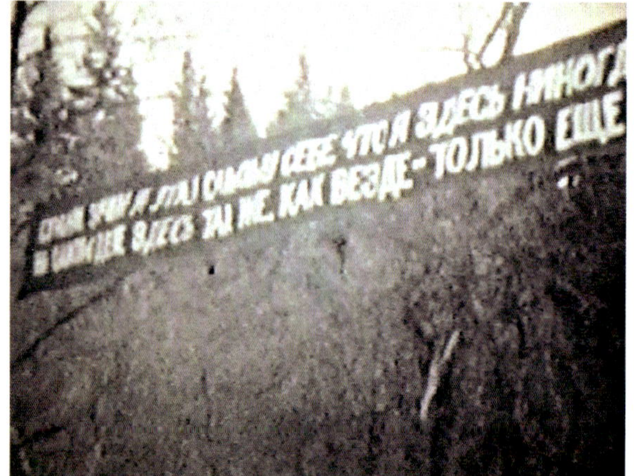
И ЗДЕСЬ НИКОГ
И ВИЖУ ЗДЕСЬ ТАК ЖЕ, КАК ВЕЗДЕ — ТОЛЬКО ЕЩЕ

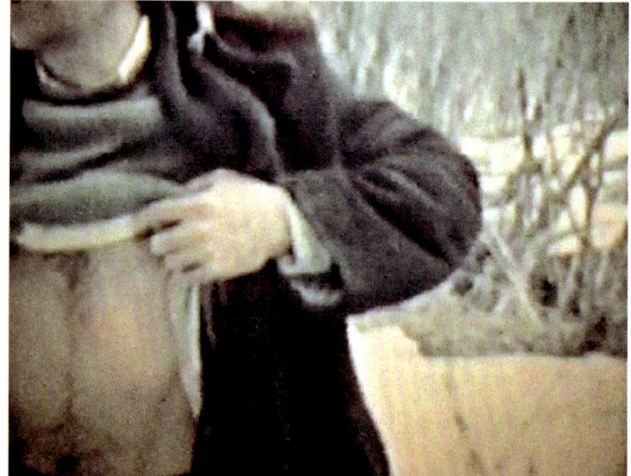

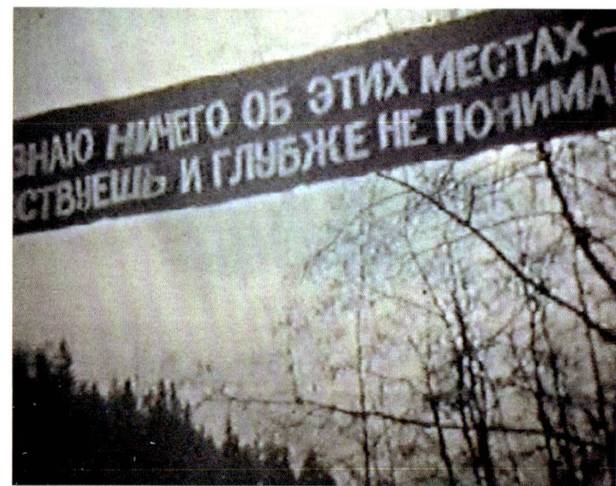
ЗНАЮ НИЧЕГО ОБ ЭТИХ МЕСТАХ —
СТВУЕШЬ И ГЛУБЖЕ НЕ ПОНИМА

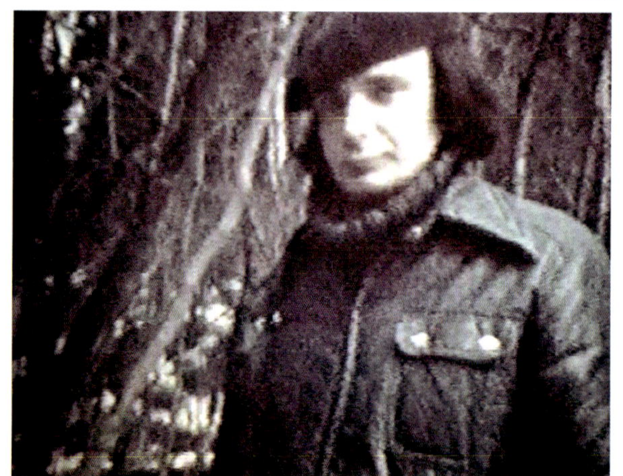

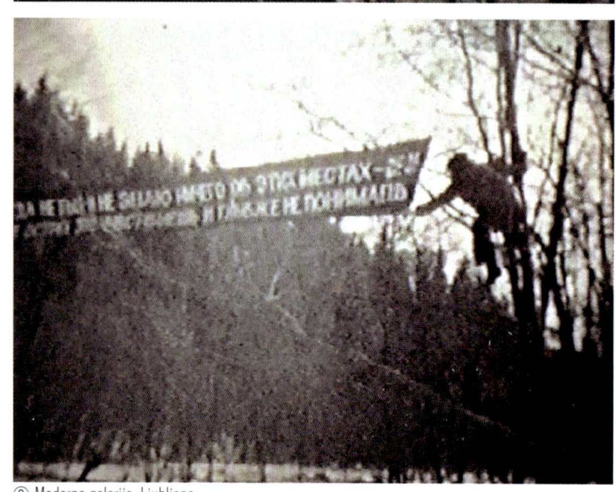
НЕ ЗНАЮ НИЧЕГО ОБ ЭТИХ МЕСТАХ —
И ГЛУБЖЕ НЕ ПОНИМАЕШЬ

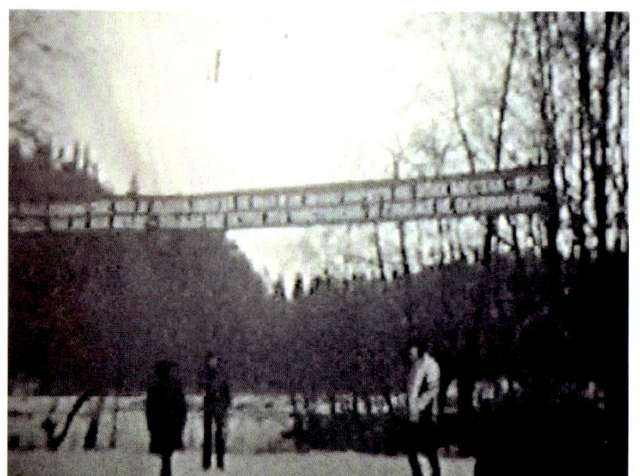

Collective Actions

(1976, Moscow, USSR, now Russia)

The Slogan

1978

16 mm film on DVD, 4'26"

Courtesy Moderna galerija, Ljubljana

Founded in 1976 and comprising, at various times, Andrei Monastyrsky, Nikita Alexeev, Elena Elagina, George Kiesewalter, Igor Makarevich, Nikolai Panitkov, Sergei Romashko, and Sabine Haensgen, Collective Actions is one of the most important groups of the Moscow Conceptualist movement. The group's performances involved traveling out of Moscow with a selected audience to Kievogorskoe Field, where performances were conducted in the form of esoteric rites. At the end of each performance, the audience was asked to make a written description and interpretation of what they had seen. Monastyrsky would then invite the artists and the audience to his flat for further discussion. All of these discussions were documented and filed. Years later, the files were published in a series of volumes as *Journeys to the Countryside*. It then became apparent that the audience only saw part of the performance, and that more salient events took place outside their field of vision.

The performance *The Slogan* took place on April 8, 1978 and involved Andrey Monastyrsky, Nikita Alexeev, Igor Yavorsky, Valery and Ludmila Veshnevsky, and George Kiesewalter. A dark blue banner, 12 m×1 m, was hung between trees on a river bank. The slogan, in white letters, read "It's strange. Why did I lie to myself that I've never been here and don't know anything about this place? In fact here is the same as everywhere else, only here you feel it more sharply and understand even less."

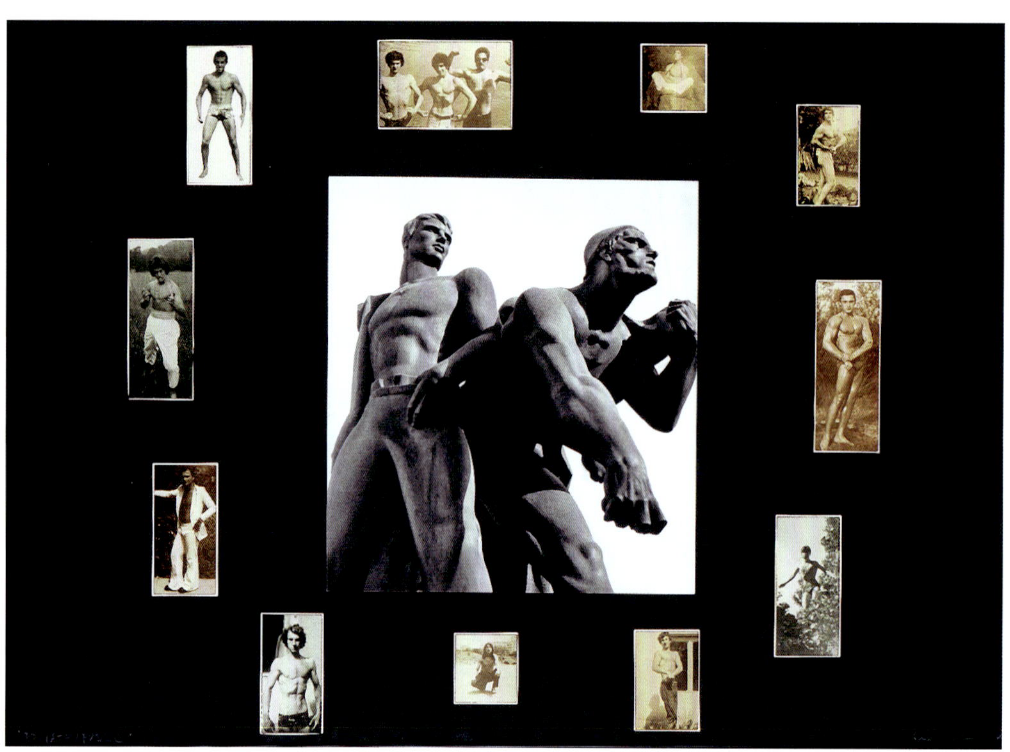

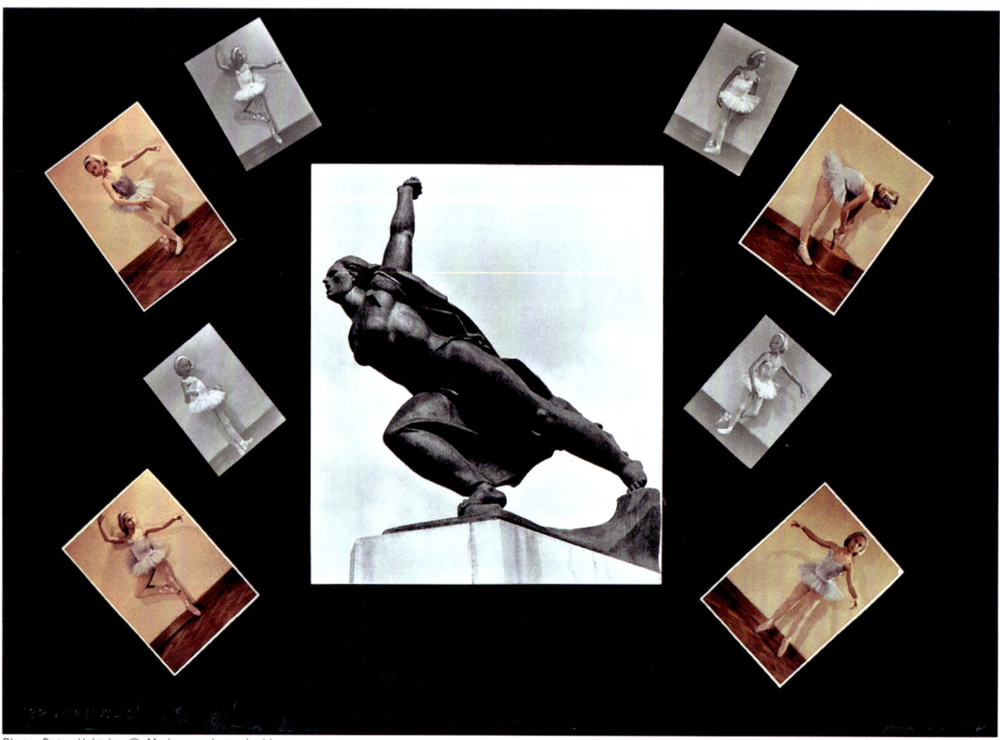

Photo: Dejan Habicht. © Moderna galerija, Ljubljana

Sanja Iveković

(b. 1949, Zagreb, Yugoslavia, now Croatia)

Private – Public (Man's Pictures – Woman's Pictures)
1981
Photocollage, 52×72cm
Courtesy Moderna galerija, Ljubljana

Sanja Iveković is one of the key representatives of the generation known in Croatia as the New Artistic Practice, a feminist, activist, and video pioneer.

From the early 1970s onwards, her work—ranging from conceptual photomontages and videos to performances and installations—has been focused on the issues of the politics of power, gender roles, and collective memory. Her works pay special attention to the role of women in society, especially in the context of the transition from socialism to capitalism, and examine the effects this transformation had on how women are represented in the mass media and, consequently, perceived in public.

Iveković already questioned the concepts of public and private space in her performative work *Triangle* (1979), documented by four photographs juxtaposed in a triangular shape. The topics of normative gender roles and of how the personal is interwoven with the political are further explored in, among others, *Private – Public (Man's Pictures – Woman's Pictures)* from 1981, where images of ideal masculinity and femininity as represented by socialist public monuments are juxtaposed with images of male models and female ballerinas.

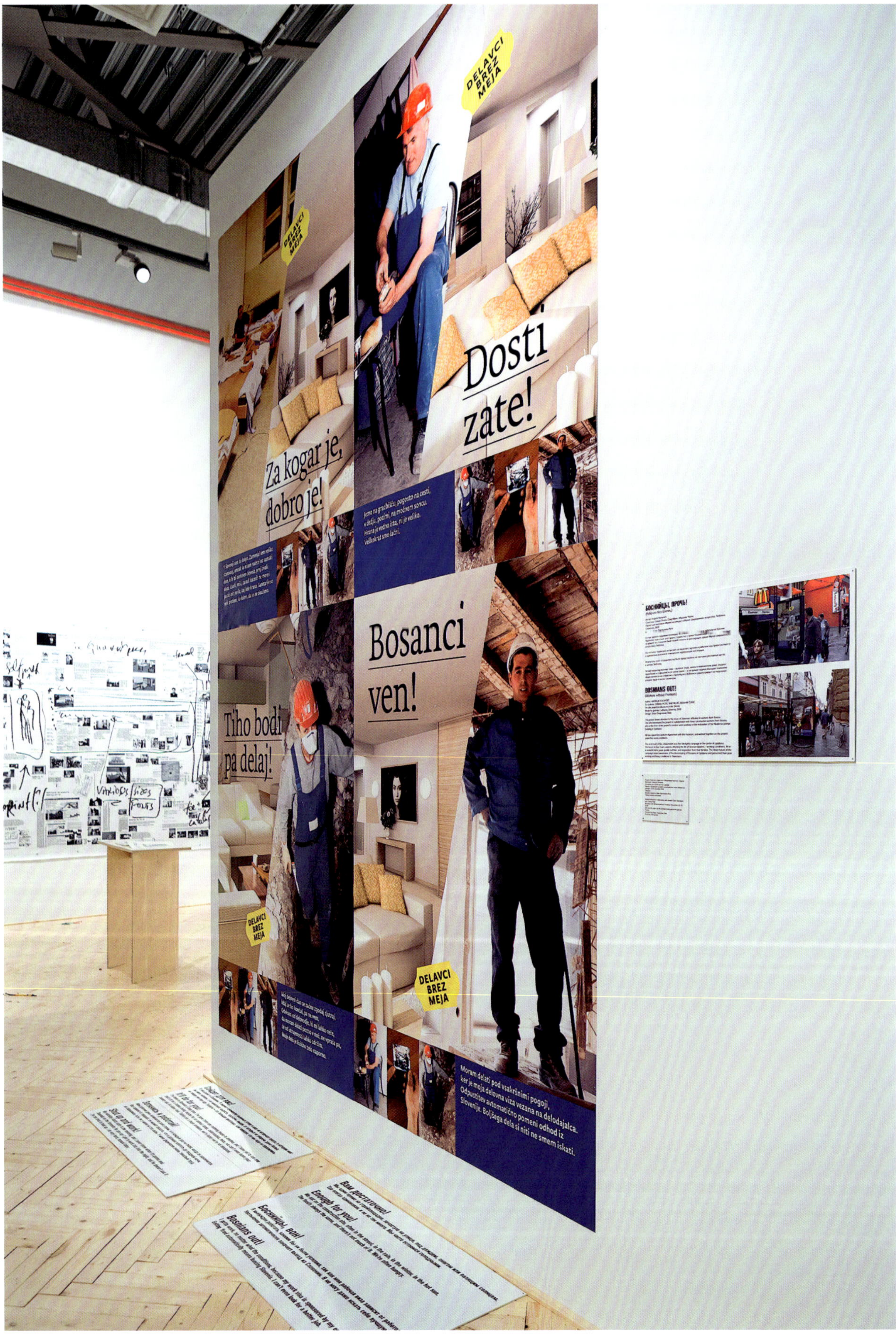

Andreja Kulunčić

(b. 1968, Subotica, Yugoslavia, now Serbia)

Bosnians Out! (Workers without Frontiers)

2008
Site-specific project for the exhibition *Museum in the Streets*, Ljubljana
In collaboration with Ibrahim Ćurić, Said Mujić, and Osman Pezić
Posters, 200×100 cm
Poster design: Dejan Dragosavac-Ruta
Courtesy of the artists

In 2008, while the building of Moderna galerija was undergoing renovation, the exhibition project *Museum in the Streets* was organized in Ljubljana. The invited artists, theoreticians, and activists explored and intervened in those aspects of the city that are both present and simultaneously invisible, marginalized, and repressed. These aspects were made visible in a new, artistic context.

The project *Bosnians Out!* referred to one of the three main topics of the exhibition, "Urban margins: parallel strategies of survival, self-organizing practices, migrants, workers' hostels, prisons…" It focused on the living and working conditions of migrant workers in Slovenia. Andreja Kulunčić developed the project in collaboration with three migrant workers from Bosnia who were employed at the Moderna galerija construction site. Kulunčić explained that her goal was "to include the workers, who have been working on the museum building for months, in co-creating the content of the museum, and to open a new channel of communication for them, creating an active dialogue with the public regarding their situation in Ljubljana." The collaboration resulted in an intervention using advertising light boxes in the city center. The workers chose four main topics for the campaign: working conditions, life in workers' hostels, poor nutrition, and separation from their families. They decided to use their own photographs and set the campaign's direct and ironical tone. In a manner reminiscent of advertising, the campaign juxtaposed their stories and their substandard living conditions (in image and text) with stereotypical representations of ideal home interiors (as found in interior design magazines) that they were building.

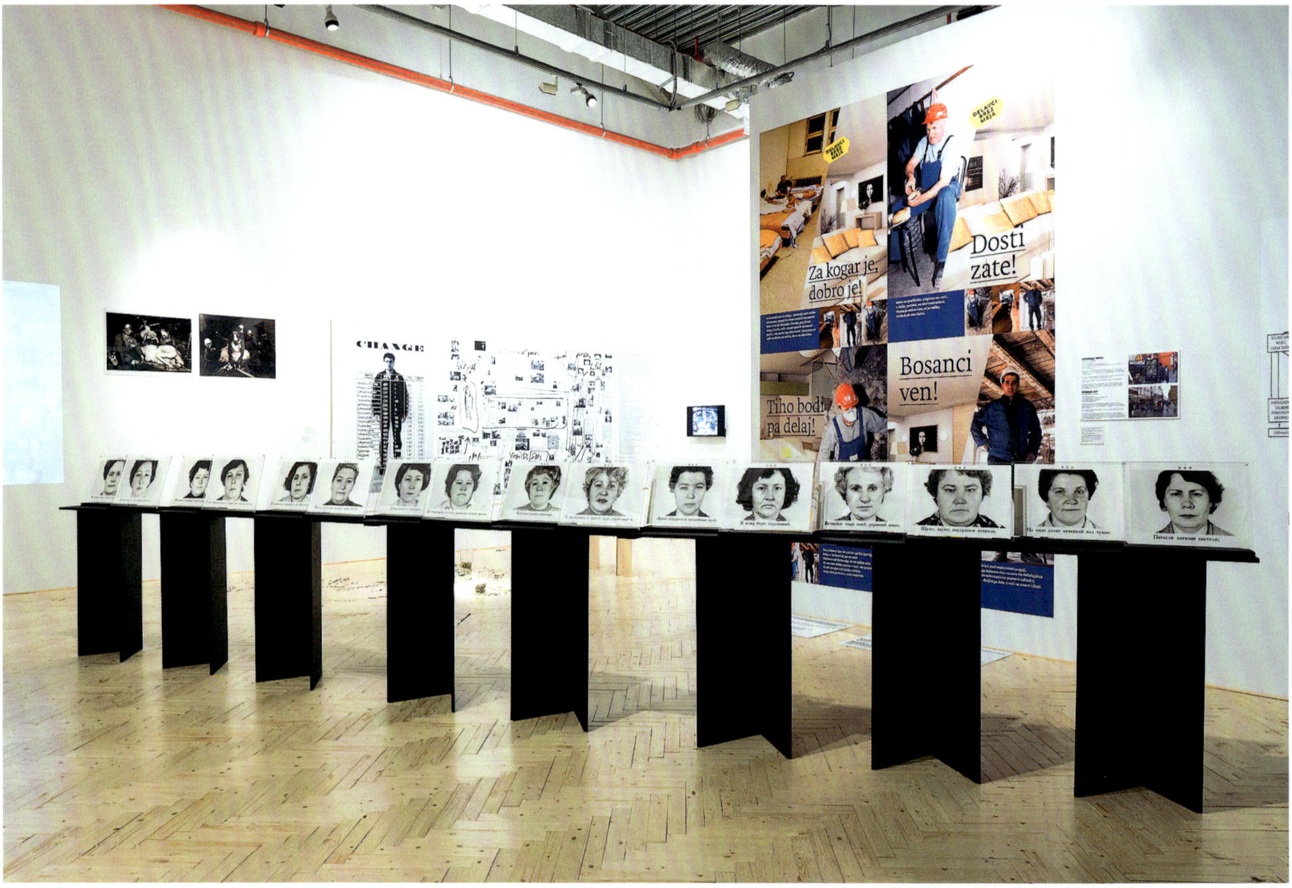
CHANGE
Za kogar je, dobro je!
Dosti zate!
Bosanci ven!
Tiho bodi pa delaj!

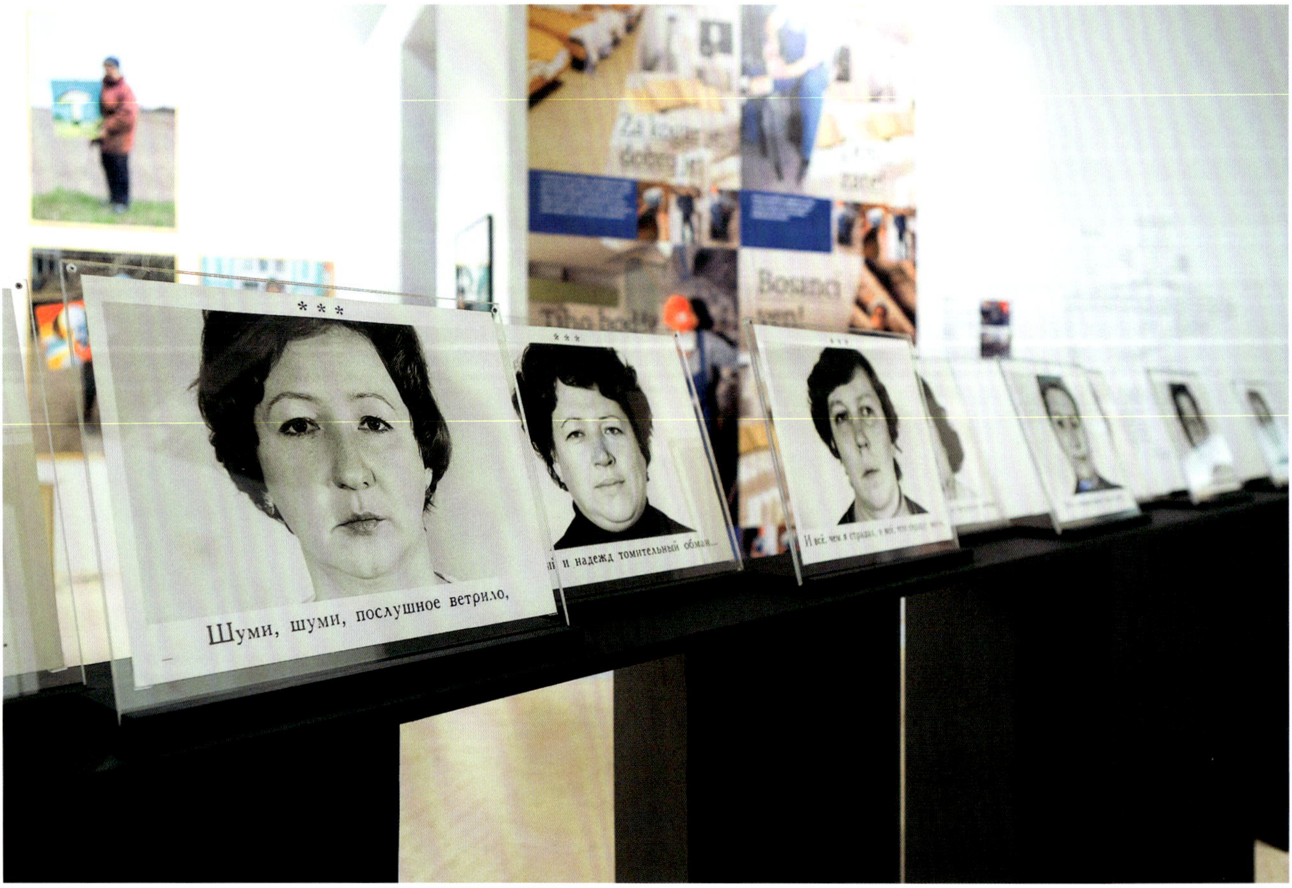
* * *
Шуми, шуми, послушное ветрило,
и надежд томительный обман...

Vladimir Kupriyanov

(1954, Moscow, USSR, now Russia—2011, Moscow, Russia)

In Memory of Pushkin

1984

Photographic installation

Courtesy Moderna galerija, Ljubljana

Photographer and artist Vladimir Kupriyanov graduated from the Moscow Institute of Culture with a degree in theater directing, which to a great extent shaped his work. Each of his projects possesses an in-built drama, with its own inner logic and figurative style. Leading critics define Kupriyanov as a "historical artist," and indeed, his whole body of work is to a certain degree connected with reflections on the historical matrix of the past. Kupriyanov's first projects date from the 1980s, the decade when the state was dissolving and the energy of the Soviet project was spent. Here there is something curiously unexpected: Kupriyanov deliberately studies the world around him, distinctively documenting things that don't seem to deserve the attention of a non-official artist of that era. In his *Metro* series, he takes viewers into the hidden, ageless world of the Moscow Metro, where the power of the Stalinist style is particularly apparent against the background of late Soviet people vanishing and reappearing. In the context of Kupriyanov's study of modernity, of particular interest is the series *Lyuberetsky Agricultural Machine Factory*, in which the artist focused on heavy industry. Another of Kupriyanov's textbook works, *Do Not Cast Me Away From Your Presence* (1989–1990), is an enormous photograph of workers taken from a factory wall newspaper. Kupriyanov, however, cut the photograph that forms the basis of the work into seven pieces—the workers were separated from one another. Space opened up between them, but the viewer notices that the separation was not smooth, and that the images of the people are literally falling apart. All of this illustrates Kupriyanov's exceptional historical intuition; throughout the final Soviet decade he soberly documented the present from a historical perspective. In the series *In Memory of Pushkin*, he combined honor roll photographs of Soviet women with romantic lines by the great poet which are taught in schools ("Extinguished is the orb of day…"). It is difficult to say how ironic this project is. What is indisputable is the work's grounding in Russian history—Kupriyanov subtly combines the ephemeral and the eternal, reconciling the recent past with the immutable and everlasting, which in the end creates a penetrating, nostalgic image.

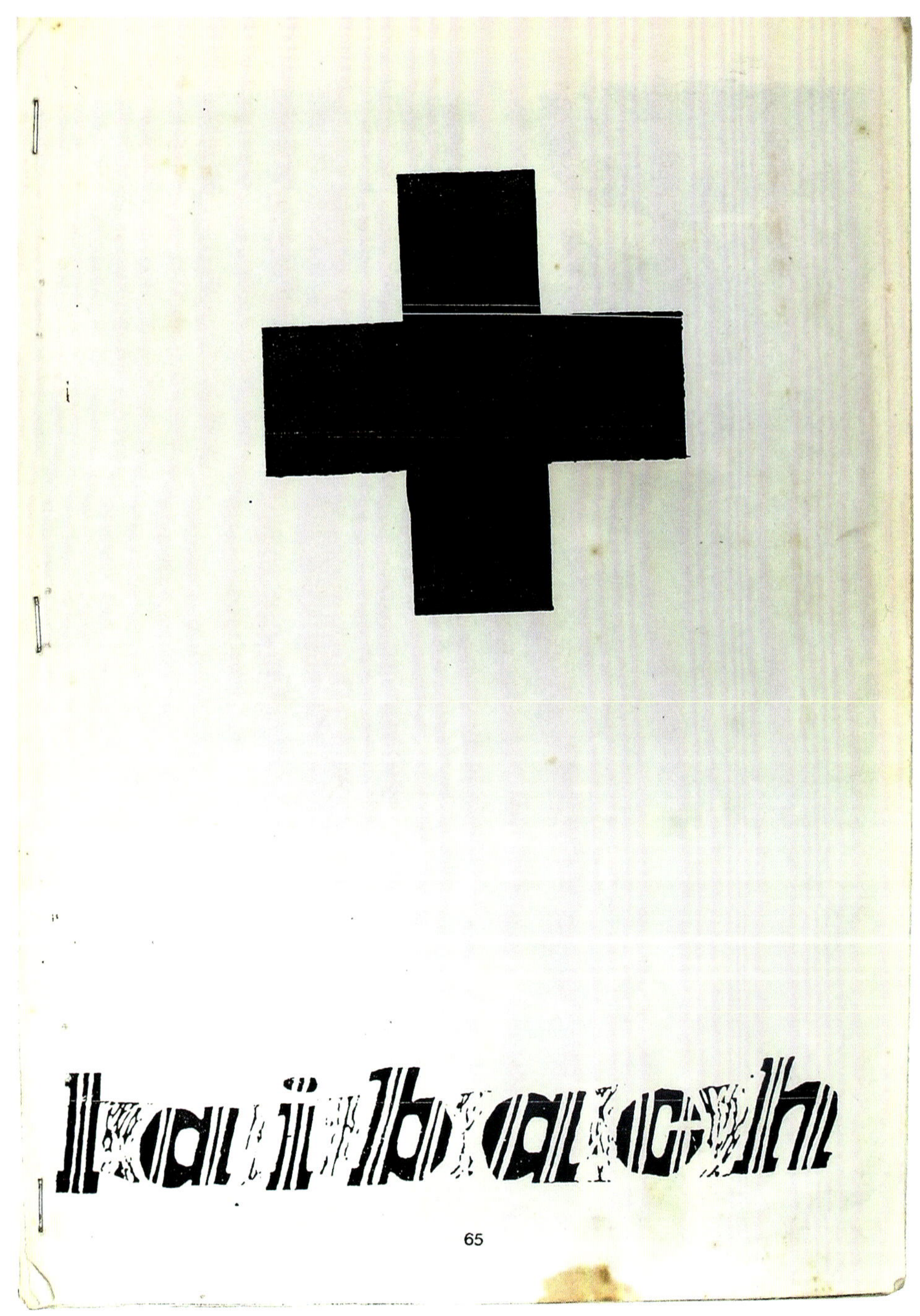

65

Laibach

(1980, Trbovlje, Yugoslavia, now Slovenia)

Laibach fanzine
1981
Xerox, paper, 28×20 cm
Courtesy of the artists

In June 1981 the first *Ausstellung Laibach Kunst* exhibition took place in Belgrade's Srećna Nova Umetnost gallery, considered the focal point of fanzine production at the time. Among the exhibited works were paintings, works on paper, and texts. The music that was playing was recorded on cassettes, and the first Laibach fanzine was created. Its final form was the result of censorship, which came into play as a result of a series of photographs which included images of Hitler, Stalin, and Tito. Two controversial images that took the form of posters, and which group members had put up on the streets of Trbovlje a year earlier in a so-called "poster action," were also part of the fanzine. The two posters announced the first public manifestation of the Laibach group—an exhibition and a concert—which was banned as a result of the illegal and irresponsible use of symbols. The posters were removed or covered by other posters the very next day. The cover of the fanzine featured an image of the first poster showing a simple black cross, associated with the Suprematist cross of Kazimir Malevich, with the German word "Laibach" written underneath. The second poster was on the back cover of the fanzine and was much less ambiguous. It depicted a person's eyes being poked out, taken from a scene in John Carpenter's film *Halloween*. The first pages comprised photographs of a workers' rally, then a section of text taken from a chronicle of the city, in which group members were depicted along with four maimed faces. The body of the fanzine covers the themes of workers' revolts, military dictatorships, the depiction of industrial objects, and the torture of Liberation Front activists. The fanzine was made using a Xerox, resulting in white, grainy images. It raised the topics of the reach of public freedom, manipulation of the masses and the individual, the question of totalitarianism and democracy, torture, and subordination. Laibach disseminated its message with provocative imagery. Using the theme of the Trbovlje mine workers' movement and their resistance, it sent a clear message that the revolution was still underway.

3   The power of collaboration

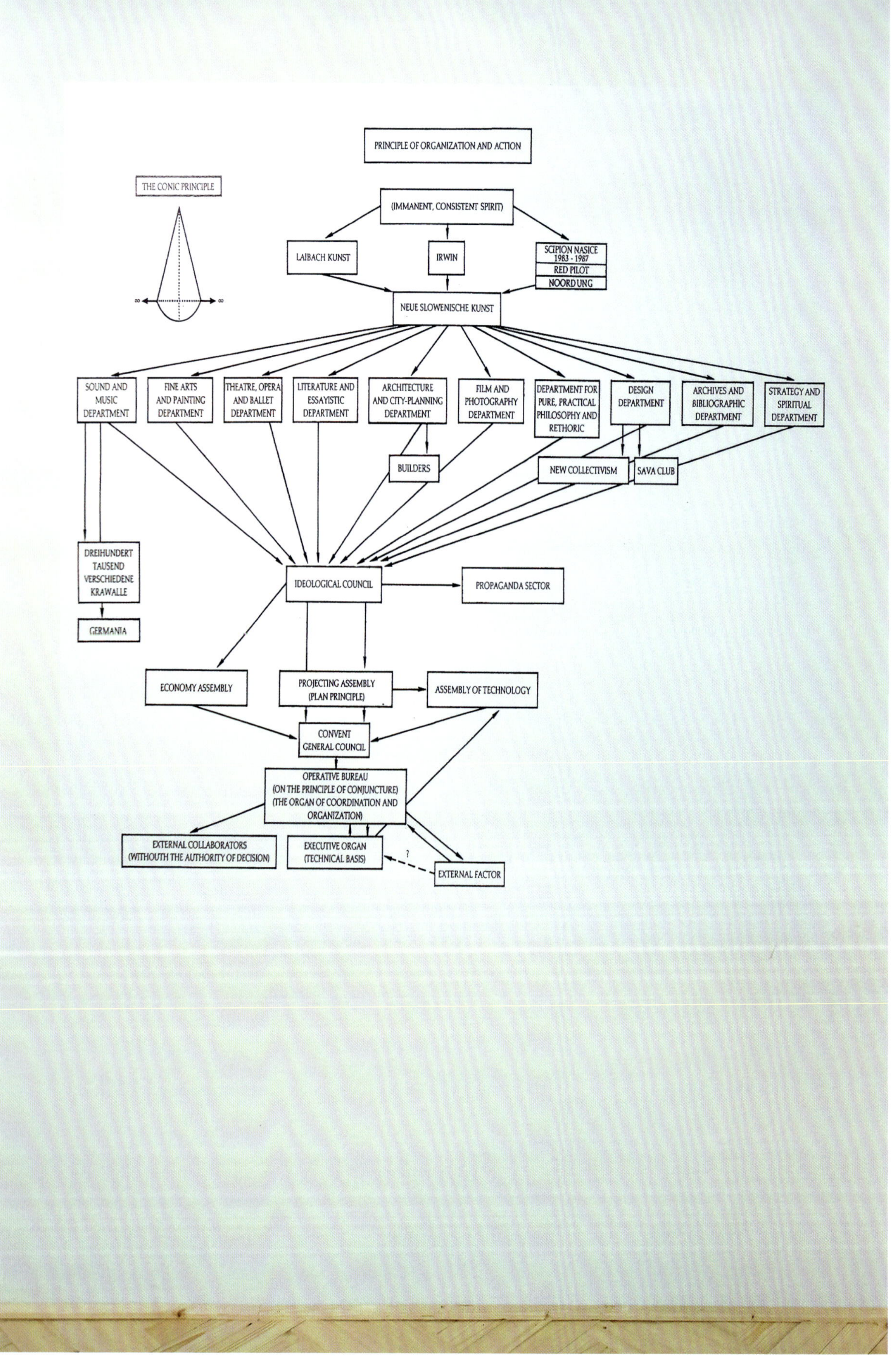

PRINCIPLE OF ORGANIZATION AND ACTION
THE CONIC PRINCIPLE
∞
∞
(IMMANENT, CONSISTENT SPIRIT)
LAIBACH KUNST
IRWIN
SCIPION NASICE
1983 - 1987
RED PILOT
NOORD UNG
NEUE SLOWENISCHE KUNST
SOUND AND MUSIC DEPARTMENT
FINE ARTS AND PAINTING DEPARTMENT
THEATRE, OPERA AND BALLET DEPARTMENT
LITERATURE AND ESSAYISTIC DEPARTMENT
ARCHITECTURE AND CITY-PLANNING DEPARTMENT
FILM AND PHOTOGRAPHY DEPARTMENT
DEPARTMENT FOR PURE, PRACTICAL PHILOSOPHY AND RETHORIC
DESIGN DEPARTMENT
ARCHIVES AND BIBLIOGRAPHIC DEPARTMENT
STRATEGY AND SPIRITUAL DEPARTMENT
BUILDERS
NEW COLLECTIVISM
SAVA CLUB
DREIHUNDERT TAUSEND VERSCHIEDENE KRAWALLE
GERMANIA
IDEOLOGICAL COUNCIL
PROPAGANDA SECTOR
ECONOMY ASSEMBLY
PROJECTING ASSEMBLY (PLAN PRINCIPLE)
ASSEMBLY OF TECHNOLOGY
CONVENT GENERAL COUNCIL
OPERATIVE BUREAU (ON THE PRINCIPLE OF CONJUNCTURE) (THE ORGAN OF COORDINATION AND ORGANIZATION)
EXTERNAL COLLABORATORS (WITHOUTH THE AUTHORITY OF DECISION)
EXECUTIVE ORGAN (TECHNICAL BASIS)
?
EXTERNAL FACTOR

Neue Slowenische Kunst (NSK)

(1984, Ljubljana, Yugoslavia, now Slovenia)

The NSK Organigram
1984
Wall poster, 170×140 cm
Courtesy Moderna galerija, Ljubljana

The Neue Slowenische Kunst (New Slovenian Art) collective was established in 1984, when Slovenia was still part of Yugoslavia. NSK has been active in the fields of music, visual, and performative art, its founding groups being Laibach, IRWIN, and the Scipion Nasice Sisters Theater. By using foreign (German) language and symbols, NSK was (and still is) evoking the traumatic history and complicated relationship the Slovenes had with the Germans. Employing strategies of appropriation and copying, their practice debunked the notions of originality and authenticity, thus challenging the myth of (any) national identity by destabilizing its phantasmatic ground.

The NSK Organigram (an organizational diagram showing principles of organization and activities), which has been made public on several occasions, clearly shows the hierarchical structure of this "state." At the head of NSK there is cooperation on an equal footing between IRWIN and the Red Pilot Cosmokinetic Theater in a tripartite council led by the ICS (Immanent Consistent Spirit). The collective leadership is rotational, the members are interchangeable. The structure of the state is based on the principles of the relation between ideology and the individual. Inside the state there is freedom. It is absolute and is never questioned by the state. Everyone plays their role. The head is the head, the hand is the hand, and the differences between them are organic and manifest themselves painlessly.

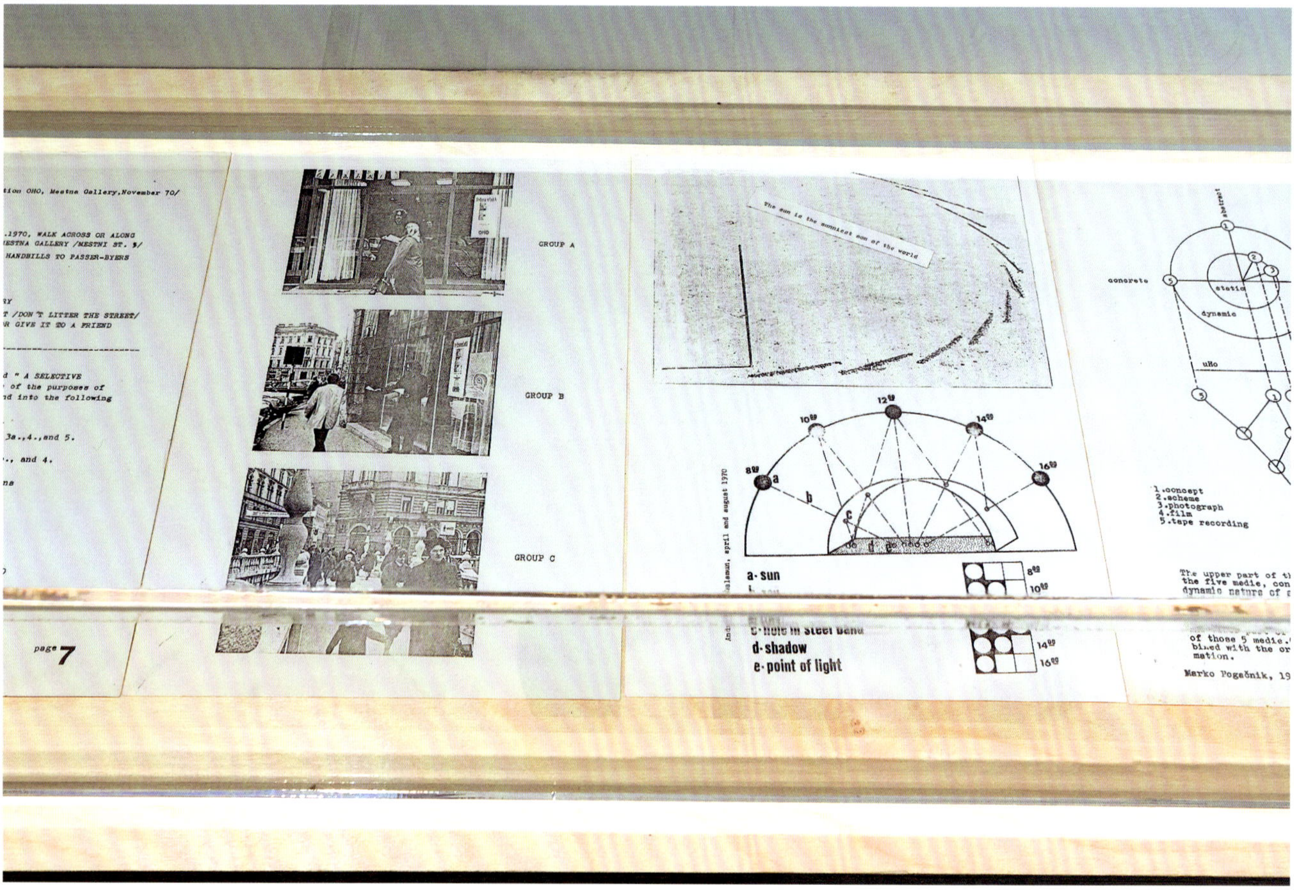

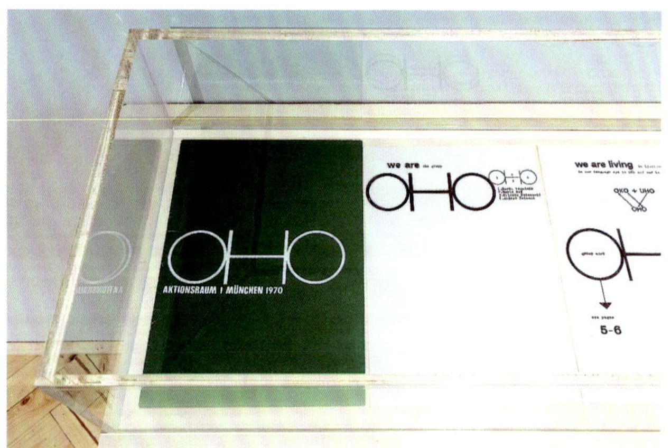

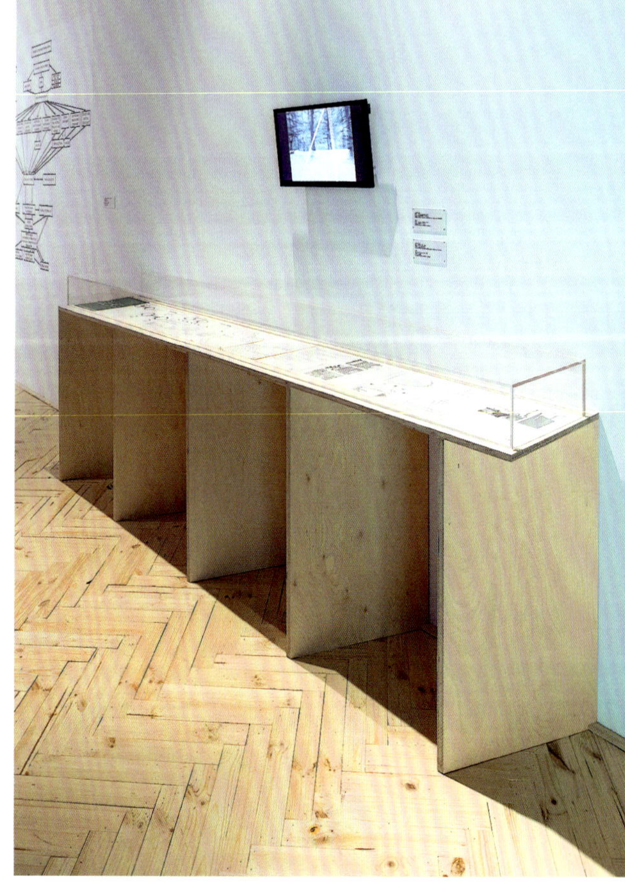

OHO (Milenko Matanović, David Nez, Marko Pogačnik, and Andraž Šalamun)

(1966–1971, Yugoslavia, now Slovenia)

OHO – Summer Projects
1970
Film, b/w, no sound, 28' 46"

We are the Group OHO
1970
11 A4 papers, in paper folder, 29.5×21cm
Courtesy Moderna galerija, Ljubljana

The OHO group was formed in the 1960s from a broader movement of visual artists and writers whose activities encompassed concrete poetry and visual works ("items"), installations, environments, happenings, films, and "OHO editions." The transformation of OHO's activities and applied aesthetic concepts coincided with the transfiguration of the broader generational movement into an art group and finally into a commune. After initially working on "reism," the principles of "poor" art (Arte Povera), and the thematization of the gallery space, the members of the group, which at the time had already formed into a closely-knit group of four, crossed first into the urban space and then into nature.

The film *OHO – Summer Projects* documents the group's works that, as a specific version of land art, arose from the group's earlier practice and from the landscape in which members intervened without any lasting consequences for the environment. Documentation played an important role, as it relayed to the audience—and sometimes even completed— these ephemeral projects that took place exclusively in the presence of the group's closest actors.

We are the Group OHO is one of the titles of the presentation schemes that were designed as an accompanying publication to the exhibition at the Aktionsraum 1 gallery in Munich. Organized in a file, the schemes look like promotional material, OHO as a packaging material for new ideas and messages published in the name of a product, or a cause, or an idea, or a person, or even an institution. In Munich, a few projects of some of the group's members were presented, all of which can be labeled as "transcendental conceptualism." This relates to the final stage of their creative activity, which aimed to surpass the transpersonal aspect and resulted in the self-termination of the group and the establishment of the so-called Šempas Family, which embodies the idea of fusion and inseparability of everyday life, artistic creation, and spiritual practice.

3   The power of collaboration

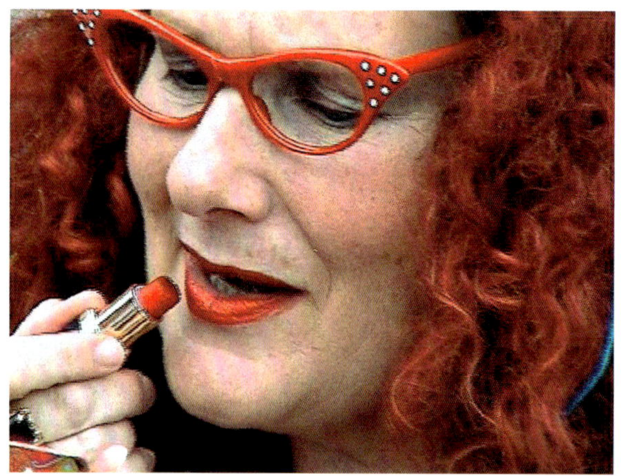

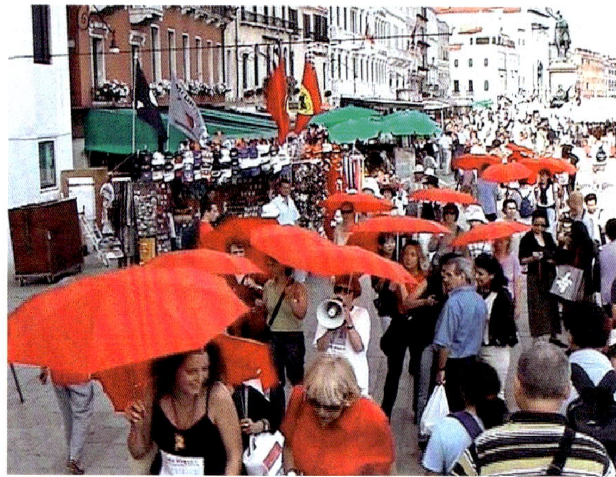

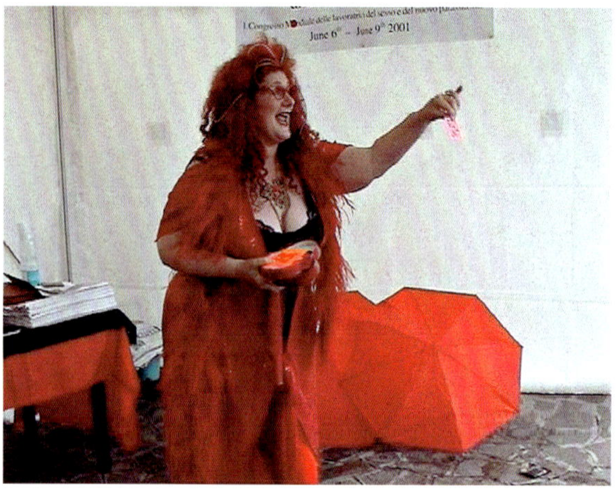

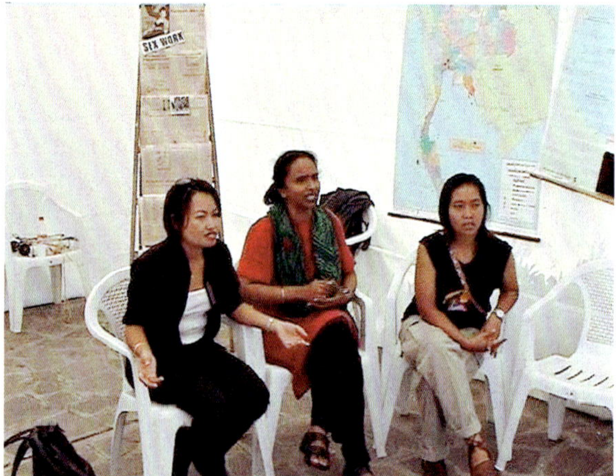

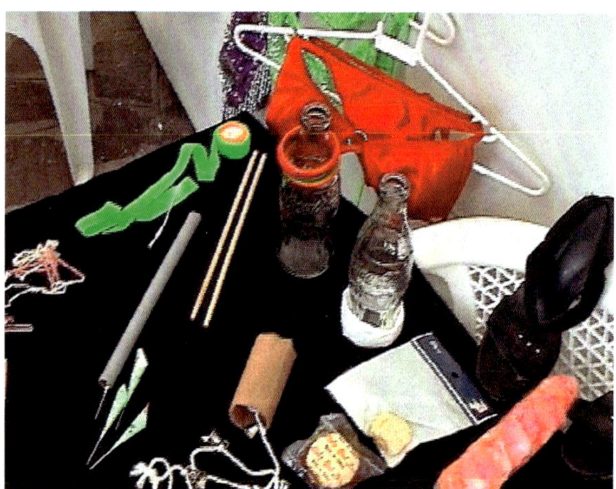

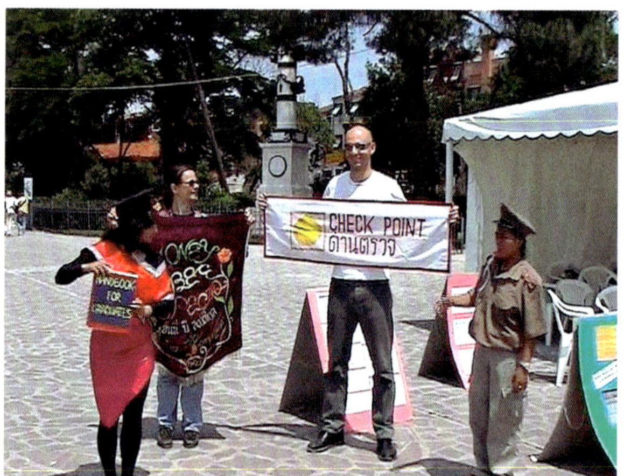

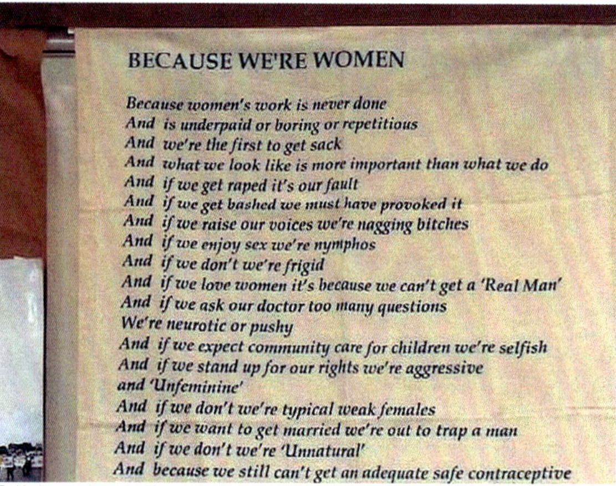

© Moderna galerija, Ljubljana

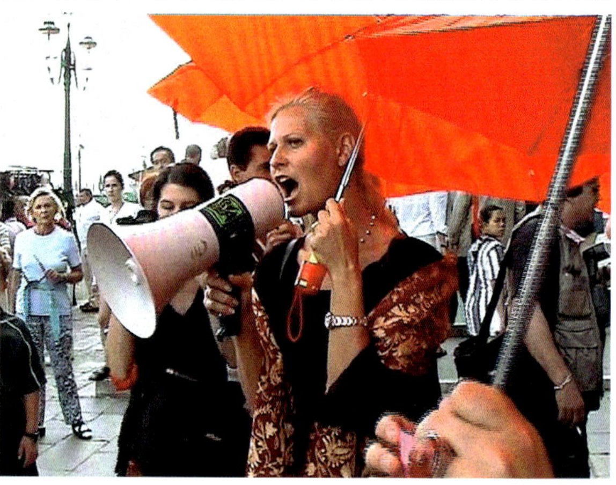

Tadej Pogačar

(b. 1960, Ljubljana, Yugoslavia, now Slovenia)

CODE:RED
I. World Congress of Sex Workers and New Parasitism
2001
Collaborative project, public action
Video, 21'32", archival materials
Courtesy of the artist

CODE:RED is a multidisciplinary, collaborative project which discusses and researches informal economy models, self-organization, global sex work, and global trafficking. It was initiated in 1999–2000 by Tadej Pogačar and the P.A.R.A.S.I.T.E. Museum of Contemporary Art. *CODE:RED* takes place within and outside the art context and encompasses various forms of joint operation with experts, scientists, and activist groups. It focuses on the topic of self-organization of marginal groups and communities which take place outside the dominant social, economic, and political frameworks.

CODE:RED activities range from research, activation, and self-help to public manifestations, actions, and exhibitions. The first public manifestation of the *CODE:RED* project was the *I. World Congress of Sex Workers and New Parasitism*, which took place from June 6 to 8, 2001 as part of the 49th Venice Biennial. In a public space in the Giardini, a tent (the Prostitute Pavilion, Padiglione delle Prostitute) was erected. The congress, conceived as a creative framework for connections, exchange, and information, emerged as a consequence of the artist's long-term co-operation with Comitato per I Diritti Civili delle Prostitute from Pordenone, one of the leading organizations for the protection of sex workers in Italy. The participating activists and groups from Cambodia, Vietnam, Thailand, Taiwan, USA, Australia, Germany, and Italy, presented current strategies in the fight for the civil rights of sex workers. Their emphasis was on the principles of organization, education, self-help, and protection. This was created through conversations, video projects, exhibitions, documentary publications, performances, activist street theater, and appearances, among others. *Congress* finished with *The Red Umbrellas March*, which publicly proclaimed solidarity with sex workers and outlined points in the suppressed and forgotten geography of the city, the geography of the social history of sex workers, from the famous Venetian courtesans Veronica Franco and Gaspara Stampa to the present day.

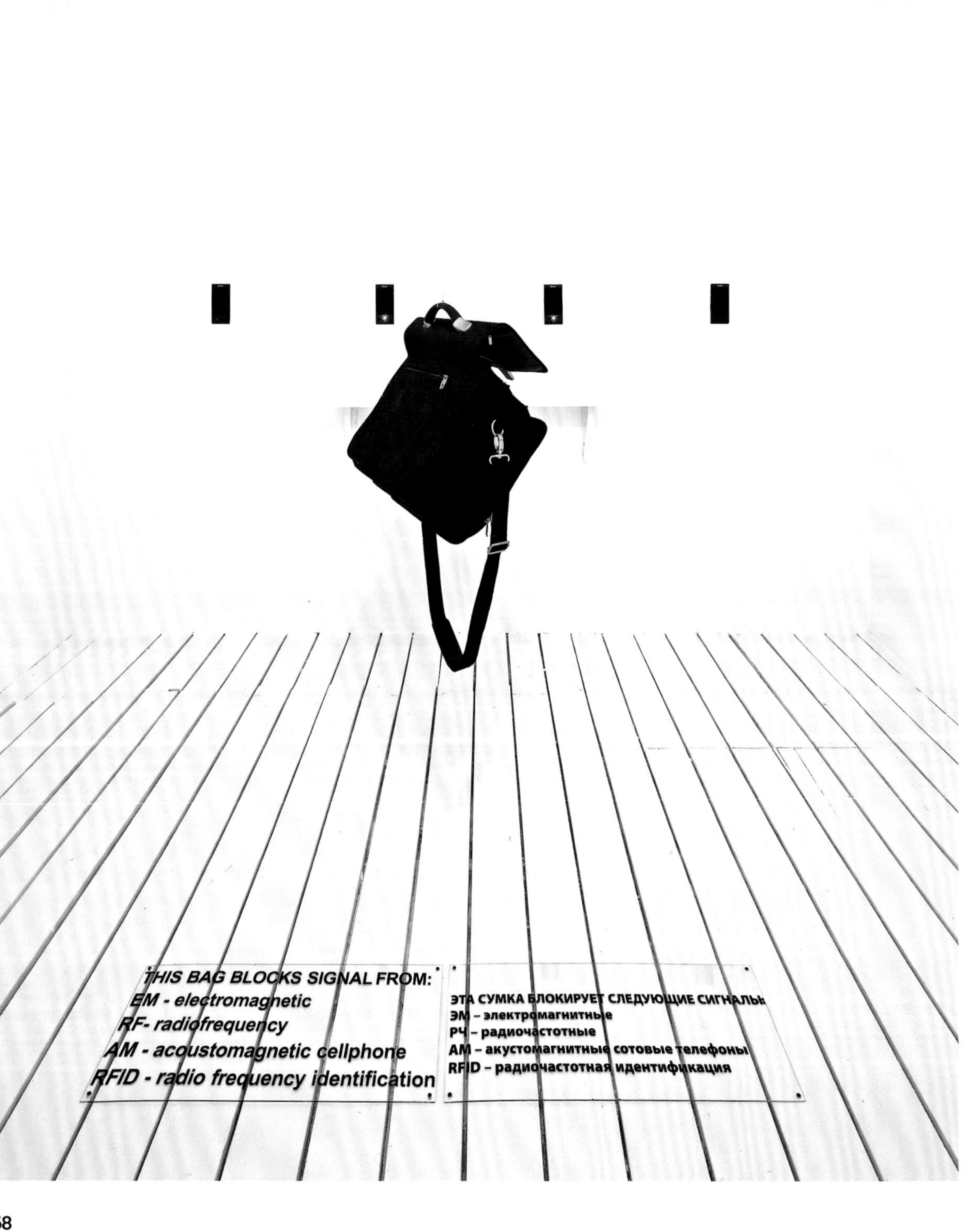

THIS BAG BLOCKS SIGNAL FROM:
EM - electromagnetic
RF- radiofrequency
AM - acoustomagnetic cellphone
RFID - radio frequency identification
ЭТА СУМКА БЛОКИРУЕТ СЛЕДУЮЩИЕ СИГНАЛЫ
ЭМ – электромагнитные
РЧ – радиочастотные
АМ – акустомагнитные сотовые телефоны
RFID – радиочастотная идентификация

Franc Purg

(b. 1955, Ptuj, Yugoslavia, now Slovenia)

Privileged Tactics I

2006

In collaboration with Sara Heitlinger

Installation

Courtesy of the artists

Privileged Tactics I (PTI) is based on the experiences the artist had with street children in Ukraine, where, since the transition to capitalism, their number has grown to several hundred thousand. This phenomenon did not exist in the Soviet Union. However, *PTI* does not simply illustrate this situation but rather questions the conditions of its existence. By taking street childrens' talent for creative survival as a model, it hopes to open up a discussion on inequalities in today's world.

The project uses cheap, low-tech methods that allow one to survive by tricking the high-tech apparatus of control and consumerism. It consists of an audio installation giving instructions for stealing and a bag that is designed to block the security alarms in shops. *PTI* asks the question, "When is stealing a criminal tactic and when is it a legal, privileged tactic?" by using the same methods as the global neoliberal capitalist system whose unregulated commerce, driven by profit alone, exploits the developing world for its natural resources and cheap labor without any regard for human values or environmental concerns. In opposition to this system, which facilitates the process where the powerful legally steal from the poor, in *PTI* theft is used as a form of survival and resistance.

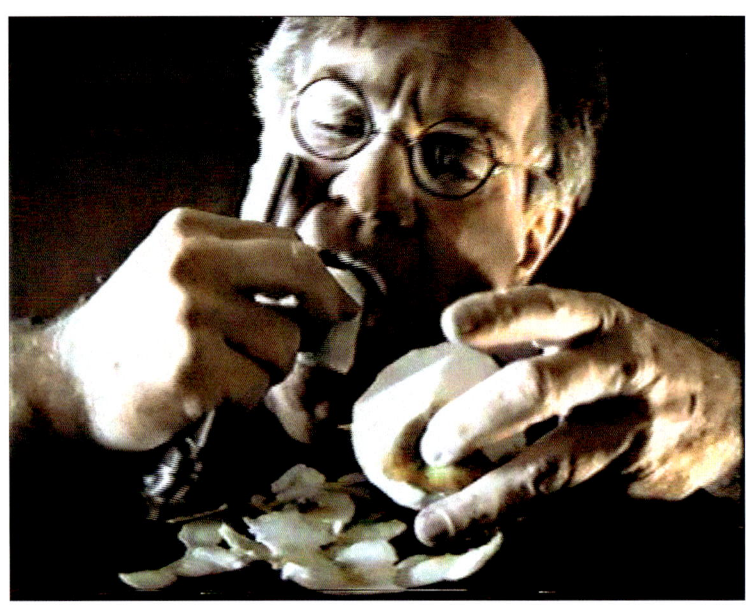

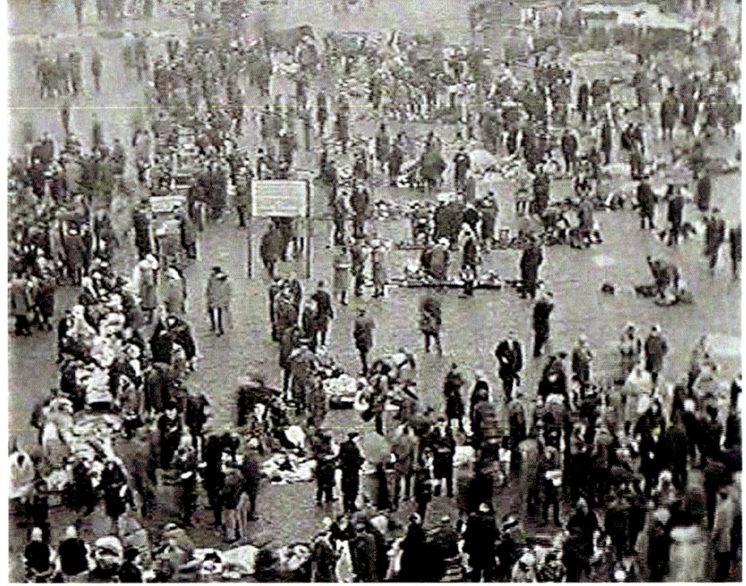

Józef Robakowski

(b. 1939, Poznań, Poland)

Market

1970

35mm film transferred to DVD, 4'20"

Production: Józef Robakowski

With Tadeusz Junak and Ryszard Meissner

Courtesy Moderna galerija, Ljubljana

Poland's Józef Robakowski is truly a jack of all trades in contemporary art. He was one of the originators of art associations such as Oko, Zero-61, and Krag, and in 1970 was a co-organizer of the Film Form Workshop. He has taught at an array of specialist institutes, helped found a number of art institutions, curated and organized numerous exhibitions, and has also been the editor of high-profile publications. Among his artworks, his first film, *6,000,000*, created in 1962, deserves special attention. It comprises a range of documentary materials about the Holocaust and was the starting point for a series of films and new media pieces—his next works were conceptual experiments at the Film Form Workshop. *Market* was the first film created at the workshop, and in it Robakowski attempts to analyse the mechanism by which illusion and reality are created in cinema. He undertakes an experiment using technology from that era, filming Łódź's Red Market with an unusual frame rate. Every five seconds Robakowski recorded only two frames (in sound films the standard rate is 24 frames a second), and in this way he used a technical means to achieve the effect of time being literally compressed, which at that moment in the film industry was considered a bold gesture.

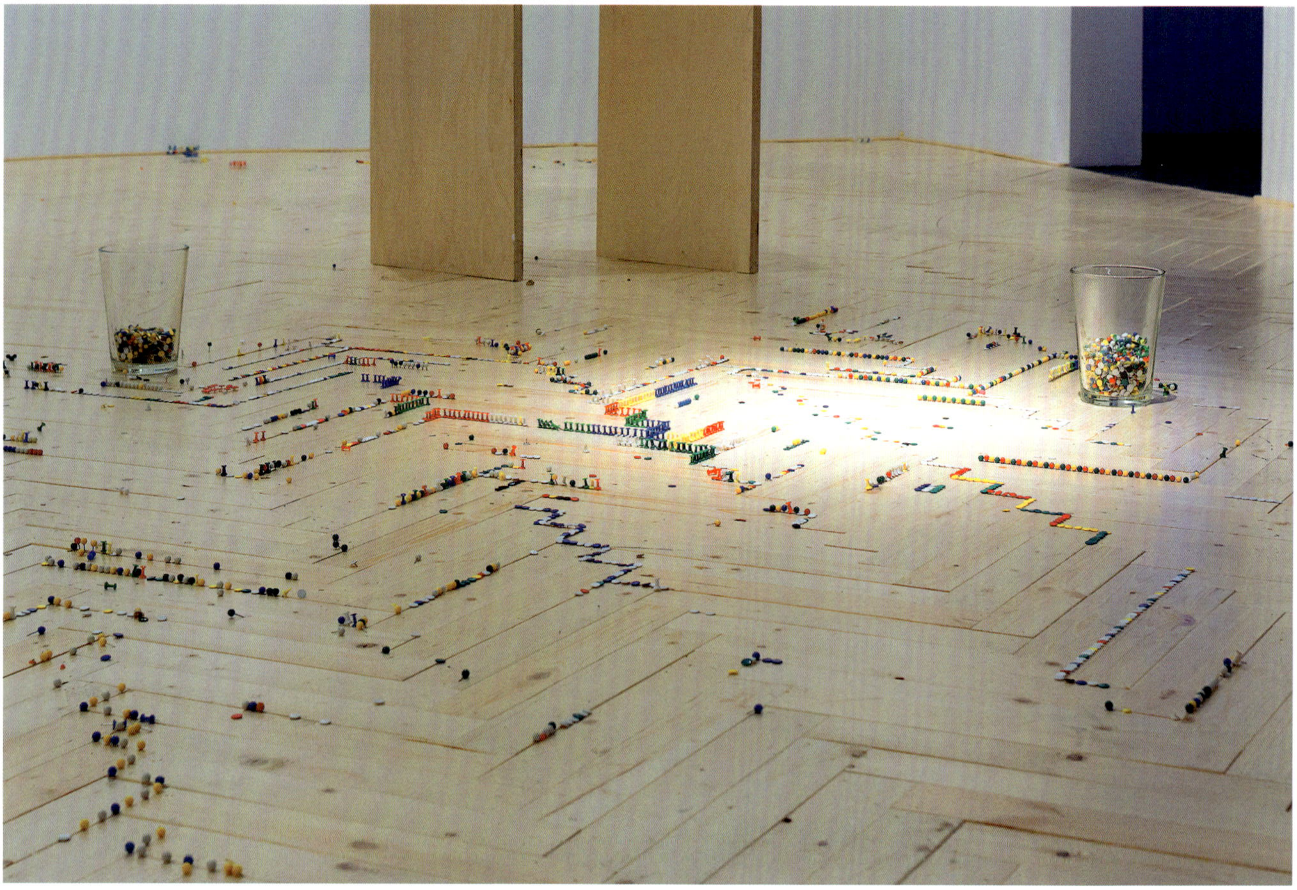

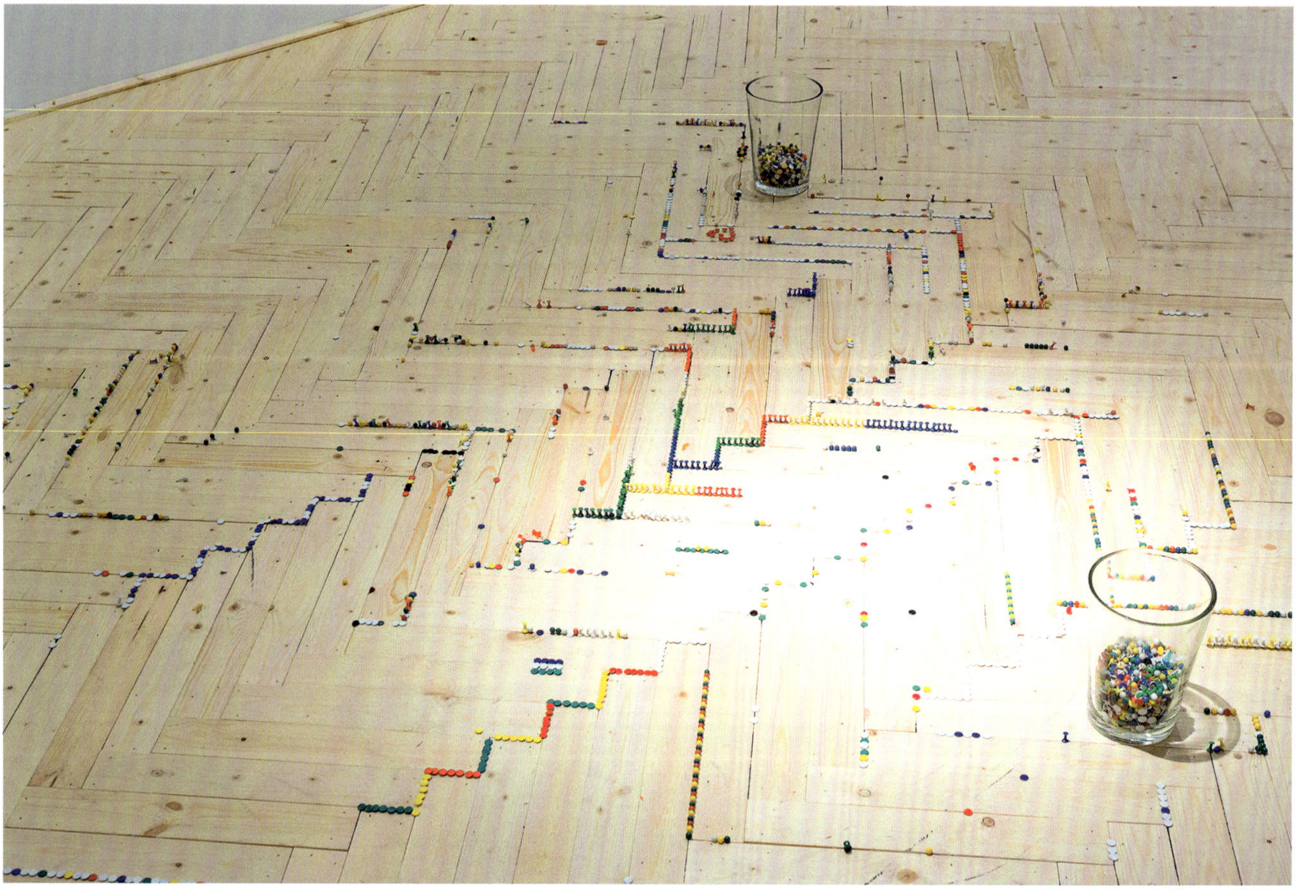

Nedko Solakov

(b. 1957, Cherven Briag, Bulgaria)

Floor
1996
Various objects, thumbtacks stuck into grooves, dimensions variable
Courtesy Moderna galerija, Ljubljana

Nedko Solakov is one of the most-recognized representatives of Eastern European art. Even though in his practice, marked by irony, humor, and absurdity, he uses the mediums of painting, video, performance, and installations, drawings are the foundation of all of his works. They often touch upon political subjects or attack demands for perfection, finality, and clarity and question collective "truths," the conditions of the art system, and the contradictions of human existence. Solakov is also a storyteller—by using visual and textual elements, his installations often create non-linear, dispersed, and multi-directional accounts that reorganize the known elements and narrative relations which are dominant in the modern world.

Floor is a simple installation, designed in 1996 for the exhibition *The Sense of Order* (*Občutek za red*) at Moderna galerija in Ljubljana. It consisted of drawing pins of various colors that were stuck into the grooves in parquet flooring. Although the work is entitled *Floor*, Solakov's intervention focuses on the grooves in the floor rather than its surface. The drawing outlined by the pins is on the one hand dictated by the pattern of the parquet boards, while on the other, it cuts into the established, given order with an arrangement of elements that follows a different logic. *Floor* points out that grooves and cracks are a constitutive part of any given order and thus subverts its universality by highlighting these gaps as a place where alternative orders might emerge. Following a logic that is characteristic of Solakov's practice, *Floor* can also be understood as a reflection on the role which the artist and his work have in the context of an art institution and, in a broader sense, in relation to the rules and limitations of the art system.

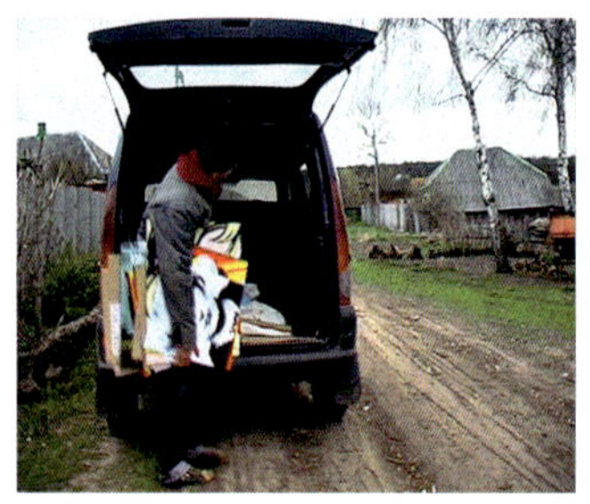
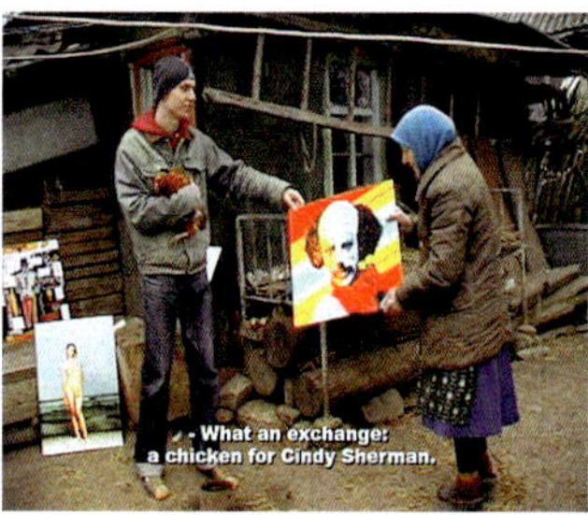
- What an exchange:
a chicken for Cindy Sherman.
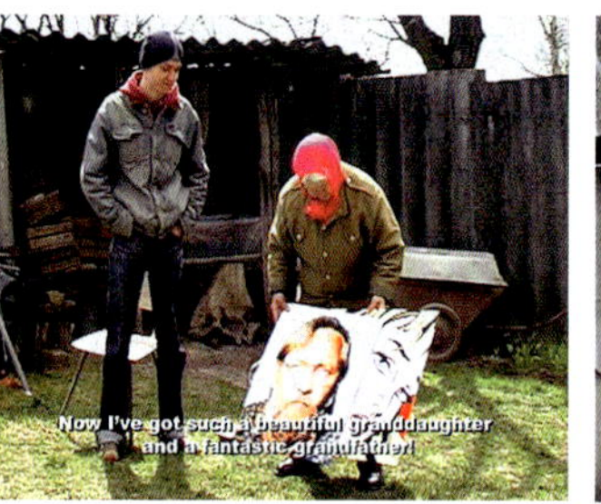
Now I've got such a beautiful granddaughter
and a fantastic grandmother!
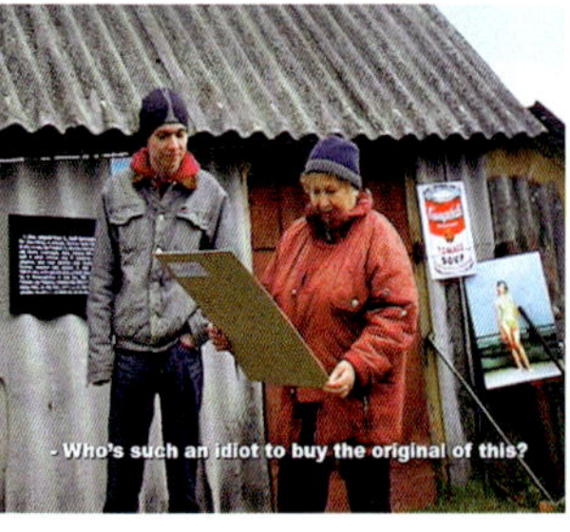
- Who's such an idiot to buy the original of this?
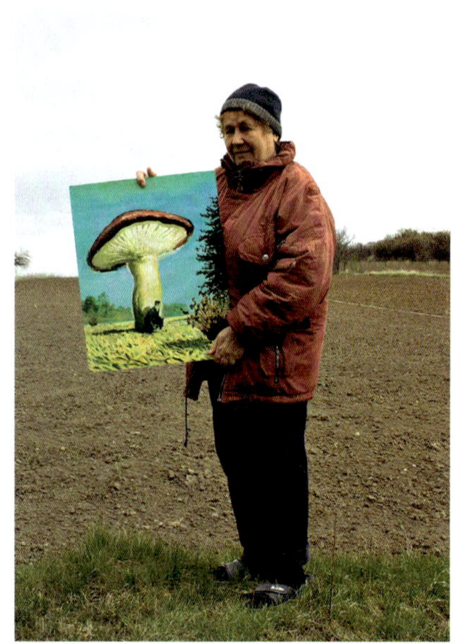
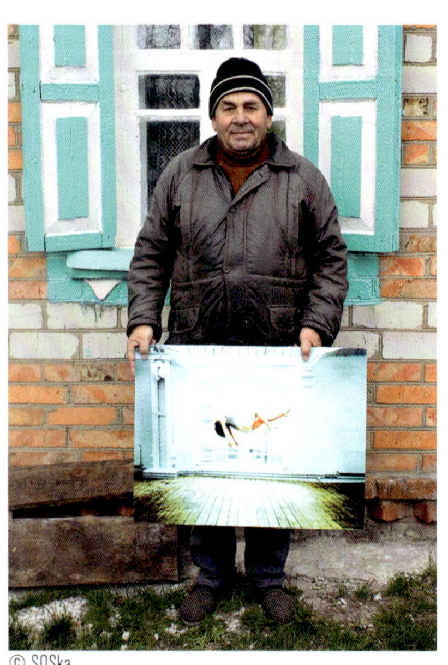
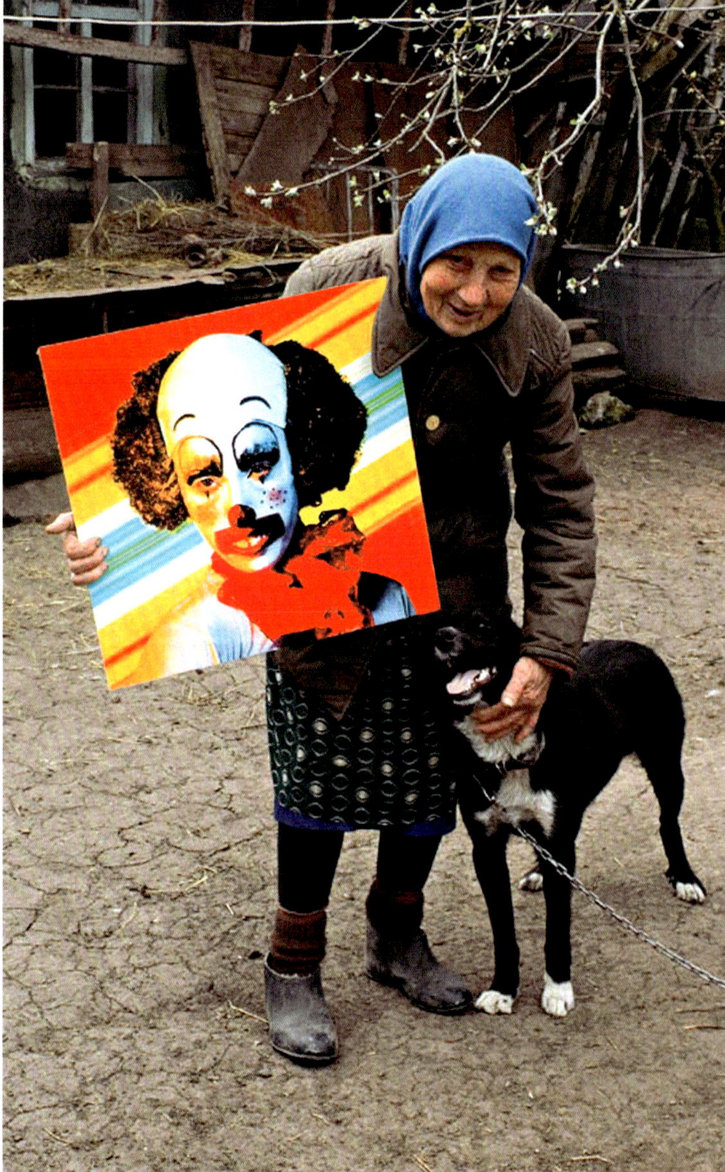

SOSka

(2005, Kharkov, Ukraine)

Barter
2007
Video, 6'54", three photographs, each 100×150 cm
Courtesy of the artists

The SOSka group originated in 2005, when Mykola Ridnyi and Anna Kriventsova began squatting in an abandoned one-story building in Kharkov, Ukraine. There they founded the SOSka gallery/laboratory with Bella Logacheva and Yelena Polyashchenko. This initiative became a focal point for Kharkov artistic life because it was essentially the only permanent, non-commercial art institution. In its work the group draws attention to socioeconomic and political issues; they evince their position through actions and their documentation, addressing poverty, social injustice, their own marginality, and post-Soviet disorder.

An excellent example is the work *They are on the Street*, when the artists, dressed as though they were homeless, wandered the streets of Kharkov and asked for money on the eve of Ukraine's 2006 parliamentary elections. They wore masks with the faces of prominent Ukrainian politicians, which in one sense was a reaction to the endless campaigning and in another was a socio-critical inversion, transforming the elite into the indigent. For the show *Impossible Community* curated by Viktor Misiano in 2011, the SOSka gallery/laboratory was recreated in a space at the Moscow Museum of Modern Art on Gogolevsky Bulvar. Adorning the walls were four photographs in which members of the group appeared alongside superstars of contemporary art Jeff Koons, Takashi Murakami, Andreas Gursky, and Damien Hirst. With this exhibition, they wanted to suggest a critical view of the landscape of the international art scene, which has become sharply stratified and is indissolubly connected with commercialism. The *Barter* performance project is also based on debunking and criticizing the art system and the power of the art market.

The artists headed to a village near Kharkov and offered locals the chance to exchange agricultural produce for prints of works by renowned contemporary artists such as Andy Warhol and Cindy Sherman, at prices set by the buyers, thereby raising the perennial issues of price and value in today's late-capitalist world.

3   The power of collaboration

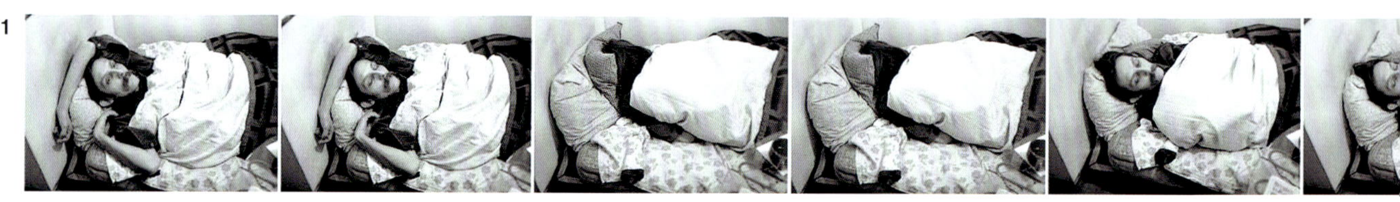

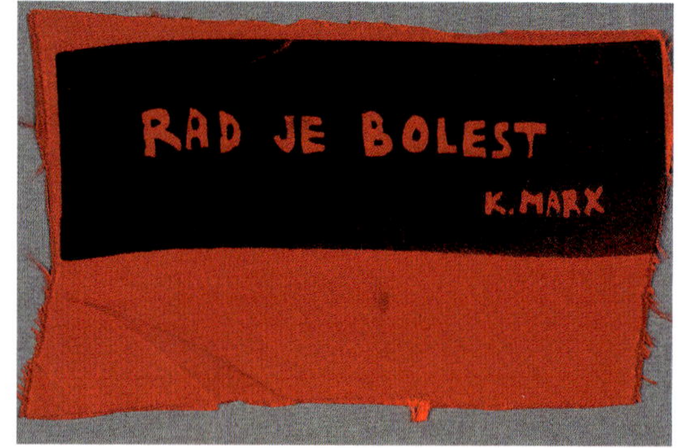

SIMBOLIKA CRVENE

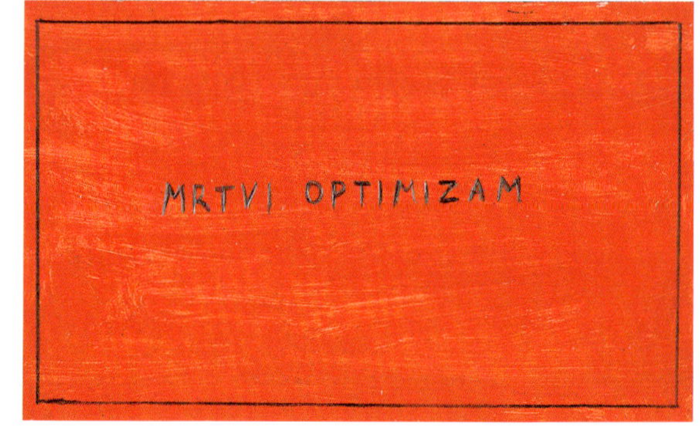

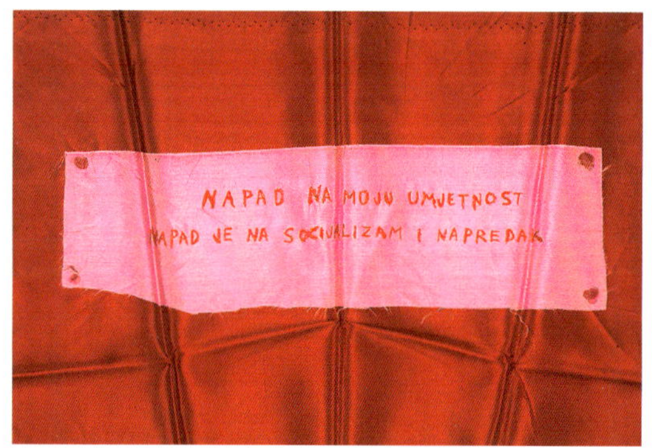

CENZURA MAŠTE

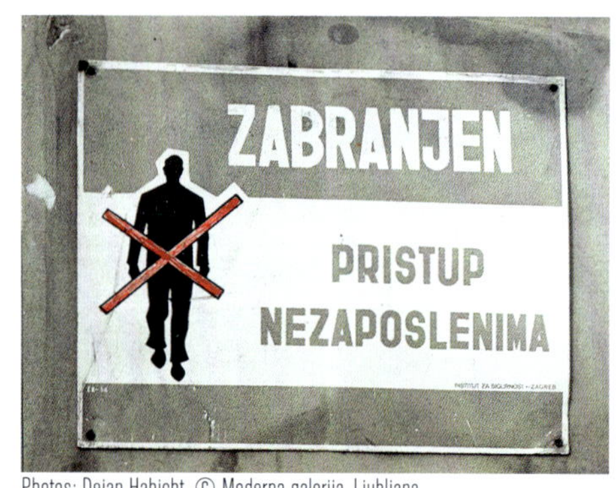

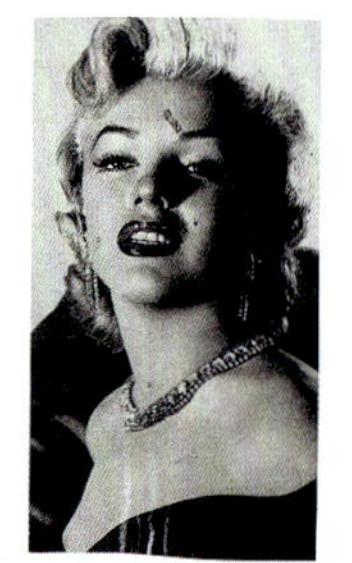

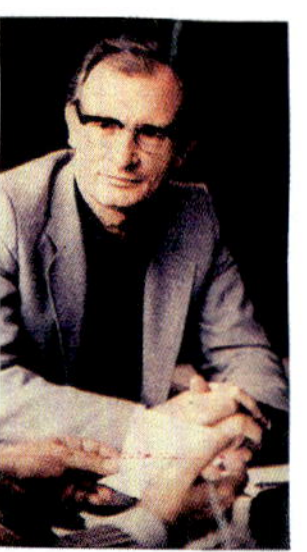

Photos: Dejan Habicht. © Moderna galerija, Ljubljana

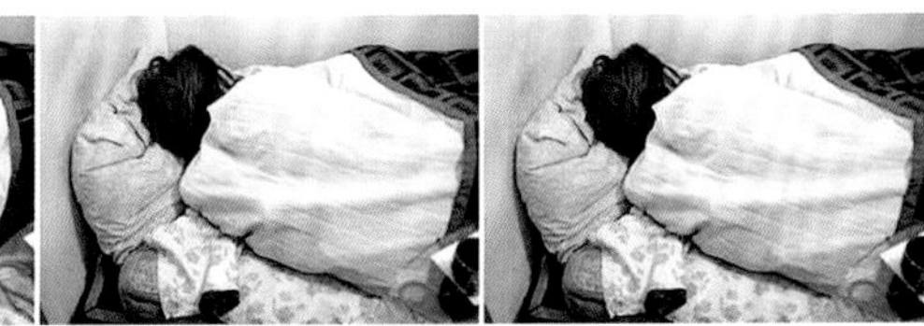

Mladen Stilinović

(b. 1947, Belgrade, Yugoslavia, now Serbia)

1
Red Era
1973-1990
8 b/w photographs, each 30×40 cm
2
Artist at Work
1977
Drawings, collage, photographs, 56 items
Courtesy Moderna galerija, Ljubljana

Mladen Stilinović is one of the founding members of the informal Group of Six Artists (Grupa šestorice autora) that was active in Zagreb from 1975 to 1979. In order to transform art and life these artists developed an alternative practice of unannounced and often humorous actions executed in public spaces in informal settings. Their works, shown outside art institutions, challenged traditional aesthetic norms, resisted the rules of the art system of the time, and criticized all forms of ideology.

From his early works onward, Stilinović has dealt with issues of social power and ideological exploitation in a humorous and ironical, yet critical, way. He has appropriated the slogans, metaphors, and symbols that are used in political and everyday speech and "exploited" them in his works in order to deconstruct their meaning and enable them to be used non-ideologically.

The color red is of special importance in his work. Besides being one of the protected and obvious socialist symbols, it is burdened with many different meanings that vary depending on the context of its use. By intensifying this plurality of meanings, Stilinović exposes their ambivalent nature and thus obstructs any meaningful reading. "If we try to read the work using our knowledge of the color red, we get an absurd reading," states the artist, who explains that by taking the color red "through a variety of contents [he] wishes to divest it of its symbolism, to make it just a color," to de-symbolise it. However, because our knowledge and symbolic networks can never be fully suppressed, we have no choice but to read his works as both "symbols and non-symbols."

In the series *Artist at Work*, one might expect to see an artist working hard in the studio, but instead we see Stilinović lying in bed. On the one hand, this is

about establishing a difference from the stereotypical notion of the lazy artist, which is often used to discredit artists' work and social status. On the other, it is a humorous way of standing up to the socialist and contemporaneous capitalist ideology of work and expanding the conception of what can be understood as work. Practicing laziness is in itself a contradictory action, through which Stilinović re-confronts us with the fact that it is impossible for work not to exist, a fact he discussed in an earlier work (*Work Cannot Not Exist*, 1976). *Artist at Work*, however, abolishes the seemingly clear line between productivity and unproductivity: if laziness can be seen as work, then work itself is marked with its own opposite. Laziness is therefore within the very essence of work.

3   The power of collaboration

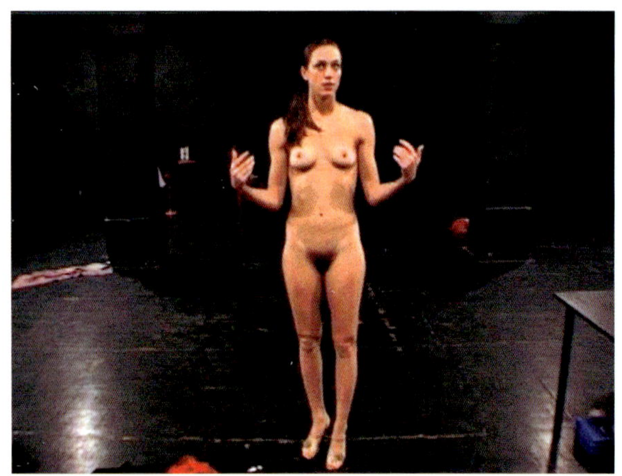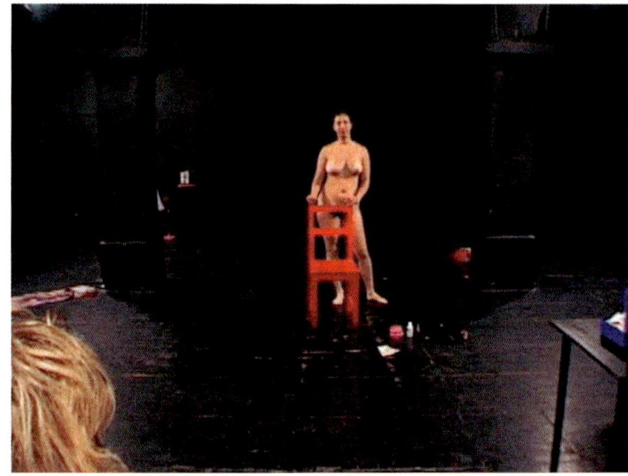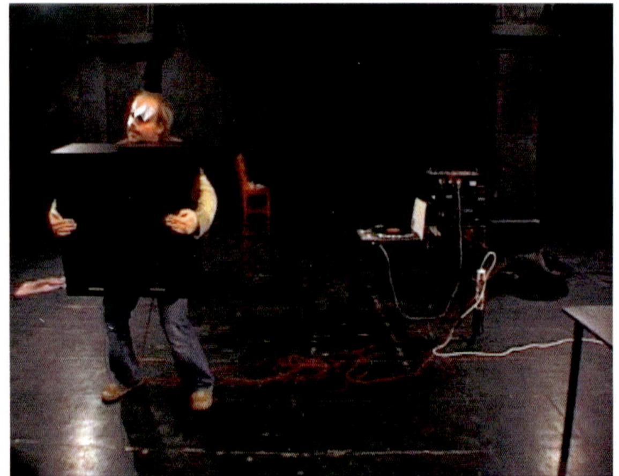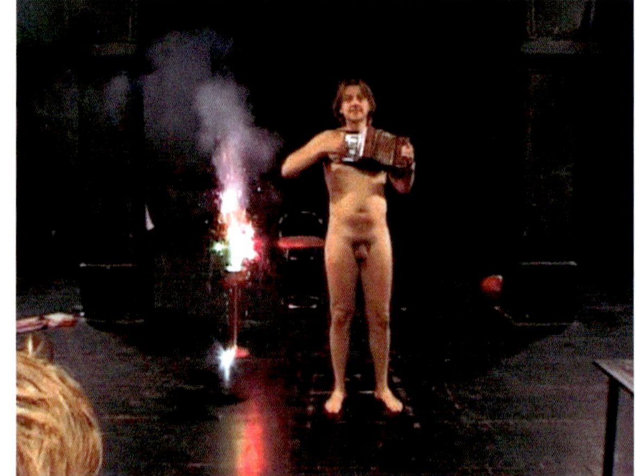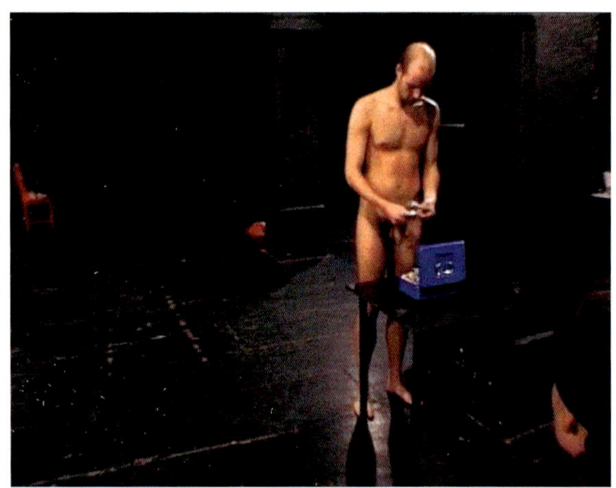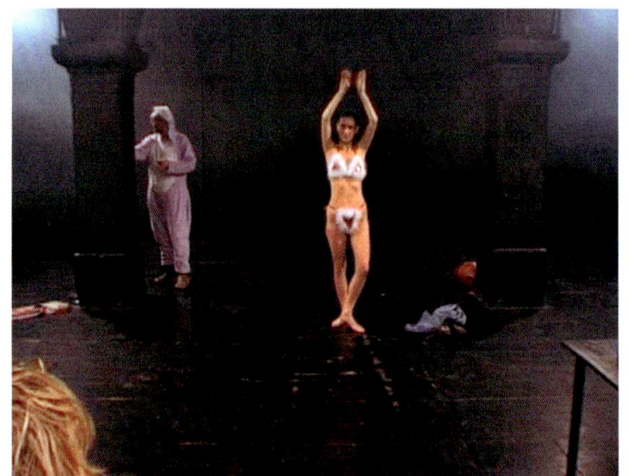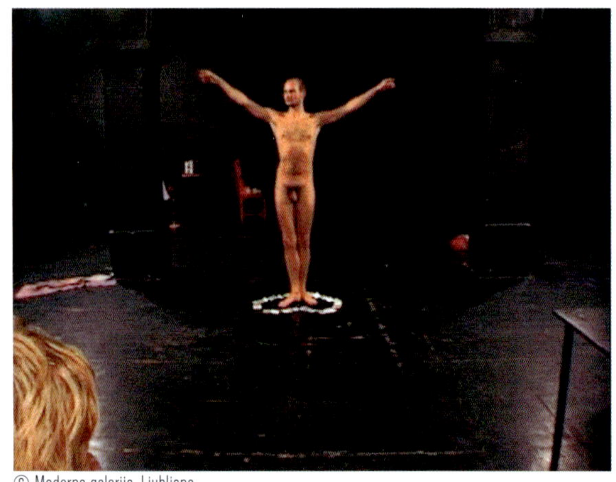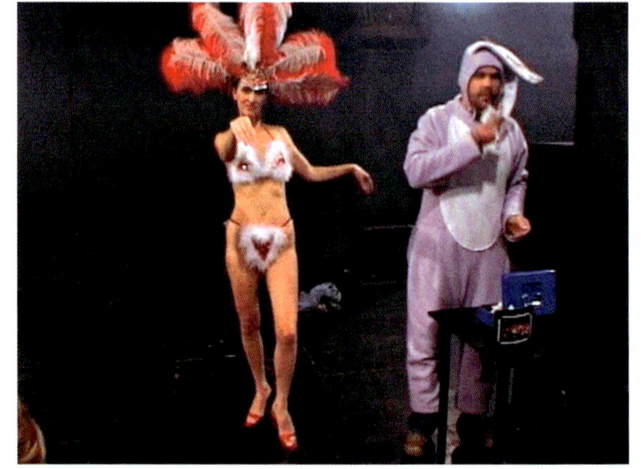

Via Negativa

(2002, Ljubljana, Slovenia)

INCASSO
2004
Video, 64'20"
Courtesy of the artists

In 2002 Bojan Jablanovec established Via Negativa, a project for contemporary theater art where the participating artists are simultaneously the performers, the authors, and the material of their performance. Although Via Negativa was active in the field of performance, the basic interests of its research remain theater and the mechanisms of theater conventions.

"Let's take a look at the present situation: you know exactly what you want for your money. You know exactly that you're not letting yourself be fooled. That you're not buying any kind of bullshit. You know exactly why you are here. You want: something beautiful, something artistic, something new, something different, something shocking, something sexual, a new interpretation, a new fascination, a new vision … You want an artistic experience. That's why you are here. And I'm here, so it's worthwhile," says Katarina Stegnar in *INCASSO*, the third of seven performances in a series entitled *Sedem smrtnih grehov* (*Seven Deadly Sins*, 2002–2008) that explores seven human characteristics: wrath, gluttony, greed, lust, sloth, envy, and pride. *INCASSO* aims to re-articulate and transform the relationship with money. The performers use the entrance fee not as payment for their work but as material for the performance. The usual circulation of money is thus interrupted in order to enable the performers to create a personal relationship with money instead of a commercial one. Every scene is a personal statement that reveals shifts, cracks, and short-circuits in the performer's identity, produced by their relationship with money.
INCASSO was directed by Bojan Jablanovec and performed by Kristian Al Droubi, Petra Govc, Jaka Lah, Sanela Milošević, Mateja Pucko, Matej Recer, Katarina Stegnar, and Grega Zorc, but was conceived and devised by the whole group.

3   The power of collaboration

Lesson 5:
The potential for uniting through adversity

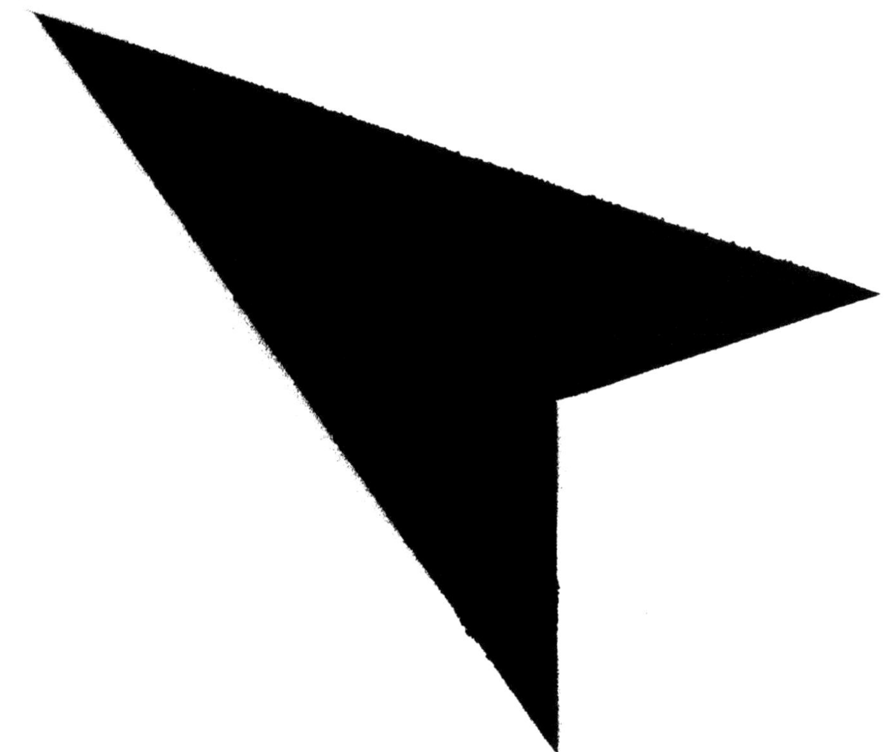

Identifying common "enemies" in times of conflict and war

The Arteast 2000+ Collection was assembled in the aftermath of a series of conflicts and wars across Eastern Europe, and many works in the collection reflect the diverse traumas that were produced by these conflicts. The artists in this final section explore existing social and political circumstances to identify more clearly common "enemies" that have emerged (and continue to do so), such as growing nationalism, religious fundamentalism, the homogenization of globalization, surveillance, and political violence, to name a few. According to the Slovene philosopher Slavoj Žižek, to clearly recognize the often invisible or generalized image of the "enemy" is of key importance in times of conflict. It is only through this that we start to share a grammar that could articulate freedom.

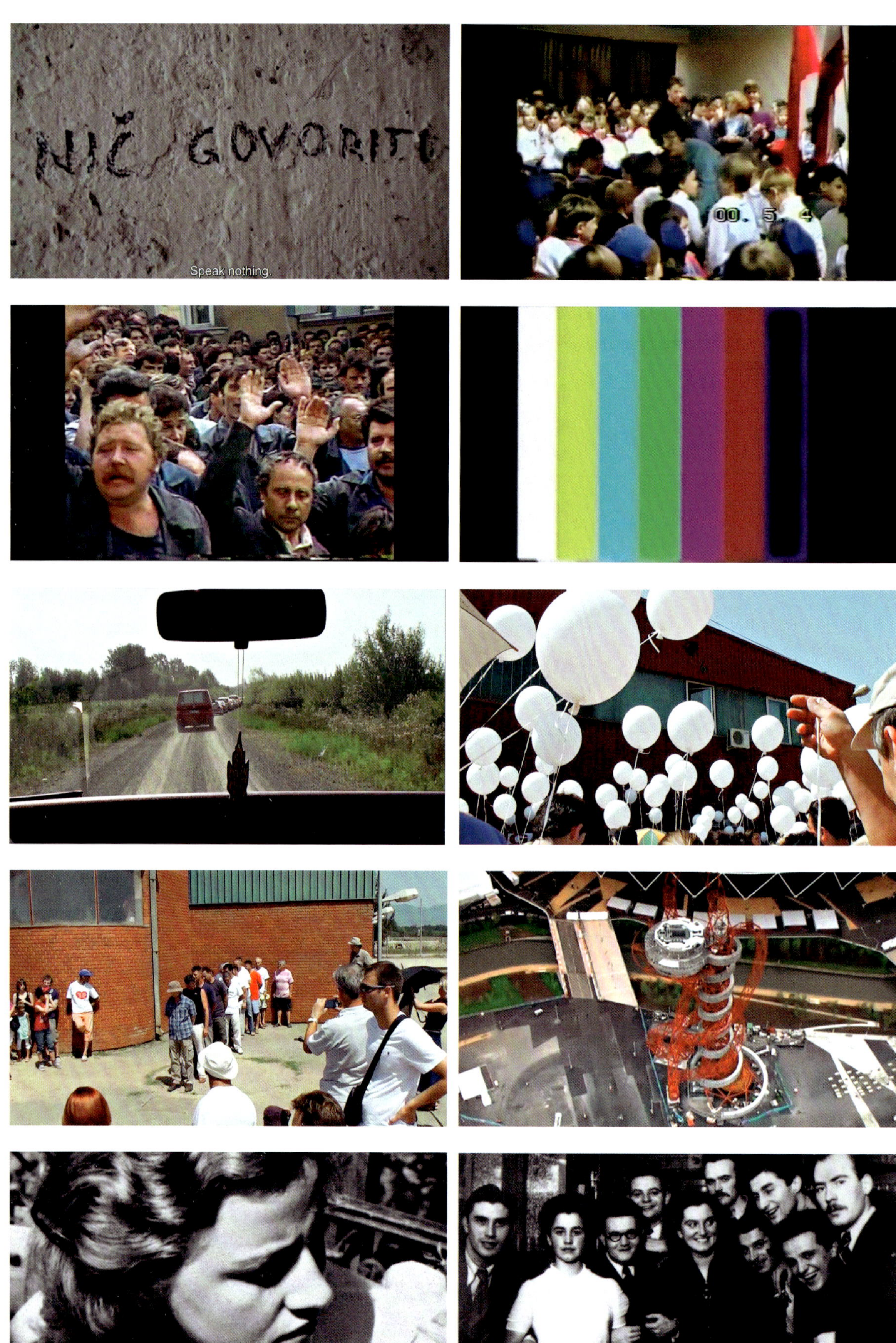
NIČ GOVORITI
Speak nothing.
Which side you are on, decide.
Which side are you on?

Nika Autor

(b. 1982, Maribor, Yugoslavia, now Slovenia)

Newsreel 55

2013

In collaboration with Marko Bratina, Ciril Oberstar, and Jurij Meden

(Obzorniška Fronta/Newsreel Front)

Video, 31'

Courtesy of the artists

As Andrej Šprah once wrote, in the former Yugoslavia newsreels as a type of subversive documentary and essayistic film practice were a rare yet precious form of political cinema. In the 1960s committed filmmakers used newsreels to probe sensitive areas that the dominant media, subordinated to the ruling ideology, did not report on. Nowadays, it is possible to re-actualize this film genre. In Slovenia a new newsreel front of political cinema is emerging, one that strives to shed light on the consequences of raging capitalism. Obzorniška Fronta (Newsreel Front), or OF for short, is an informal collective of workers from the fields of theory and art practice who try to make the question of the necessity of committed journalism topical again in various sociopolitical constellations by confronting past works and creative initiatives of the present.

Newsreel 55, a collective work by Nika Autor, Marko Bratina, Ciril Oberstar, and Jurij Meden, is a compilation of quotations, archival footage, and footage of current events relating to the territory of the former Socialist Federal Republic of Yugoslavia, with a special focus on Maribor, once the third largest industrial center in the country. It explores questions that relate to the social and political shifts of the 20th century, which shaped the city's economic, political, and social dynamics; a city of occupation, a city of industrialization and deindustrialization, and a city marked by the disintegration of the state. These periods are presented through the eyes of the generation that grew up during the transition between two systems. How can images be used today and what political impact and power do they have? Which issues do they raise with regard to the class struggle of today?

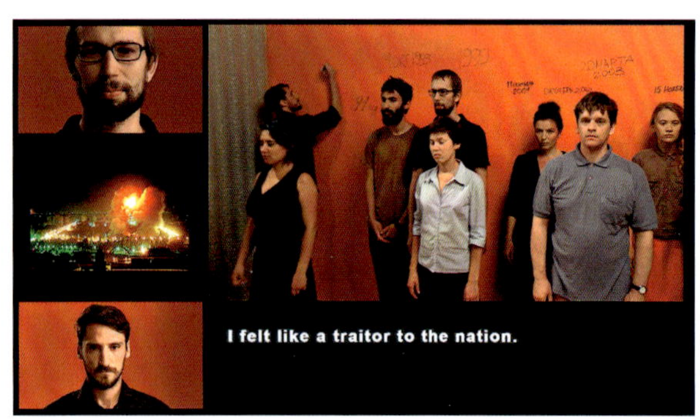
I felt like a traitor to the nation.

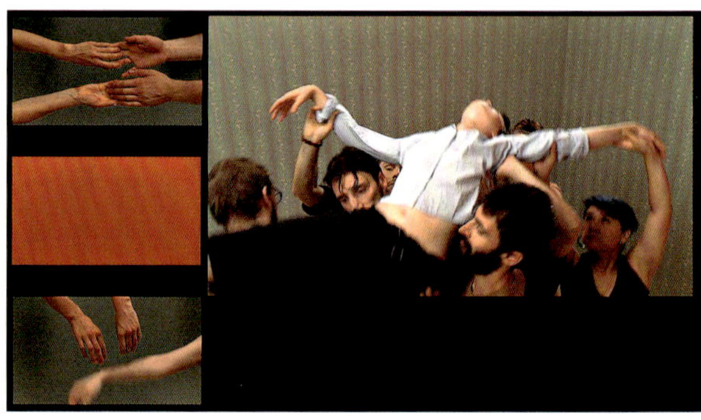

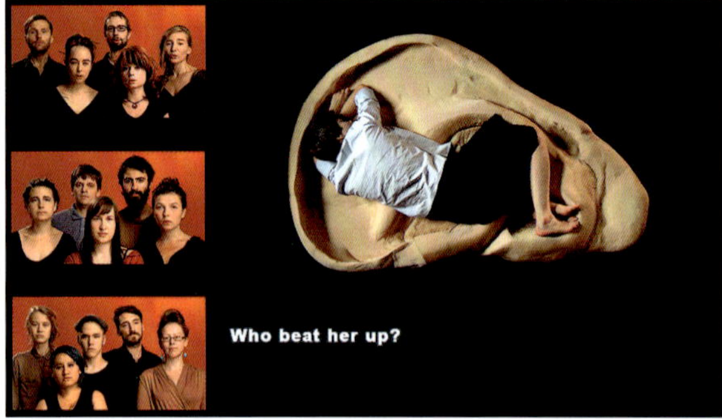
Who beat her up?

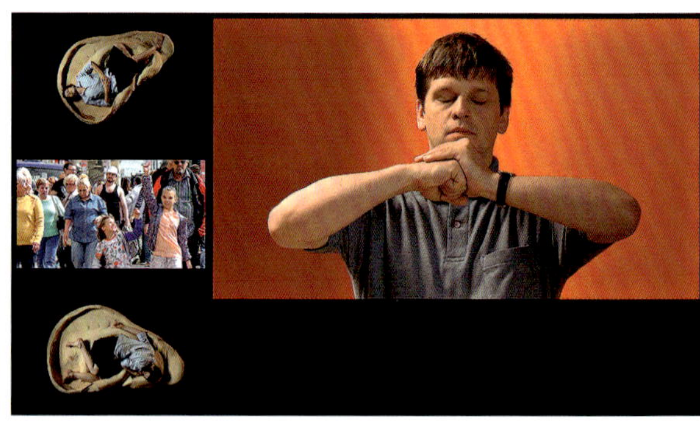

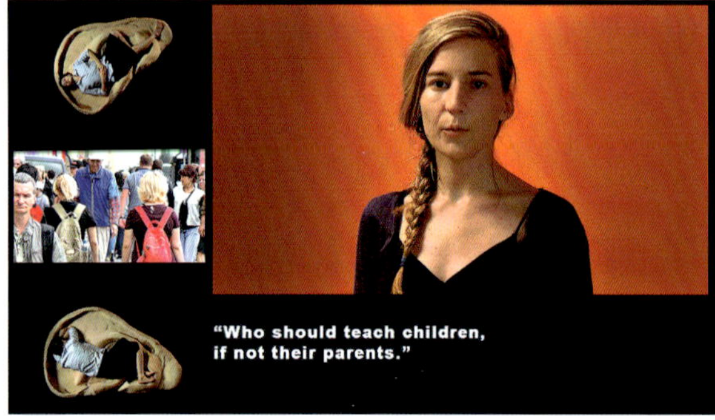
"Who should teach children,
if not their parents."

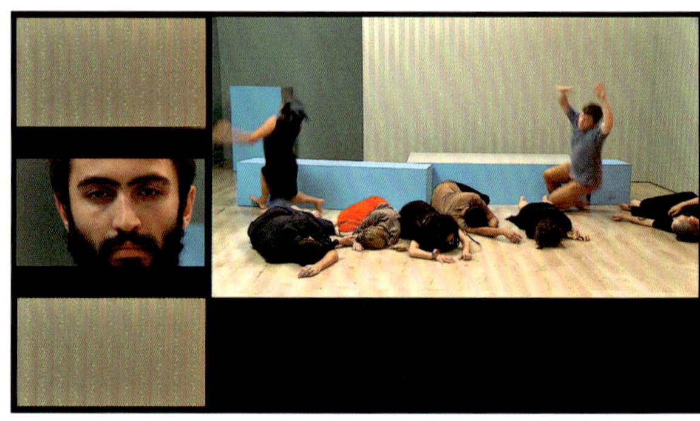

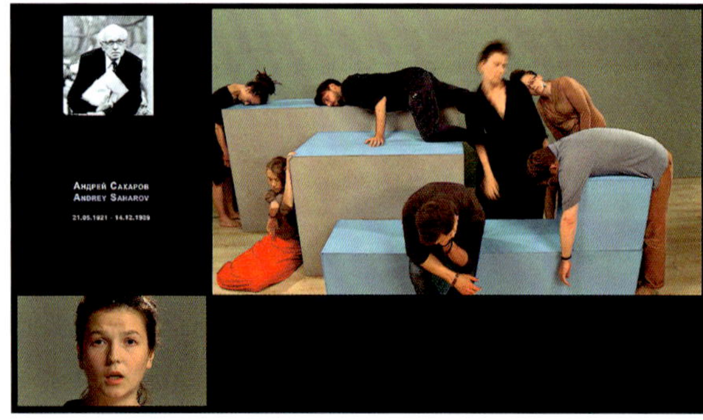
Андрей Сахаров
Andrey Saharov

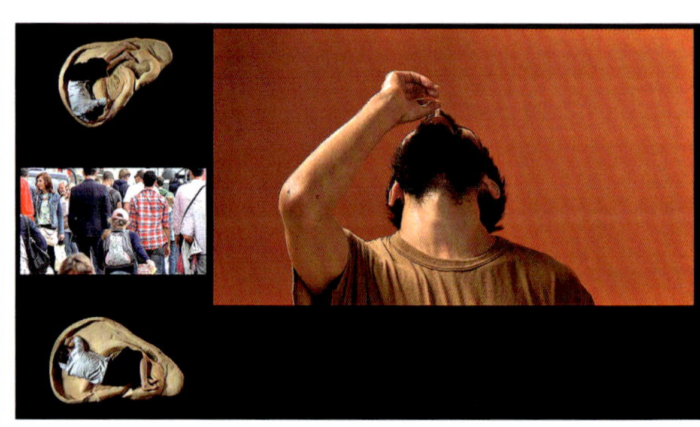

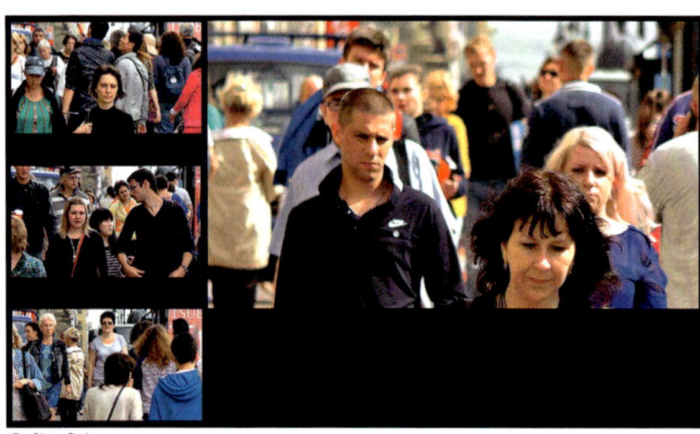

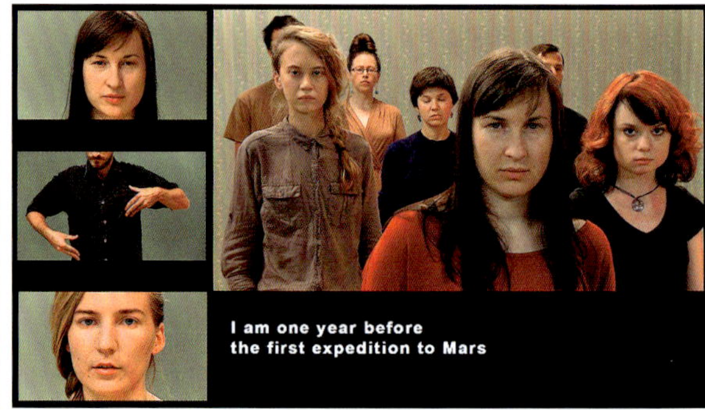
I am one year before
the first expedition to Mars

The Excluded. In a Moment of Danger
2014
Video, 56'
Film concept, design and editing: Olga Egorova (Tsaplya)
and Dmitry Vilensky
Director: Olga Egorova (Tsaplya)
Choreography: Nina Gasteva and Mikhail Ivanov
Made with the support of Secession (Vereinigung bildender KünstlerInnen
Wiener Secession); Kunstbunker – Forum für zeitgenössische Kunst,
Nuremberg; and Fundação Bienal de São Paulo
Courtesy of the artists

The group Chto Delat was founded by artists, critics, philosophers, and writers from St. Petersburg, Moscow, and Nizhny Novgorod. Its activities are varied—the members make films, stage productions, publish a newspaper, run the School of Engaged Art, and organize discussions and educational programs around the world. Owing to a creative method based on combining political theory, art, and activism, the group's work is highly critical with regard to the world around it. One of the main genres in which the group works is the social musical, the "songspiel" in Brechtian terminology, where the actors play out the most critical political issues of the day. As a rule the main narrative in the work is a specific historical event, which the artists subject to analysis and interpretation; they propose that viewers take a new view of recent history.

The film *The Excluded. In a Moment of Danger* is based on a theater performance by members of the School of Engaged Art. Thematically the work is connected with the recent social situation in Russia—the failure of citizen-led initiatives, government repression, and the overall sense of depression that has overcome people. The closed space where the action takes place evokes the claustrophobia that has paralyzed the country's public space with fear. The immutability of politics, the dashed hopes and futile expectations of which the actors speak, are also manifested in their movements and gestures, which convey a sense of the collective social body, laden with emotions.

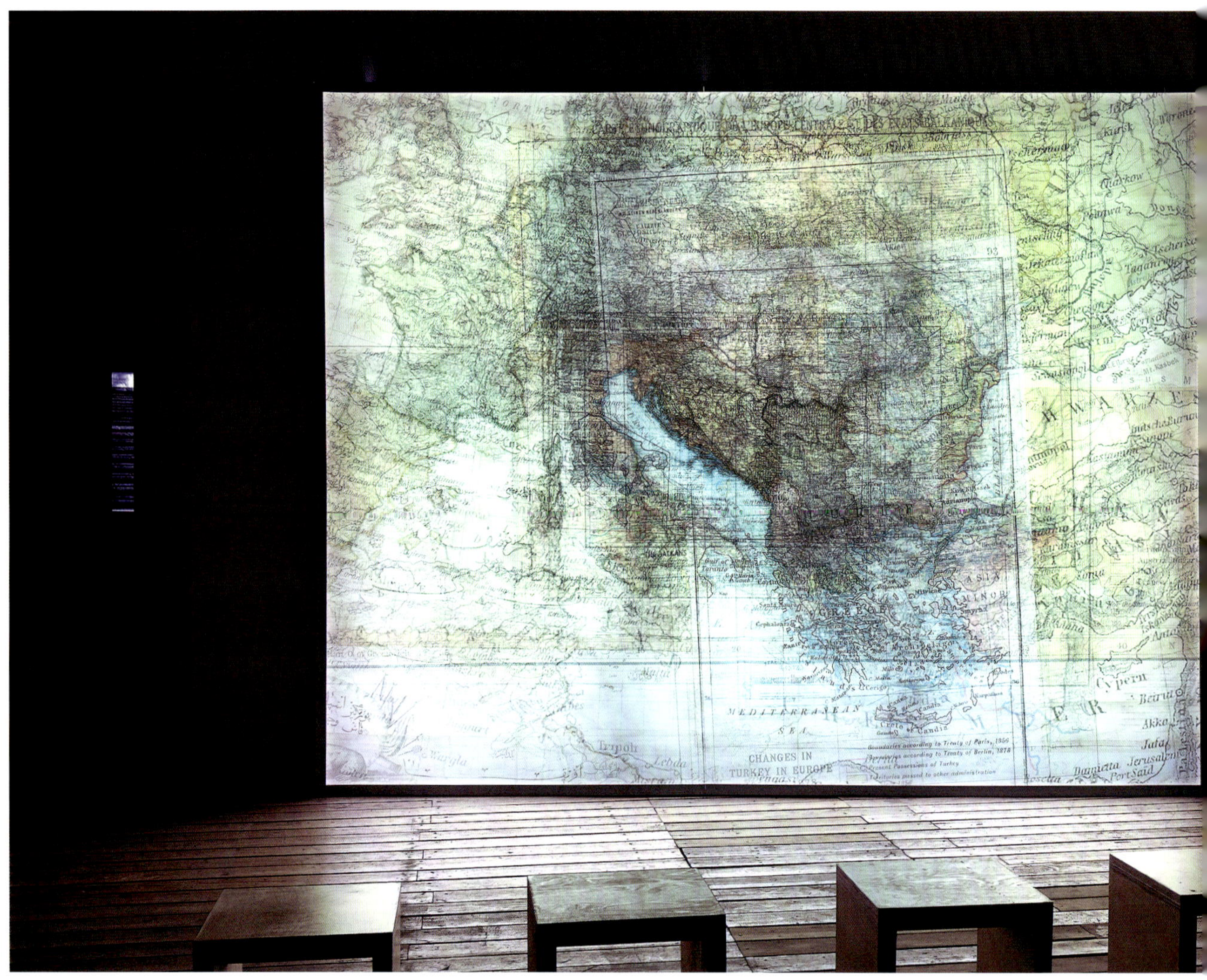
MEDITERRANEAN SEA
CHANGES IN TURKEY IN EUROPE
Boundaries according to Treaty of Paris, 1856
Boundaries according to Treaty of Berlin, 1878
Present Possessions of Turkey
Territories passed to other administration
Crete or Candia

Lana Čmajčanin

(b. 1983, Sarajevo, Yugoslavia, now Bosnia and Herzegovina)

551.35 – Geometry of Time
2014
Installation, 343×266 cm
Courtesy of the artist

551.35 – Geometry of Time confronts us with various delimitations of the territory of Bosnia and Herzegovina, whose borders were set and changed following dynamic and intense historical processes. It points out the social and political reality of Bosnia and Herzegovina by illuminating the conflictual and unstable nature of its territory. For centuries the borders were set by wars and peace treaties, while in the 19th and 20th centuries they were constituted by turbulent ideological events. At that time cartography turned into political geography and produced openly nationalistic, imperialistic, intentionally educational maps with a clearly underlined territorial nature. Besides the territory they represent, historical maps of Bosnia and Herzegovina thus also map the interests and conquest plans of cartographers throughout history.

In *551.35 – Geometry of Time* the light object that illuminates multiple layers of overlapping maps of the territories of former Yugoslav republics serves the same purpose as the special tables used in the army to enable a more precise, clearer reading of maps. Since the density of marks makes the borders unclear, the work can be read as an overlapping of all previous texts that results in illegibility and the inability to consider the sovereignty and statehood of this area as it is today through the numerous layers of the past.

5   The potential for uniting through adversity

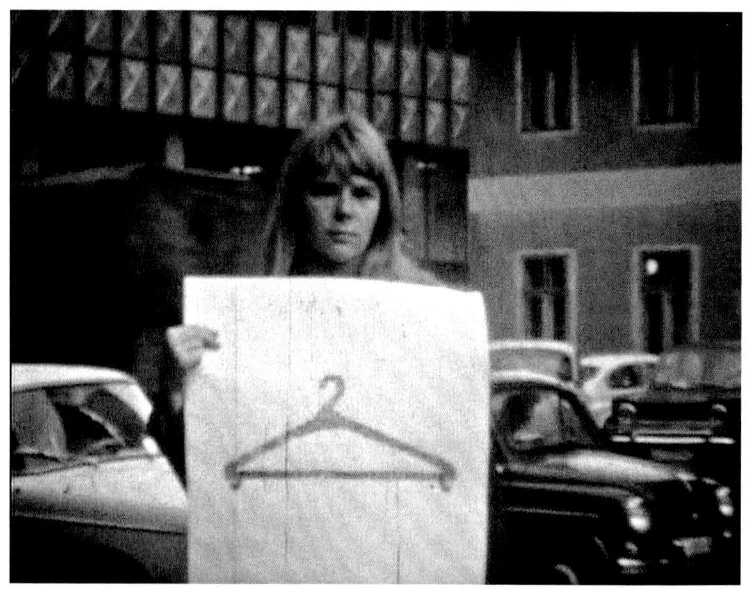

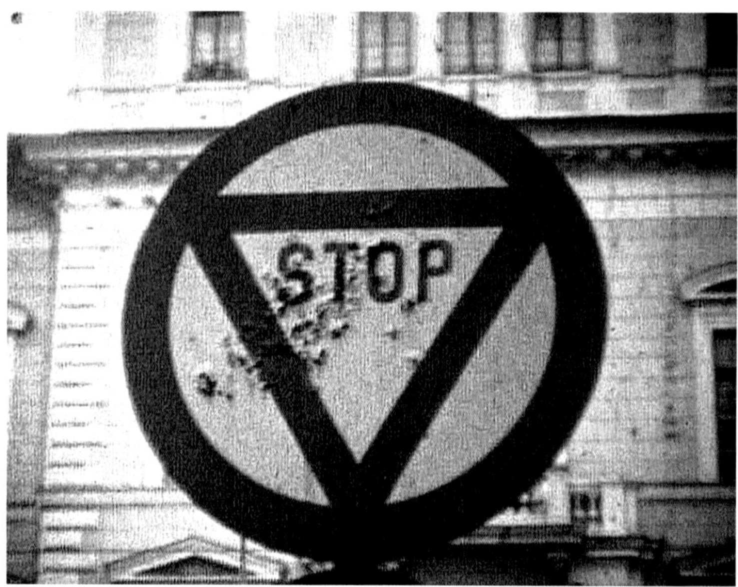

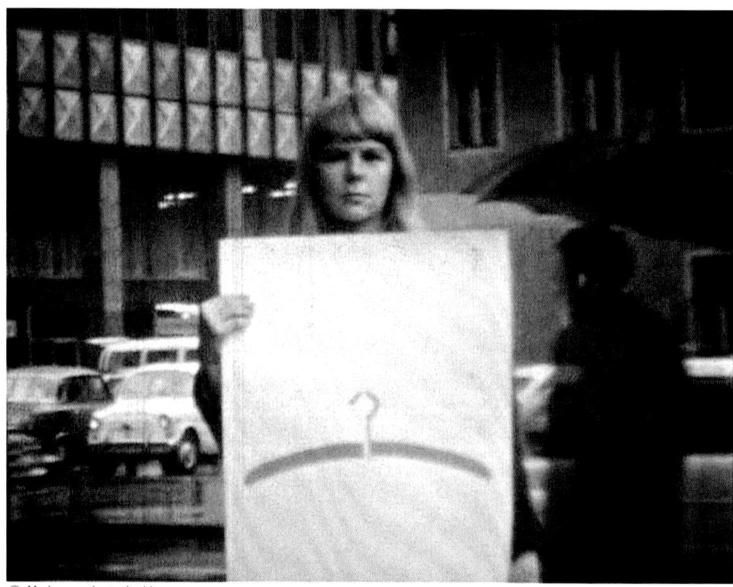

© Moderna galerija, Ljubljana

Ana Nuša and Srečo Dragan

(1943, Jesenice, Yugoslavia, now Slovenia—2011; b. 1944, Spodnji Hrastnik, Yugoslavia, now Slovenia)

RG Vietnam
1969
Film, 8 mm, b/w, sound, 2'50"
Courtesy of Srečo Dragan

In the former Yugoslavia Srečo and Ana Nuša Dragan are regarded as pioneers in the field of video art. They are the most important representatives of the so-called New Artistic Practice that in Slovenia was a continuation of the conceptual and avant-garde art of the 1960s. Their practice included the production of actions, conceptual projects, films, and videos.

The two artists were active as a duo in the late 1960s, when they filmed several original works where they took on the role of screenwriter and actor. The use of quotes from the history of filmmaking (Eisenstein, Tarkovsky, Resnais) is typical of their later works. They also strove to use sound in a different way. In their videos sound is not a mere illustration of the visual content, but a medium in itself.

RG Vietnam is based on the idea of group communication and tries to encourage the audience to help decline, in reverse order, the word "vietnam". On the one hand, *RG Vietnam* can be understood as an explicitly political work connected to a concrete historical moment, since it was created at the time when student movements and protests against the Vietnam War were organized worldwide. However the artists, as Ana Nuša said in an interview, did not want to make another boilerplate protest film about Vietnam. Active participation in the declination of the word "vietnam" makes the audience aware of the social context, seeing it as a reality which does not tolerate passivity.

5   The potential for uniting through adversity

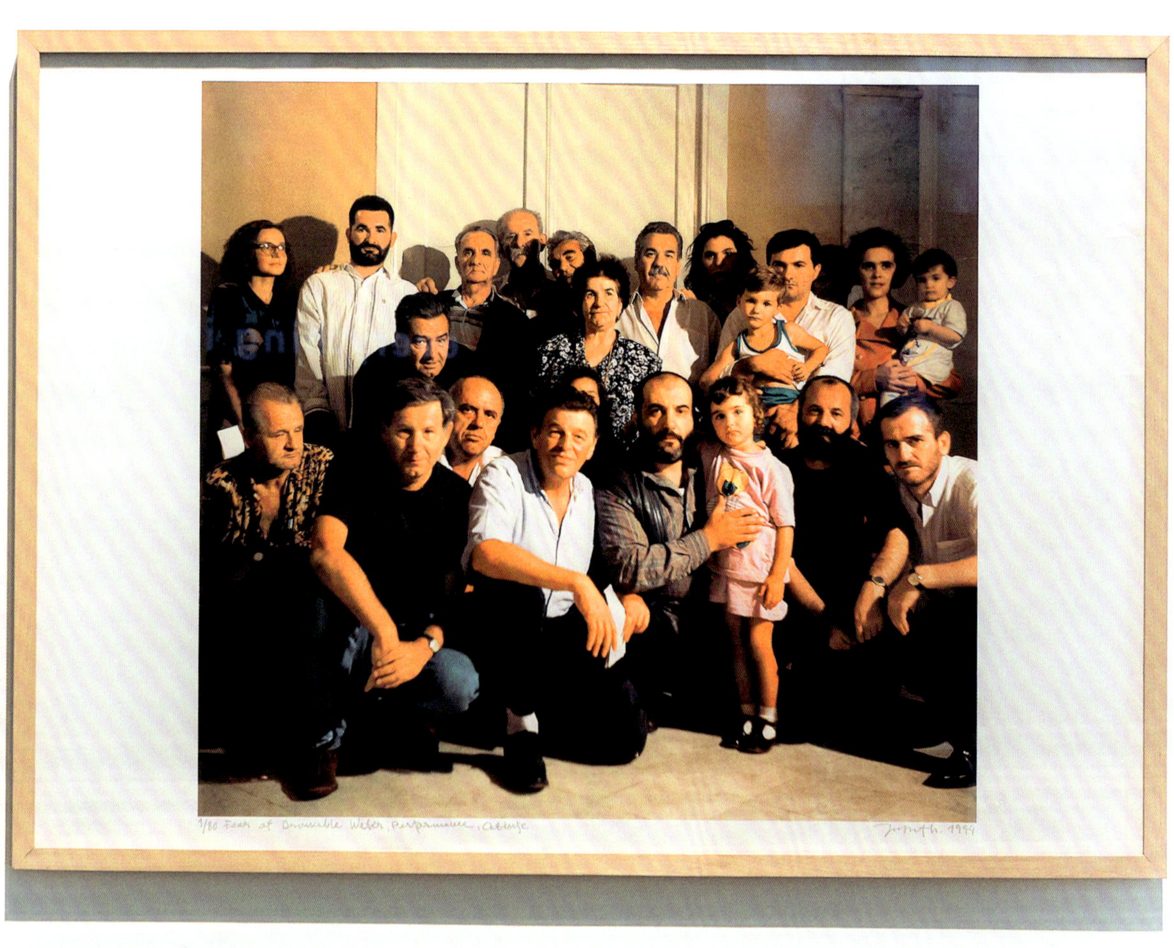

Jusuf Hadžifejzović

(b. 1956, Prijepolje, Yugoslavia, now Serbia)

The Fear of Drinking Water
1994
Silkscreen print, 70×64 cm
Courtesy Moderna galerija, Ljubljana

Jusuf Hadžifejzović began his career as a painter, but since the 1970s his main focus has been on performance and a special type of practice based on an almost "archeological" investigation of depots. He has been collecting stored items and depositing them again, rearranged, in the form of installations in exhibition spaces. Hadžifejzofić's so-called depotgraphies, as Ugo Vlaisavljević writes, have a strong political sense: they "release deposited things from captivity. To offer an exit from depots is to acknowledge the worth of things previously removedfrom the public eye. By taking them from the dark shadows of depots and putting them under the bright light of exhibition rooms, he restores their lost dignity, as if they were amnestied prisoners."

In 1994, Hadžifejzović, who was living in Belgium as a war refugee at the time, was invited to participate at the Cetinje Biennial in Montenegro as an eminent artist. Although his depotgraphic practice primarily targets gallery and museum repositories and focuses on the items that they store, at the Cetinje Biennial he decided to gather and exhibit (redeposit) his "deposited kith and kin." Instead of focusing on the repositories of the Montenegrin museums and galleries he invited all the members of his large family to attend the biennial exhibition. *The Fear of Drinking Water* is a family portrait documenting this first family reunion after a three-year separation during the war. On the basis of this photograph, Hadžifejzović later developed a series of performances with the same title that dealt with the collective trauma of separation and loss.

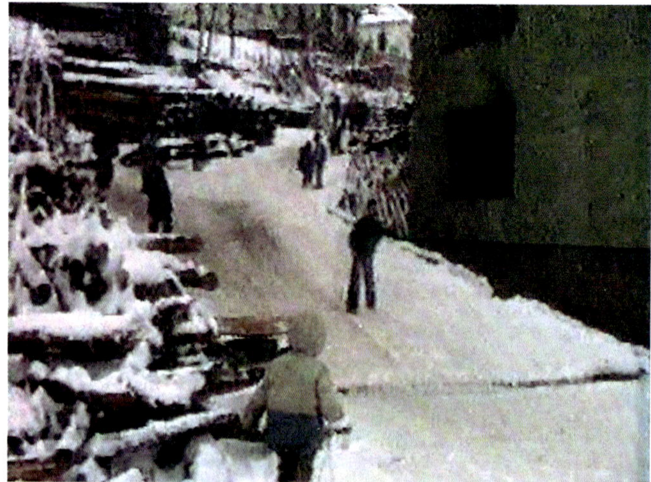 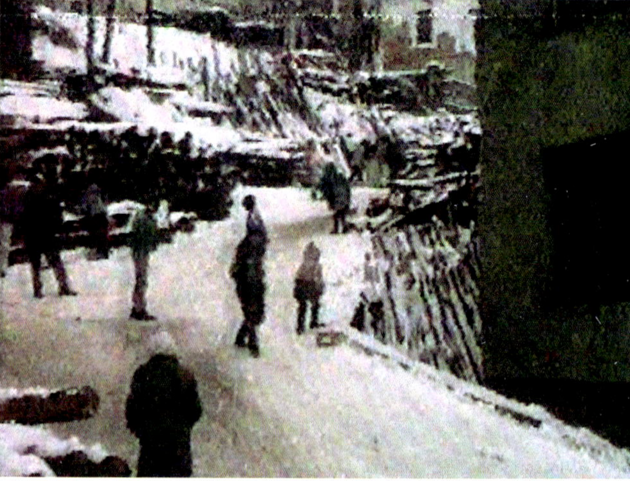

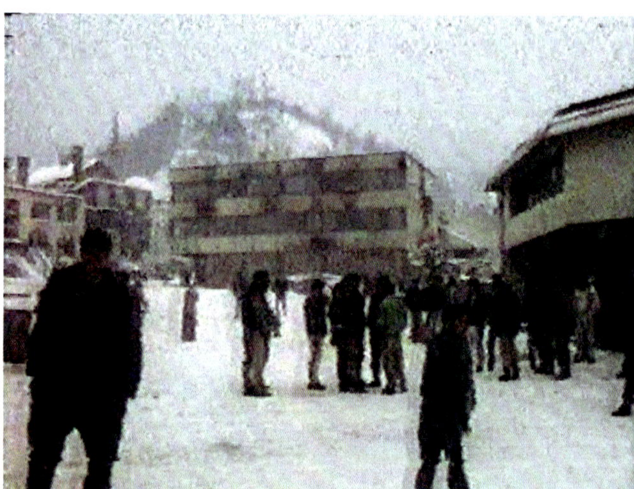 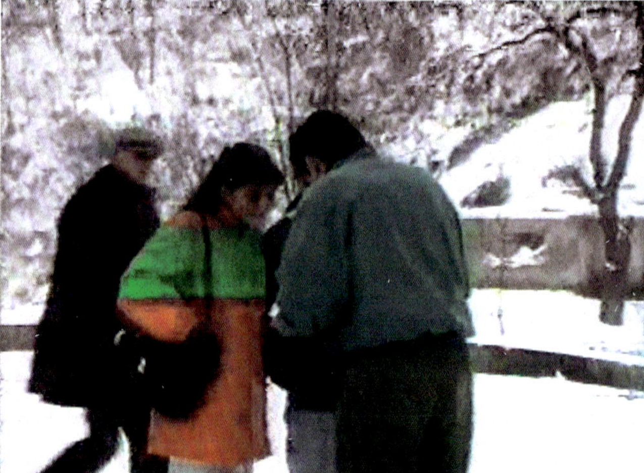

Ibro Hasanović

(b. 1981, Ljubovija, Yugoslavia, now Serbia)

30. Nov '93 – Pieter Brueghel
in the Letters of my Father
2013
Video, 3'36"
Courtesy of the artist

30. Nov '93 – Pieter Brueghel in the Letters of my Father is, as Hasanović explains, a video made from the "VHS letter" that his father sent him during the war in Bosnia. The sequences of children playing in snow closely resemble Pieter Brueghel's paintings; but while in his paintings it seems as if all children ever do is play, the fragmented sequences used by Hasanović evoke a different notion of time, especially if we consider the context in which they were recorded. As Bojana Piškur observes, the children in Hasanović's film "are completely unaware of what is going on around them, they are so absorbed in their activities that we actually feel what Agamben meant by 'invasion of life by play'. According to Agamben, the invasion in question is a change and acceleration of time. Play is not only about the present moment, it is about the destruction of the calendar, when people free themselves from regular time and, in Hasanović's case, from the time of war atrocities and suffering. Observing children at play in a war-torn town can mean only one thing: what children are playing with are not merely toys, but history as well."

The artist reorganized these very personal documents in such a way that they became "a place for imagination, for the creation of absent history. Not only for his family, but also for us, the observers in a gallery space." Hasanović's work thus reactivates "the relationship between the poetical (children playing, people talking in the streets, the almost bucolic atmosphere of a snow-covered town) and the political (the harshness of war, not evident at first glance)."

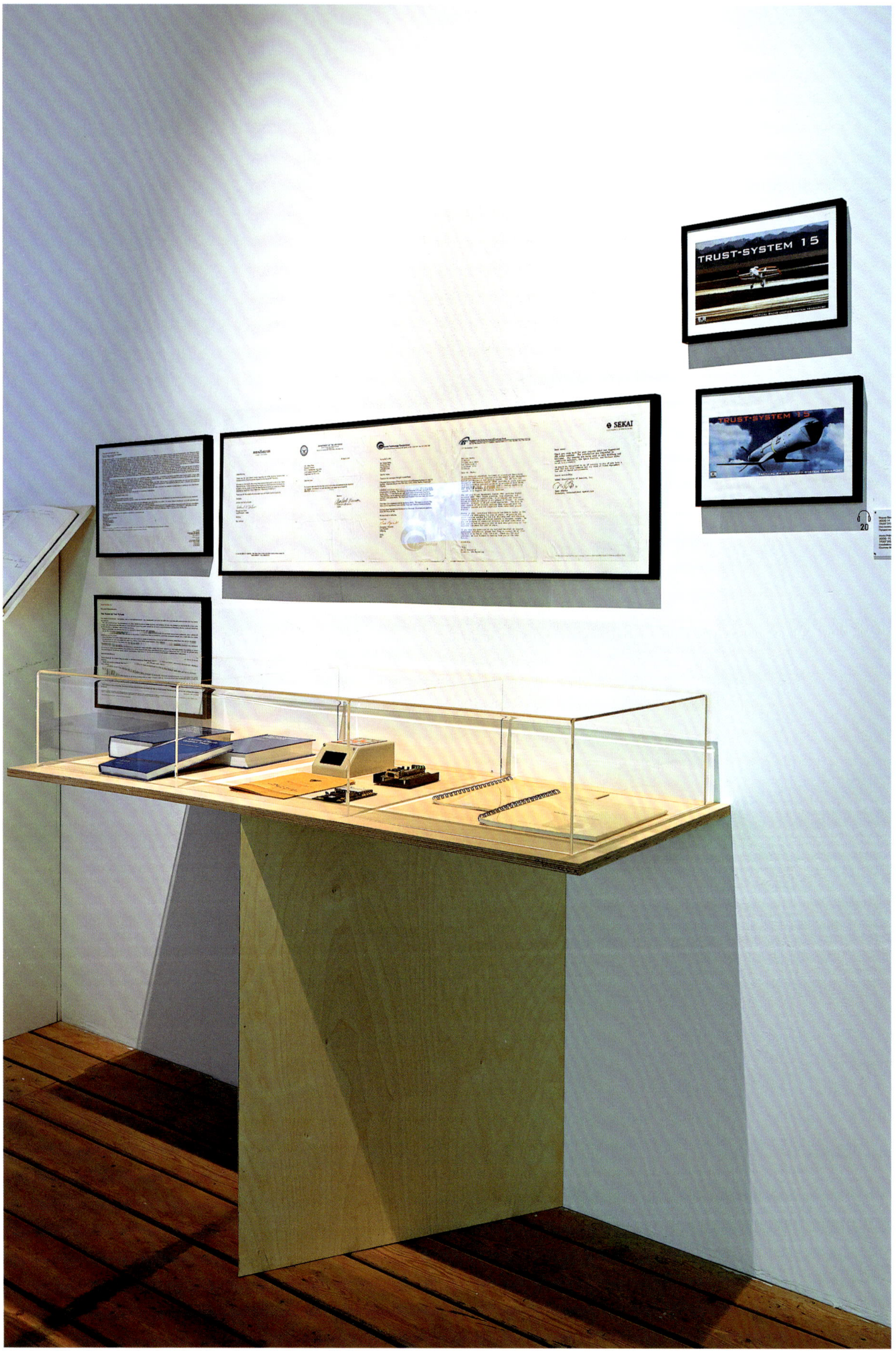

Marko Peljhan

(b. 1969, Šempeter pri Gorici, Yugoslavia, now Slovenia)

1
UCOG-14
1996
2
TRUST SYSTEM-15
1999
Mixed media
Courtesy Moderna galerija, Ljubljana

Marko Peljhan deals with questions of art, science, and technology, drawing upon the experiences of historical avant-gardes and their utopian thought. One of the key themes of his work is the relationship between humankind, nature, and technology in the context of today's society. He explored the issues of communication and control through technology in *Makrolab* (1997–2007), a project focusing on research into global dynamic systems (telecommunications, migrations, and weather), and in projects such as *UCOG-14* and *TRUST SYSTEM-15*, which form part of *Resolutions*, a series of works that focus on practical solutions to certain problems of society.

UCOG-14 (Urban Colonization and Orientation Gear 14) was developed by the technology branch of Projekt Atol called PACT SYSTEMS (founded by Peljhan in 1995) and represents one of the first participatory networked mapping projects based on Global Positioning Systems (GPS). This was the first time that GPS, a military technology, was used in the civil sector in Slovenia.

TRUST SYSTEM-15 (Tactical Radio Unified System Transport) was brought about by communication with the military-industrial complex and the collecting of documents and basic UAV (unmanned aerial vehicle) technology. The system is to be used as a mobile platform for civilian/tactical purposes—the tactical transmission of radio programs over a territory where it is impossible to do so by ordinary means due to military actions and civil repression, and the collection of intelligence for civil use. As UAVs have become a weapon in the hands of Western militaries and, as such, a means of control and repression, efforts to find an alternative use of UAV technology become urgent. Peljhan and his team are interested in how to maintain a certain level of civil control and use the technology, whose development is directed by military interest, as a tool of resistance, protection of citizens' rights, and civilian access to information.

5   The potential for uniting through adversity

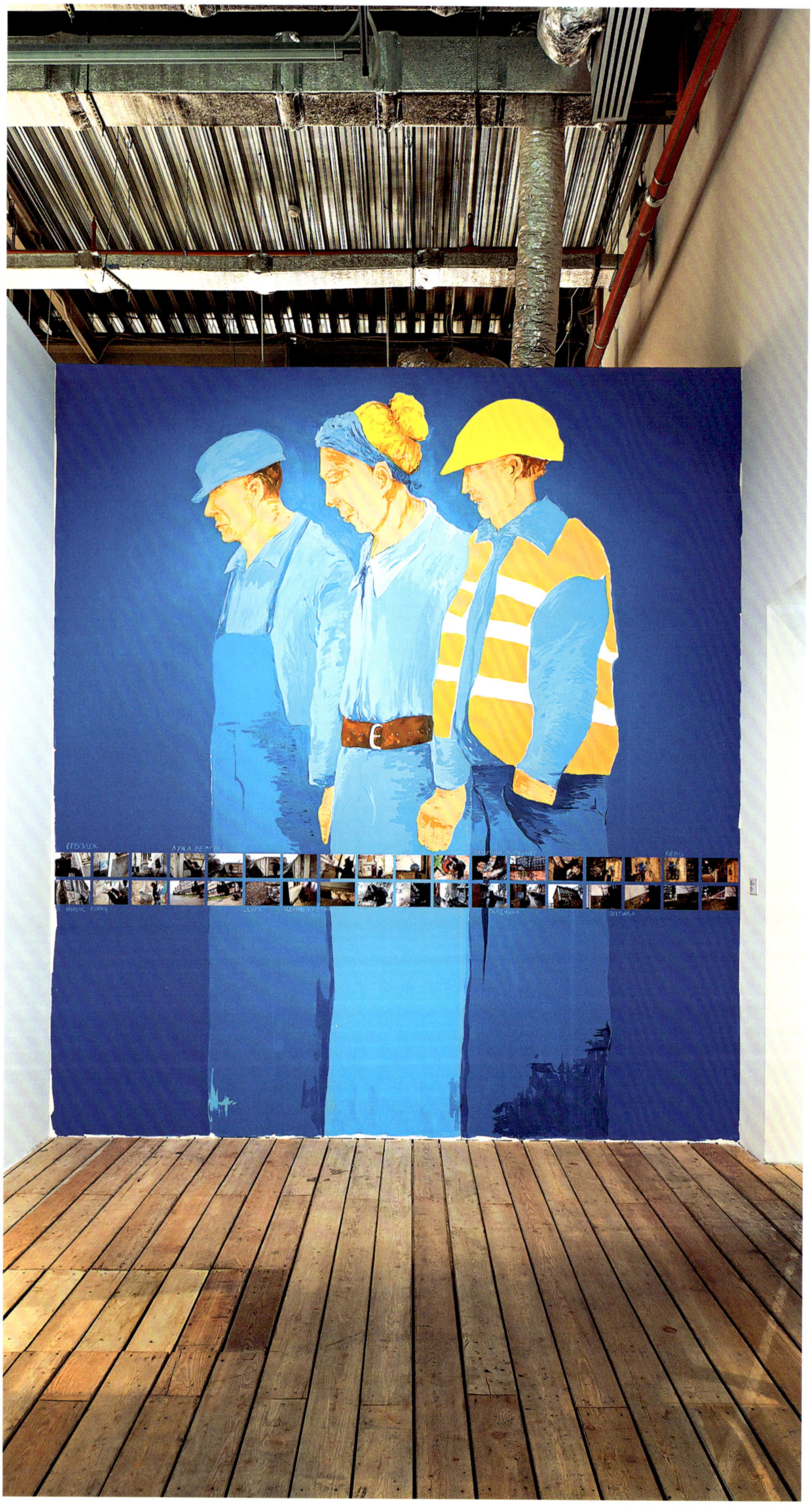

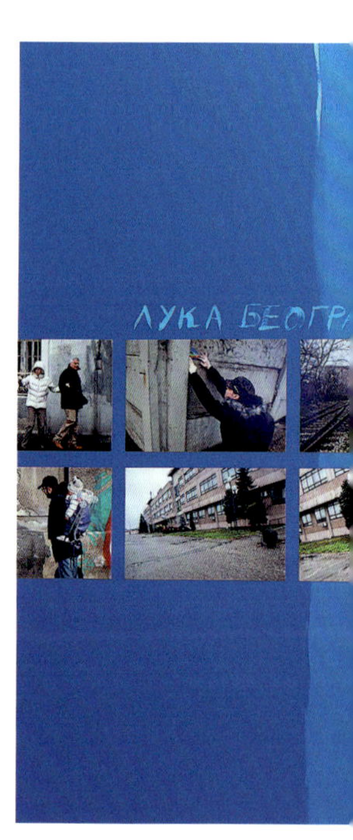

ЛУКА БЕОГРА

Darinka Pop-Mitić

(b. 1975, Belgrade, Yugoslavia, now Serbia)

Useful Idiot

2014

Mural, 36 photographs, each 13×18 cm

Photos: Nenad Kostić

Courtesy of the artist

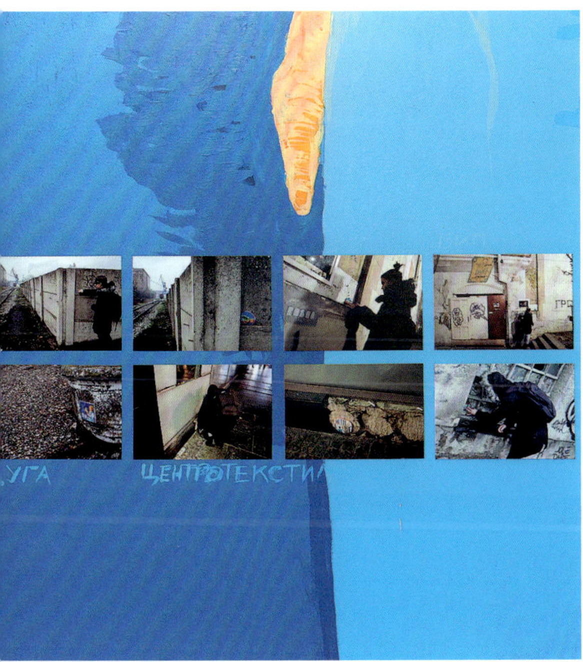

Useful Idiot, conceived by Darinka Pop-Mitić especially for this exhibition, consists of a wall painting and a number of small photographs. The photographs document several actions which the artist performed in Belgrade a few months before the opening. Her site-specific interventions consisted of painting small frescoes of iconic representations of work and then gluing them on the facades of those Belgrade buildings where the painted activities took place before the sites were privatized and began to serve a different purpose. For example, a fresco depicting sewing was glued on the wall of a former textile factory that later became a luxury office space. Pictorial elements from the fresco paintings form the basic elements of the mural painted in the gallery space.

Besides dealing with the displacement of traditional occupations in the context of transition from industrial to neoliberal societies, with this project Pop-Mitić also reflects upon the position of artists, considering them to be "useful idiots." A useful idiot is a term used in many languages to describe a person who furthers an agenda without fully realizing its consequences. She adopts this cynical remark but gives it an optimistic twist: even though she is producing objects and meanings, the consequences of which are not (yet) fully known, she hopes her artistic work will somehow prove useful or meaningful to the future of society.

5   The potential for uniting through adversity

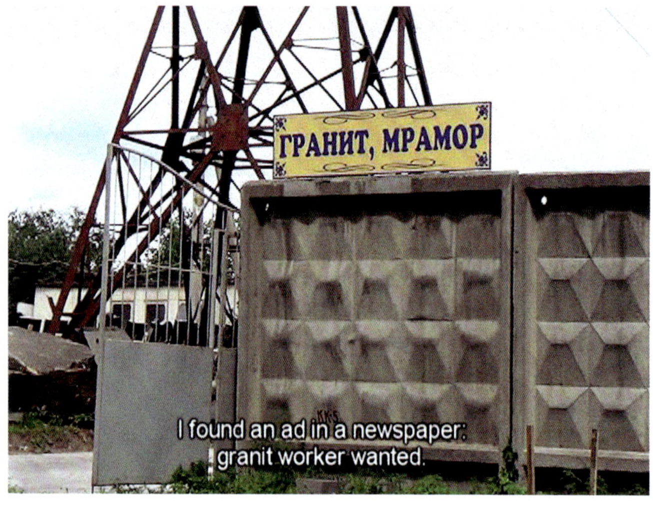
ГРАНИТ, МРАМОР
I found an ad in a newspaper:
granit worker wanted.

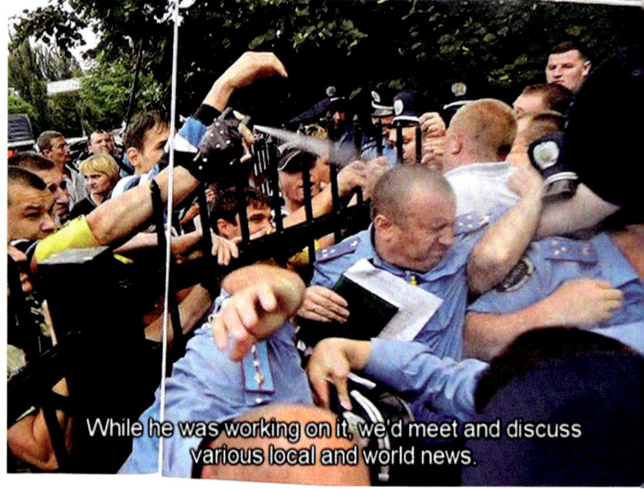
While he was working on it, we'd meet and discuss
various local and world news.

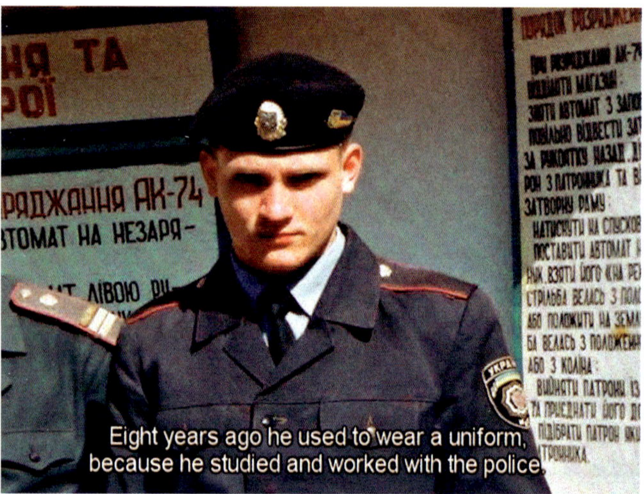
Eight years ago he used to wear a uniform,
because he studied and worked with the police.

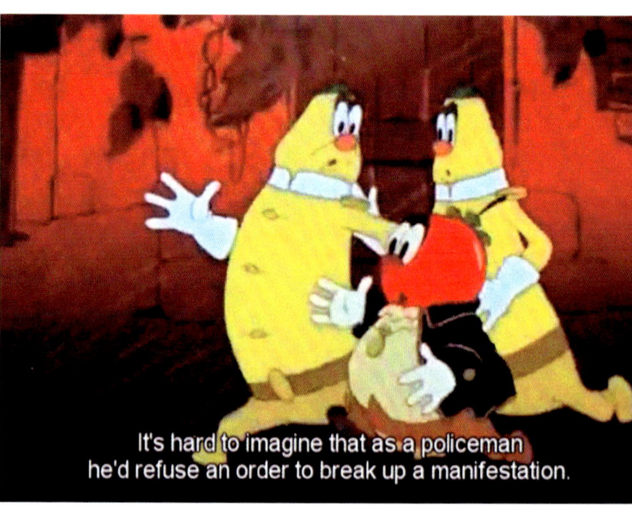
It's hard to imagine that as a policeman
he'd refuse an order to break up a manifestation.

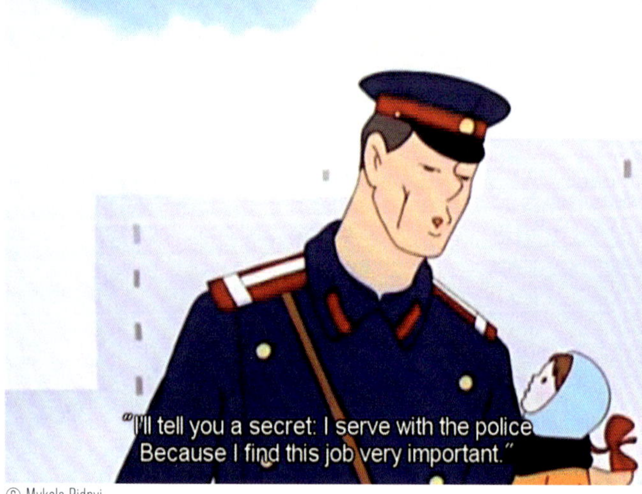
"I'll tell you a secret: I serve with the police.
Because I find this job very important."

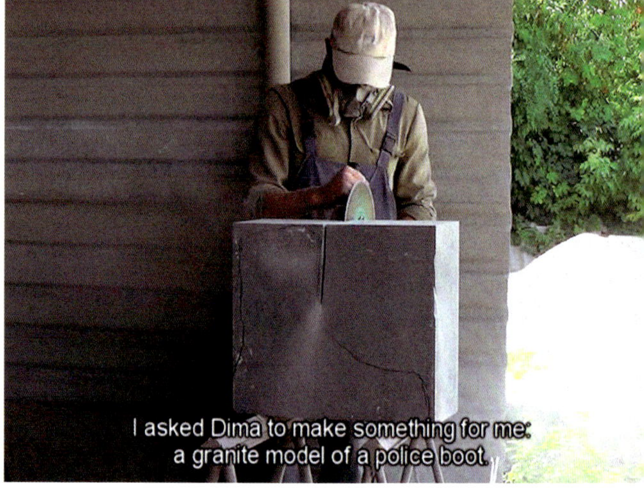
I asked Dima to make something for me:
a granite model of a police boot.

Mykola Ridnyi

(b. 1985, Kharkov, USSR, now Ukraine)

Dima. From the series
Constant Dripping Wears Away Stone
2013
Video, 7'57"
Courtesy of the artist

Mykola Ridnyi works with various genres, from sculpture to photography, film, and installations. The launch of his creative career coincided with the tense political situation in Ukraine in 2005, the Orange Revolution. Together with other member of the SOSka group, Ridnyi took part in street actions that suggested a different way of seeing the world and showed the absurdity of what was going on. Ridnyi is one of those artists who combines rejection and participation in his practice, art with political activism. Having been involved in numerous demonstrations and pickets, Ridnyi explores the form of the protest movement, tracing the mechanisms of the relationship between the regime and the people expressing their opposition to the established order. The artist's focus is on the broad panorama of public space on the one hand and narrows in to private histories on the other, revealing a collective reality through a vital and very personal narrative.

The film *Dima* is from the three-part project *Constant Dripping Wears Away Stone*. The first part comprises video sketches of various protests and demonstrations that took place in Ukraine in 2012 and 2013. The second part includes several sculptures of police boots. The third is a video interview with a former policeman named Dima who, having left the force, works as a granite cutter and takes orders from the artist. In a confidential conversation Dima reflects on the painful political situation in the country, the agonies of the regime, and the impossibility of fulfilling one's professional duties under the present circumstances. This film is striking not only for the man's surprising personal story—he made a decision to change his fate— but also for its somewhat naïve and yet frightening predictions, which have come true today.

5   The potential for uniting through adversity

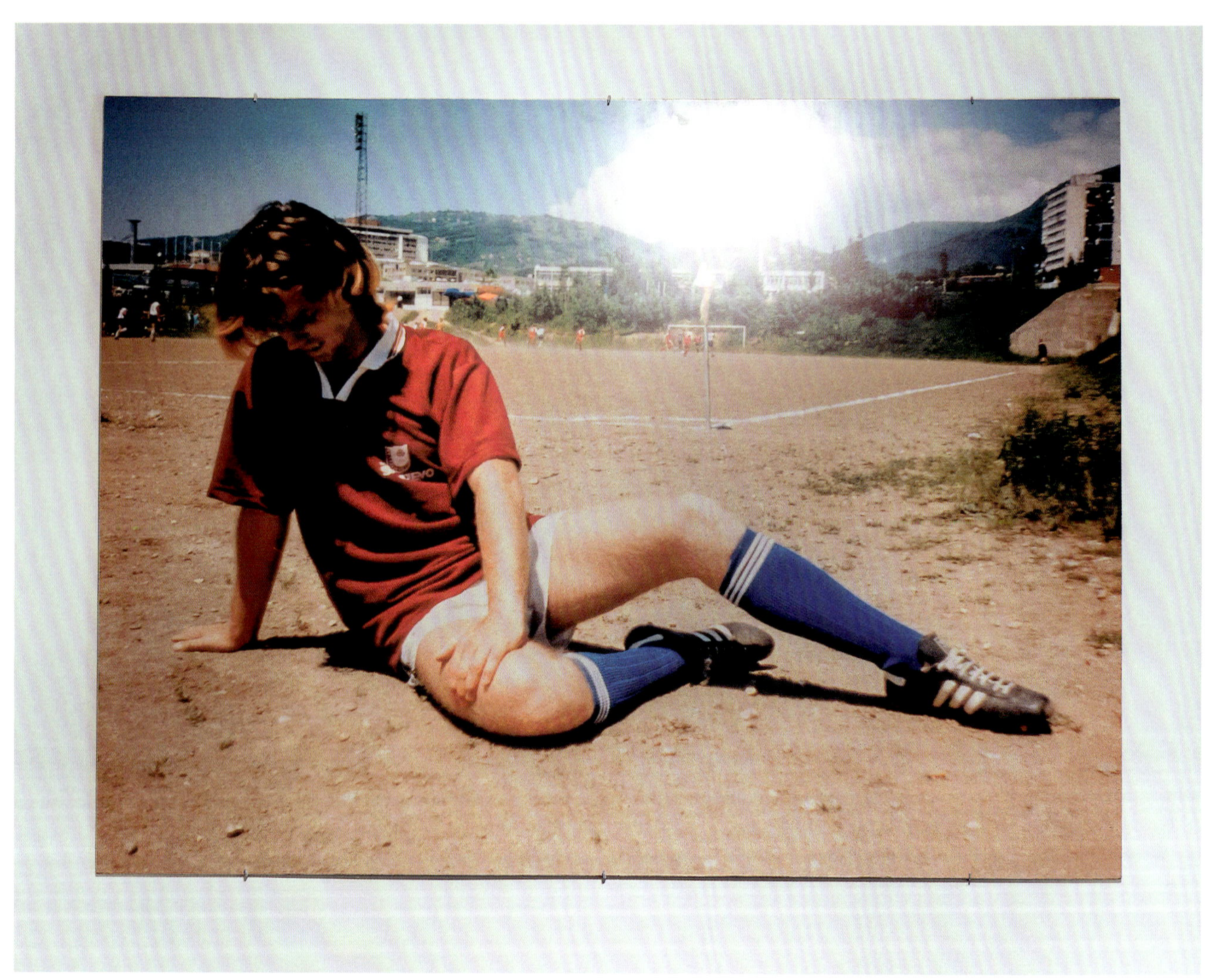

Nebojša Šerić-Šoba

(b. 1968, Sarajevo, Yugoslavia, now Bosnia and Herzegovina)

Tragedy
1999
Photograph on cardboard, 200×150 cm
Courtesy Moderna galerija, Ljubljana

One of Nebojša Šerić-Šoba's basic artistic strategies is to bring together elements from very different historical and sociopolitical contexts to find surprising parallels and connections between them. In his work, where he questions the postwar political and social realm in Bosnia and Herzegovina, he frequently appears as the main character, associating personal stories with painful collective experiences.

Tragedy, made for Šerić-Šoba's show at Škuc Gallery in Ljubljana in 1999, combines the imagery of contemporary mass culture with the high tradition of Classical sculpture. The picture shows a football player from a small town, a provincial club, in total despair after his team has been defeated. His posture is immediately recognizable as the posture of the Dying Gaul. This sculpture is not only a representation of a dying soldier; the Gaul is, above all, a personification of the bitterness and despair of defeat. In the overall context of the celebration of Roman victories, the sculptor of the Dying Gaul succeeded in imbuing this image of despair and defeat with a particular moral dignity. The parallel of the sculpture and the football player is more than just a witty idea. Journalists often use the word "tragedy" to describe a badly defeated team. As Šerić-Šoba shows in his work, such descriptions should be taken literally. Sports teams and their fans are emotionally and symbolically invested in the battles of contemporary sport, and a defeat can be a very real tragedy for them.

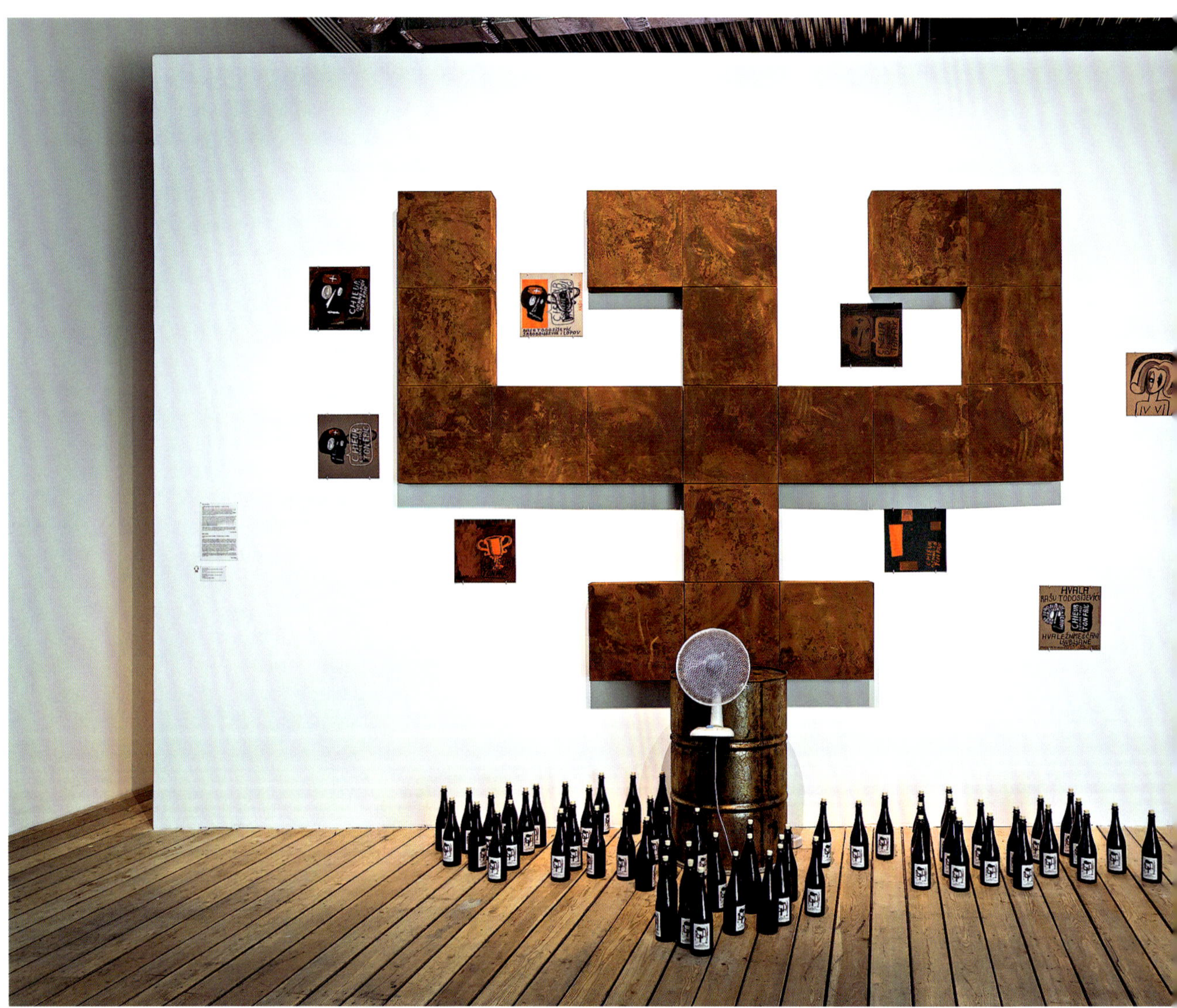

Raša Todosijević

(b. 1945, Belgrade, Yugoslavia, now Serbia)

Special Thanks to Raša Todosijević — The Grateful Citizens of Ljubljana
2000
Installation
Courtesy Moderna galerija, Ljubljana

Special Thanks to Raša Todosijević — The Grateful Citizens of Ljubljana is one of many different manifestations in the *Gott Liebt die Serben (God Loves the Serbs)* series that Todosijević began in the late 1980s. In the 1990s the series coincided with the war in the Balkans and the consequent collapse of the socialist system. At that time, Todosijević started to use the swastika and transformed it many times in his work in order to expose the unstable nature of the meaning of symbols. By taking ideologically burdened symbols and removing them from their context, Todosijević shifted their traditional meaning and thus interfered with their interpretation, exposing it as a process completely dependent on the changing historical context.

The juxtaposition of inverted totalitarian symbols with national ones, as in the case where he served his guests traditional Serbian dishes on a swastika shaped table, and the use of the German language in the enunciation "Gott Liebt die Serben" that appeared on different elements of his installations, served as a tool of provocation directed at Serbian nationalism.

Special Thanks to Raša Todosijević — The Grateful Citizens of Ljubljana, which was exhibited at Moderna galerija in Ljubljana, inherited the above-mentioned strategies. However, an important addition appeared: "Thank you Raša Todosijević!" With this exclamation, Todosijević ironically awarded himself for his work in the name of the citizens of Ljubljana and thus commented on his own position and role in society and in the system of art.

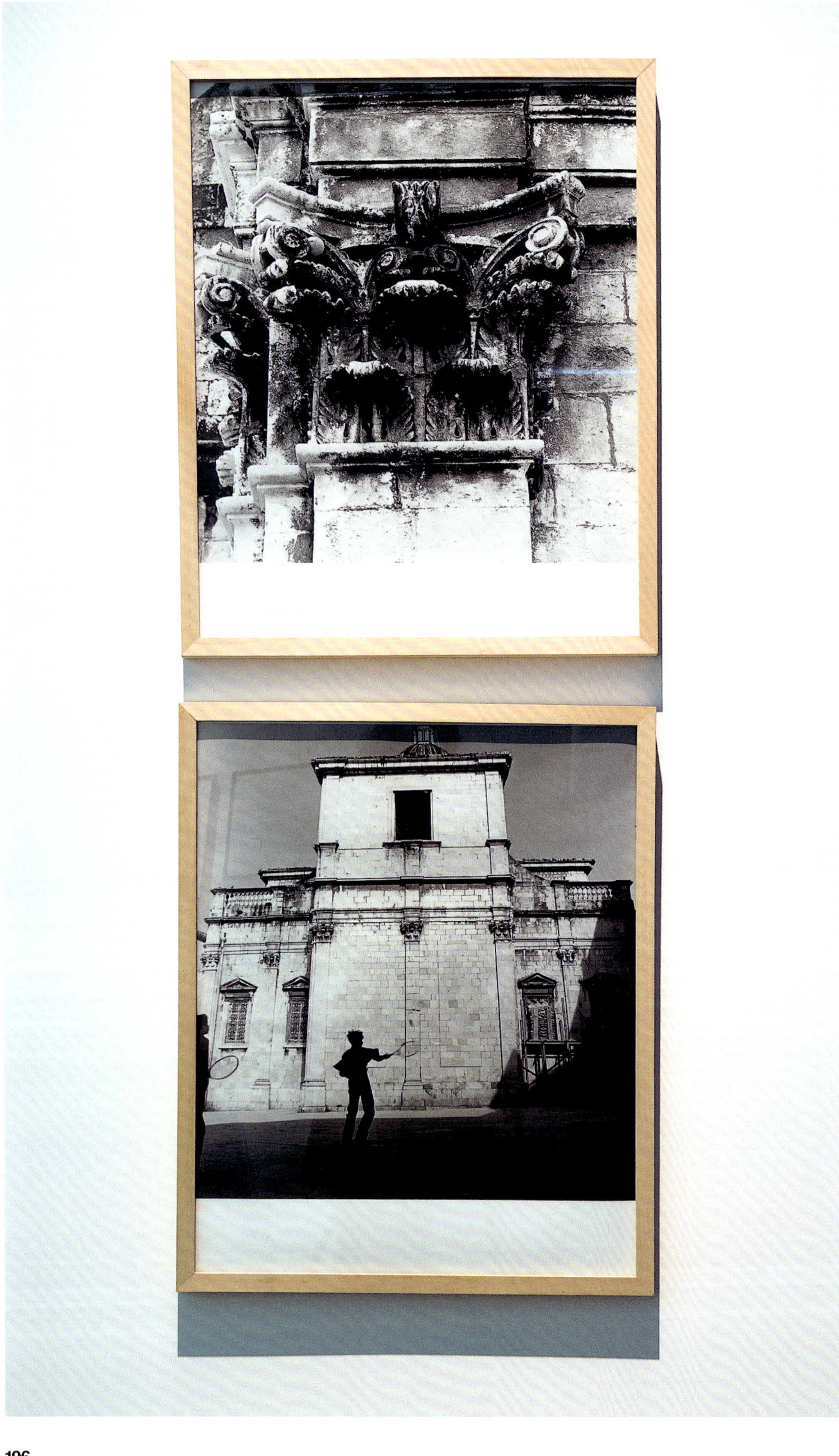

Slaven Tolj

(b. 1964, Dubrovnik, Yugoslavia, now Croatia)

Interrupted Games or Pax. Vobis. Memento Mori Qui. Ludetis Pilla.

1993

Readymade, Bunićeva poljana, Dubrovnik

B/w photographs, each 50×60 cm

Photos: Boris Cvijetanović

Courtesy Moderna galerija, Ljubljana

In Slaven Tolj's *Interrupted Games,* photographs are not mere documents of the witnessed scene. They create a suggestive image of a specific political and historical context: in front of Dubrovnik Cathedral, at Bunićeva poljana, children often play a game of hitting a ball against the wall of the cathedral with a racquet. Their game is interrupted and comes to an end once their ball gets stuck in the Baroque decoration of the cathedral's pillars.

At the time the photographs were shot, the city of Dubrovnik was under siege. The title *Pax. Vobis. Memento Mori Qui. Ludetis Pilla* (*Peace Be With You. Remember You are Mortal, You, Who Play with a Ball*) actually comes from a 16th century graffiti that, as the story goes, a priest who was fed up with children playing with a ball carved into the stone wall of a house somewhere in Dubrovnik. The title thus serves as a reminder that at the time, in the time of war, the game was interrupted in a much more brutal and dangerous way: to play in the square could be fatal. Like the old inscription, the interrupted children's game and the stuck tennis ball became a memento mori, a reminder of one's own mortality, but, as Antun Maračić notes, the metaphor also bears a more permanent meaning. It corresponds to "a postmodernist artistic amalgam" that the artist himself understood as a very concrete, multilayered metaphor of the imprisonment of modernity by classical beauty. "You will stay here as a postmodernist sign," he says.

5   The potential for uniting through adversity

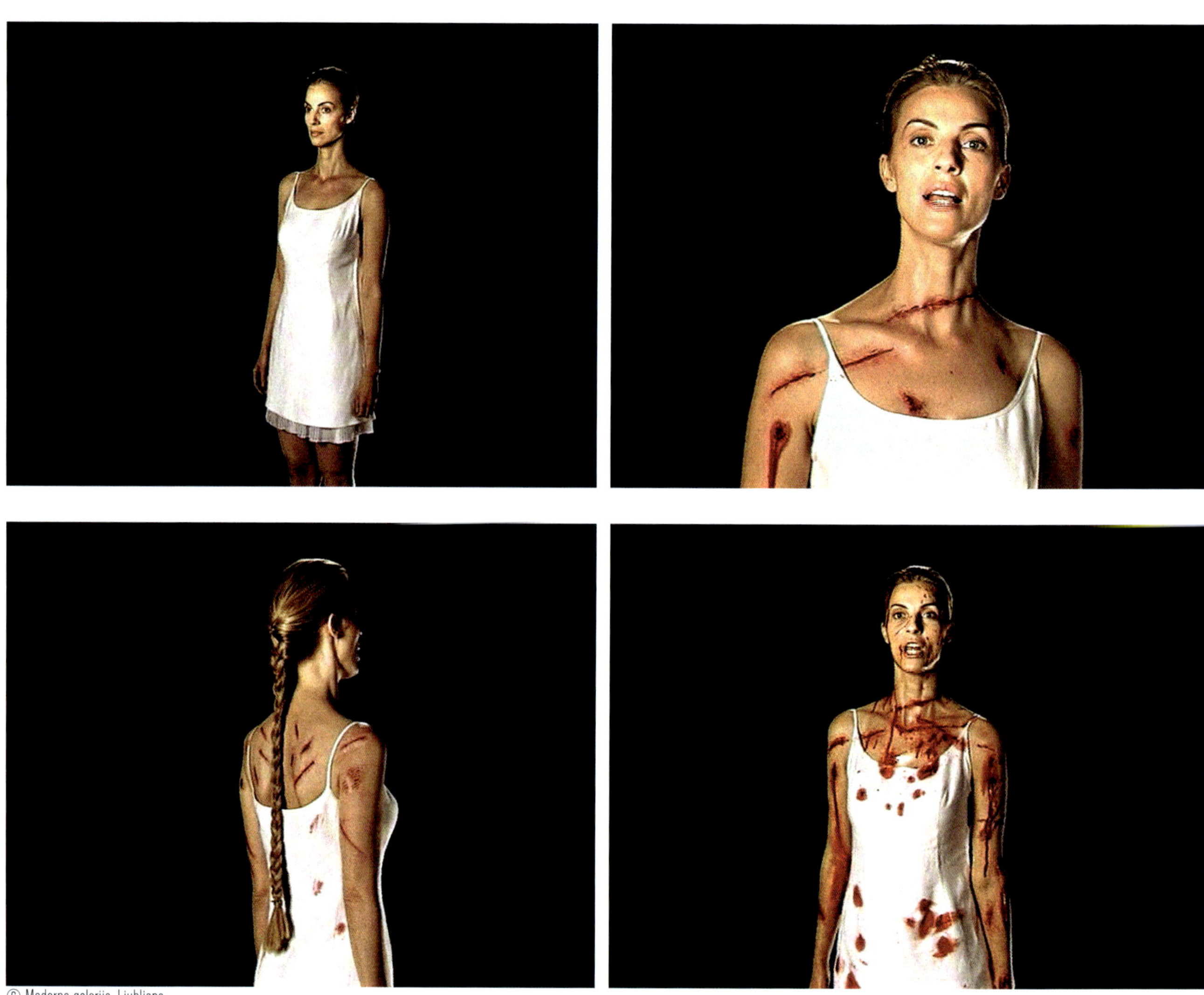

Milica Tomić

(b. 1960, Belgrade, Yugoslavia, now Serbia)

I Am Milica Tomić

1999

Video installation, sound, 9'58", loop

Courtesy Moderna galerija, Ljubljana

The video installation *I Am Milica Tomić* features the artist who, standing, appears to be bleeding from open wounds inflicted by flagellation while saying, calmly and in a rhythmic voice, the following sentences, "I am Milica Tomić, I am Norwegian. I am Milica Tomić, I am Korean…Austrian…" The installation dates from 1998, when the Milošević regime was still in place, and is a clear commentary on pan-Serbian nationalism which, like other forms of archaism in the Balkans, emerged at a time (and partly as a consequence) of fully-fledged globalization. These opposites form the broader contextual framework of *I Am Milica Tomić*.

The work reflects the virtual connectedness of the world and the fragmentation and intertwining of various identities, while warning against the possibility of a return to the old world of opposing and limiting identities. Tomić does not see connectedness in the harmonious terms of the new myth of multiculturalism. Instead, she sees a cleft that determines our foundations and decides our acts of violence.

The work is a response to the collective psychosis which attaches to Serbian identity and to the entire national, cultural, and historical heritage. All those who, during the Milošević regime, did not feel Serbian in the way prescribed by the governing ideology were declared the scum of the nation and a wound on the nation's healthy body. In her work, Tomić finds national identity important at a personal level but denies its public existence, speaking openly from the position of the wound. Through exposure of the process of identification—by means of true and false identity statements—the work rises far above the level of purely declarative condemnations of war to reveal the true foundations of war and violence: identification as exclusion of the other.

5   The potential for uniting through adversity

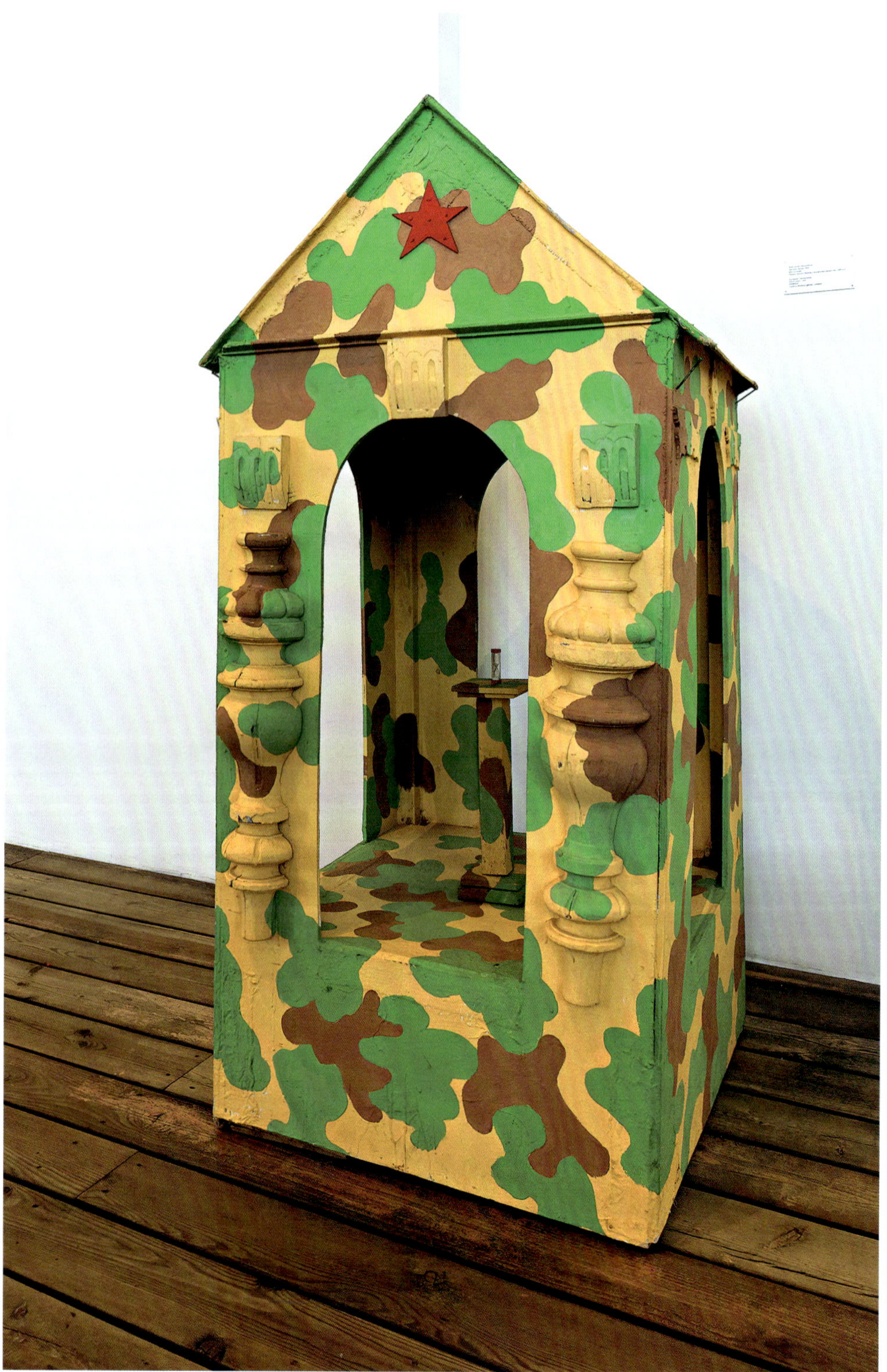

Konstantin Zvezdochotov

(b. 1957, Moscow, USSR, now Russia)

Clock Tower

1994

Installation, 80×155×86 cm

Courtesy Moderna galerija, Ljubljana

Konstantin Zvezdochotov is without a doubt a central figure in Russian art. While he was studying production at Moscow Art Theater School in the late 1970s and early 1980s, he worked intensively as part of the renowned Toadstools group. Along with his comrades he quickly came to the attention of the KGB, but he would not renounce his principles, and as a result he found himself in the Soviet Army in the Far North facing appalling conditions. His spark was not extinguished, however, and after his return he continued to produce ironic and humorous works. In his book of poetry *Ephemerides,* Zvezdochotov announced his desire to become the supreme being and remake the universe. From the mid-1980s his folkloric, kitsch art gradually obtained an almost grotesque emotional cast. In his paintings and installations, Zvezdochotov depicted the imaginary world of Perdo, which lay beyond barbed wire, and also created the most important figure in this made-up place, a pioneer called The Boy Nipper-Pipper. A shrewd observer, Zvezdochotov closely followed the fate of the Balkans, a place with which he has a long history. *Clock Tower* was influenced by the tragic sociopolitical events in Yugoslavia in 1991 and 1992, and the camouflage paint is a direct reference to the armed conflicts of that era. This installation was first shown at the second Cetinje Biennale, but the artist remade it especially for Moderna galerija in Ljubljana. Here there is another historical echo: Moderna galerija's new space was previously an army barracks.

Biographies

Marina Abramović
(b. 1946, Belgrade, Yugoslavia, now Serbia)
Lives and works in New York, USA. Selected solo exhibitions: *Marina Abramović*, Serpentine Gallery, London, UK , 2014; *The Artist is Present*, Garage Museum of Contemporary Art, Moscow, Russia; *The Artist is Present*, Museum of Modern Art (MoMA), New York, USA, 2010; *Seven Easy Pieces*, Solomon R. Guggenheim Museum, New York, USA. Selected group exhibitions: 37th and 47th Venice Biennales, Venice, Italy (1976, 1997); documenta 6, 7 and 9, Kassel, Germany (1977, 1982, 1992).
p. 35

Yuri Albert
(b. 1959, Moscow, USSR, now Russia)
Lives and works in Cologne, Germany and Moscow, Russia. Selected solo exhibitions: *Fragen der Kunst: Moskauer Abstimmung*, Studienzentrum für Künstlerpublikationen, Universität Bremen, Bremen, Germany, 2014; *What Did the Artist Mean to Say by That?* (with Ekaterina Degot), Moscow Museum of Modern Art, Russia, 2013; *Painting, Sculpture, Works on Paper*, Stella Art Foundation, Moscow, Russia, 2008. Selected group exhibitions: *Counterpoint. Russian Contemporary Art*, the Louvre, Paris, France, 2010; 3rd Moscow Biennale for Contemporary Art, Moscow, Russia, 2009; 3rd Istanbul Biennale, Istanbul, Turkey, 1992.
p. 37

Nika Autor
(b. 1982, Maribor, Yugoslavia, now Slovenia)
Lives and works in Ljubljana, Slovenia. Selected solo exhibitions: *Film d'Actualités — l'Actu est à Nous*, Jeu de Paume, Paris, France, 2014; *Asad is Going Home*, Alkatraz Gallery, Ljubljana, Slovenia, 2008. Selected group exhibitions: 7th Triennale of Contemporary Art in Slovenia U3, Ljubljana, Slovenia, 2013; *This Is No Longer the Country My Uncles Talked About: Margin (al) Notes on Solidarity, Survival and Life*, Galerija Škuc, Ljubljana, Slovenia, 2011; 16th Biennale of Young Artists from Europe and the Mediterranean (BJCEM), Brussels, Belgium, 2009.
p. 175

Yuri Avvakumov
(b. 1957, Tiraspol, USSR, now Moldova)
Lives and works in Moscow, Russia. Selected solo exhibitions: *Games*, Stella Art Foundation, Moscow, Russia, 2007; *Beautiful Corner*, Stella Art Foundation, Moscow, Russia, 2006; Russian Pavilion, 6th Architectural Biennale, Venice, Italy, 1996. Selected group exhibitions: *This Obscure Object of Art*, Kunsthistorisches Museum, Vienna, Austria, Ca' Rezzonico, Venice, Italy, 2008–2009; 50th Venice Biennale, Venice, Italy, 2003; 6th Architectural Biennale, Venice, Italy, 1996.
p. 103

Jože Barši
(b. 1955, Ljubljana, Yugoslavia, now Slovenia)
Lives and works in Ljubljana, Slovenia. Selected solo exhibitions: *Jože Barši*, Museum of Modern Art Metelkova (MSUM), Ljubljana, Slovenia, 2013; *House*, Mala galerija, Ljubljana, Slovenia, 1999; Slovene Pavilion, 47th Venice Biennale, Venice, Italy, 1997. Selected group exhibitions: 2nd and 6th Triennales of Contemporary Art in Slovenia U3, Ljubljana, Slovenia (1997, 2010); *7 Sins*, Moderna galerija, Ljubljana, Slovenia, 2004; 4th Istanbul Biennale, Turkey, 1995.
p. 39

Luchezar Boyadjiev
(b. 1957, Sofia, Bulgaria)
Lives and works in Sofia, Bulgaria. Selected solo exhibitions: *Local Warming*, Friends Gallery, Ruse, Bulgaria, 2011; *5 Views to Mecca*, Galerie Feinkost, Berlin, Germany, 2006; *The Fountain of Europe: Luchezar Boyadjiev*, Galleries of the Center for Curatorial Studies, Bard College, Annandale-on-Hudson, USA, 1994. Selected group exhibitions: 1st Kiev Biennale for Contemporary Art ARSENALE 2012, Kiev, Ukraine, 2012; *The Global Contemporary*, ZKM, Karlsruhe, Germany, 2011; Manifesta 4, Frankfurt am Main, Germany, 2002.
p. 141

Geta Brătescu
(b. 1926, Ploiești, Romania)
Lives and works in Bucharest, Romania. Selected solo exhibitions: *MATRIX 254/Geta Brătescu*, Berkeley Art Museum and Pacific Film Archive, Berkeley, USA, 2014; *Geta Brătescu: Los Talleres de la Artista*, Museo de Arte Contemporáneo de Castilla y León (MUSAC), Leon, Spain, 2013; *Spaces, 1971–2005*, Ivan Gallery, Bucharest, Rumania, 2009. Selected group exhibitions: 5th Moscow Biennale for Contemporary Art, Moscow, Russia, 2013; 55th Venice Biennale, Venice, Italy, 2013; Romanian Pavilion, 30th Venice Biennale, Venice, Italy, 1960.
p. 41

Alexander Brener and Barbara Schurz
(b. 1957, Alma-Ata, USSR, now Kazakhstan; b. 1973, Klagenfurt, Austria)
In collaboration since the late 1990s. They live and work in Vienna, Austria. Selected solo exhibitions: *Claim Against Fame*, Knoll Gallery Budapest, Budapest, Hungary, 2013; *Last Seen Entering the MUMOK*, Knoll Galerie Wien, Vienna, Austria, 2006; *Women and Pigs*, Knoll Galerie Wien, Vienna, Austria, 2006. Selected group exhibitions: *Russian Renaissance*, Hilger BROTKunsthalle, Vienna, Austria; *Political/Poetical*, Tallinn Art Hall, Tallinn, Estonia, 2007; *Never Stop the Action*, < rotor > association for contemporary art, Graz, Austria, 2001.
p. 73

Olga Chernysheva
(b. 1962, Moscow, USSR, now Russia)
Lives and works in Moscow, Russia. Selected solo exhibitions: *Keeping Sight*, Museum of Modern Art in Antwerp (M HKA), Antwerp, Belgium, 2014; *Compossibilities*, Kunsthalle Erfurt, Erfurt, Germany, 2013; *Zone of Happiness*, State Russian Museum, Saint Petersburg, 2003. Selected group exhibitions: *Ostalgia*, New Museum, New York, USA, 2011; 6th Berlin Biennale, Berlin, Germany, 2010; Russian Pavilion, 49th Venice Biennale, Venice, Italy, 2001.
p. 75

Chto Delat (What is to be Done)
(2003, St. Petersburg, Russia)
Core members: Dmitry Vilensky, Olga Egorova (Tsaplya), Nikolai Oleinikov, Natalia Pershina-Yakimanskaya (Glyuklya), Kirill Shuvalov, Alexander Skidan, Oxana Timofeyeva, Artyom Magun, Alexei Penzin, David Riff, Nina Gasteva (as of 2012). Selected solo exhibitions: *Time Capsule. Artistic Report on Catastrophes and Utopia*, Secession, Vienna, Austria, 2014; *Chto Delat: Was tun?*, Brandenburgischer Kunstverein, Potsdam, Germany, 2014; *The Urgent Need to Struggle*, Institute of Contemporary Art, London, UK, 2010; Selected group exhibitions: 31st Bienal Internacional de Arte de São Paulo, São Paulo, Brazil, 2014; Bergen Assembly art triennial, Bergen, Norway, 2013; 10th Gwangju Biennale, South Korea, 2012.
p. 177

Lana Čmajčanin
(b. 1983, Sarajevo, Yugoslavia, now Bosnia and Herzegovina)
Lives and works in Sarajevo, Bosnia and Herzegovina.

Selected solo exhibitions: *Blank Maps*, Cultural Centre Tobačna 001, Ljubljana, Slovenia, 2014; *Bedtime Stories*, 90-60-90 Gallery, Zagreb, Croatia, 2013; *World with my Eyes*, ARTATAK/Centre for Contemporary Art, Sarajevo, Bosnia and Herzegovina, 2008. Selected group exhibitions: 4th Moscow International Biennale of Young Art, Moscow, Russia, 2014; *Feminism is Politics!*, Beursschouwburg, Brussels, Belgium, 2013; … *Was ist Kunst?…*, Halle für Kunst & Medien, Graz, Austria, 2013.
p. 179

Collective Actions
(1976–, Moscow, USSR, now Russia)
Group members: Nikita Alexeev (to 1983), Elena Elagina (from 1979), Sabina Haensgen (from 1985), George Kiesewalter (to 1989), Igor Makarevich (from 1979), Andrei Monastyrsky, Nikolai Panitkov, Sergei Romashko (from 1979). Selected solo exhibitions: Russian Pavilion, Venice Biennale, 2011; *Performing the Archive*, Zimmerli Art Museum, New Brunswick, USA, 2009; *Collective Creativity*, Kunsthalle Fridericianum, Kassel, Germany, 2005. Selected group exhibitions: *Performance in Russia: A Cartography of its History*, Garage Museum of Contemporary Art, Moscow, Russia, 2014; *Field of Action. The Moscow Conceptual School in Context*, Ekaterina Foundation, Moscow, Russia, 2010 and Calvert 22, London, UK, 2011; *Moscow Conceptualism and its Influence*, M HKA, Antwerp, Belgium, 2005.
p. 143

Vuk Ćosić
(b. 1966, Belgrade, Yugoslavia, now Serbia)
Lives and works in Ljubljana, Slovenia. Selected solo exhibitions: *Future Past Now*, Aksioma Project Space, Ljubljana, Slovenia, 2012; *ASCII History of Moving Images*, Berkeley Art Museum and Pacific Film Archive, Berkeley, USA, 2010; *Out of Character*, Threshold Artspace, Horsecross, Perth, Scotland, 2009. Selected group exhibitions: 3rd and 6th Triennales of Contemporary Art in Slovenia U3, Ljubljana, Slovenia (2003, 2010); *Maquinas y Almas*, Museo Nacional Centro de Arte Reina Sofía, Madrid, Spain, 2008; Slovene Pavilion, 49th Venice Biennale, Venice, Italy, 2001.
p. 105

Goran Đorđević
(b. 1950, Dragaš, Yugoslavia, now Kosovo)
Lives and works in New York, USA. Selected solo exhibitions: *Scenes of Modern Art*, Galerija Škuc, Ljubljana, Slovenia, 1985; *Bilder uber Bilder*, Wilhelm-Hack-Museum, Ludwigshafen am Rhein, Germany, 1984; *Copies*, Galerija Škuc, Ljubljana, Slovenia, 1984. Selected group exhibitions: *Artists Call*, Judson Memorial Church, New York, USA, 1984; *The Ritz*, WPA & Collab Projects NY, the Ritz Hotel, Washington, USA, 1983; Arteder '82, Bilbao, Spain, 1982.
p. 77

Ana Nuša Dragan
(1943, Jesenice, Yugoslavia, now Slovenia–2011)
Lived and worked in Ljubljana, Slovenia. Selected solo exhibitions: *Ana Nuša Dragan (1943–2011)*, Museum of Modern Art Metelkova (MSUM), Ljubljana, Slovenia, 2012; *Nuša Dragan*, Galerija Media Nox, Maribor, Slovenia, 1994; Selected group exhibitions: *Museum of Parallel Narratives*, Museu d'Art Contemporani de Barcelona (MACBA), Barcelona, Spain, 2011; *This is All Film!*, Moderna galerija, Ljubljana, Slovenia, 2010; *As Soon as I Open My Eyes, I See a Film*, Museum of Modern Art, Warsaw, Poland, 2008.
p. 181

Srečo Dragan
(b. 1944, Spodnji Hrastnik, Yugoslavia, now Slovenia)
Lives and works in Ljubljana, Slovenia. Selected solo exhibitions: *Time is Out of Joint — Srečo Dragan 1968–2000*, Moderna galerija, Ljubljana, Slovenia, 2000; *Rotas Sator*, Equrna Equrna, Ljubljana, Slovenia, 1997; *Srečo Dragan Neo Geo VII*, Mala galerija, Ljubljana, Slovenia, 1989. Selected group exhibitions: *Museum of Parallel Narratives*, Museu d'Art Contemporani de Barcelona (MACBA), Barcelona, Spain, 2011; *This is All Film!*, Moderna galerija, Ljubljana, Slovenia, 2010; *As Soon as I Open My Eyes, I See a Film*, Museum of Modern Art, Warsaw, Poland, 2008.
p. 181

Vadim Fishkin
(b. 1965, Penza, USSR, now Russia)
Lives and works in Ljubljana, Slovenia. Selected solo exhibitions: *Light Matters 4*, Galerija Škuc, Ljubljana, Slovenia, 2013; Slovene Pavilion, 51st Venice Biennale, Venice, Italy, 2005; Russian Pavilion (together with Evgeny Asse and Dmitry Gutov), 46th Venice Biennale, Venice, Italy, 1996. Selected group exhibitions: Manifesta 10, St. Petersburg, Russia, 2014; 50th Venice Biennale, Venice, Italy, 2003; Manifesta 1, Rotterdam, the Netherlands, 1996.
p. 107

György Galántai
(b. 1941, Bikács, Hungary)
Lives and works in Budapest and Kapolcs, Hungary. Selected solo exhibitions: *Life Works*, Ernst Museum, Budapest, Hungary, 1993; *György Galántai*, DAAD Gallery, Berlin, 1989; *György Galántai*, Ferencváros Basement Gallery, Budapest, Hungary, 1975. Selected group exhibitions: *Art Has No Alternative*, tranzit.sk, Bratislava, Slovakia, 2015; *Gender Check*, Museum of Modern Art Ludwig Foundation (MUMOK), Vienna, Austria, 2009; *Fluxus East*, Ludwig Múzeum, Budapest, Hungary, 2008.
p. 79

Gorgona
(1959–1966, Zagreb, Yugoslavia, now Croatia)
The group existed from 1959 to 1966. Selected solo exhibitions: *Gorgona, Gorgonesco, Gorgonico*, Villa Pisani, Venice, Italy, 1997; *Gorgona*, Regional Fund for Contemporary Art (FRAC) Bourgogne, Art Plus University, Dijon, France, 1989; *Gorgona*, Student Cultural Centre Gallery, Belgrade, Yugoslavia, 1986. Selected group exhibitions: *Museum of Parallel Narratives*, Museu d'Art Contemporani de Barcelona (MACBA), Barcelona, Spain, 2011; *Les Promesses du Passé*, National Museum of Modern Art — Centre Pompidou, Paris, France, 2010; *Kollektive Kreativität*, Museum Fridericianum, Kassel, Germany, 2005.
p. 81

Tomislav Gotovac
(1937, Sombor, Yugoslavia, now Serbia–2010, Zagreb, Croatia)
Lived and worked in Zagreb, Croatia. Selected solo exhibitions: Croatian Pavilion (together with BADco), 54th Venice Biennale, Venice, Italy, 2011; *It All Started On The Rio Grande…*, Museum of Modern Art, Warsaw, Poland, 2012; *Zameo ih vjetar/Prohujalo sa vihorom/V vrtincu/Gone With the Wind*, Moderna galerija, Ljubljana, Slovenia, 2009. Selected group exhibitions: *Personal (Hi-) stories*, Garage Museum of Contemporary Art, Moscow, Russia, 2014; *Museum of Parallel Narratives*, Museu d'Art Contemporani de Barcelona (MACBA), Barcelona, Spain, 2011; *Les Promesses du Passé*, National Museum of Modern Art — Centre Pompidou, Paris, France, 2010; 50th Venice Biennale, Venice, Italy, 2003.
p. 43

Ion Grigorescu
(b. 1945, Bucharest, Romania)
Lives and works in Bucharest, Romania. Selected solo exhibitions: *In the Body of the Victim 1969–2008*, Museum of Modern Art, Warsaw, Poland, 2009; *Am Boden*, Salzburger Kunstverein, Salzburg, Austria, 2006; Romanian Pavilion, 47th Venice Biennale, Venice, Italy, 1997. Selected group exhibitions: *Performing Histories (1)*, Museum of Modern Art (MoMA), New York, USA, 2012; Romanian Pavilion, 54th Venice Biennale, Venice, Italy, 2011; documenta 12, Kassel, Germany, 2007.
p. 45

Marina Gržinić and Aina Šmid
(b. 1958, Rijeka, Yugoslavia, now Croatia; b. 1957, Ljubljana, Yugoslavia, now Croatia)
The artists live and work in Ljubljana and have been in collaboration since 1982. Selected solo exhibitions: *City of Women: Hi-Res*, Stara Elektrarna, Ljubljana, Slovenia, 2006; *Marina Gržinić & Aina Šmid*, Rote Fabrik, Zurich, Switzerland, 1994; *A Retrospective of Video Works, 1982–1992*, Moderna galerija, Ljubljana, Slovenia, 1992. Selected group exhibitions: *Museum of Parallel Narratives*, Museu d'Art Contemporani de Barcelona (MACBA), Barcelona, Spain, 2011; 13th Sydney Biennale, Sydney, Australia, 2002; 25th Bienal de São Paulo, São Paulo, Brazil, 2002.
p. 109

Dmitry Gutov
(b. 1960, Moscow, USSR, now Russia)
Lives and works in Moscow, Russia. Selected solo exhibitions: *To Be Surprised At Nothing*, Moscow Museum of Modern Art, Moscow, Russia, 2013; *Repeat, Canon, Return, Delay, Stupefaction*, State Tretyakov Gallery, Moscow, Russia, 2006; Russian Pavilion (together with Evgeny Asse and Vadim Fishkin), 46th Venice Biennale, Venice, Italy, 1996. Selected group exhibitions: 52nd Venice Biennale, Venice, Italy, 2007; documenta 12, Kassel, Germany, 2007; Manifesta 1, Rotterdam, the Netherlands, 1996.
p. 111

Jusuf Hadžifejzović
(1956, Prijepolje, Yugoslavia, now Serbia)
Lives and works in Sarajevo, Bosnia and Herzegovina. Selected solo exhibitions: *Depotgraphia Roma*, Museo Laboratorio di Arte Contemporanea (MLAC), Rome, Italy, 2009; *Objects-*

Installations, Museum of Modern and Contemporary Art, Rijeka, Croatia, 2003; *Ljubljana Dépôt*, Galerija Škuc, Ljubljana, Slovenia, 1995. Selected group exhibitions: *Gender Check*, Museum of Modern Art Foundation Ludwig (MUMOK), Vienna, Austria, 2009; Pavilion of Bosnia and Herzegovina, 50th Venice Biennale, Venice, Italy, 2003; 4th Istanbul Biennale, Istanbul, Turkey, 1995.
p. 183

Tibor Hajas
(1946, Budapest, Hungary—1980, Szeged, Hungary)
Lived and worked in Budapest, Hungary. Selected solo exhibitions: *Use My Voice, April 8, 1973*, Galerie Volker Diehl, Berlin, Germany, 2006; *Tibor Hajas (1946–1980) — Emergency Landing*, Ludwig Múzeum, Budapest, Hungary, 2005. Selected group exhibitions: 10th Shanghai Biennale, Shanghai, China, 2014; *Personal (Hi-)stories*, Garage Museum of Contemporary Art, Moscow, Russia, 2014; *Ostalgia*, New Museum, New York, USA, 2011.
p. 47

Ibro Hasanović
(b. 1981, Ljubovija, Yugoslavia, now Serbia)
Lives and works in Pristina, Kosovo. Selected solo exhibitions: *Letters*, Cultural Centre Tobačna 001, Ljubljana, Slovenia, 2013; *A Short Story*, Turku Museum of Art, Turku, Finland, 2012; *Stories*, A plus A, Venice, Italy, 2011. Selected group exhibitions: *Attention Economy*, Kunsthalle Wien, Vienna, Austria, 2014; *Out of the Blue, a Sense of Public Mindedness*, National Gallery of Kosovo, Prishtinë, Kosovo, 2014; *…Was ist Kunst?…*, Halle für Kunst & Medien, Graz, Austria, 2013.
p. 185

IRWIN
(1983, Ljubljana, Yugoslavia, now Slovenia)
Group participants: Dušan Mandič, Miran Mohar, Andrej Savski, Roman Uranjek, and Borut Vogelnik. Selected solo exhibitions: *Back to the USA*, Galerija Škuc, Ljubljana, Slovenia, 2013; *Construction of the Context*, Kumu Art Museum, Tallinn, Estonia, 2012; *NSK Passport Office New York*, Museum of Modern Art (MoMA), New York, USA, 2012. Selected group exhibitions: Manifesta 9, Genk, Belgium, 2012; 50th Venice Biennale, Venice, Italy, 2003; Manifesta 1, Rotterdam, the Netherlands, 1996.
p. 113

Sanja Iveković
(b. 1949, Zagreb, Yugoslavia, now Croatia)
Lives and works in Zagreb, Croatia. Selected solo exhibitions: *Sweet Violence*, Museum of Modern Art (MoMA), New York, USA, 2011; *Urgent Matters*, Van Abbemuseum, Eindhoven, the Netherlands, BAK, basis voor actuele kunst, Utrecht, the Netherlands, 2009; *Alerta General. Obres 1974–2007*, Fundació Antoni Tàpies, Barcelona, Spain, 2007. Selected group exhibitions: *Ostalgia*, New Museum, New York, USA, 2011; documenta 8, 11, 12, 13, Kassel, Germany (1987, 2002, 2007, 2012); Manifesta 2, Luxemburg, 1998.
pp. 49, 145

Ilya and Emilia Kabakov
(b. 1933 and 1945, Dnepropetrovsk, USSR, now Ukraine)
The artists live and work in New York, USA. In collaboration since 1988. Selected solo exhibitions: Monumenta 2014, Grand Palais, Paris, France, 2014; *Moscow Retrospective. Alternative History of the Arts and other projects*, various platforms, Moscow, Russia, 2008; *Chance in the Museum and other installations*, The State Hermitage, Saint Petersburg, Russia, 2004. Selected group exhibitions: 1st Kiev Biennale for Contemporary Art ARSENALE 2012, Kiev, Ukraine, 2012; 47th, 49th, 50th, 52nd Venice Biennale, Venice, Italy (1997, 2001, 2003, 2007); documenta 9, Kassel, Germany, 1992.
p. 115

Kapiton
(2008–2009, Moscow, Russia)
Participants: Yuri Leiderman, Andrei Monastyrsky, Vadim Zakharov. The results of the group's ten meetings over the period of its existence are published in the book *Kapiton* (Moscow: Pastor Zond Editions, 2009).
p. 83

Vitaly Komar and Alexander Melamid
(b. 1943 and 1945, Moscow, USSR, now Russia)
The artists worked together from 1967 to 2004. They live and work in New York, USA. Selected solo exhibitions: *Asian Elephant Art and Conservation Project*, Galleries at Moore College of Art & Design, Philadelphia, USA, Berkeley Art Museum and Pacific Film Archive, Berkeley, USA, 2000–2001; Russian Pavilion, 48th Venice Biennale, Venice, Italy, 1999; *The Most Wanted — the Most Unwanted Picture*, Museum Ludwig, Cologne, Germany, 1997. Selected group exhibitions: *Counterpoint. Russian Contemporary Art*, The Louvre,

Paris, France, 2010; 47th Venice Biennale, Venice, Italy, 1997; documenta 8, Kassel, Germany, 1987.
p. 117

Alexander Kosolapov
(b. 1943, Moscow, USSR, now Russia)
Lives and works in New York, USA. Selected solo exhibitions: *Freedom of Vodka*, Galerie Sébastien Bertrand, Geneva, Switzerland, 2014; *Alexander Kosolapov*, Galerie Vallois, Paris, France, 2014; *SOTSART*, Leonard Hutton Galleries, New York, USA, 2011. Selected group exhibitions: *Museum of Parallel Narratives*, Museu d'Art Contemporani de Barcelona (MACBA), Barcelona, Spain, 2011; *Russia!*, Solomon R. Guggenheim Museum, New York, USA, 2005; *7 Sins*, Moderna galerija, Ljubljana, Slovenia, 2004.
p. 119

Jarosław Kozłowski
(b. 1945, Śrem, Poland)
Lives and works in Poznań, Poland. Selected solo exhibitions: *Decompositions*, Atlas Sztuki, Łódź, Poland, 2014; *African Standards — Postcolonial Version*, Galeria AT, Poznań, Poland, 2011; *Episodes*, Ujazdów Castle — Centre for Contemporary Art, Warsaw, Poland, 1997. Selected group exhibitions: *Fluxus East*, Ludwig Múzeum, Budapest, Hungary, 2008; 4th Istanbul Biennale, Istanbul, Turkey, 1995; 8th Sydney Biennale, Sydney, Australia, 1990.
p. 85

Katarzyna Kozyra
(b. 1963, Warsaw, Poland)
Lives and works in Warsaw, Poland, Trento, Italy, and Berlin, Germany. Selected solo exhibitions: *Katarzyna Kozyra*, National Museum in Krakow, Krackow, Poland, 2011; *Casting*, Zachęta — National Gallery of Art, Warsaw, Poland, 2010; Polish Pavilion, 48th Venice Biennale, Venice, Italy, 1999. Selected group exhibitions: *International Women´s Day*, Worker and Collective Farm Woman Museum and Exhibition Center, Moscow, Russia, 2013; *Polish!*, Kunstlerhaus Bethanien, Berlin, Germany, 2011; 17th Sydney Biennale, Sydney, Australia, 2010.
p. 51

Oleg Kulik
(b. 1961, Kiev, USSR, now Ukraine)
Lives and works in Moscow, Russia. Selected solo exhibitions: *Chronicles. 1987–2007*, Central House of Artists, Moscow, Russia, 2007; *Museum*, XL Gallery, Moscow, Russia, 2002; Yugoslav Pavilion, 49th Venice Biennale, Venice,

Italy, 2001; Selected group exhibitions: 1st Kiev Biennale for Contemporary Art ARSENALE 2012, Ukraine, 2012; 51st Venice Biennale, Venice, Italy, 2005; Manifesta 1, Rotterdam, the Netherlands, 1996.
p. 53

Zofia Kulik
(b. 1947, Wroclaw, Poland)
Lives and works in Łomianki, Poland. Selected solo exhibitions: *Instead of Sculpture, Sequences 1968–1971*, ŻAK | BRANICKA Gallery, Berlin, Germany, 2014; *From Siberia to Cyberia and Other Works*, Kunstmuseum Bochum, Bochum, Germany, Kunsthalle Rostock, Rostock, Germany, 2005; Polish Pavilion, 47th Venice Biennale, Venice, Italy, 1997. Selected group exhibitions: *British British Polish Polish*, Ujazdów Castle — Centre for Contemporary Art, Warsaw, Poland, 2013; *Museum of Parallel Narratives*, Museu d'Art Contemporani de Barcelona (MACBA), Barcelona, Spain, 2011; documenta 12, Kassel, Germany, 2007.
p. 55

Andreja Kulunčić
(b. 1968, Subotica, Yugoslavia, now Serbia)
Lives and works in Zagreb, Croatia. Selected solo exhibitions: *To Begin the Best We Can*, Gallery Nova, Zagreb, Croatia, 2014; *Conquering and Constructing the Common*, Museo Universitario Arte Contemporáneo (MUAC), Mexico City, Mexico, 2013; *Are You Optimistic About the Future?*, MADRE — Museo de Arte Contemporáneo Donna Regina, Naples, Italy, 2011. Selected group exhibitions: 8th Istanbul Biennale, Istanbul, Turkey, 2003; documenta 11, Kassel, Germany, 2002; Manifesta 4, Frankfurt am Main, Germany, 2002.
p. 147

Vladimir Kupriyanov
(1954, Moscow, USSR, now Russia—2011, Moscow, Russia)
Lived and worked in Moscow, Russia. Selected solo exhibitions: *Facades of the Volga*, Arsenal, Nizhny Novgorod, Russia, 2006; *Central Russian Antiquity. The Last Judgement*, Gallery WAM, Moscow, Russia, 2004; *Lists*, Moscow House of Photography, Moscow, Russia, 2002. Selected group exhibitions: *Museum of Parallel Narratives*, Museu d'Art Contemporani de Barcelona (MACBA), Barcelona, Spain, 2011; *Time of the Storytellers*, Kiasma, Helsinki, Finland, 2007; *Progressive Nostalgia*, Centro per l'arte contemporanea Luigi Pecci, Prato, Italy, 2007.
p. 149

KwieKulik
(1971–1987, Poland)
Group members: Sofia Kulik and Przemyslaw Kiwek. Selected solo exhibitions: *A Complicated Relation: KwieKulik*, Index — The Swedish Contemporary Art Foundation, Stockholm, Sweden, 2011; *Aktivitäten mit Dobromierz*, ŻAK | BRANICKA Gallery, Berlin, Germany, 2010; *Form is a Fact of Society*, Gallery of Contemporary Art BWA Wroclaw, Wroclaw, Poland, 2009. Selected group exhibitions: *Museum of Parallel Narratives*, Museu d'Art Contemporani de Barcelona (MACBA), Barcelona, Spain, 2011; 11th Istanbul Biennale, Istanbul, Turkey, 2009; documenta 12, Kassel, Germany, 2007.
p. 57

Laibach
(1980, Trbovlje, Yugoslavia, now Slovenia)
Musical group and platform for interdisciplinary performance. Selected solo exhibitions: *Laibach Kunst Perspectives*, Maribor Art Gallery, Maribor, Slovenia, 2011; *Ausstellung Laibach Kunst – Recapitulation 2009*, Muzeum Sztuki, Łódź, Poland, 2009. Selected group exhibitions: 2nd Biennial of Contemporary Art D-0 Ark Underground, Sarajevo, Bosnia and Herzegovina, 2013; *Museo de las Narrativas Paralelas*, Museu d'Art Contemporani de Barcelona (MACBA), Barcelona, Spain, 2011; 7 Sins. Ljubljana-Moscow, 2004.
p. 151

Yuri Leiderman
(b. 1963, Odessa, USSR, now Ukraine)
Lives and works in Berlin, Germany. Selected solo exhibitions: *Portrait dans les Roseaux*, Michel Rein, Paris, France, 2013; *Die Visionen des Hans Castorp*, Galerie Gregor Podnar, Berlin, Germany, 2010; *Die Ehre hüt von Jugend auf*, Museum Folkwang, Essen, Germany, 2009. Selected group exhibitions: Bergen Assembly Art Triennial, Bergen, Norway, 2013; 50th Venice Biennale, Venice, Italy, 2003; Manifesta 1, Rotterdam, the Netherlands, 1996.
p. 121

Kazimir Malevich
Biographical details for the artist are lacking, with the exception of a letter published in *Art in America*, reprinted in the collection catalogue *Arteast 2000+ — The Art of Eastern Europe: A Selection of Works for the International and National Collections of Moderna galerija, Ljubljana*, folio, 2001, pp. 136–137. Selected solo exhibitions:

Fiction Reconstructed, Galerija Škuc, Ljubljana, Slovenia, 2000; *New Paintings*, Hereford Salon, London, UK, 1997; *Retroavangarda*, Visconti Fine Art Kolizej, Ljubljana, Slovenia, 1994. Selected group exhibitions: *Arteast 2000+ Collection: The Art of Eastern Europe in Dialogue with the West*, Moderna galerija, Ljubljana, Slovenia, 2000; *Aspects/Positions*, Museum des 20. Jahrhunderts, Vienna, Austria, 1999; *Who Choses Who*, New Museum, New York, USA, 1994.
p. 87

Yerbossyn Meldibekov
(b. 1964, Tyulkubas railway station, USSR, now Kazakhstan) Lives and works in Almaty, Kazakhstan. Selected solo exhibitions: *Mountains of Revolution*, Rossi & Rossi, Hong Kong, China, 2014; *The Revolution in the Mountains*, Jozsa Gallery, Brussels, Belgium, 2013; *Peak of Lenin*, Galleria Nina Lumer, Milan, Italy, 2013. Selected group exhibitions: 1st Kiev Biennale for Contemporary Art ARSENALE 2012, Kiev, Ukraine, 2012; *Progressive Nostalgia*, Centro per l'arte contemporanea Luigi Pecci, Prato, Italy, 2007; Central Asian Pavilion, 51st and 54th Venice Biennale, Venice, Italy (2005, 2011).
p. 59

Jan Mlčoch
(b. 1953, Prague, Czechoslovakia, now Czech Republic)
Lives and works in Prague, Czech Republic. Selected solo exhibitions: *Gratis Slapen*, De Appel, Amsterdam, the Netherlands, 1980; *Tre Artisti Cecoslovacchi*, Laboratorio, Milan, Italy, 1977; *Karel Miler, Jan Mlčoch, Petr Štembera*, Galeria Remont, Warsaw, Poland, 1975. Selected group exhibitions: *Personal (Hi-)stories*, Garage Museum of Contemporary Art, Moscow, Russia, 2014; *Museum of Parallel Narratives*, Museu d'Art Contemporani de Barcelona (MACBA), Barcelona, Spain, 2011; Prague Biennale, Prague, Czech Republic, 2007.
p. 61

Ivan Moudov
(b. 1975, Sofia, Bulgaria)
Lives and works in Sofia, Bulgaria. Selected solo exhibitions: *Ivan Moudov*, Museum of Modern Art Foundation Ludwig (MUMOK), Vienna, Austria, 2013; *Ivan Moudov*, Museo d'Arte Moderna e Contemporanea in Udine, Udine, Italy, 2012; *The 1st at Moderna: Ivan Moudov*, Moderna Museet, Stockholm, Sweden, 2008. Selected group exhibitions: *Art Has No*

Alternative, tranzit.sk, Bratislava, Slovakia, 2015; 1st Moscow Biennale for Contemporary Art, Moscow, Russia, 2005; Manifesta 4, Frankfurt am Main, Germany, 2002.
p. 89

Neue Slowenische Kunst (NSK)
(1984, Ljubljana, Yugoslavia, now Slovenia)
This collective is made up of the groups Laibach and IRWIN and the theatre company Scipion Nasice Sisters. Selected group exhibitions: *The Mediterranean Experience: The Mediterranean as a Spatial Paradigm for the Circulation of Ideas and Meaning*, Macedonian Museum of Contemporary Art (MMCA), Thessaloniki, Greece, 2013; 2nd Athens Biennale, Athens, Greece, 2009; *7 Sins*, Moderna galerija, Ljubljana, Slovenia, 2004.
p. 153

Timur Novikov
(1958, Leningrad, USSR, now St. Petersburg, Russia — 2002, St. Petersburg, Russia)
Lived and worked in St. Petersburg, Russia. Selected solo exhibitions: *Timur Novikov and MMOMA*, Moscow Museum of Modern Art, Moscow, Russia, 2013; *Space of Timur*, The State Hermitage, St. Petersburg, Russia, 2008; *Retrospective, 1978–1998*, State Russian Museum, St. Petersburg, Russia, 1998. Selected group exhibitions: *Manifesta 10*, St. Petersburg, Russia, 2014; *Russia!*, Solomon R. Guggenheim Museum, New York, USA, 2005; *Moskva — Berlin/Berlin — Moskau 1950–2000*, Martin-Gropius-Bau, Berlin, Germany, State Historical Museum, Moscow, Russia, 2003–2004.
p. 123

OHO
(1966–1971, Yugoslavia, now Slovenia)
Group participants: Marko Pogačnik, Iztok Geister, Marjan Ciglič, Naško Križnar, Aleš Kermauner, Milenko Matanović, Drago Dellabernardina, David Nez, Andraž Šalamun, Srečo Dragan, and others. Selected solo exhibitions: *Hidden Histories of the OHO Group*, P74 Gallery, Ljubljana, Slovenia, 2009; *OHO Retrospective*, Moderna galerija, Ljubljana, Slovenia, 1994; *OHO 1966–1971*, Galerija Škuc, Ljubljana, Slovenia, 1978. Selected group exhibitions: *Museum of Parallel Narratives*, Museu d'Art Contemporani de Barcelona (MACBA), Barcelona, Spain, 2011; 6th Triennale of Contemporary Art in Slovenia U3, Ljubljana, Slovenia, 2010; *Eye on Europe*, Museum of Modern Art (MoMA), New York, USA, 2006.
p. 155

Anatoly Osmolovsky
(b. 1969, Moscow, USSR, now Russia)
Lives and works in Moscow, Russia. Selected solo exhibitions: *Cadavre Exquis and Dodici Suicidi*, Thomas Brambilla, Bergamo, Italy, 2013; *Convergence of Parallels* (together with Pawel Althamer), Casa dei Tre Oci, Venice, Italy, 2013; *Wares*, Stella Art Foundation, Moscow, Russia, 2006. Selected group exhibitions: documenta 12, Kassel, Germany, 2007; Manifesta 3, Ljubljana, Slovenia, 2000; 45th and 52nd Venice Biennales, Venice, Italy (1993, 2007).
p. 125

Marko Peljhan
(b. 1969, Šempeter pri Gorici, Yugoslavia, now Slovenia)
Lives and works in Ljubljana, Slovenia. Selected solo exhibitions: *Coded Utopia: From Makrolab to the Arctic Perspective Initiative* (as part of the project Makrolab), Moderna galerija, Ljubljana, Slovenia, 2011; *Territory 1995*, Museum of Modern Art, Belgrade, Serbia, 2010; *Situational Awareness*, Lentos Kunstmuseum Linz, Linz, Austria, 2007. Selected group exhibitions: 11th Istanbul Biennale, Istanbul, Turkey, 2009; 50th Venice Biennale, Venice, Italy, 2003; Manifesta 2, Luxemburg, 1998.
p. 187

Dan Perjovschi
(b. 1961, Sibiu, Romania)
Lives and works in Bucharest, Romania. Selected solo exhibitions: *What Happens to US? Project 85*, Museum of Modern Art (MoMA), New York, 2007; *The Room Drawing*, Tate Modern, London, UK, 2006; Romanian Pavilion (together with SubReal), 48th Venice Biennale, Venice, Italy, 1999. Selected group exhibitions: 52nd Venice Biennale, Venice, Italy, 2007; 9th Istanbul Biennale, Istanbul, Turkey, 2005; Manifesta 2, Luxemburg, 1998.
p. 63

Tadej Pogačar
(b. 1960, Ljubljana, Yugoslavia, now Slovenia)
Lives and works in Ljubljana, Slovenia. Selected solo exhibitions: *Hills and Valleys and Mineral Resources* (together with the P.A.R.A.S.I.T.E. Museum of Contemporary Art), Moderna galerija, Ljubljana, Slovenia, 2014; *The Big Archive*, Croatian Association of Artists (HDLU), Zagreb, Croatia, 2013; *This Is Not America*, P74 Gallery, Ljubljana, Slovenia, 2009. Selected group exhibitions:

10th Istanbul Biennale, Istanbul, Turkey, 2007; Slovene Pavilion, 49th Venice Biennale, Venice, Italy, 2001; Manifesta 1, Rotterdam, the Netherlands, 1996.
p. 157

Darinka Pop-Mitić
(b. 1975, Belgrade, Yugoslavia, now Serbia)
Lives and works in Belgrade. Selected group exhibitions: 9th Gwangju Biennale, South Korea, 2012; *Working Title. Tytuł Roboczy*. Ujazdów Castle — Centre for Contemporary Art, Warsaw, Poland, 2009; 11th Istanbul Biennale, Istanbul, Turkey, 2009.
p. 189

Zoran Popović
(b. 1944, Belgrade, Yugoslavia, now Serbia)
Lives and works in Belgrade, Serbia. Selected group exhibitions: *Politicization of Friendship*, Museum of Modern Art Metelkova (MSUM), Ljubljana, Slovenia, 2014; *Staging Action: Performance in Photography since 1960*, Museum of Modern Art (MoMA), New York, USA; *THIS IS ALL FILM! Experimental Film in Former Yugoslavia 1951–1991*, Moderna galerija, Ljubljana, Slovenia, 2010; *Micro-narratives: Tentation des Petites Réalités*, Museum of Modern Art in Saint-Étienne, Saint-Étienne, France; *Performans 1968–1978*, Vojvodina Museum of Modern Art, Novi Sad, Serbia, 2007.
p. 91

Dmitri Prigov
(1940, Moscow, USSR, now Russia—2007, Moscow, Russia)
Lived and worked in Moscow, Russia. Selected solo exhibitions: *Dmitri Prigov: From the Renaissance to Conceptualism and Beyond*, State Tretyakov Gallery, Moscow, Russia, 2014; *Dmitri Prigov: Dmitri Prigov*, Università Ca' Foscari, Venice, Italy, 2011; *Citizens, Do Not Forget, Please!*, Moscow Museum of Modern Art, Moscow, Russia, 2008. Selected group exhibitions: *Adventures of the Black Square*, Whitechapel Gallery, London, England, 2015; *Ostalgia*, New Museum, New York, USA, 2011; *Moskva — Berlin/Berlin — Moskau 1950–2000*, Martin-Gropius-Bau, Berlin, Germany, State Historical Museum, Moscow, Russia, 2003–2004.
p. 127

Franc Purg
(b. 1955, Ptuj, Yugoslavia, now Slovenia)
Lives and works in London, UK. Selected solo exhibitions: *Coming Soon, the Future!*, Centre for Contemporary Art, Celje, Slovenia, 2011; *BE+FAST*, Golden Thread Gallery, Belfast, UK, 2002. Selected group exhibitions: Kunst Macht Frei, Galerija Equrna, Ljubljana, Slovenia, 2014; *Consume,* Exit Art, New York, USA, 2010; 5th Triennale of Contemporary Art in Slovenia U3, Ljubljana, Slovenia, 2006.
p. 159

Mykola Ridnyi
(b. 1985, Kharkov, USSR, now Ukraine)
Lives and works in Kharkov and Kiev, Ukraine. Selected solo exhibitions: *Shelter*, Centre for Visual Culture, Kiev, Ukraine, 2014; *Labor Circle*, Ujazdów Castle — Centre for Contemporary Art, Warsaw, Poland, 2012; *Documents*, Mystetskyi Arsenal, Kiev, Ukraine, 2011. Selected group exhibitions: Ukrainian Pavilion, 55th Venice Biennale, Venice, Italy, 2013; *Global Activism*, Karlsruhe, Germany, 2013; 1st Kiev Biennale for Contemporary Art ARSENALE 2012, Kiev, Ukraine, 2012.
p. 191

Guia Rigvava
(b. 1956, Tbilisi, USSR, now Georgia)
Lives and works in Vienna, Austria. Selected solo exhibitions: *Cut in the Matter*, Galerie Mosel und Tschechow, Munich, Germany, 1995; *I Hate the State*, Gallery 1.0, Moscow, Russia, 1994; *Are you Powerless?! Or on the Whole Things Really aren´t that Bad*, Art Media Centre TV Gallery, Moscow, Russia, 1993. Selected group exhibitions: *Objects in Mirror Are Closer than They Appear*, Futura, Prague, Czech Republic, 2010; *Get Connected*, Künstlerhaus Wien, Vienna, Austria, 2009; *Moskva — Berlin/Berlin — Moskau 1950–2000*, Martin-Gropius-Bau, Berlin, Germany, State Historical Museum, Moscow, Russia, 2003–2004.
p. 129

Józef Robakowski
(b. 1939, Poznań, Poland)
Lives and works in Łódź, Poland. Selected solo exhibitions: *The Handshake*, ZKM, Karlsruhe, Germany, 2012; *My Own Cinema*, Ujazdów Castle — Centre for Contemporary Art, Warsaw, Poland, 2012; *View from my Window*, Frankfurter Kunstverein, Frankfurt am Main, Germany, 2000. Selected group exhibitions: *Ostalgia*, New Museum, New York, USA, 2011; 2nd Moscow Biennale for Contemporary Art, Moscow, Russia, 2007; documenta 6, Kassel, Germany, 1977.
p. 161

Alexander Roitburd
(b. 1961, Odessa, USSR, now Ukraine)
Lives and works in Kiev, Ukraine. Selected solo exhibitions: *Imaginarium*, Dymchuk Gallery, Kiev, Ukraine, 2013; *Scrabble*, M & J Guelman Gallery, Moscow, Russia, 2010; *Roitburd vs Caravaggio*, Kollektsiya Gallery, Kiev, Ukraine, 2010. Selected group exhibitions: 3rd Odessa Biennale for Contemporary Art, Odessa, Ukraine, 2013; *New Ukrainian Painting*, Whitebox Art Center, New York, USA, 2008; 49th Venice Biennale, Venice, Italy, 2001.
p. 131

Arsen Savadov
(b. 1962, Kiev, USSR, now Ukraine)
Lives and works in Kiev, Ukraine. Selected solo exhibitions: *Blow-Up*, PinchukArtCentre, Kiev, Ukraine, 2011; *Recent Works*, Daneyal Mahmood Gallery, New York, USA, 2007; *Parliament Lights*, Stella Art Foundation, Moscow, Russia, 2005. Selected group exhibitions: 1st Kiev Biennale for Contemporary Art ARSENALE 2012, Kiev, Ukraine, 2012; Ukrainian Pavilion, 49th Venice Biennale, Venice, Italy, 2001; Manifesta 1, Rotterdam, the Netherlands, 1996.
p. 163

Kalin Serapionov
(b. 1967, Vratsa, Bulgaria)
Lives and works in Sofia, Bulgaria. Selected solo exhibitions: *Choose Training*, Contemporary Space, Varna, Bulgaria, 2014; *As Far Away as Near*, Institute of Contemporary Art, Sofia, Bulgaria, 2013; *Video Stills*, Un Cabinet d'Amateur, Sofia, Bulgaria, 2012. Selected group exhibitions: *Breaking Walls — Building Networks*, Macedonian Museum of Modern Art, Salonika, Greece, 2010; *From Ideology To Economics*, State Central Museum of Contemporary History of Russia, Moscow, Russia, 2009; Manifesta 4, Frankfurt am Main, Germany, 2002.
p. 93

Nebojša Šerić-Šoba
(b. 1968, Sarajevo, Yugoslavia, now Bosnia and Herzegovina)
Lives and works in New York, USA. Selected solo exhibitions: *Battlefields*, Dumbo Arts Centre (DAC), New York, USA, 2010; *Any Given Place*, Galerija Miroslav Kraljevic, Zagreb, Croatia, 2004; *Tragedy*, Museum of Modern Art, Roudnice nad Labem, Czech Republic, 1999. Selected group exhibitions: *Greater New York 2005*, MoMA PS1, New York, USA, 2005. Pavilion of Bosnia and Herzegovina, 50th Venice Biennale, Venice, Italy, 2003; Manifesta 2, Luxemburg, 1998.
p. 193

Alexei Shulgin
(b. 1963, Moscow, USSR, now Russia)
Lives and works in Moscow, Russia. Selected solo exhibitions: *Requiem. Farewell Exhibition* (together with Aristarkh Chernyshev), Multimedia Art Museum, Moscow, Russia, 2012; *Criti-Pop* (together with Vladislav Yefimov and Aristarkh Chernyshev), Moscow Museum of Modern Art, Moscow, Russia, 2008; *Beauty Inside*, XL Gallery, Moscow, Russia, 2005. Selected group exhibitions: 4th Moscow Biennale for Contemporary Art, Moscow, Russia, 2011; *Wolfgang von Kempelen. Mensch- [in der] -Maschine*, ZKM, Karlsruhe, Germany, 2007; *Moskva — Berlin/Berlin — Moskau 1950–2000*, Martin-Gropius-Bau, Berlin, Germany, State Historical Museum, Moscow, Russia, 2003–2004.
p. 105

Nedko Solakov
(b. 1957, Cherven Bryag, Bulgaria)
Lives and works in Sofia, Bulgaria. Selected solo exhibitions: *All in Order, with Exceptions*, Municipal Museum of Modern Art (S. M. A. K.), Ghent, Belgium, 2012; *The Freedom of Speech (or How to Argue Properly)*, Castello di Rivoli, Turin, Italy, 2009; Bulgarian Pavilion, 48th Venice Biennale, Venice, Italy, 1999. Selected group exhibitions: documenta 13, Kassel, Germany, 2012; Manifesta 1, Rotterdam, the Netherlands, 1996; 45th, 49th, 50th, and 52nd Venice Biennales, Venice, Italy (1993, 2001, 2003, 2007).
p. 165

SOSka
(2005, Kharkov, Ukraine)
Group participants: Mykola Ridnyi, Serhiy Popov, Ganna Krivetsova. Selected solo exhibitions: *Memorial*, Project WE, Turin, Italy, 2010; *Barter*, The Cardboard Gallery, New York, USA, 2009; *Dreamers*, PinchukArtCentre, Kiev, Ukraine, 2008. Selected group exhibitions: *Verticals of Power, Plywood Colonnades*, Ukrainian Ministry of Foreign Affairs, Kiev, Ukraine, 2014; *Global Activism*, ZKM, Karlsruhe, Germany, 2013; *Impossible Society*, Moscow Museum of Modern Art, Moscow, Russia, 2011.
p. 167

Ilja Šoškić
(b. 1934, Dečani, Yugoslavia, now Kosovo)
Lives and works in Rome, Italy. Selected solo exhibitions: *Nove Ore Dopo*, Museo Laboratorio di Arte Contemporanea (MLAC), Rome, Italy, 2005; *Brottheater*,

Gallery Brotundspiele, Berlin, Germany, 2000; *Ilja Šoškić*, Happy Gallery, Belgrade, Serbia, 1992. Selected group exhibitions: *Museum of Parallel Narratives*, Museu d'Art Contemporani de Barcelona (MACBA), Barcelona, Spain, 2011; Montenegrin Pavilion, 54th Venice Biennale, Venice, Italy, 2011; *Body and the East*, Exit Art, New York, USA, 2001.
p. 65

Petr Štembera
(b. 1945, Plzeň, Czechoslovakia, now Czech Republic)
Lives and works in Prague, Czech Republic. Selected solo exhibitions: *Petr Štembera*, Galerie Papala, Karlsruhe, Germany, 1980; *Petr Štembera*, Studio 16/e, Turin, Italy, 1976; *Petr Štembera*, New Reform Gallery, Antwerp, Belgium, 1974. Selected group exhibitions: *Beyond Corrupted Eye*, Zachęta — National Gallery of Art, Warsaw, Poland, 2012; *Museum of Parallel Narratives*, Museu d'Art Contemporani de Barcelona (MACBA), Barcelona, Spain, 2011; *Subversive Praktiken*, Wuerttembergischer Kunstverein, Stuttgart, Germany, 2009.
p. 67

Mladen Stilinović
(b. 1947, Belgrade, Yugoslavia, now Serbia)
Lives and works in Zagreb, Croatia. Selected solo exhibitions: *Mladen Stilinović*, Museum of Modern Art (MSU), Zagreb, Croatia, 2013; *Sing!*, Ludwig Múzeum, Budapest, Hungary, 2011; *I Have No Time*, Museum of Modern Art, Warsaw, Poland, 2010. Selected group exhibitions: *Ostalgia*, New Museum, New York, USA, 2011; documenta 12, Kassel, Germany, 2007; 50th Venice Biennale, Venice, Italy, 2003.
p. 169

Krasimir Terziev
(b. 1969, Dobrich, Bulgaria)
Lives and works in Sofia, Bulgaria. Selected solo exhibitions: *Cosmopolis*, Institute of Contemporary Art, Sofia, Bulgaria, 2012; *Background Action*, Wuerttembergischer Kunstverein, Stuttgart, Germany, 2008; *Background Action*, Sofia Municipal Art Gallery, Sofia, Bulgaria, 2007. Selected group exhibitions: *Beyond Credit*, Sanat Limani, Antrepo, Istanbul, Turkey, 2010; *Breaking Walls — Building Networks*, Macedonian Museum of Modern Art, Salonika, Greece, 2010; *From Ideology To Economics*, State Central

Museum of Contemporary History of Russia, Moscow, Russia, 2009.
p. 95

Raša Todosijević
(b. 1945, Belgrade, Yugoslavia, now Serbia)
Lives and works in Belgrade, Serbia. Selected solo exhibitions: Serbian Pavilion, 54th Venice Biennale, Venice, Italy, 2011; *Raša Todosijević*, Ottilia Pribilla Gallery, Antwerp, Belgium, 2006; *Compli Citys*, Gallery 99, Glasgow, Scotland, 1994; *Raša Todosijević*, Institute of Contemporary Art, Brisbane, Australia, 1984. Selected group exhibitions: *…Was ist Kunst?…*, Halle für Kunst und Medien, Graz, Austria, 2013; *Museum of Parallel Narratives*, Museu d'Art Contemporani de Barcelona (MACBA), Barcelona, Spain, 2011.
pp. 69, 195

Slaven Tolj
(b. 1964, Dubrovnik, Yugoslavia, now Croatia)
Lives and works in Dubrovnik, Croatia. Selected solo exhibitions: *Ahilova Peta*, Radnicka Galerija, Zagreb, Croatia, 2014; *Citius, Altius, Fortius*, Museum of Arts and Crafts (MUO), Zagreb, Croatia, 2013; *Slaven Tolj*, Museum of Modern Art, Dubrovnik, Croatia, 2006. Selected group exhibitions: *Art Has No Alternative*, tranzit.sk, Bratislava, Slovakia, 2015; *Anarchy.Utopia.Revolution*, Ludwig Múzeum, Budapest, Hungary, 2014; documenta 10, Kassel, Germany, 1997.
p. 197

Milica Tomić
(b. 1960, Belgrade, Yugoslavia, now Serbia)
Lives and works in Belgrade, Serbia. Selected solo exhibitions: *One Day, Instead of One Night, a Burst of Machine-Gun Fire Will Flash, If Light Cannot Come Otherwise*, Turku Arts Museum, Turku, Finland, 2012; *One Day*, Museum of Modern Art, Belgrade, Serbia, 2010; Serbian Pavilion, 50th Venice Biennale, Venice, Italy, 2003. Selected group exhibitions: 3rd Odessa Biennale for Contemporary Art, Odessa, Ukraine, 2013; *Expanded Cinema 3*, Moscow Museum of Modern Art, Moscow, Russia, 2013; *Reflecting Fashion*, Museum of Modern Art Foundation Ludwig (MUMOK), Vienna, Austria, 2012.
p. 199

Goran Trbuljak
(b. 1948, Varaždin, Yugoslavia, now Croatia)
Lives and works in Zagreb, Croatia. Selected solo

exhibitions: *GT: Monogram, Monograph, Monochrome, Monologue…*, P420, Bologna, Italy, 2014; Croatian Pavilion, 46th and 51st Venice Biennales, Venice, Italy (1995, 2005); *Goran Trbuljak: 1973–2004*, P74 Gallery, Ljubljana, Slovenia, 2004. Selected group exhibitions: *Art Has No Alternative*, tranzit.sk, Bratislava, Slovakia, 2015; *Museum of Parallel Narratives*, Museu d'Art Contemporani de Barcelona (MACBA), Barcelona, Spain, 2011; *Scenes from Zagreb*, Museum of Modern Art (MoMA), New York, USA, 2011.
p. 97

Miha Turšič
(b. 1975, Ljubljana, Yugoslavia, now Slovenia). Lives and works in Ljubljana, Slovenia. Selected group exhibitions: *Neighbours*, Istanbul Modern, Istanbul, Turkey, 2014; 6th Triennale of Contemporary Art in Slovenia, U3, Ljubljana, Slovenia, 2010; *7 Sins*, Moderna galerija, Ljubljana, Slovenia, 2004.
p. 133

Via Negativa
(2002, Ljubljana, Slovenia)
Project founded by theater director Bojan Jablanovec. Selected solo presentations: *No-One Should Have Seen This*, Moderna galerija, Ljubljana, Slovenia, 2012; *Naked Presence*, Kunsthalle Düsseldorf, Düsseldorf, Germany, 2010. Selected group presentations: *New Territories: Scotland's International Festival of Live Art*, Glasgow, Scotland, 2011; Eurokaz Festival of New Theatre, Museum of Modern Art, Zagreb, 2010; Ex Ponto Festival, City Museum, Ljubljana, Slovenia, 2009.
p. 171

Sašo Vrabič
(b. 1974, Slovenj Gradec, Yugoslavia, now Slovenia)
Lives and works in Ljubljana, Slovenia. Selected solo exhibitions: *Fairly Accessible Paintings*, Galerija Equrna, Ljubljana, Slovenia, 2010; *Let's Go Away for a While*, A plus A, Venice, Italy, 2004; *Privat (e)*, Galerija P74, Ljubljana, Slovenia, 2003. Selected group exhibitions: *We Want to be Free as the Fathers Were*, International Centre for the Graphic Arts (MGLC), Ljubljana, Slovenia, 2010; *Old Habits Die Hard*, Hamburger Bahnhof Museum, Berlin, Germany, 2004; *7 Sins*, Moderna galerija, Ljubljana, Slovenia, 2004.
p. 99

Dragan Živadinov
(b. 1960, Ilirska Bistrica, Yugoslavia, now Slovenia)
Lives and works in Ljubljana, Slovenia. Selected group exhibitions: *Neighbours*, Istanbul

Modern, Istanbul, Turkey, 2014; 6th Triennale of Contemporary Art in Slovenia U3, Ljubljana, Slovenia, 2010; *7 Sins*, Moderna galerija, Ljubljana, Slovenia, 2004.
p. 133

Dunja Zupančič
(b. 1963, Ljubljana, Yugoslavia, now Slovenia). Lives and works in Ljubljana, Slovenia. Selected group exhibitions: *Neighbours*, Istanbul Modern, Istanbul, Turkey, 2014; 6th Triennale of Contemporary Art in Slovenia, U3, Ljubljana, Slovenia, 2010; *7 Sins*, Moderna galerija, Ljubljana, Slovenia, 2004.
p. 133

Konstantin Zvezdochotov
(b. 1958, Moscow, USSR, now Russia)
Lives and works in Moscow, Russia. Selected solo exhibitions: *Couldn´t Hold It In*, Moscow Museum of Modern Art, Moscow, Russia, 2009; *Normal Civilisation*, XL Gallery, Moscow, Russia, 2009; *Losses*, XL Gallery, Moscow, Russia, 2005. Selected group exhibitions: Russian Pavilion, 50th Venice Biennale, Venice, Italy, 2003; documenta 9, Kassel, Germany, 1992; 44th Venice Biennale, Venice, Italy, 1990.
p. 201

Published to mark
the exhibition *Grammar
of Freedom/Five Lessons:
Works from the Arteast 2000+
Collection*
Garage Museum of
Contemporary Art
February 6–April 19, 2015

Curators:
Zdenka Badovinac,
Snejana Krasteva,
Bojana Piškur

Project Manager:
Asya Shishkova

Exhibition Design:
Anastasia Komarova

Garage Team:
Anton Belov, Director
Kate Fowle, Chief Curator
Anastasia Tarasova, Head
of Exhibition, Education and
Research Projects
Darya Kotova, Head of
Development and Marketing
Brittany Stewart, International
Project Manager

With:
Yana Babanova
Evgeniya Bobyleva
Vika Dushkina
Anastasia Evtushenko
Olga Federyagina
Kit Hell
Anna Ignatenko
Ekaterina Istratova
Maria Kalinina
Vlad Kolesnikov
Elena Melkumova
Anastasia Mityushina
Dmitry Nakoryakov
Dmitry Nikitin
Amina Nmadzuru
Galina Novotortseva
Maria Nosova
Iva Ostistaya
Darya Ostratenko
Alexey Pevzner
Egor Sanin
Maria Sarycheva
Sofia Seiranyan
Valery Serikov
Alena Solovyova
Nastya Tarasova
Evgenia Tsygankova
Anastasia Shamshaeva
Ekaterina Valetova
Alexander Vasilyev
Alesya Veremyeva
Ekaterina Vladimirtseva
Yuri Volkov
Mila Yakovenko
Elena Zabelina

Catalogue

Editors:
Ruth Addison
Kate Fowle
Snejana Krasteva

Texts:
Ruth Addison
Yulia Aksenova
Zdenka Badovinac
Snejana Krasteva
Andrey Misiano
Viktor Misiano
Tjaša Pogačar

Translators:
Andrey Fomenko
Alastair Gee
Gelya Morozova
Miha Šuštar
Katja Zakrajšek

Proofreader:
Brittany Stewart

Design, layout and pre-press:
Igor Kochergin
Fedor Khorikov
Pavel Ermakov

Project Manager:
Anastasia Makarenko

Production and coordination:
Holloway UK Ltd

ISBN 978-5-905110-51-1

The exhibition organizers would
like to thank:
Moderna galerija, Ljubljana and
personally: Nina Dorič-Majdič,
Tomaž Kučer, Nada Madžarac,
Teja Merhar, Ana Mizerit,
Sabina Povšič, Anja Radović,
Marko Rusjan, Igor Španjol,
Rebeka Vegelj, Ana Žan,
Adela Železnik

Tomislav Gotovac Institute,
Zagreb

Artpool Art Research Center,
Budapest

Barcelona Museum of
Contemporary Art

Vladimir Antonichuk, collector

Olga Alekseenko, photographer

Participating artists:
Marina Abramović, Yuri Albert,
Nika Autor (in collaboration with
Marko Bratina, Ciril Oberstar,
and Jurij Meden (Obzorniška
Fronta/Newsreel Front),
Yuri Avvakumov, Jože Barši,
Luchezar Boyadjiev,
Geta Brătescu,
Alexander Brener
and Barbara Schurz,
Olga Chernysheva,
Chto Delat, Lana Čmajčanin,
Collective Actions, Vuk
Ćosić (in collaboration
with Alexei Shulgin
and Andreas Broeckmann),
Goran Đorđević,
Ana Nusa and Srečo Dragan,
Vadim Fishkin, György Galántai,
Gorgona, Tomislav Gotovac,
Ion Grigorescu, Marina
Gržinić and Aina Šmid,
Dmitry Gutov (in collaboration
with Konstantin Bokhorov),
Jusuf Hadžifejzović,
Tibor Hajas, Ibro Hasanović,
IRWIN, Sanja Iveković,
Ilya and Emilia Kabakov,
Kapiton, Vitaly Komar
and Alexander Melamid,
Alexander Kosolapov,
Jarosław Kozłowski,
Katarzyna Kozyra, Oleg Kulik,
Zofia Kulik, Andreja Kulunčić
(in collaboration
with Ibrahim Ćurić, Said Mujić,
and Osman Pezić),
Vladimir Kupriyanov, KwieKulik,
Laibach, Yuri Leiderman,
Kazimir Malevich,
Yerbossyn Meldibekov,
Jan Mlčoch, Ivan Moudov,
Via Negativa, Neue
Slowenische Kunst (NSK),
Timur Novikov, OHO,
Anatoly Osmolovsky,
Marko Peljhan, Dan Perjovschi,
Tadej Pogačar,
Darinka Pop-Mitić,
Zoran Popović, Dmitri Prigov,
Franc Purg and Sara Heitlinger,
Guia Rigvava, Józef Robakowski,
Alexander Roitburd,
Mykola Ridnyi, Arsen Savadov,
Kalin Serapionov,
Nebojša Šerić-Šoba,
Nedko Solakov, SOSka,
Ilija Šoškić, Petr Štembera,
Mladen Stilinović,
Krassimir Terziev,
Raša Todosijević, Slaven Tolj,
Milica Tomić, Goran Trbuljak,
Josip Vaništa, Sašo Vrabič,
Dragan Živadinov
with Dunja Zupančič
and Miha Turšič,
Konstantin Zvezdochotov

Installation shots of
the exhibition *Grammar
of Freedom/Five Lessons:
Works from the Arteast
2000+ Collection* (Garage
Museum of Contemporary
Art, Moscow, 2015): Olga
Alekseenko
© Garage Museum of
Contemporary Art: pp. 6-7,
8-9, 10-11, 12-13, 34, 36-37,
38, 40, 50, 54, 60, 62, 66, 76,
86-87, 96, 98, 102, 106, 110-111,
112-113, 114, 116, 118, 120, 122-
123, 124, 126, 132-133, 140-141,
146, 148, 152, 154, 158, 162, 164,
178-179, 182, 186, 188-189,192,
194-195, 196, 200.

All posts are correct at date
of publication.

Corporate Patron

Sotheby's